DISCARD

Arkansas

Arkansas

AN ILLUSTRATED HISTORY OF

THE LAND OF OPPORTUNITY

C. Fred Williams

Picture Research by Lynn Ewbank

Partners in Progress By Starr Mitchell

Sponsored by the Arkansas State Capitol Association

Windsor Publications, Inc.
Northridge, California

Page three: *The dramatic beauty of Arkansas' Lake Conway is captured in this photograph by Matt Bradley.*

Page six: *The beauty of Little Rock's evening sky-line is pictured in this John McDermott photo-graph.*

Windsor Publications, Inc.—History Book Division

Publisher: John M. Phillips
Editorial Director: Teri Davis Greenberg
Design Director: Alexander E. D'Anca

Staff for *Arkansas: The Land of Opportunity*

Senior Editor: Susan L. Wells
Assistant Editor: Marilyn Horn
Director, Corporate Biographies: Karen Story
Assistant Director, Corporate Biographies: Phyllis Gray
Editor, Corporate Biographies: Judith L. Hunter
Layout Artist, Corporate Biographies: Mari Catherine Preimesberger
Sales Representatives, Corporate Biographies: Marcus Black,
    Curtis Courtney, John Neff, Ron Sutton
Editorial Assistants: Kathy M. Brown, Laura Cordova, Una FitzSimons, Marcie Goldstein,
    Pam Juneman, Susan Muhler, Pat Pittman
Designer: J. Vasquez
Layout Artist: Ellen Ifrah

Library of Congress Cataloging-in-Publication Data

Williams, C. Fred
    Arkansas, an illustrated history of the Land of
Opportunity.

    Bibliography: p.
    Includes index.
    1. Arkansas—History. 2. Arkansas—Description and
travel. 3. Arkansas—Industries. I. Arkansas State
Capitol Association. II. Title.
F411.W55   1986   976.7   86-22376
ISBN 0-89781-182-8

Contents

To Laura Beth, Brad, and Libby,
with Love

As the demand for cars grew, car dealerships began to spring up. Robert E. Dove was the owner of this Willys-Knight Overland dealership in Texarkana. Courtesy, Arkansas History Commission

Preface

Capturing the spirit of Arkansas in the state's sesquicentennial year is difficult. A prominent public official once commented that "Arkansas is one of the best kept secrets in the nation." Perhaps this is true. Certainly there are periods in the state's past that even historians know little about and trying to interpret the Arkansas mosaic is indeed a challenge. Maybe this volume will provide at least an overview of the state's accomplishments. What is not fully developed in the narrative will hopefully be covered by the photographs and illustrations. This volume has been prepared with the general reader in mind and is not intended to provide the definitive word on all aspects of Arkansas history.

Certain individuals have played important roles in developing this project. Thanks go to Lynn Ewbank, who sorted through thousands of photographs to select the ones most appropriate for the text; to Starr Mitchell, who did her usual fine job in writing the business histories; and to Susan Wells, whose patience as an editor is perhaps unmatched.

Special thanks go to Cheryl Patterson and Peggy Fitzgerald, who typed portions of the manuscript, and to Barbara Malott without whose dedication this project would not have been completed. I owe a special debt of gratitude to my wife Janet.

CFW
Little Rock
1986

When he arrived at the
Mississippi River,
Hernando De Soto still
had not located the gold
he sought in America.
Artist G.C. Widney's in-
terpretation of the event
was printed in a supple-
ment to the St. Louis
Globe Democrat *February
9, 1902. Courtesy, University of Arkansas at Little
Rock Archives and Spe-
cial Collections*

The Land of the Arkansas

CHAPTER I

Arkansas' identity in the family of states stems from its unique geography and its cultural development. Both geography and culture have made it difficult to identify modern-day Arkansans and to place them in context with the United States. Some people consider Arkansas a part of the South, others see it as part of the West. Some try to compromise and say southwest or mid-south. But, while there is an element of truth in each of these descriptions, no label seems to fit completely. Through the years, Arkansans have wrestled with this lack of identity.

On a map, the state is easy to locate. Its northern border is drawn along 36° 30' north latitude. The southern boundary is 30° north latitude. Its eastern border is identified by the Mississippi River and its western border basically follows the ninety-fourth parallel west longitude.

Within those boundaries, some 53,000 square miles, Arkansas is almost evenly divided between highlands and lowlands. The highlands are subdivided between two mountain regions, bisected by the Arkansas River. To the northwest is the Ozark mountain range. To the southwest the Ouachitas. The Ouachitas and the Ozarks were both created by an uplift in the earth's strata. The Ozarks are considered to be the oldest mountains in the state because of their plateaus and valleys, while the Ouachitas are more recent in origin because of their sharp, almost vertical uplift, and their narrow ridges and valleys. The lowlands are bisected by the Arkansas River. On the southeast and northeast is an area called the Delta or the Mississippi Alluvial Plain, which was formed by centuries of flood deposits from the Mississippi River. To the southwest is the West

Named for Herbert Crowley, an early settler, Crowley's Ridge stretches from Helena into Missouri. Soil erosion of the ridge can be seen in this Works Progress Administration photograph. Courtesy, Arkansas History Commission

Gulf Coastal Plain, the result of much of the land surface of Arkansas.

Within the broad categories of highlands and lowlands there are a number of other unique features about the state's geography. A curious anomaly in the eastern part of the state is an area called Crowley's Ridge, named for early settler, Herbert Crowley, which begins near Helena and stretches to the state's northern border into the Missouri boot hill. This ridge was constructed by dust particles carried by the wind from the deserts of the Southwest, that have been deposited for centuries, accumulating into a formation. It ranges in width from one to twelve miles and in height from 400 to 500 feet above sea level. Most of the principal cities in the Delta are built along Crowley's Ridge.

In the Delta too, is an area known as the Grand Prairie—a vast treeless region of more than 500,000 acres slightly uplifted from the floodplain. The prairie was a favorite location for hunters and graziers who first inhabited the region.

The Arkansas landscape is bisected by five principal river systems ranging from the Mississippi on the east followed by the White, Arkansas, Ouachita, and the Red. These rivers flow in a general northwest to southeast direction and were the principal avenues of settlement for the early inhabitants of the state.

The contrast in Arkansas' historical fabric continued with the cultural developments that took place on the land. Long before written records, a group of people now called Paleo-Indians made their appearance in the Ozark Mountains on the upper headwaters of the White River and established crude dwellings in the cliffs and bluffs overlooking the riverbanks. These dwellers perhaps came from the west as early as ten or twelve thousand years ago. Although lacking in technology, they did develop crude weapons and mastered the art of weaving. It is unclear as to why or when they declined, but evidence left behind in a few of the bluff shelters indicate that these early dwellers had domesticated the dog, buried their dead in a flex position, and from all appearances were hunters and fishermen in their day to day existence.

Almost contemporary to the Bluff Dwellers was a group of people to the southeast. These individuals built villages along the streams and riverbanks of most of Arkansas' inland waters and were known as Mound Builders. Their culture was characterized by earthen mounds, some as high as twenty feet, covering several acres,

which they built for specific purposes. Anthropologists have been able to identify at least three types of mounds, all of which apparently were present in Arkansas. A common and early mound discovered was the burial mound. A second variety has been called ceremonial, which perhaps was used as a religious temple, and a third type was for everyday living. These Mound Builders apparently were not advanced in technology. They left no evidence of weapons and from all appearances lived a quiet, peaceful life. Their economy was built around subsistence agriculture and fish gleaned from the rivers around the villages. Anthropologists are uncertain as to what happened to the Mound Builders. One common theory is that they were simply overrun by the arrival of new groups of people who made their appearance in Arkan-

Indians in the Ozarks of northwest Arkansas used bluffs like this one in Bella Vista for living quarters. The overhang provided protection from the weather. It also helped preserve some woven belongings, which have enabled archaeologists to learn something about how the Indians lived. Courtesy, the Shiloh Museum

Arkansas' Indian mounds drew national attention with this 1883 issue of Frank Leslie's Illustrated Newspaper. *Existing mounds are fewer and less recognizable now than they were a hundred years ago. Courtesy, Arkansas History Commission*

This 1857 German lithograph illustrates Arkansas' Grand Prairie about thirty years after Arkansas' Indian population had vacated the area. Courtesy, University of Arkansas at Little Rock Archives and Special Collections

sas sometime prior to the sixteenth century.

The first of these people to arrive appear to have been a group called Quapaw—from which the state takes its name. These Indians spoke a Siquan dialect and were one of twelve tribes from the Dakota family who originally made their homes in the upper headwaters of the Ohio River. Sometime prior to 1500, they made their way down the Ohio and Mississippi rivers to the mouth of the Arkansas. There they built shelters made of wood characterized by an oval design. Poles were implanted in the ground and the tops bent and tied together, which were then reinforced and covered with bark. The size of these structures varied but could accommodate four to five families. Some provided shelter for as many as twenty families.

At the same time the Quapaw were arriving in the southeast, another tribe, the Osage, were moving into Central Missouri. The Osage also spoke the Siquan dialect and were

from the same Dakota family. Although they never made permanent homes in Arkansas, they did use the mountainous highlands in the Arkansas River Valley to hunt deer and buffalo. Physically large, they were known as a reckless and warlike tribe that spent much of its time in hostile conflict with both white and red nations alike. Many were described as being more than six feet tall who were not only great hunters and warriors but noted for their endurance.

While the Quapaw and the Osage were making their appearance on the scene in the southeastern and northwestern parts of the state, a new unrelated tribe was migrating into the southwest. The Caddo, as its people were known, occupied southwestern Arkansas from near Arkadelphia along the Ouachita River to Hot Springs and southwest in the Red River Valley. A few apparently came into the Arkansas River Valley west of Little Rock. Although their origin is unclear, the Caddo are believed to have come from Texas and were related to the Indians of Mexico. They apparently took over the sites first settled by the Mound Builders and developed a society that centered around farming and pottery making. Their skill in pottery was renowned, and became a trade item for many of the tribes in the southeast. The Caddo on occasion were also quite warlike, as the Spanish Conquistadores were to find out. They lived in multi-family dwellings that included as many as fifteen to twenty people per structure. A Caddo house was a cone-shaped structure, something like a beehive. Within the structure each family was assigned a space around the circumference of the building. Only the fire was shared in common.

Although there were other Indian tribes that later came to live in Arkansas, notably the Cherokee and the Choctaw, in reality the Quapaw, the Osage, and the Caddo were the indigenous tribes of the state. It was from these people that Arkansas' cultural history begins. Their life-style was first preserved in the written record

by the "Gentleman from Elvas," a member of Hernando De Soto's band of Spanish explorers. De Soto arrived on the bank of the Mississippi River probably just downstream from the present-day town of Helena late in the spring of 1541.

In planning for his expedition to the New World, De Soto was motivated by the usual conquistador incentives of God, gold, and glory. But months of traveling in the southeastern part of what is now the United States had left his original group of 600 men, traveling with 200 horses, a number of hogs, and other livestock, demoralized and even confused. The river was larger than anything they had encountered and to cross it was no easy task. De Soto named it Rio de Grande or Mississippi, the "father of the waters" as the French would call it later. But, after several days of deliberation, De Soto devised a plan to build rafts and ford the river.

While preparing the rafts, however, the Spanish were challenged each afternoon by a band of some 200 Indian

warriors in canoes who approached from the other side of the river. They came almost within bow-shot range, then fired arrows in the general direction of the Spanish workers. This action was inconsequential except to create growing apprehension on the part of De Soto's men. Despite the apparent opposition, when the rafts were completed, De Soto ordered the move across the river. The current was swifter than any in the group had accounted for and it took some effort to get across. But other than the physical task, the fording was without incident.

On the Arkansas side of the river, the Spanish found the Indians not hostile, as they had anticipated, but rather receptive to their visit. The explorers traveled in a northwesterly direction and eventually came to a small village near the river apparently just south of present-day Helena. There the Indians told them that a larger village lay to the northwest. In De Soto's inquiries about gold he was assured by the Indians that gold was available in the other villages. De Soto only spent the night in the first village and then moved in the northwesterly direction up the bank of the river toward what is now Helena. There he encountered a large village that the Gentleman from Elvas described as being "in the midst of a plain surrounded by walls and a ditch filled with water." But the story remains much the same for De Soto in many of the villages where he stopped. In most places he found an abundance of grain and other food supplies, but not the gold that he so eagerly anticipated. After spending a few days at Casquin he moved to the southwest to what most historians believe to be Arkansas Post, called Quiguite. There he encountered the Arkansas River.

He then moved up the north bank of the river to a spot probably near today's Little Rock. There the group crossed the river and traveled in a southwesterly direction, the route eventually bringing them to Hot Springs, where De Soto's lieutenants took note of the mineral water, the warm springs, and commented on how eagerly the horses drank the water. They also reported that a number of Indian settlements were located nearby. Upon interrogation, the Spanish learned that Indians from throughout the region considered the area sacred and used the water for medical purposes.

After spending a few days at the springs to rest, De Soto moved to the southwest. Being in the mountains had rekindled the men's excitement about finding gold. However, near present-day Caddo Gap, the party encountered fierce resistance from the Caddo Indians. Their fury and fighting forced the Spaniards to retreat and alter their course to a more southerly direction. Following the Ouachita River, they moved downstream to near present-day Camden where they discovered another Indian village and inquired about gold, of which the natives had no knowledge. Disappointed, the group moved into Northern Louisiana.

By the time De Soto had left Arkansas, he had become quite ill. The travel and the stress of being involved in various encounters with the Indians left his body weak and his morale broken; he died in Northern Louisiana. His men, fearing the Indians would attack if they knew De Soto was dead, kept his death a secret and the body concealed until they reached the Mississippi River, where the conquistador was buried in what was perhaps his greatest discovery. The remaining members of the party then moved down the river and ultimately returned to Florida and Cuba.

De Soto's foray into Arkansas during the summer, winter, and spring of 1541-1542 began the historical period of Arkansas culture. The accounts left by his lieutenants provided the first written description of the Indian villages, the general terrain, and the expectations the Spanish had for the region. However, as far as lasting influence, the Spanish left little.

De Soto's expedition became the basis for Spanish colonial policy in the lower Mississippi River Valley for more than two centuries. His failure to find any minerals of consequence caused Spanish officials to lose interest in the region and refocus their attention on other parts of the New World.

For more than a century, the native residents of Arkansas were undisturbed by outsiders. However, in the latter part of the seventeenth century, a new group of Europeans—the French—arrived. French motives in North America were similar to those of the Spanish. They were interested in the religious welfare of the Indians and desired to find an all-water route to the Orient for trade, and many believed there was an outside chance for gold or silver. But, more than anything else, they wanted to develop economic ties with the Indians—particularly through the fur trade.

Although France's claims on North America had been established in the early sixteenth century, the first French contact with Arkansas came in July 1673 when an expedition led by Jacques Marquette and Louis Joliet visited an Indian village on the Mississippi River near present-day Helena. This site was probably the

same village visited by De Soto more than 100 years earlier. Marquette, a Jesuit missionary, had tried for several years to get permission for a missionary visit to the Indians in the south. Marquette received permission because church leaders knew of his interest in working with the Indians in the southwest, and his experience working with Indians in the Great Lakes region. Joliet, who had trained early in his career for the priesthood before leaving to earn a reputation as an explorer and fur trapper, built important political connections in Canada. He used those connections to join Marquette and plan the venture down the Mississippi River.

After Joliet was appointed to head the expedition, the pair began their journey in May 1673. Despite warnings from Indians in the Great Lakes

Following De Soto, the next white men to visit Arkansas were Jacques Marquette and Louis Joliet. In this scene Father Marquette talks to Indians the expedition met near the site of present-day Helena. From Reynolds, Makers of Arkansas History, *1918. Courtesy, Arkansas History Commission*

Robert Cavelier, Sieur de La Salle, journeyed down to the mouth of the Mississippi River in 1682. Claiming the entire Mississippi valley for France, he named the area Louisiana, honoring King Louis XIV. From Chesnel, History of Cavelier de La Salle 1643-1687, 1932. Courtesy, Arkansas History Commission

region about dangerous tribes downstream and hazards, such as excessive heat and a demon that guarded the mouth of the river, Marquette and Joliet nevertheless took two canoes, five men, a supply of Indian corn and smoked meat, and set out down the river. For the first several days, the trip was uneventful. Both men noted the beauty of the landscape and the abundance of wild animals. No major activities occurred until they reached a place on the river near present-day Helena. At that point, the party was approached by a delegation of Indians, one of whom carried a calumet—the peace pipe.

This friendly encounter led to an invitation to the explorers to visit the village. According to Marquette, the party "sat down with the old men and warriors [and] fortunately found among them a young man who spoke Illinois much better than the interpreter whom we had brought with us." It was from this interpreter that Arkansas received its name. Marquette, translating the Indian dialect into French, called the tribe the Arkansea. Although there have been at least seventy different spellings of the name, the General Assembly in 1881 officially adopted the spelling as Arkansas. The Frenchmen learned that they were only a few days from the mouth of the river. The leaders of the village warned of hostile Indians further down the river and encouraged the group to turn back. After discussing the issue, Marquette and Joliet concluded that since they were so close to the mouth of the river, it could not possibly be a route to the Orient. Consequently, they began their return trip to Canada. Unfortunately, much of the information about their discoveries was lost when the canoe carrying Marquette's exten-

sive notes about the expedition overturned and he was forced to write his report primarily from memory.

Even though Marquette and Joliet established that the Mississippi River emptied into the Gulf of Mexico and did not present a water route to the Orient, many Frenchmen were not satisfied. A group that included Robert Cavelier, Sieur de La Salle, who had been trying for several years to get a commission to the New World, used the Marquette report to make another plea with the King of France for a trade expedition. La Salle was particularly interested in establishing a commercial colony in America. He also wanted to continue the search for a trade route through the Gulf of Mexico that would lead to the Orient. Finally, he thought that it was important to build a city at the mouth of the river that would guard the Mississippi—similar to the way Quebec controlled the St. Lawrence River.

La Salle was given permission to

institute his plans in 1678. He traveled to Canada, organized an expedition of fifty men and began his descent down the river in December 1681. The group included Henri de Tonti, an Italian, whom La Salle appointed as chief assistant.

As with Marquette and Joliet, La Salle's trip down the river was largely uneventful. By March, the party had arrived at a site now identified as Chickasaw Bluffs, present-day Memphis, Tennessee, where they encountered a dense fog and were forced to go ashore. There La Salle decided to build a fort for protection in case of Indian attacks. However, when the fog lifted later in the day, it became apparent that the party had landed on an island in the Mississippi and were in no immediate danger. From the island, La Salle was able to see an Indian village further downstream on the south bank of the river. He sent a delegation to meet with the Indians and to confirm that they were friendly. Although he was unaware

of it at the time, La Salle had encountered the same village that Marquette, Joliet, and De Soto had previously visited. After a cordial visit, La Salle told the Indians, whom he called the Acansa (Arkansas), that he intended to claim possession of all the Mississippi Valley in the name of his King Louis XIV and that the name of the region would be Louisiana. The Acansa agreed to provide La Salle help in time of war with other Indian tribes and La Salle in turn promised the protection of the French government to the Indians. To commemorate the agreement, he erected a large post with a lead plate bearing the French Coat of Arms and proclaimed the region under the control of the King of France.

La Salle then set out to find the mouth of the river. Guided by two Acansa Indians, he reached the Gulf in a short time and then returned to Canada and then France to get a new appointment to build the inland empire he envisioned. La Salle got his new appointment in 1685 and outfitted three ships to travel by way of the Gulf of Mexico. He planned to enter the mouth of the river and ascend it from the Gulf. He also dispatched Chief Lieutenant Henri de Tonti down the river to prepare for the main party's arrival. De Tonti chose a site on the river near present-day St. Louis to wait for La Salle's arrival. But La Salle's venture fell on hard times. To begin with, the ships missed the mouth of the Mississippi River as it emptied into the Gulf. As they sailed on along the Texas coast, the group encountered a severe storm. One of the ships was sunk and another damaged. La Salle then decided to go ashore and attempt to locate the mouth of the river by traveling overland. Taking a small party he

Henri de Tonti (1650-1704) founded Arkansas Post in 1686. Courtesy, Arkansas History Commission

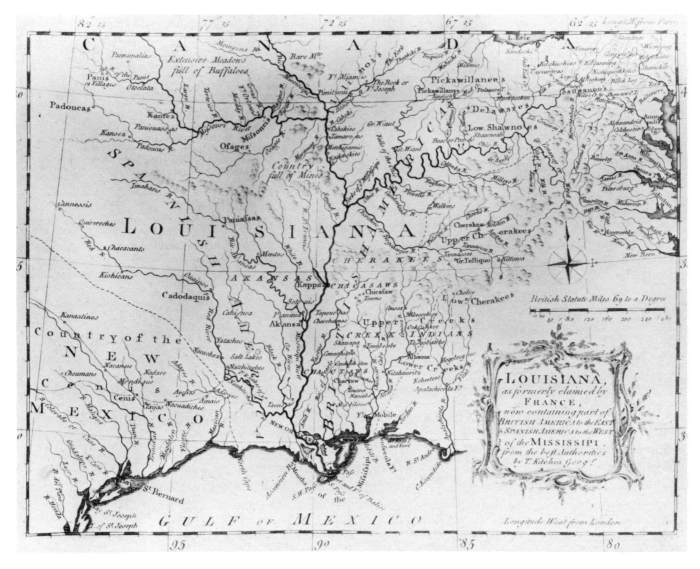

Geographer T. Kitchin produced this map including Arkansas that was printed in London Magazine. *Courtesy, Arkansas History Commission*

Annie Hatley's 1904 painting pays tribute to Arkansas Post, the first permanent European settlement in the lower Mississippi valley. The Post of Arkansas was established by the French in 1686. Courtesy, Arkansas History Commission

marched to the northeast only to encounter another tragedy. After only a few days of travel, La Salle's men mutinied and assassinated their leader. Thus, La Salle's vision for the great inland empire for France in North America was brought to a violent end.

In the meantime, de Tonti grew impatient waiting and set out down the river in an effort to locate La Salle. Near the confluence of the Arkansas and Mississippi rivers, he again stopped and decided to await La Salle's return. La Salle had awarded de Tonti several leagues of land along the Arkansas River, and so he finally decided to establish a claim to the region by building a village and way station. This settlement, commissioned the Arkansas Post, became the first permanent European settlement west of the Mississippi River. After again waiting several days, de Tonti gave up and moved back up the river, ultimately returning to France. Only then did he learn of the fate of his

partner. Ironically, remnants of La Salle's expedition made their way overland and eventually arrived at Arkansas Post.

The collapse of La Salle's adventure brought a temporary end to the French interest in North America. Like the Spanish, they too had become quite disappointed.

Arkansas did not again figure in French plans until the early part of the eighteenth century. The new plan was proposed by Scottish financier John Law, and included a scheme to pay off the French national debt. Law's idea was to found a colony in the new Louisiana Territory, sell shares in the company to wealthy French noblemen, and allow them to colonize and develop the area agriculturally. Even though Law had never seen the region he publicized it to the French nobility as an area rich in resources that would produce bountiful harvest.

After receiving authorization from the French government to go forward

John Law, a Scottish financier, tried to establish a French colony near Arkansas Post in 1717 with German settlers. The Germans soon abandoned Arkansas and moved to a settlement north of Baton Rouge. This drawing of the Biloxi colony is an example of how the Law Colony in Arkansas might have been laid out. Courtesy, Arkansas History Commission

with such a plan, including a generous land grant in the Louisiana Territory, Law made an effort to recruit colonists. Unfortunately, French noblemen did not want to immigrate and Law was forced to utilize German farmers to develop his colony in the New World. A large group of these Germans, perhaps 700 including 500 black slaves, came to the new land and established a colony just upstream from the confluence of the Arkansas and Mississippi rivers. The Germans planted crops, primarily wheat, and built a few semi-permanent houses. But Law's inability to provide the resources that he had promised caused many of the German farmers to become discouraged. To complicate matters, he lost the confidence of the French court and was forced to leave the country for fear of arrest. The Germans abandoned their farms in Arkansas and moved further down the Mississippi River to a spot just north of Baton Rouge and reestab-

lished a settlement. The French, in the meantime, concentrated their attention at the mouth of the river where the city of New Orleans was finally established in 1718 as a guard post.

Further French interest in Arkansas in the eighteenth century stemmed more from speculation and adventure than it did economic and political planning. In 1719 French explorer Bernard La Harpe made a trip up the Arkansas River to identify the resources of the region—including the wild animal population. He hoped to establish a center for supplying food to New Orleans. As La Harpe made his way up the river, he learned about the Indian rumor of a giant emerald embedded in a rock somewhere upstream. In anticipation of that, La Harpe eagerly searched the banks of the Mississippi and the Arkansas rivers looking for rock formations that might have the emerald. Unfortunately, he was unable to find any rock formation from the time he left New Orleans until he ascended the Arkansas River to a point near present-day Little Rock. La Harpe was so anxious to make this discovery that, upon seeing this small outcropping of rock on the south bank of the river, he anxiously wrote in his journal about the "point of rocks on the Arkansas River." A few miles upstream he encountered a giant cliff on the north side of the river that he named "French Rock." In eager anticipation of finding the emerald, he and his men went ashore, scaled the rocky cliff to the top, and searched in vain for the precious stone. The remainder of La Harpe's trip proved uneventful.

Although he did not find the emerald he so anxiously sought, La Harpe did note an abundance of wildlife and was happy to record that there was ample food available in the upper regions of the Arkansas River to supply the city of New Orleans. He also encouraged French officials to establish a trading post in the region to carry on fur trade with the Indians. Perhaps the most significant result of La Harpe's expedition was the "point of rocks," which came to be known as the "Little Rock" to distinguish it from the Big Rock. The Little Rock, on the south bank of the river, came to be a main landmark for travel on the river.

While La Harpe made a second expedition, the French made no other major effort to develop the region of Louisiana above New Orleans—at least where Arkansas was concerned. Finally, in 1763 at the end of the French and Indian War, France ceded all claims in North America, including Louisiana, to Spain. But, while the French were here, their presence did not go unnoticed. Unlike De Soto's

First named "French Rock" by Bernard La Harpe in the early 1700s, Big Rock on the Arkansas River now supports Fort Roots. Courtesy, Arkansas History Commission

earlier ill-fated venture, the French did leave behind a number of contributions, such as a political system for the region. Louisiana was identified as a separate entity subdivided into political units. A law system was established to replace Indian tribal law and later became the basis for Anglo-American law, particularly in reference to the slave code. The French also established strategic posts along the river systems, particularly at Arkansas Post, and identified a number of place names in the Arkansas region, such as Arkansas Post Ecore Faber (Camden). In addition, they made the first maps of the region that became the basis for later exploration.

The French also made some social and economic contributions. In addition to establishing a system of trade, they gave technology to the Indians, particularly the Osage, by providing them with guns and knives. The French also provided a written description of the region and, from an architectural standpoint, built the first European structure in the region. Their relationship with the Indians, particularly the Quapaw, became the model for later race relations, as they established a good neighbor policy and worked closely with the Quapaw for mutual benefit. Finally, the French established the Catholic religion in the region. Even though the grand schemes of La Salle, the anxious adventures of La Harpe and others, failed to reach their full potential, the French nevertheless left behind a cultural legacy that still has identity in Arkansas.

When Spain reassumed control of the Louisiana Territory in 1763, it did little to follow up on the policies that France had enacted. In fact, Arkansas figured only nominally in Spanish policy in the New World. Other than dispatching a few commanders to occupy Arkansas Post, Spanish influence was minimal at best. During the American Revolution, there was a brief attack on the post led by British agents and Chickasaw Indians, but the Spanish garrison there, with the aid of the Quapaw Indians, were able to repel the attack and preserve Spanish control of the region.

Following the American Revolution, Spanish officers at New Orleans made some effort to develop trade with the growing number of Anglo-Americans moving into the eastern Mississippi Valley. The French, with the driving force of Napoleon Bonaparte, revived plans for a great commercial empire in the New World. Napoleon actively pursued plans for redeveloping the area and pressured Spanish officials to cede Louisiana back to France. This the Spanish did in the secret Treaty of San Ildefonso in 1800. Unfortunately, war with England drained his treasury of revenues and disruptions in other parts of his empire caused Napoleon to sell the Louisiana Territory to the United States in 1803.

The United States, under the leadership of Thomas Jefferson, had become quite interested in the Louisiana Territory. Not only did western farmers use the river for transportation, but allowing a foreign nation to control the river posed a threat to the fledgling United States. Therefore, Jefferson authorized a delegation to proceed to France and negotiate the purchase, initially just of New Orleans. However, once in Paris the American representatives learned of Napoleon's interest in selling all of Louisiana. They readily accepted this offer and Arkansas, by virtue of this purchase, became part of the United States in 1803.

The new policies enacted by the United States government were quite different from what Arkansas had experienced under Spanish and French rule. For instance, the Anglo-Americans were very interested in settling the land, which led to a conflict between the United States and the Indian nations in the region. At first, American officials tried to establish organized trade with the Indians called the factory system, a plan begun in the late eighteenth century. However, by the early part of the nineteenth century it was apparent that the system was not functioning well. Even so, after the Louisiana Purchase, Indian factories were established in various points west of the Mississippi River including three in Arkansas. Those established in Arkansas were Arkansas Post, where efforts were made to develop trade with the Quapaw Indians; at Sulphur Springs near present-day Texarkana for trade with the Caddo Indians; and at Illinois Bayou, near present-day Russellville, for trade with the Osage and then the Cherokee Indians.

By the time the United States acquired the Louisiana Territory, the Indians in Arkansas had become well-established, although their numbers had decreased substantially from the time the Spanish had first observed them. The Quapaw, usually the first to encounter any European travelers because of their location on the Arkansas River, had established villages near the mouth of the Arkansas River not far from Arkansas Post. Their hunting grounds and individual settlements stretched up the river to perhaps as far as present-day Pine Bluff. The Caddo had continued to maintain their holdings in the southwest and established villages near Arkadelphia, Hot Springs, Murfreesboro, and Camden. Although the Osage did not construct permanent villages, they nevertheless established strong hunting claims in the upper Arkansas River Valley in the Ozark and Ouachita mountains. Because of their special relationship with the French, the Osage became the middlemen in relations between Europeans and Indians and controlled trade in the lower Mississippi Valley.

As the Indians were to learn, the new American government was interested in possessing the land the Indians had occupied for centuries. One by one efforts were made to negotiate treaties with individual tribes, to convince them to relinquish land in Arkansas and accept lands further west. This had been a pattern that had developed east of the Mississippi River and now continued in the West. The Osage were the first to go. In 1808 a delegation from the tribe met with Meriwether Lewis, governor of the Territory of Missouri, at Fort Clark in western Missouri. By the Treaty of Fort Clark, the Osage gave up their claims in Arkansas except for that land lying west of the line beginning at Fort Clark and running in a southeasterly direction passing just east of Fayetteville and intersecting the Arkansas River at Frog Bayou near the southeast corner of Crawford County. In exchange for these lands the Osage were to receive $1,200 in cash and $1,500 in merchandise annually. Revisions were made in this treaty in 1818 and again in 1825. In the latter year, the Osage population, having declined to perhaps 1,200, moved entirely from Arkansas Territory.

The Quapaw Indians were the next to face demands on their territory. In

When the Osage Indians signed the Treaty of Fort Clark in 1808, giving up their claims to land in Arkansas, they became the first of Arkansas' four principal tribes to leave. By 1863 the Quapaw, Choctaw, and Cherokee had also left. Fort Clark is depicted in this aquatint after a watercolor by Karl Bodmer in February 1834. From McDermott, Travelers on the Western Frontier, *1920. Courtesy, Arkansas History Commission*

1818 a delegation of Quapaw chiefs accepted an invitation to attend a meeting in St. Louis to discuss land claims. There, in negotiations with federal Indian agents, tribal leaders agreed to reduce their claims in Arkansas and accept a reservation. As a result of this treaty, the Quapaw were assigned lands between the Arkansas and the Saline rivers and joined on the south by Arkansas Post and the north by Little Rock. In 1824 the Quapaw agreed to give up their claims even to this reservation and accept new land among the Caddo on the Red River. Finally, in 1833, the Quapaw gave up all of their claims in Arkansas and relocated in Indian territory.

The Caddo was the last indigenous tribe to surrender its claims in Arkansas Territory. Their settlement in the southwestern part of the state, an area less accessible than the Arkansas River Valley, allowed the Caddo to remain undisturbed until 1835. By that time, white population in the region had increased to the point that demands were made to also force the Caddo to move. In response to this pressure, a delegation from the tribe met with federal agents in St. Louis to negotiate a removal treaty and relocate to Texas.

Although the three indigenous tribes may have given up their claims to Arkansas prior to statehood, there were nevertheless other Indians who had an interest in Arkansas. For example, the Cherokee and the Choctaw both established substantial claims to lands in Arkansas in the late territorial period. The Cherokee had perhaps the most significant claim of the two new tribes. They began arriving in Arkansas as both individuals and small bands some time after the American Revolution. By

the time of the Treaty of Fort Clark the Cherokee had established a strong claim to land in Arkansas both along the St. Francis River in the northeast and along the Arkansas River near present-day Morrilton.

The Cherokee were in almost constant conflict with the Osage over hunting rights and hunting grounds. When the Treaty of Fort Clark caused the Osage to give up their claims in Arkansas, the Cherokee readily occupied that land and claimed it as their own. Nevertheless, they were not satisfied with the arrangement because of constant intrusion by whites. In 1815 a delegation went to Washington to ask for a formal treaty with the United States government that would recognize Cherokee land in Arkansas. That treaty was formally negotiated in 1817 and created a Cherokee reservation in Arkansas that was bounded on the north side between the Arkansas and White rivers, and a line beginning on the Arkansas River at Point Remove Creek near Morrilton and running in a northeasterly direction to a point on the White River near Batesville. Similarly, the western boundary line of the Cherokee reservation began at a point near present-day Fort Smith and ran in a northeasterly direction to present-day Harrison. This Cherokee reservation appeared to be in contradiction with the prevailing Indian policy of the United States government. The Osage, Quapaw, and ultimately the Caddo were removed from the region, ironically, just as the Cherokee were being established.

However, there was a master plan in the federal government's policy. In truth, the Cherokee living east of the Mississippi had land that was anxiously coveted by the white population. A move to create a Cherokee reservation in the West was seen as a prelude to moving all the eastern Cherokee to the west into Arkansas Territory. But this was a plan the Cherokee nation as a whole did not share. In fact the tribe became badly divided between those who remained in the east in their traditional homelands and those who accepted lands in the new reservation in Arkansas Territory. Two nations developed within the Cherokee nation, the Cherokee West in Arkansas and the Cherokee East—about two-thirds of the tribe that remained in their ancestral homes.

For a time, the western Cherokee settled down in their new reservation, began extensive cultivation, and built villages. They had the distinction of building the first school in the territory—a mission named Dwight established by Cephas Washburn near Russellville in 1821. Washburn, a Protestant missionary from Connecticut, traveled to the Arkansas Territory for the specific purpose of establishing a mission among the Cherokee Indians. At one point Dwight Mission had as many as one hundred structures, about as many students, and was one of the most advanced educational institutions of its kind west of the Mississippi River.

Ironically, the Cherokee's success in Arkansas Territory proved to be their undoing. Anglo neighbors observed the cultivated fields and the structures being built on the reservation; in time, they came to have an interest in those improvements for themselves. Plans were made to negotiate the removal of these western Cherokees to a new location further west. It was at this point that federal Indian policy came together again for the Cherokee. In a coordinated effort, plans were launched to move both the eastern and western segments of the tribe simultaneously to establish a new reservation.

In May 1828 a delegation of Cherokee chiefs went to Washington to negotiate a second treaty with federal officials. Under the new terms they agreed to give up all of their claims to the lands established in the 1817 Treaty of Fort Clark in exchange for land in Indian territory. Removal began soon afterwards and by the end of the summer Arkansas was free of Cherokee Indian claims.

In an experience similar to the Cherokee, the Choctaw also established a reservation in Arkansas as part of the removal process. In October 1820 representatives of the Choctaw tribe met with Andrew Jackson, general of the United States Army in the West and Thomas Hines, commissioner for the United States government, and signed an agreement whereby the Choctaw accepted lands in the Arkansas Territory in exchange for land they occupied in present-day Mississippi.

In Arkansas the Choctaw reservation was adjacent to the Cherokee reservation beginning on the south bank of the Arkansas River. The boundary at Point Remove Creek was extended south until it intersected the Red River about three miles below the mouth of the Little River. The northern boundary line of the reservation began at the intersection of the Cherokee reservation line near Fort Smith and extended west to the South Canadian River. This meant that the Choctaw occupied a large section of Arkansas land claimed by the Caddo, in addition to land occupied by some white settlers.

Arkansas' political representatives made strong protests to such a generous land grant to the Choctaw in the territory. The *Arkansas Gazette* com-

Cephas Washburn (1793-1860), a Protestant missionary to the Western Cherokees, established Dwight Mission near present-day Russellville in 1820. This portrait was painted by Washburn's son, Edward Payson Washburn, of Arkansas Traveler *fame. Courtesy, Arkansas History Commission*

plained bitterly that a large percentage of the white population was now inside the Choctaw reservation. This statement was untrue but it was not fully investigated by the federal government. In any event, because of these protests, it became necessary to negotiate a second treaty with the Choctaw to redefine the boundary between the Choctaw reservation and the Arkansas Territory.

The Choctaw reservation created controversy in Arkansas not only because of the large portion of land it occupied, and the illegal settlers there, but also because it disrupted the western boundary of the Arkansas Territory. This line had been established by an act of Congress when it created the Arkansas Territory in 1819; the new treaty compromised that line. Therefore, the federal officials through Secretary of War John C. Calhoun summoned the principal chiefs of the Choctaws to Washington in January 1825 and began discussions about renegotiating the Choctaw reservation as it applied to Arkansas Territory. By common consent the Choctaw agreed to give up their claims to most of Arkansas Territory in a region defined by a line beginning 100 paces east of Fort Smith and proceeding in a due southerly direction until the line intersected the Red River. The Choctaw surrendered all their claims to lands east of that line and recommitted their interest and attention to the area west of the line in Indian territory.

As a result of this series of treaties with both the indigenous tribes and the relocated tribes—the Cherokee and the Choctaw— by the mid-1830s the United States government had redistributed the land of the Arkansas and opened the door for Anglo settlement.

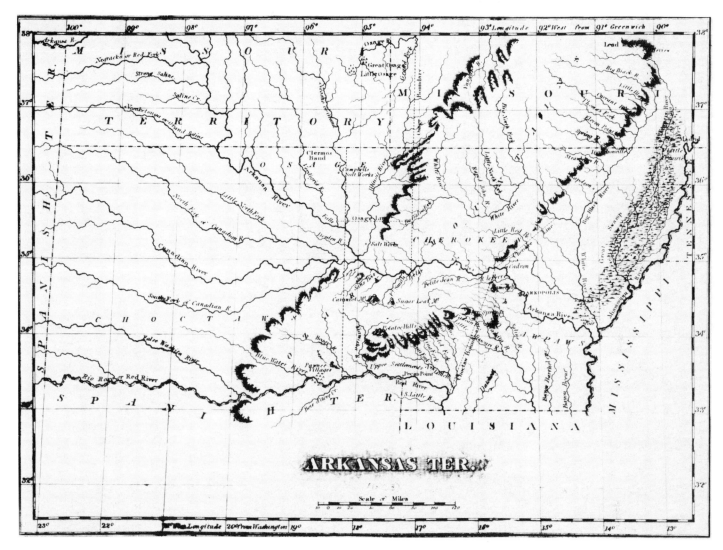

With the Louisiana Purchase of 1803, Arkansas became a part of Louisiana Territory, before the creation of Arkansas Territory in 1819. Courtesy, Arkansas History Commission

Some Arkansans followed the railroads going west, hiring themselves and their teams to the railroad companies while their wives and families camped nearby. Artists Frenzeny and Tavernier recorded their lifestyle for Harper's Weekly. Courtesy, University of Arkansas at Little Rock Archives and Special Collections

The Bear State Experience

CHAPTER II

Soon after the United States acquired the Louisiana Purchase from France, government officials in Washington made plans to organize the region west of the Mississippi River into distinct political units. The initial move was to divide the region into two sections: the area south of the thirty-third parallel was identified as the District of Orleans, and the region north of that was called the Territory of Louisiana.

Arkansas gained its political identity in 1806, when a District of Arkansas was organized in the Louisiana Territory. When the Territory of Orleans petitioned for statehood in 1812, requesting the name Louisiana for the state, the region north of the thirty-third parallel had to be renamed and reorganized. The new territory was called Missouri, and Arkansas became a political unit in the new structure. In 1814 the District of Arkansas was upgraded to a full-scale county. The next year, the county was subdivided to form another county. Arkansas County retained its identity on the south, and a new county, Lawrence, was carved out of the northern section. By 1818 there were five counties, the original District of Arkansas, now Arkansas County, Lawrence County, then Pulaski in the center of the territory, Clark to the southwest, and Hempstead even further to the southwest. The organization of these counties was a reflection of a growing population pattern into the region—one that primarily followed the river systems.

Access to Arkansas proved extremely difficult. The normal pattern of progression and migration had followed an east to west plain, usually along the same parallel. Unfortunately, Arkansas was in the Mississippi floodplain; as the Mississippi River emptied out of the region south of Cape Girardeau, Missouri, the river overflowed into Arkansas, and during flood season, a band of water forty miles wide extended the full length of the state's boundaries between the thirty-third parallel. Hence, as pioneers moved west toward Arkansas, their migration pattern had to be diverted to avoid the floodplain or else endure considerable hardship in crossing. Travelers frequently complained about swamps and bayous, and the difficulty in moving across Arkansas from the east. The majority of the travelers came from Tennessee during the fall and spring months when the rivers were most prone to be flooded and access into Arkansas proved to be most difficult. The stream of migration then tended to come up the Mississippi River into the Arkansas and White rivers or up the Red River in the southwest, and population during the territorial period flowed along the river systems more than any other route. This presented a unique problem. Both the Arkansas and the Red rivers were notorious for their inconsistency as far as floods and dry riverbeds were concerned. Also, both had an abundance of snags that presented severe problems for boating on the rivers. Migration from the north was hampered by the Ozarks. While not presenting the same problems as rivers or the Mississippi floodplain, the mountains nevertheless were a formidable barrier to access into the state. The barriers posed by the Ozark Mountains in the north and the Mississippi floodplain on the east were simply other indications of the contributions that geography has made to the state's development.

A normal migration pattern had been to follow the Ohio River to the Mississippi and then from the Mississippi west by way of the Missouri River and through the Rockies to the west coast. There was also a pattern of settlement that moved through the Cumberland Gap into Tennessee and followed the Natchez Trace from Nashville, Tennessee, down to Natchez, Mississippi, and then down the Mississippi to New Orleans and west through Texas. Both of these routes to the major arteries to the west bypassed Arkansas. That geographical feature, coupled with the political decision of the federal government to designate the area adjacent to Arkansas' western borders as Indian territory, proved a severe barrier for western settlement. Unlike Missouri, which had claimed the role as Mother of the West through which thousands of people passed yearly, Arkansas had the distinction of being isolated from the major arteries and as a result the population growth was very irregular; those people who came into the state did so more out of choice than because of any planned part of the normal progression of westward expansion.

The first Anglo-Americans to arrive in the Arkansas Territory were predominantly hunters and trappers who were attracted to Arkansas because of the abundance of game—bear, deer, buffalo, and a variety of smaller animals. The Anglo hunters found this to be no exception. These hunters and trappers had a life-style that was primarily nomadic. Building very crude shacks, they spent a short time in one region before they moved on to hunt and trap in another area. In time, some began to grow small gardens to supplement their diet of meat, wild berries, and fruit and some began to bring in livestock. The majority of these hunters and trap-

pers came into the Arkansas Valley, and the early population centered upstream from Arkansas Post where the vast treeless region of the Grand Prairie provided ideal grazing area for cattle and of course abundant feed for hogs.

By the time Arkansas was officially organized as a territory in 1819 it had accumulated a population of approximately 14,000 people. These were spread out in the various geographical zones beginning at Arkansas Post, up the Arkansas River, on the White River as far as Batesville, in the area along the St. Francis, known as Davidsonville, in the northwest area around Fayetteville, and also in the southwest along the River River, inland near Washington, on the Ouachita River near Camden, and later at Arkadelphia. These population centers became the basis for political agitation for territorial status.

The desire for territorial status was

not a goal shared by everyone. Many of the independent hunters and trappers were content with their independent life-styles but in the more organized settlements there was a growing body of people who felt that political organization was essential to maintain law and order and to establish some symbolism of institutional development within the state. Hence, petitions were circulated in the key population areas of the territory, signatures gathered, and ultimately a proposal presented to the United States Congress for acceptance. The issue that sparked the petition drive was Missouri's move for separate statehood. Arkansans felt it was important to their cause that Missouri be organized as a state and have a separate identity.

When the petitions were presented to the United States Congress there was a mixed reaction. It was fairly evident that the territory did not have

In 1833 Captain Henry Shreve began clearing away the "Red River Raft," a dense accumulation of logs, fallen trees, and floating vegetation, that extended 200 miles, making water transportation impossible. This formidable task, completed in 1840, allowed improved river transportation and economic expansion. Courtesy, Arkansas History Commission

In his book, The First Report of a Geological Reconnoissance [sic] of the Northern Counties of Arkansas, *David Dale Owen depicts various views of Arkansas. Pictured here are two views of Sugar Loaf Mountain, one in Marion County, above; and the other in bordering Searcy County, facing page, top. Also shown are Mammoth Spring in Fulton County, left; and Calico Rock in Izard County, facing page, bottom. Courtesy, University of Arkansas at Little Rock Archives and Special Collections*

Arkansas' first inhabitants were hunters and trappers who came because of the abundance and variety of game. They gradually added small gardens, and over the years Arkansas grew to be primarily an agricultural state. Courtesy, Arkansas History Commission

sufficient population to merit admission or organization as a territory, if the traditional formula adopted in the northwest territories was followed. There was also the issue of slavery, which was becoming an increasingly heated subject in Congress, and the representatives and senators were almost evenly divided between those who favored slavery and those who opposed its expansion. Because of these complications the petition to create Arkansas Territory was debated at length in the House of Representatives. Ultimately, a compromise reached between representatives of the Northern states and those of the Southern states allowed Arkansas Territory to be admitted as a slave territory, but slavery in the remaining part of the Louisiana Territory would be forbidden.

Organizing a territory brought changes to Arkansas, especially the increasing role of federal government. Not only did the President appoint

public officials of the new territory—judges, the governor, and the secretary to the territory—but also a federal payroll became considerably important to the economy of the region. And, in addition to assuming responsibility for paying the salaries of public officials—essentially the governor, the secretary, and the judges—the federal government paid for internal improvements, such as making the rivers more navigable, building levees along the rivers for flood control, and building interior roads. These federal roads were usually referred to as military roads because of the use of the United States Army Corps of Engineers in their construction. In the early 1820s plans were launched to build a wagon road from Memphis into Little Rock through the Mississippi floodplain—a task that proved difficult but successful. By 1827 the road had been completed to Little Rock and was later extended up the Arkansas River to Fort Smith and to the southwest to Fulton on the Red River, and passed near Arkadelphia and Washington.

The federal government also began paying increased attention to the western frontier in the 1820s. Since Arkansas' western border lay adjacent to Indian territory and because the Texas region of Mexico was international territory, the federal government watched the region closely. Troops were dispatched near Fort Smith initially to control and keep an eye on the Indians in the region, and later became more concerned with the Mexican influence on the southwest along the Red River.

However, the area in which federal influence was perhaps most evident was in the disposal of the public domain. Of all the reasons for people

migrating west, land was perhaps the key driving force, and in Arkansas this was no exception.

As the population grew it became increasingly apparent that land titles were becoming essential. The federal government opened land offices, initially one in Batesville and one in Little Rock, and then later extended to other parts of the territory for the specific purpose of selling public land and recording deeds of land purchased. The federal government had in fact begun surveying in the territory in 1815. The first surveys west of the Mississippi in the Louisiana Territory began in Arkansas Territory in a spot just west of Helena.

The federal government was of course a dominating influence in the territory period, but local government

Early settlers raised and hunted wild hogs. Harper's Weekly *published this Gilbert Gaul drawing titled* Hunting Wild Hogs in Arkansas, *which shows an early hog hunt. Courtesy, Arkansas History Commission*

After achieving territorial status, Arkansas was eligible for federal funds for roads. One such road was the heavily traveled Southwest Trail. The Old Stagecoach House near Little Rock, built in 1836 or earlier, was a stage stop on the Southwest Trail, which was also called the Military Road. Courtesy, Arkansas History Commission

also had areas of specific importance. One key issue considered by the 1819 Territorial Legislature meeting at Arkansas Post was to establish a permanent site for the capital of the new territory. Because of its location on the banks of the Arkansas River, which was subject to flooding, and its distance away from the center of the territory, most of the political leadership recognized that Arkansas Post would not be suitable for a capital. Before adjourning in the spring of 1820 the legislature appointed a special committee to study the needs for the permanent capital and to make recommendations when the legislature reconvened in the fall. The committee made several months of study and in its initial report was prepared to recommend an early fur-trapping post on the Arkansas River just west of present-day Conway as a permanent capital site. However, there was a group of individuals with considerable land ownership around the point of rocks that became quite interested in having the capital located there. The group was led by Virginian-born William Russell, who had moved to Little Rock where he purchased a Spanish grant and a preemption claim from an early trapper, Edmund Hogan, who had claimed the region. Russell used his Spanish grant and his preemption claim as a basis for ownership of land around the point of rocks, now commonly referred to as the "little rock."

A group led by Stephen Austin also purchased claim to the region by buying new land claims. Both Russell and Austin worked actively to influence the legislature and special committee to make recommendation to Little Rock. When the legislature reconvened in October 1820 the special committee recommended that Little

Rock be chosen as the capital. As the committee reported, Little Rock had several advantages, including its location on the river—above the floodplain. There was a good harbor free from the current of the river, which could be navigated almost all year around. The location of Little Rock was also on a road leading from Missouri to the Red River and there was an abundant supply of timber and spring water to support a large population. After making its report the legislature voted six to three to locate the capital in Little Rock. What was not recorded at the time was that a number of the committee members held title to real estate lots around Little Rock. La Harpe's "Point of Rocks" became the permanent capital and has never seriously been challenged since that time as the permanent seat of government.

Other issues considered by the Territorial Legislature included creating additional counties and chartering towns. In 1819 the territory had five counties; by the end of the territorial period in 1836, there were thirty-four. Creation of these new counties was the cause of considerable political concern. Not only did the counties represent an organized political unit, but they also meant a payroll, an opportunity for individuals to be elected to political office, an increase in sales, and an increased price of real estate. Therefore, the Territorial Legislature was bombarded by requests for additional counties. The county system was also an important way for aspiring political leaders to develop a political network built around favors granted to local officials.

Other issues of concern to the legislature revolved around law and order, particularly Arkansas' problem of violence. Dueling, most common among

John Miller of New
Hampshire was appointed
Arkansas' first territorial
governor in 1819 by Pres-
ident James Monroe.
Courtesy, Arkansas His-
tory Commission

the gentry class, was of such concern that the legislature outlawed the practice as one of its early items of business—although in truth the number of duels did not decrease; they were simply conducted outside the territory. Horse stealing and brawling were problems the legislature addressed itself to as well, and horse stealing was made a capital offense. Another dimension to the law and order issue was the fact that it was very difficult to get federal judges to serve in the district. Because of its isolation and the independent tradition already established by the territory, judges found it difficult to hold court in the territory itself. Of the three judges originally appointed by the President to serve in the county, two resigned their seat rather than serve, and the third was frequently absent. This prompted the legislature to protest vigorously to the President, but the inconsistent court system continued in the territorial period.

One issue that had an impact on territorial politics was that of personalities. In the region there were a number of political opportunities, but there were even more people who wanted to take advantage of those opportunities—inevitably personality conflicts began to develop. One of the first conflicts that became apparent was the internal conflict between the territorial governors and the secretary to the territorial governor. John Miller was appointed as the first territorial governor in 1819 by President James Monroe. At the same time, Robert Crittenden, a lawyer from Kentucky, was appointed secretary to the territory. Miller, a New Hampshire native, had established a reputation in the War of 1812 and was known as the "Hero of Lundy's Lane" when he successfully led a charge against the British battery. However, he had not had a political career before and was slow to recognize the political implications of his appointment.

Robert Crittenden, a young man of twenty-one, had not only seen limited experience in the War of 1812 and the Seminole War, but saw clearly the political opportunities available to him. Making it a top priority to get to the territory as quickly as possible following his appointment, Crittenden arrived on the scene several months in advance of the governor. By contrast, Miller first went to Washington to formally accept his appointment, traveled to Pittsburgh to pick up arms and ammunition to be used in frontier defense, and eventually made a leisurely trip down the Ohio and Mississippi rivers. His military reputation had preceded him and a number of communities along the river held celebrations for him as his barge, appropriately named the *Arkansas,* made its way down the river systems. The result was that by the time Miller arrived in Arkansas Crittenden had already organized the first legislature, held elections, and had the territory well on the way in its political development. Miller was inclined to resist Crittenden's actions, but after he heard the opinions of the people involved, decided that the majority will was represented and chose to agree. Miller, unaware of the various opportunities to build a political base in the Arkansas Territory, spent much of his time away on personal business. Even though he was reappointed for a second term, he resigned early to accept a position of customs collector at the Port of Salem in Massachusetts. During Miller's absences, Crittenden had served as acting governor and continued to

Robert Crittenden (1797-1834) organized Arkansas' territorial government at Arkansas Post in 1819. That same year he was appointed secretary of the territory, a position he held until 1829. Courtesy, Arkansas History Commission

exert a strong influence over the territory, so strong that a Crittenden faction began to develop within the political community. This factionalism became even more evident under Miller's successor, George Izard, a highly educated man who had served as commander of the West Point Military Academy prior to coming to Arkansas as governor.

When Izard arrived in Arkansas he complained that public affairs in the territory were in a state of chaos. Miller had been gone from the state for at least six months and acting governor Robert Crittenden was also out of the state while a number of issues needing immediate attention had gone unsettled. For example, the federal treasury had forwarded a considerable sum of money to the territory to be used in compensation for the various Indian removal agreements. One draft in the amount of $10,500 was in Little Rock and another of $3,000 was on deposit with

William Montgomery at Montgomery's Point at the mouth of the Arkansas River. Izard complained that no attention had been given to dispensing these funds and he of course was concerned about the security. Izard also discovered other problems related to the money; when he tried to cash the $10,500 note, none of the merchants had enough funds to cover it—and there was no bank. As Izard was to find out, he would have to go all the way to Memphis to collect that amount of money.

On another occasion Izard complained to one of the local citizens about the chaos in the territory. To that the citizen replied, "Oh, everybody does about as he pleases anyhow and we get along just as well when the governor is absent as we do when he is here." This, of course, Izard did not appreciate. Trained in the military, Izard was accustomed to order and procedure. Not only did his difficulties with Crittenden continue but he was also confronted with conflict with the legislature. The legislature was unimpressed with the governor's attention to detail and order and tended to act on its own agenda. When Izard commented on their lack of discipline and direction, the Assembly responded with a series of resolutions and announced the governor was a dictator. But all of Izard's experiences in the territory were not unpleasant or ended in frustration; he had highly successful negotiations with the Indians, particularly in resolving difficulties with the Cherokee and the Quapaw about a treaty agreement with the federal government.

Conflict between the governor's office and the legislature subsided somewhat in 1827 with another dispute involving two of the state's leading political leaders—Robert Crittenden and Congressman Henry Conway. Conway had been elected as the territory's second delegate in 1821 after the first congressional delegate, Henry Woodson Bates, decided not to seek reelection. In the years following 1821 Conway came to have significant influence in the state. While he and Crittenden were initially friends, their political ambitions began to strain the relationship. From his position as secretary of state, Crittenden watched as Conway strengthened his political base. And while Crittenden was not actively involved in national politics, he did use influence with friends to see particular issues advance. In the 1827 congressional race, Crittenden threw his support to Robert Oden, a Little Rock lawyer who opposed Conway, and the campaign proved to be one of the most bitter in the territory's brief political history. As charges were hurled by each opponent against the other, the

Ambrose H. Sevier, the "Father of Arkansas Statehood," served as a delegate to Congress (1827-1836) and U.S. senator (1836-1848). As a special envoy to Mexico, Sevier negotiated the Treaty of Guadalupe Hidalgo, which ended the Mexican War in 1848. Courtesy, Arkansas History Commission

most telling was a charge levied by Crittenden against Conway for misuse of federal funds in his office as territorial delegate. Conway had in fact deposited a federal bank draft to his own personal account while in Washington, but had rewritten the draft once he arrived back in the territory; while he had not actually used the money, it had been mixed up with his own personal funds for a short time. This charge was printed in the newspaper, and even though Crittenden's name was not used it soon became apparent to most of the territory who was behind the story. Conway bitterly denounced the claim and charged that Crittenden had insulted him. There were other complaints but in the end Conway was able to keep his seat in Congress, and won reelection by a fairly comfortable margin. But the controversy was far from over. Crittenden challenged Conway to a duel and the two met on a sandbar on the Mississippi River just offshore from Montgomery's Point. During the exchange of gunfire Conway was killed and Conway's bullet amazingly passed through Crittenden's coat but did not pierce his body. Conway's political career thus ended, his successor proved to be his relative by marriage. Ambrose Sevier, also a Tennessean, had strong connections with the political family of Tennessee, and was a close friend of Andrew Jackson. Sevier was reelected in 1829 and in fact stayed in office until the territory became a state; he was elected as one of the first senators from the new state of Arkansas.

Factionalism later went beyond just personalities and had some measure in issues as well. And as the state matured, different needs had to be met. Up until this time the territorial government had met in various locations, chiefly in the Baptist and Presbyterian churches in town. However, as additional counties were added and as the General Assembly continued to grow in size, meeting space became an increasing problem. Governor John Pope, soon after coming to the state, received authorization from the federal government to sell ten sections of land, and use the proceeds to build a territorial capitol. Soon after, the Territorial Legislature received a proposal from Robert Crittenden, who offered to trade his large brick house in Little Rock in exchange for the ten sections of land. It seemed apparent that Crittenden had influenced the legislators, and even passed out favors including Kentucky hams, in an effort to get votes. Indeed, the General Assembly passed a resolution authorizing the exchange of the ten sections of land for Crittenden's house—and making it the new territorial capitol. However, Governor Pope vetoed the As-

sembly's action, which brought sharp criticism from the legislators, even to the point of asking that the governor be censured. President Andrew Jackson, however, supported Pope's efforts and in the years that followed Pope began selling the land and ultimately received proceeds in excess of $30,000. Crittenden's house sold a year after the legislature made its resolution for $6,000. This controversy about the capitol demonstrated a continuing split within the state's political line-ups. Crittenden increasingly reflected a minority position best expressed nationally by the Republican Party leader John Quincy Adams. Pope, however, continued to reflect the Democratic Party in terms of Andrew Jackson.

The final evidence of factionalism in the territory was demonstrated in the move to grant the territory statehood. As early as 1831 letters began to appear in the *Arkansas Gazette* advocating Arkansas petitioning for statehood. The established political leadership, however, did not make any move to follow up on these suggestions. In fact, as late as 1833 Ambrose Sevier, who had been reelected as congressional delegate that year, made no mention of the issue in his campaign, but to the surprise of many, when he resumed his seat in Washington, he introduced a resolution requesting that the Committee on Territories consider making Arkansas a state. The basis for Arkansas becoming a state was argued by many as a proven ability to be organized and independent as a sovereign state, able to elect their own officials, particularly their governor and the congressional delegation, and not being dependent upon federal appointments directly. Critics of statehood, however, pointed out that costs of in-

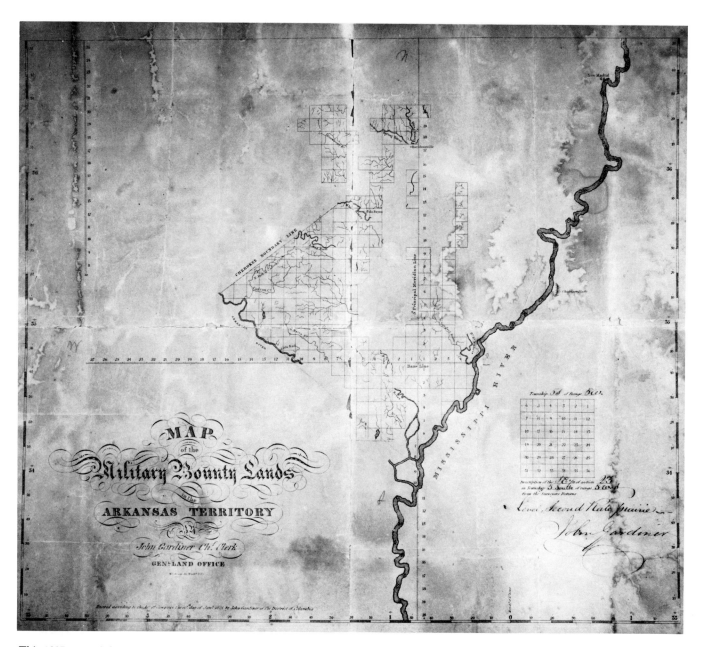

This 1837 map of the surveying district of Arkansas was completed by Edward Cross (1798-1887), surveyor general of public lands from 1836-1838. Cross later served as U.S. representative, 1839-1845; associate justice of the Arkansas Supreme Court, 1845-1846; and president of the Cairo and Fulton Railroad, 1855-1862. Courtesy, Arkansas History Commission

On June 15, 1836, President Andrew Jackson signed this bill making Arkansas a state. The new, twenty-fifth state of the Union was admitted as a slave state. Courtesy, Arkansas History Commission

S. 178.

IN SENATE OF THE UNITED STATES.

MARCH 22, 1836.

Mr. BUCHANAN, from the select committee on the subject, reported the following bill; which was read, and passed to a second reading.

A BILL

For the admission of the State of Arkansas into the Union, and to provide for the due execution of the laws of the United States within the same, and for other purposes.

1   Whereas the people of the Territory of Arkansas did, on

2   the thirtieth day of January, in the present year, by a con-

3   vention of delegates called and assembled for that purpose,

4   form for themselves a constitution and State Government,

5   which constitution and State Government, so formed, is re-

6   publican: and whereas the number of inhabitants within the

7   said Territory exceeds forty-seven thousand seven hundred

8   persons, computed according to the rule prescribed by the

9   constitution of the United States; and the said convention

10   have, in their behalf, asked the Congress of the United States

11   to admit the said Territory into the Union as a State, on an

12   equal footing with the original States:

STATE OF REGNANT POPULI ARKANSAS

ternal improvements, such as roads, and river systems, and frontier defense against the Indians, were now borne by the federal government and would have to be assumed by the state; the state simply did not have sufficient population and tax base to support that kind of service. Nevertheless, Sevier persisted with his request and the Democrat-controlled Congress quickly moved ahead in 1834 with the plan to make Arkansas a member of the family of states.

The statehood debate focused on the controversy of slavery. As with the Arkansas Territorial Bill, when Arkansas had little choice in the decisions made to identify the region as a slave territory, so now in 1834 was the decision made that Arkansas would be admitted as a slave state.

This was done in part to try and keep parity between the slave states and the non-slave states. As Sevier would say later, his reason for petitioning for statehood in 1833 was prompted primarily because Michigan was preparing to apply for admission to statehood at that time, and he saw an opportunity for Arkansas as a slave state to be paired with Michigan as a non-slave state. Also, the Territory of Florida was preparing to apply for admission as a state and Sevier felt that if Arkansas did not move to pair itself with Michigan, there was a possibility that Florida would, making it that much more difficult for Arkansas.

The approaching 1836 Presidential election was of some concern as well. Andrew Jackson did not seek reelection in 1836, and had already selected

Ballou's Pictorial featured Arkansas in its April 7, 1855, issue. The article cited 1850 census reports stating that more than two-thirds of the 209,897 Arkansans were farmers. There was one banker, one bookbinder, and one musician. Physicians and lawyers were more abundant, with 449 and 224 respectively. In addition, there were 105 harness makers, ninety-four printers, and four editors. Courtesy, University of Arkansas at Little Rock Archives and Special Collections

49

his successor, Martin Van Buren from New York. Jackson and the Democrats were somewhat concerned about Van Buren's ability to draw votes in the South. Arkansas was seen as a potential slave state that would give additional votes for Van Buren and the Democratic Party, assuming the state could be admitted under the Democratic administration of Andrew Jackson. In the United States Congress, Arkansas' bid for statehood ran into the usual controversy regarding slavery and slave expansion west of the Mississippi River. The old argument raised at the time of the Arkansas Territorial Bill was brought up again and the committee on territories debated at length whether or not to admit Arkansas as a slave state.

While this debate was going on in Washington, citizens in the territory took matters into their own hands and proceeded to call a constitutional convention and draft a document that would be reflective of the interest of all other people in the territory. Governor William S. Fulton was quite concerned about this action by the people and at first refused to sanction their efforts. The proceedings of the convention and the final document drafted by that body was printed in the *Arkansas Gazette.* The document that was drafted was typical of the frontier at the time; not particularly progressive but not too conservative, it was similar to the documents drafted in Tennessee and Missouri. Charles Fenton Mercer Noland, a delegate to the convention and representative from Batesville, was authorized to take the official document to Washington for presentation to the United States Congress. Noland was delayed on his trip on January 30, and because of high waters did not reach Washington until

March 8. In the meantime, Ambrose Sevier received a copy of the *Arkansas Gazette* with the constitution printed in it and used that information to introduce the request to Congress for admission as a state.

The United States Congress was somewhat reluctant to act upon such an official document but given the pressing needs of the time and the influence of Jacksonian supporters in Congress they were able to get the Arkansas Constitution accepted.

The issue was not really settled, however, because Territorial Governor Fulton still debated whether or not the convention was legal. He asked the United States attorney general for an opinion, who responded that while only Congress could authorize the people of the territory to call a constitutional convention, if the convention did represent the interest and desires of the people, there was no law that could prevent them from holding a peaceful assembly or petition the United States Congress. He interpreted the constitution as simply a petition from a body of citizens in the territory, and therefore legally acceptable. President Andrew Jackson signed the Arkansas Statehood Bill into law on June 15, 1836, making Arkansas the twenty-fifth state in the Union.

Following statehood, the first action was to hold statewide elections for new officers as called for in the constitution. The elections were scheduled for August and a spirited campaign developed among the Democrats, led by friends of Ambrose Sevier including James Conway, brother of second territorial delegate Henry Conway. The ticket included Archibald Yell, a lawyer and federal judge from Ozark who accepted the nomination from the party as the congressional delegate. The governor's race and the race for U.S. representative were the only statewide contests. Sevier had his eye on the United States senator post, for which he would have to wait until the General Assembly was elected to choose him, as this was prior to the direct election process of senators. The Democrats were opposed by members of the Whig Party, led by Absalom Fowler, who ran for governor, and William Cummings, who sought the representative position.

The elections were scheduled for the first Monday in August and all the candidates except Conway campaigned actively throughout the state. Although Conway complained he did not have time for campaigning, in the end it didn't really make a great deal of difference. The wisdom of the Democrats in pushing Arkansas to statehood, perhaps prematurely, came to be demonstrated in the elections, and Conway and Yell won easily over Fowler and Cummings. The first of what would be a long string of Democratic officeholders were inaugurated in Little Rock.

As governor, Conway faced the basic needs of establishing state government, getting the essential institutions into operation, and perhaps most importantly, establishing a state banking system. Because the federal bank had gone out of existence in 1836, it became increasingly necessary for states to adopt a state banking system in order to deal with state revenues. Another economic matter that had the attention of both the governor and the General Assembly was the need for revenue to operate state government. So, for this purpose, both Conway and the General Assembly worked together with the legislators to pass a bill levying a .25

Archibald Yell, Arkansas' second governor (1840-1844), came to Arkansas from Tennessee. After the Mexican War broke out, Yell resigned to go to war, and was killed at the battle of Buena Vista February 23, 1847. Courtesy, Arkansas History Commission

percent tax on real estate property. Even though the state's population was still below the national formula of 60,000, the tax collection proved to be more than enough to run state government. By the end of the second year of Conway's term as governor he could report that there was a surplus of $16,000 in the state treasury. This prompted the legislators to reduce the tax base to .12 percent—but in a short period of time the state experienced a deficit and so the original tax levy was reimposed.

With the state's finances in order, Conway and the Assembly could address the state's institutional needs. In addition to continuing some basic things already developed in the territorial period, mainly creating counties and towns, the General Assembly moved to establish a state penitentiary. While there was no great need, it was nevertheless important, and in 1838 the Assembly appropriated $20,000 to establish a state penitentiary, specifying that it must be at least five miles away from downtown Little Rock. The site chosen on Robert Crutchfield's farm is now occupied by the state capitol. Construction soon began, but the $20,000 was only enough for the foundation, and it took an additional appropriation of $45,000 to finish the structure in 1840.

Much of Conway's administration was overshadowed by controversy and by his own personal limitations. His health became a factor before the end of his term and his interest in the office greatly decreased. One controversy that particularly plagued him centered upon Miller County in the southwestern part of the state. Miller County had been chartered by the Territorial Legislature, but its loyalty had been divided between Arkansas and the Republic of Texas. The residents were increasingly more loyal to the Republic of Texas, and in fact, representatives from Miller County were elected to both the Texas Legislature and the Arkansas Legislature.

The dispute came to a head in 1837 when the State of Arkansas attempted to collect taxes through the new revenue bill passed by the legislature. After citizens of the county refused to pay, Conway ordered the sheriff to collect the taxes. The sheriff, who was unable to collect the taxes, resigned his position and took an oath of allegiance to the Republic of Texas. The problem heightened when the circuit judges appointed by the governor were unable to reach Miller County because of heavy spring rains that flooded the Red River. The Miller County dispute was not resolved until an appeal was made before the United States Supreme Court, which handed down a decision in which the majority of the land was

assigned to Texas and the Miller County boundary was redrawn to present-day specifications.

Conway also faced the continuation of a usual problem in the territory—namely law and order. In the 1830s the Cherokee Indians were moved from east to west and the resulting merge of the eastern and western factions brought increased hostility. In an area outside Fayetteville, a bloody massacre occurred, which local authorities generally attributed to conflict between the two factions. The suspected murderers escaped into Indian territory and were never brought to trial. This instability on the frontier contributed to the general nervousness of the residents in the western counties and added to Conway's difficulties as governor.

The various trials and tribulations of the new state of Arkansas combined to present serious problems for Conway's administration. Those problems, coupled with his declining health, caused Conway to decide not to seek reelection in 1840. Instead, Archibald Yell decided to give up his seat as the state's congressional delegate to run for the office of governor. The Democrats then nominated Edward Cross to run for the House of Representatives. Yell and Cross provided the team for the Democratic Party. The Whigs did not choose to nominate anyone for the office of governor, but they did endorse Absalom Fowler for the office of the state congressional delegate.

In the campaign that followed Yell proved to be one of the most effective politicians the state had produced. He was generally identified as the man of the people—equally at home debating the issues or participating at a community social event—and received a wide majority of votes in the

1840 election. As governor he called attention for the first time to the needs of the state for an improved education system, a public education law. In his inaugural speech he said, "As the public mind is elevated on the scale of learning, so are the means of advancing the morals and intellectual progress increased and rendered stable. Hence, self-preservation should be a sufficient incentive to lay deep and broad the foundation of universal education." With that prodding, the General Assembly passed a public school law requiring every township to elect three commissioners to oversee the sale or rent of land in each township in the county to finance the public schools, build buildings, and hire teachers. It was the responsibility of local officials to enforce the law and in truth there was wide disparity between the original law and its application. For the most part schools were kept open only a few months out of the year even though the law specified they be kept open five months. The commissioners were to visit the school once a month, but this proved unenforceable; in reality Arkansas' public education did not develop prior to the Civil War.

The missing ingredient for education was state funding. The funds to operate the school were left primarily at the local level although the legislature did authorize the sale of some public lands to finance public education. But, by and large, the function of the law was left in local hands and no effort was made by the legislature to reinforce it or to establish an institution of higher education, even though there was some debate on the

During the days of early statehood, public education was undeveloped. As a result, private schools such as Sophia Sawyer's Fayetteville Female Seminary were established. Courtesy, Arkansas History Commission

Before becoming Arkansas' fifth governor in 1852, Elias Nelson Conway (1812-1892), the youngest of the Conways' sons, served Arkansas as United States deputy surveyor and auditor. Conway served eight years as governor. Courtesy, Arkansas History Commission

need for one.

Other issues of concentration in Yell's administration included internal improvement, the continued development of the state's institutional system, and the establishment of the office of attorney general. Improvements were made to construct levees along the Mississippi River to help control floods and improve river transportation and navigation, and improve public roads. During Yell's administration coal was discovered in Johnston County and the first state geological survey was taken to identify the state's mineral resources. Yell spent much of his time trying to deal with the controversial banking issue. By 1840 both the state bank and the real estate bank had fallen into bankruptcy, and serious charges and counter-charges were hurled about who was responsible. Yell called for an investigation to examine the bank's books and try to determine the problems within the system. However, it became apparent that most of the state's influential leaders, including members of the General Assembly, had stock in the banks and Yell's call for investigation grew very unpopular. The real estate bank went as far as turning its affairs over to a group of private trustees. When Yell challenged their actions he filed suit in Pulaski County Circuit Court, which upheld the action of the real estate bank. Yell then appealed to the U.S. Supreme Court but unfortunately Yell's term as governor ended before he got a hearing, and the bank issue was not resolved.

As Yell neared the end of his first term as governor it became apparent that the state's Democratic Party was deeply divided. The leadership roles were held by a group referred to as "the family," which hailed from

William E. Woodruff (1795-1885) of New York founded the Arkansas Gazette *in 1819. Courtesy, Arkansas History Commission*

Henry Conway, who was elected as the state's congressional delegate. He and his brother, first governor James Conway, as well as their relatives by marriage and blood relation—namely Ambrose Sevier and Richard Johnson—had joined forces to control most of the state's significant political offices. The increased immigration after statehood in 1836 had caused a number of people in the outlying areas of Little Rock to become more concerned about "the family" and its control of the state's policies. At the 1844 Democratic convention the family nominated Elias Conway, James' brother, as governor, and Daniel Chapman to the office of congression-

Thomas S. Drew (1801-1879) followed Archibald Yell in the governor's office, after he was elected in 1844. Although Drew was elected to a second term, he resigned in January 1849 because of financial problems. Courtesy, Arkansas History Commission

al delegate from the state. However, only sixteen of the state's forty-six counties were represented at the convention—and an open dispute soon developed. William Woodruff, the influential editor of the *Arkansas Gazette,* charged the family with being unrepresentative of the state's party as a whole. In a dramatic move, Woodruff broke with party officials and walked out of the meeting. The Whigs, observing the split within the Democratic Party, met in their convention and nominated Lorenzo Gibson, a physician from Hot Springs,

for governor, and David Walker, an influential lawyer from Fayetteville, for congressional delegate. This slate promised to be the strongest that the Whigs could offer, and, coupled with the division within the Democratic Party, caused the family to ask for a new convention.

At the new convention the family members changed their strategy and persuaded Chapman to run for governor, dropping Elias Conway from the ticket, and asked Archibald Yell to run again for his old seat of congressional delegate. Yell agreed, and the Chapman-Yell ticket was then forged to oppose the Gibson-Walker ticket of the Whigs. Unfortunately, Chapman became ill in the course of the campaign and had to drop out. The Democratic Party then chose Thomas Drew to replace him in a hasty caucus. Drew was from Tennessee and had worked at a variety of jobs before finally settling in Lawrence County to open a fairly large farm. With the Drew-Yell ticket the Democrats won, although by a close margin, over the Whigs.

The gubernatorial election had hardly been over before the so-called "Texas question" began to be discussed in the state and national press. This issue had first come to the attention of state citizens in 1836 when Texas won independence from Mexico and appeared to be preparing for application for admission as a state in the United States. However, the slavery issue, coupled with Arkansas' statehood, made Texan admission appear impossible, so Texas withdrew its request and established itself as an independent republic. It remained the "Lone Star Republic" until 1844 when national pressures reopened the debate and pushed for Texan statehood. One complication

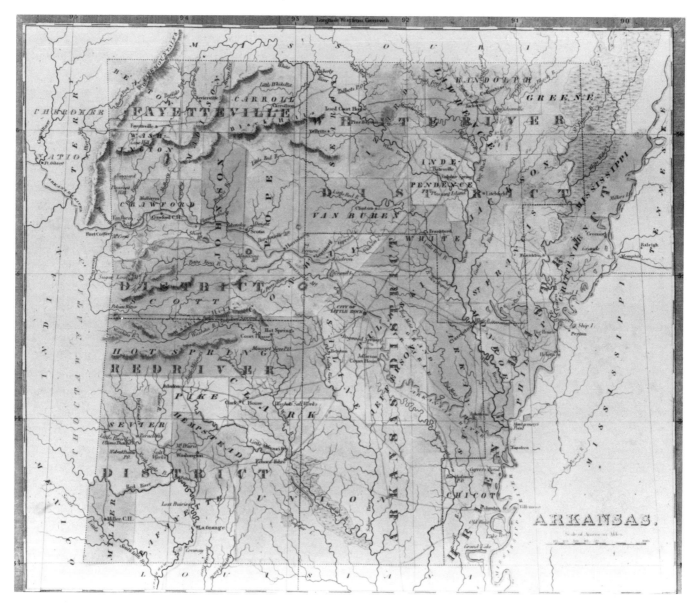

In his 1842 map of Arkansas, Greenleaf showed the state's land districts. With offices listed in parentheses, the districts were: the Fayetteville District (Fayetteville), the Red River District (Washington), the White River District (Batesville), the Arkansas District (Little Rock), and the Helena District (Helena). Courtesy, Arkansas History Commission

Prominent Little Rock attorney and land speculator Chester Ashley (1791-1848) served as U.S. senator from 1844 until his death in 1848. Courtesy, Arkansas History Commission

was the position taken by Mexico, which stated that annexation of Texas by the United States would be taken as an act of war.

As the national political leaders considered what direction to take regarding Texas, Arkansans observed Texas' close proximity to their border and wondered what the impact would be. Proponents of annexation argued that admitting Texas would in fact attract more immigrants into Arkansas as they moved toward Texas. Admitting Texas would also bring in more slave territory, providing opportunity for slavery expansion, which would continue to increase the value of slaves. This of course was also an argument against admitting Texas, as anti-slavery forces rallied for their cause. Others thought the admission of Texas would bring trade with Sante Fe, therefore improving prices for Arkansas flour, pork, and horses.

When war was officially declared with Mexico in May 1845, President James K. Polk called for volunteers. Many Arkansans quickly responded. Secretary of War William Marcy requested that Arkansas furnish a regiment of cavalry for combat duty and also a batallion of mounted riflemen to guard the frontiers of the state. A cavalry unit was easily put together with a number of volunteers including Archibald Yell, who resigned his seat in Congress to enlist in the regiment as a private.

However, not long after he enlisted, Yell received word from Secretary of War Marcy that he was to be made a commanding officer. The Arkansas unit proceeded to the Rio Grande, joined forces with the general army of Zachary Taylor, marched across the river, and saw action in a number of small skirmishes. The major battle came at Buena Vista. During that

58

battle the American forces were brought to a standstill by the Mexican Army. Unfortunately, Archibald Yell was killed in that battle and the other ranking officer, Solon Borland, was taken prisoner and brought to Mexico. After the battle American forces pushed forward and won the war with Mexico. After the Treaty of Guadalupe Hidalgo was signed in 1848, Texas became a part of the United States.

Arkansas politics following the Mexican War were unsettled and extremely volatile. Yell's death had taken away one of the state's most popular politicians and Sevier resigned his senate seat to go with the peace commission to negotiate the Treaty of Guadalupe Hidalgo. To make matters worse, Governor Drew, although re elected in 1848, resigned at the end of the first legislative session when the legislature refused to propose a salary increase for him.

Moreover, after Solon Borland was freed from a Mexican prison he returned to the state, as did Ambrose Sevier following the conclusion of the peace conference. They both tried for the same senate seat that Sevier had just vacated. At the same time, Senator Chester Ashley died, leaving the other senate seat vacant, but Sevier wanted his old seat back and refused to stand for an election for Ashley's seat. Borland was ultimately selected by the state General Assembly, and William Case Sebastian was chosen to fill Ashley's seat. Sevier died a year later. Ultimately the Assembly called a special election for the governorship, and John S. Roane was elected to replace Thomas Drew. With all posts filled, the state was again ready to move forward, but the political dust was still trying to settle.

Another factor contributing to the

Elias N. Conway (1812-1892) began his political career as state auditor from 1835 to 1849. In 1852 he was elected governor and remained in that office until 1860. As governor, Conway strengthened the railroad system, led the state to assume control of the Blind School, and began a geological survey. Courtesy, Arkansas History Commission

unsettled nature of the state's political scene was the discovery of gold in California. Gold had actually been discovered a few weeks following the signing of the peace treaty ending the Mexican War, but was kept secret for a time, only becoming public knowledge in December 1849. President James K. Polk's announcement in his State of the Union message that gold had been discovered in California in the lands recently gained from Mexico touched off a mass migration of people moving west to the California goldfields. Many of those people traveled through Arkansas on the way. Some chose to stay and for the first time the state benefited from the overland migration routes. But those who stayed were outnumbered by those who left the state to go to the goldfields on their own. The drain was significant enough to prompt Governor Roane to estimate that more than 1,000 people had left the state in 1850, and, as he commented, if each took only $200 in hard money, the state would suffer a great deal because of it.

As Arkansas survived its political instability and shifting population, the state strengthened. Politics in the 1850s did eventually become more stable. This was due primarily to the 1852 election of Democrat Elias N. Conway, the youngest member of the Conway family. A strong member of the family organization, Elias was also one of the most conservative governors in the pre-Civil War period. He opposed building railroads because of the tax monies it would require and instead lobbied for improvement of dirt roads, earning the nickname "Dirt Roads Conway." He was also a strong advocate of economy and government, and due to his conservative management of the state's

budget, he left a sizable surplus in the treasury upon leaving the governorship in 1860. He also concentrated his attention on trying to repay the loans left by the real estate and state banks and was successful in getting more than two million dollars of the debt repaid. However, there still remained a balance on the bonds, an issue that continued into the late nineteenth century.

During the 1850s, particularly after the first wave of the gold rush interest had passed by, Arkansas experienced a time of growth and development. A large influx of immigrants, most owning slaves, caused the state's population to increase. It had doubled between 1840 and 1850, but the decade of the 1850s saw the largest increase of the state's population, doubling again by 1860. These new immigrants also added to the political problems within the state, at least as far as family control of the many political offices was concerned. In 1850 the population of the state had become large enough to merit a second seat in the United States Congress,

and the family had increased difficulties controlling its nominees and getting them elected in the congressional races; by 1856 it became apparent that the family control was all but gone. The newcomers were simply not bound by the same traditions as the voters who had resided in the state since and before statehood. By 1860 Arkansas' political developments were coming to reflect a greater diversity of interest and the new settlers were bringing new ideas and new interests into the political scene.

Conway did not seek reelection in 1860, but a relative by marriage, Henry M. Rector, chose to run as an independent candidate, defeating the family-backed candidate. Rector's election not only signaled the final break in the family's control, at least for the immediate period, but also the beginning of shattering events for Arkansas. Because of his strong advocacy for slavery, Rector began an active campaign to lead the state into seceding from the Union to join with the sister states in the South to form a Confederacy.

Confederate Brigadier General N.B. Burrow called Arkansans "To Arms!" on February 25, 1862, from his headquarters in Fort Smith. All were ordered to report or suffer the consequences. Courtesy, Arkansas History Commission

TO ARMS ! TO ARMS !

HEADQUARTERS 3RD BRIGADE 1ST DIVISION ARKANSAS MILITIA, } Fort Smith, Arkansas, February 25th, 1862. }

By order of the Governor and Commander in Chief of the Militia, and President of the Military Board of Arkansas, every man subject to military duty is required to report himself forthwith to the Commanding officer of his company, armed and equiped as the law directs.

Those who refuse to report themselves must be made to comply, or treated as deserters, who desert in the face of the enemy. Such persons cannot be left behind safely! All suspicious persons will be arrested and kept under guard and moved forward with the Militia. Black Republican spies, deserters, vagrants, and sympathizers with the North, if there be such in the land, cannot be trusted in the rear when the Militia moves forward! All must, therefore, move together or be dealt with as law directs.

All are entreated by their honor, their homes, and their families to act promptly.

Officers will lay aside all other business, and devote themselves exclusively to the public service—rally their men, borrow, purchase or seize all the arms in the hands of non-combatants and march to the places appointed for rendezvous.

N. B. BURROW,
Brig. Gen. Commanding.

This illustration by H.B. Mollhausen was lithographed by Sarony, Major & Knapp of New York for the twelve-volume set Reports of Explorations and Surveys to Ascertain the Most Practicable and Economic Route for a Railroad from the Mississippi River to the Pacific Ocean *published between 1855 and 1861. Courtesy, Arkansas History Commission*

*In the March 29, 1862, is-
sue of* Harper's Weekly,
*the Battle of Pea Ridge
fought earlier that month
was recorded. Because it
was the largest west of
the Mississippi, that im-
portant battle has been
called the "Gettysburg of
the West." Courtesy, Ar-
kansas History Com-
mission*

Arkansas in the Civil War and Reconstruction

CHAPTER III

Few events have made a more graphic impact on Arkansas than the Civil War and the Reconstruction period that followed. More has been written about the war than any other topic in the state's history, and the process of reconstructing political, social, and economic institutions galvanized opinion and shaped political developments as perhaps no other event has in the state's history.

Soon after Governor Henry Rector assumed office, he made a strong plea for legislators to join the states of South Carolina and Georgia to secede from the Union. During the legislative session, representatives from both South Carolina and Georgia came to Arkansas and lobbied the legislators to join with the governor in seceding. Members of the General Assembly, however, were not as motivated for secession as the governor and his cohorts appeared to be. Rather than vote immediate secession the assembly members decided instead to call a special convention to discuss the matter. Delegates were elected in February 1861 who met in Little Rock for the first secession convention. Debates lasting for several days ultimately decided not to secede. However, it did leave the issue open and empowered convention president David Walker from Washington County, to reconvene the convention at a future date should conditions merit. Following its adjournment Arkansans watched anxiously as the events in South Carolina moved closer to open conflict with the federal government.

The decisive action came in April 1861. President Abraham Lincoln was determined to send support to federal forces in Fort Sumter, off the coast of Charleston, South Carolina. When shore batteries of the city of Charleston fired upon supply ships, the

opening gunfire of the Civil War had begun. President Lincoln called South Carolina's act a domestic rebellion and called for 75,000 federal troops to mobilize and remain in a state of readiness in an effort to put down the disturbance. In a telegram to Arkansas Governor Henry Rector, the President asked that Arkansas contribute soldiers to the federal effort. Governor Rector, however, refused to honor the President's request for troops and instead stated in a returned telegraph that "from Arkansas none would be taken."

Following the firing on Sumter, David Walker reconvened the delegates of the secession convention. The act was considered serious enough to vote whether or not to secede from the Union. As the delegates met in the state capitol in Little Rock on May 7, 1861, there was strong sentiment in favor of secession on the basis that South Carolina's state's rights had been violated by the federal government. On the first ballot that was taken, all but five of the delegates voted for secession and in the second motion to make it

unanimous, all but one, Isaac Murphy, a delegate from Madison County, agreed. Murphy stood alone and refused to vote secession.

With Arkansas' move to secede, formal action of war was now under way. The secession convention stayed in session to organize preparations to join the Confederacy and pursue the war effort against the United States. To assist in the planning, the convention created a special committee, a board made up of the governor and two appointed members, who would be responsible for overseeing the ac-

Facing page, left: *Henry Massie Rector (1816-1899) was elected governor in 1860, defeating Richard H. Johnson. After secession Arkansas' constitution was rewritten and the governor's term shortened to two years. Rector lost his 1862 reelection campaign to Harris Flanagin. Courtesy, Arkansas History Commission*

Facing page, right: *Editor of the* States Rights Democrat *at Helena and a U.S. representative (1856-1861), Thomas C. Hindman served as a major general in the Confederate Army. Hindman commanded at the Battle of Prairie Grove in 1862. Courtesy, Arkansas History Commission*

Right: *This "extra" proclaimed the beginning of the Civil War just three days after Confederates fired on Fort Sumter. Courtesy, Arkansas History Commission*

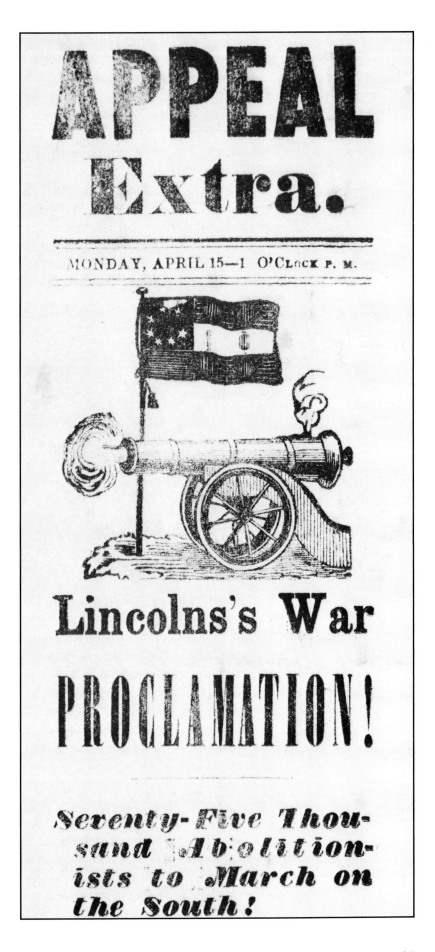

tivities. The convention also called for volunteers to join the Arkansas state militia and to prepare for frontier and home defense.

Throughout the Civil War, Arkansas' political leaders wrestled with the problem of how to maintain security within the state and at the same time contribute to the greater war effort east of the Mississippi River. It was not an easy decision for Rector or any of the other political leaders to make.

Encouraging Arkansans to volunteer for the Confederate Army almost in Arkansas, the Confederate States of America moved to prepare for war throughout the nation, especially in the western region. General Ben McCullough, commander of the Confederate forces in Texas, was ordered to move toward Fort Smith and begin preparation for an invasion of Missouri. He was to be joined there by the Arkansas unit headed by Brigadier General N.B. Pierce. After joining Pierce and the Arkansas troops at Fort Smith, McCullough made plans to move north into Missouri, which

surely meant that they would be taken from the state and assigned positions in the eastern battlefields. Such a move would no doubt leave the state unprotected and invite attack from the Indian tribes on the state's western border. By contrast, if the state encouraged citizens to join the state in frontier defense, then Arkansas would have to shoulder the responsibility of outfitting and paying the salaries of these soldiers—an expense the state was not ready to bear. Nevertheless, there was much enthusiasm for the war effort and in short order a group of volunteers had been organized as a unit from Arkansas.

While events were moving forward was particularly important to the Confederate cause. It not only contained the most important water and land routes west, but also the state had become a political rallying cry for the slave interest; it was the Missouri Compromise that had established slavery in Missouri, while excluding it from the balance of the Louisiana territory. Missouri also held strategic value for the Confederacy because of its lead and zinc deposits. These items, together with the salt deposits in neighboring Oklahoma and Kansas, were particularly important for making ammunition. There was also some concern for the psychological, morale-building aspects of the Con-

Facing page: *As secession sentiment grew in Arkansas, the state government demanded the surrender of the United States arsenal in Little Rock. After troops called in from around the state threatened a forced takeover, Governor Henry M. Rector persuaded the federal commander to evacuate. The building now houses the Museum of Science and History at MacArthur Park. Courtesy, Arkansas History Commission*

Right: *Because supplies were in high demand during the Civil War and funds were low, benefits such as this performance sponsored by the Pine Bluff Histrionic Club were held to raise money. Sometimes the funds went to help a specific company in the area. Courtesy, Arkansas History Commission*

A lucky shot caused severe damage to the Union gunboat Mound City, which was bringing relief to the troops under General Samuel A. Curtis, but failed to prevent the capture of St. Charles in July 1862. Courtesy, Arkansas History Commission

federacy being able to take Missouri.

Missouri's secession convention had refused to secede following its vote in St. Louis. A few individuals who sympathized with the Confederate cause sought to organize an independent unit to attempt an overthrow of the existing government in Missouri. Sterling Price, who had a significant role in the Mexican War and who had also served as president of the secession convention, joined with the governor to lead efforts to move Missouri into Confederacy.

Price reestablished his military skills and organized a group of volunteers in the southwestern portion of the state, which by 1861 had grown to about 6,000. McCullough and Arkansas General Pierce decided on the strategy of marching north from Fort Smith to link up with Price and his volunteers, hoping to control Missouri and wrest it from federal hands. The three units organized just south and west of Springfield, Missouri, and began plans for an attack upon federal

troops stationed in Springfield. Those troops, under the command of General Nathaniel Lyon, who had come from St. Louis to accept the command, numbered some 6,500 troops and were determined to stop the Confederacy from taking Missouri.

Although outnumbered, Lyon soon discovered an advantage he had in facing his Confederate opponents—namely opposition and dissension within the ranks. Price, commanding only a militia movement, nevertheless had outranked McCullough in the Mexican War and continued to show his lack of support or respect to McCullough, even though he had an official command from the Confederate States of America. Pierce, in the Arkansas militia, also argued for a greater role in the decision-making process. While the three generals argued over strategy, Lyon moved his troops out of Springfield and, just after daybreak, at the community known as Wilson's Creek, Lyon led his surprise attack on the combined

Although Albert Pike was a Confederate brigadier general in charge of the Indian territory, he is probably better known as a leader in Freemasonry. In addition, Pike was a lawyer, a poet and, in 1864, an associate justice of the Arkansas Supreme Court. Courtesy, Arkansas History Commission

Lithographers Currier and Ives produced a print of Union General Franz Sigel at the Battle of Pea Ridge, March 8, 1862, where Confederates met defeat. Courtesy, University of Arkansas at Little Rock Archives and Special Collections

forces of McCullough, Pierce, and Price. The battle lasted several hours, and after Lyon was killed on the battlefield trying to rally his men, the federal troops began a hasty retreat back into Springfield. Senior commander McCullough, although urged by Sterling Price to pursue the retreating forces, refused to do so, and the Union forces were able to retreat into Springfield. McCullough not only refused to pursue the retreating Union forces, but he also grew uneasy about his position in southern Missouri, fearing he would run out of supplies and become prey of the regrouped Union Army. Consequently, McCullough ordered a general retreat of the Confederate Army back into Arkansas toward Fayetteville, where they took up winter quarters.

Lyon was replaced as commander of the Union troops by General Samuel A. Curtis. Curtis, during the winter of 1861-1862, prepared to move south, attack McCullough, and break up the Confederacy's effort to penetrate and control Missouri.

With a new group of men, the army marched south in March 1862. As he proceeded south Curtis' army was detected by a McCullough unit, and plans were made to stop the federal troops' advance. The site chosen for the defense by McCullough, Pierce, and Price was the area outside Elkhorn Tavern known as Pea Ridge. Arriving early, McCullough and his forces took up defensive positions around an open field just south of the ridge. As Curtis' troops approached, McCullough and the Confederate Army launched a major attack. Their first charge was beaten back; McCullough was killed on the field and his second in command, James McIntosh, who led the effort to recover McCullough's body, was also killed. This

left in charge the third in command, Albert Pike, who had been designated commissioner of Indian affairs to the Indians of the region west of Arkansas' western boundaries. Pike had been given the responsibility of negotiating a treaty to enlist as much Indian support as possible and had brought a band of Cherokee and Choctaw warriors into the battlefield. However, he was out of position from the main body of the Confederate troops and did not learn of McCullough's and McIntosh's deaths until late in the day—too late to effectively plan a counter-strategy. The end result of Pea Ridge is somewhat the reverse of Wilson's Creek. The Confederate Army chose to withdraw after suffering severe losses in its leadership and the Union Army held the day at Pea Ridge. McCullough's army retreated as best it could and was ultimately placed under the command of Earl VanDorn.

After weighing the strengths of Curtis, VanDorn concluded that it was impossible to beat Curtis with his group and withdrew from Arkansas, taking Confederate troops east of the Mississippi River. Most of the Arkansas militiamen stayed behind, although their morale suffered considerably, and there was little for them to do in the state. In truth, it became increasingly difficult for the state to effectively outfit any other militia units.

After VanDorn's removal of regular Confederate troops from the state, Curtis made a leisurely drop across northern Arkansas, eventually making his way to the Delta. He moved across the northern counties on his way to Batesville, where he took control, and then moved on to take control of Helena. In each case, while militia units worked actively to try to

Like these five, Arkansas men volunteered eagerly for service in the Confederate Army. Arkansas women also joined in the war effort by supplying clothing, blankets, and bandages. Courtesy, Arkansas History Commission

resist the federal army, the Confederate Army was able to contribute very little because so many of its soldiers were deployed to areas east of the river. Curtis was then in position to control the area north of the Arkansas River. At Helena, however, he was placed under the command of a new officer, General Frederick Steele.

Steele made plans to march on Little Rock and take control of the capital city but he was delayed somewhat due to persistent rumors about the size and strength of the Confederate

march in. General Steele led the Union troops to occupy Arkansas, at least the area north of the Arkansas River, in September 1863.

For a few months after Steele's occupation of Little Rock, the war settled down into a stalemate. The Union Army controlled most of the state north and east of the Arkansas River while the Confederate Army, under the command of Sterling Price, controlled the region to the south and west of the Arkansas River. Price had been brought back from east of the

Helena was occupied early in the war by Union General Samuel A. Curtis. The heavy artillery moved in by the Federals can be seen in the pyramids of cannonballs and the cannon in the foreground. Courtesy, Arkansas History Commission

Army and the Arkansas volunteers. Nevertheless, in late summer of 1863 Steele moved his troops from Helena toward Little Rock. The General Assembly had determined earlier it would not stay in the war zone and had all the state's official records moved to the community of Washington in the southwestern corner of the state. Also, the legislators themselves had agreed to move and set up the capital in the courthouse at Hempstead County in Washington. In the meantime, plans were made to evacuate the city of Little Rock and not resist the efforts of the Union troops to

Mississippi to assume control of the Arkansas militia and the other Confederate units in the region. Arkansas was still under the general control of the Trans-Mississippi District of the Confederacy under the general command of Kirby Smith, who was stationed at Shreveport. During this lull in the actual fighting in the fall of 1863 and the winter of 1864, the state became somewhat nomadic in many sections. Bushwhackers and jayhawkers fought vigilante actions in the northern Ozarks and many innocent Arkansans came to be the prey of the lawless band of men who rode back

THE WAR IN THE BORDER STATES.

As the war raged on, more soldiers left home to go to war, and as blockades cut off supplies from the industrial North, the situation in the South became grim. Harper's Weekly ran emotional depictions of hunger and suffering. Courtesy, Arkansas History Commission

and forth in the unpatrolled regions, living off the land. Many did so in the name of the Confederate Army and many simply used their own strength and might to take what they desired.

The Civil War was particularly difficult for families. Three long years of hostilities had brought severe strains on family members, when often one member fought for the Union and the other for the Confederate Army. Not infrequently a type of guerilla warfare broke out between these families over land titles, lost livestock, or simply

disagreement about the war effort itself.

It was also during this time that one of the most celebrated spy stories in the state developed. While Steele was occupying Little Rock, a youth by the name of David O. Dodd, who had grown up southwest of Little Rock, was charged with spying for the Confederacy. Dodd and his family had moved to Camden in southern Arkansas when the war began. Dodd had returned to Little Rock to visit with friends in the fall of 1863 not long after Steele occupied the city.

David Owen Dodd is known as the "boy martyr of the Confederacy." Born in 1846, Dodd was just a teenager when he was hanged as a Confederate spy by the Union forces at Little Rock on January 8, 1864. Courtesy, Arkansas History Commission

Earlier in his youth Dodd had worked for a brief time in the telegraph office and had apparently learned the basic rudiments of Morse Code. As he was preparing to return to Camden, he was stopped by a sentry on the outskirts of Little Rock, searched, and was discovered to have a coded message. He was arrested and brought back to Steele's headquarters in Little Rock where his message was decoded. In a very general way the message seemed to describe the number and location of Steele's troops in Little Rock. Dodd was charged with spying and with making an attempt to carry classified information to enemy lines. He was arrested and confined. A court martial was convened in a military court and a ruling on the evidence found Dodd guilty and sentenced him to be hanged. As a youth of sixteen his arrest and the publicity surrounding his activities captured the attention of many residents in the city who had known him personally as he grew up outside of the town. Several women of Little Rock approached Steele and asked that he grant leniency to Dodd and spare his life. The general, however, stated that the youth had been found guilty of being a spy and the only recourse he had was capital punishment. Dodd was subsequently hanged, his death making him a local hero and martyr. A monument was erected in Little Rock's MacArthur Park.

Steele's army headquartered in Little Rock in the fall and winter of 1863. In the southwest part of the state, Sterling Price, in command of the Arkansas units, stayed in the general vicinity of Washington. Little military action was seen until the spring of 1864 when the federal armies determined to make a major strike into the Trans-Mississippi District in an effort to crush the remaining Confederate force there. As outlined by federal strategy, Steele was to march southwest of Little Rock to rendezvous with Nathaniel Banks, who would be leading an expedition up the Red River from Baton Rouge. Most of Banks' expedition was to board steamboats and join Steele near Monroe, Louisiana, in preparation for an attack on Shreveport.

Unknown to Steele, Banks' movement upriver encountered numerous difficulties, including floodwaters on the Red River, which made travel extremely difficult. Increasing opposition from Confederate units along the river ultimately forced Banks to turn back without reaching his objective in Monroe.

Meanwhile, Steele launched his part of the campaign, which came to be known in Confederate annals as the Red River Campaign, or Southern Campaign in Arkansas. Steele marched toward Hot Springs and gave all the appearances that he was planning to attack the new capital of Washington. Price and his units began preparing to defend Washington and attacked Steele's troops periodically with Confederate cavalry units. Steele's strategy was to push the Confederate armies back to the southwest away from the general vicinity of Monroe so that he could link up with Nathaniel Banks. For a period of weeks the plan seemed to work successfully. Price and General I.S. Marmaduke did stage the southwest drive, and Steele made his march toward the south in a more southeasterly direction. At a strategic moment, Steele turned and marched toward Camden to take that city as a supply base in preparation for moving on to Monroe.

His rapid change in direction was

successful and he was able to get to the city of Camden and capture it without any major incidents ahead of the more superior Confederate forces. After a few days in Camden, however, intelligence sources began to indicate the mounting Confederate opposition to the south and west. Moreover, Steele's supplies began to run short as he encountered increasing difficulties in getting supply trains from Little Rock into Camden because of Confederate cavalry activity.

While waiting in Camden, Steele learned of a large supply of corn near the vicinity of Poison Springs and decided to send a forage band of some 700 men to capture the corn supply and bring it back to camp. As they marched out, the group, which included the first Kansas "colored infantry regiment," were attacked by a large band of Confederates and driven back to camp. The first Kansas colored regiment lost almost 50 percent of its members and the so-called Battle of Poison Springs ended in disaster for the Union foragers. Back in Camden, supplies running dangerously low, Steele was forced to make alternative plans to get support. He sent word for new supplies to be routed through Pine Bluff by way of Marks' Mills and subsequently a large caravan of some 240 wagons started to Pine Bluff to bring supplies into Camden. Again, the Confederate forces learned of the movement, attacked the wagon train near the community of Marks' Mills, and succeeded in capturing the entire unit.

Supplies rapidly dwindling, Steele determined to abandon the Red River Campaign and turn back to the safety of Little Rock. In early spring of 1864 he started with his men out of Camden and moved in an easterly direction toward Little Rock. His numbers by this time had dwindled to some 5,000 men and he was pursued by a total group of some 10,000 Confederates. The Confederates were not as well organized, which allowed Steele to march more rapidly and gain the advantage in distance as he made his way back toward Little Rock. Upon reaching the Saline River, however, Steele discovered that the river was flooded, posing a serious problem for crossing. In efforts to bridge the river as quickly as possible, his engineering corps began to build a pontoon bridge, just as the Confederate forces began approaching. There followed a running battle that lasted several hours, known as the Battle of Jen kins Ferry. Fortunately, Steele and his men were able to hold off the Confederate Army until the pontoon bridge was completed. Steele and his troops escaped across the river, destroying the bridge as they left and for the time being, at least, preventing Confederate pursuit. Steele was able to make his way back into Little Rock and then enjoyed the safety and comfort of the city.

Major efforts were made to restore order as quickly as possible and city authorities who were loyal to the federal government were allowed to remain in office. Trade was also resumed quickly for merchants. Steele received some pressure from his field commanders to mount a campaign to take all of Arkansas, and when he did not receive orders to follow such a plan, he began efforts to recruit Union support in the state by promising peace and security, by adding to the rumors that the Confederacy planned to abandon Arkansas, and suggesting that peace would help end crime and violence and return economic stability to the state.

Perhaps Steele's efforts began to

Arkansas' Confederate officials moved to Washington in Hempstead County to conduct governmental business for the remainder of the war as Union forces occupied Little Rock in September 1863. This house served as the state capitol. Courtesy, Arkansas History Commission

pay off because within a month after the capture of Little Rock, Union meetings were held in various parts of the state—Fort Smith, Van Buren, and Little Rock—all in the month of October. In Little Rock central Union clubs formed and a committee of five was appointed to draft a proclamation to work for a peaceful establishment of state government. Most of the Union meetings followed a similar pattern. There was an initial pledge of support for the United States government, agreement to abolish slavery, and a pledge to cooperate with the Union and the military. Ultimately, as the meetings became more defined, plans were made to elect delegates to a new state constitutional

convention that would meet in Little Rock and reorganize the state. The President was kept informed of the developments in Arkansas through military reports.

President Lincoln appeared to respond to Arkansas' effort when he issued his Ten Percent Plan in December of 1863. In Lincoln's plan, any state in which 10 percent of the voters in the 1860 election would take the loyalty oath to the federal government could be readmitted to the Union. Soon after hearing the President's announcement, citizens from twenty or thirty counties, all north and east of the Arkansas River, met again in Fort Smith to discuss readmission. There it was decided to call

The only Arkansas legislator to vote against secession in 1861 was Isaac Murphy (1799-1882) of Madison County, who was elected governor in 1864, and served until 1868. Courtesy, Arkansas History Commission

for an election of delegates for a constitutional convention to meet in Little Rock. The convention opened in 1864 and remained in session for about three weeks. In the proceedings that followed a committee of twelve drafted the Constitution of 1864, which was essentially the same as that of 1836 with the slavery provision modified. The constitution was then submitted to the voters for ratification and passed by an overwhelming margin. At the same time the constitution was being voted on, individuals were being elected for the various state offices provided for in the constitution. Candidates were also elected to reestablish the federal government in Arkansas.

Isaac Murphy, the only member of the secession convention to refuse to vote for secession, was elected governor under the new constitution. Murphy had been forced to leave the state soon after the vote but returned following Steele's capture of the city

the previous fall. Isaac Murphy was born in Pittsburgh and educated in eastern schools, later moving to Tennessee where he taught school. He came to Arkansas in 1834 where he established residence near Fayetteville, resuming his teaching career. By 1840 he had become one of the best-known teachers in the northwestern part of the state and also studied law. In 1849 he achieved some recognition by going to the gold rush in California, and later admitted he returned poorer than when he had started. Murphy served in the state senate in 1856 from Benton and Madison counties, and stayed in the office of governor for four years. As he told the legislature in his first address to the General Assembly in April of 1864, "The state has not a dollar in her treasury" and so the officers of the provisional government remained in the same condition. However, through his frugal management and the slow return of prosperity to the state, Murphy was able to report by the time he left office that a surplus of more than $220,000 had accumulated in the treasury.

While Murphy and the federal sympathizers were in the process of reestablishing some federal control in a region north of the Arkansas River, the Confederate government of Harris Flanagin continued to operate in Washington. By 1864, however, the representation in the Confederate Assembly had declined to the point that the Supreme Court was asked to give a special opinion of what constituted a quorum for transacting business. The Constitution of 1861, the document the Confederate government had enacted, required a two-thirds majority of the delegates to be a quorum. Because of the disruption of the war effort, however, the Confederate

Des Arc, Arkansas, fell under Union control during the Civil War. Courtesy, Arkansas History Commission

Supreme Court ruled that only two-thirds of those present at the time of voting were needed in order to form a quorum. With that interpretation, Flanagin and the members of the Confederate Legislature continued to transact business.

In reality, there was little the Confederate Legislature could do in 1864. It did authorize elections for delegates to the Confederate Congress and state and local elections were held, but in reality, most recognized the days of the Confederacy were numbered. Morale sank and there was little effort made by the Confederate officials in Arkansas to expand its control of the territory beyond the southwest part of the state. In the

1864 Congressional election to the Confederate Congress only 615 people voted. David Carroll was elected Arkansas' representative. By contrast, in 1861 more than 4,000 people had voted in the Congressional election.

The election simply illustrated the overall problem—the lack of commitment to the Confederacy. Robert E. Lee's surrender at Appomattox Court House on April 9, 1865, convinced many people that further resistance was simply unacceptable. Confederate troops in the Trans-Mississippi District also surrendered to the Union Army in Baton Rouge. While there was some talk by Thomas Hindeman and others about starting guerilla warfare, in truth no responsible offi-

Although occupied by Union forces until the end of the Civil War, Helena seems to have fared quite well. Homes in the background seem undisturbed by the soldiers, who are in formation by their tents in the lower left. Courtesy, Arkansas History Commission

cial advocated such a course. In the words of the editor of the *Washington Telegraph,* "We can see nothing in guerilla warfare that seems of violence, attended by the utter dissolution of all noncombats." This sentiment perhaps expresses the feelings of those who had been loyal to the Confederacy.

In one of his last official acts as Confederate governor, Flanagin issued a proclamation for the people to maintain law and order and protect private property and individual rights. A mass meeting of citizens turned out in Washington in response to Governor Flanagin's proclamation and passed a resolution pledging their loyalty to the Union and to the support of Governor Murphy in Little Rock. Murphy adopted a policy of malice toward none and made it a point to recognize all the local officials and the positions they held in the Confederate States of America until the next general election, which was scheduled to be held the first

Monday in August 1866. Murphy's fairness policy prompted the editor of the *Washington Telegraph* to write, "Many of us who were true to the Confederacy until the last of the independence of the South had vanished are constrained to congratulate ourselves on the organization of the present state government."

Unfortunately, there were a number of national events that were to prevent a peaceful transition. Perhaps the most significant was the assassination of President Lincoln. His successor, Andrew Johnson, encountered a number of problems with the United States Congress almost from the beginning of his term. For example, in the summer of 1864, while Congress was out of session, Johnson pledged to go forth with Lincoln's plan of reconstruction for those states that had reorganized and adopted new constitutions. Johnson asked that they elect congressmen and senators who were to be prepared to assume their seats in the United States Congress

Although the Civil War ended in the spring of 1865, the news did not reach the Indian territory until late June. Troops returned home after being mustered out, like these Union volunteers at Little Rock. Courtesy, Arkansas History Commission

when it reconvened in the fall of 1864. Arkansas joined with several of the other Confederate states to elect these congressional delegates. On the basis of its population Arkansas was allowed three congressional seats and the usual two senators. The General Assembly chose Elisah Baxter, a judge from Batesville, and William Fishback, a lawyer from Fort Smith, to be the U.S. senators from Arkansas. William Buyers from Independence County was elected to represent the First District, G.H. Cyle of Dallas County to represent the Second District, and J.N. Johnson of Pulaski County was elected to represent the Third District. This delegation of five men made their way to Washington to present their credentials to the United States Congress. Unfortunately, all were denied their seats, as were representatives from other Southern states.

In the autumn and winter of 1866 conditions deteriorated between the President and Congress. The President had encouraged the Southern states to reorganize and reapply for admission into the Union as soon as possible; however, Congress refused to comply with these efforts, and the states were caught in the middle. Congress' primary objections to the new delegates from the Southern states were that many had been Confederate officers or Confederate sympathizers. Congress, dominated by Northern representatives, was simply not prepared to accept the return to Congress of these so-called traitors. In the winter and spring of 1866, while Arkansas and the other Southern states waited, the President and Congress became involved in a great struggle for power over the direction of reconstructing the Southern states. Congress passed a Civil Rights bill

that the President vetoed, but Congress promptly overrode his veto and moved to incorporate the language of that bill into an amendment to the Constitution—the Fourteenth Amendment.

By July 1866 Congress had completed its work on the Fourteenth Amendment and submitted it to the Southern states for their approval. The President advised the Confederate states to ignore the amendment, however, suggesting that they could obtain better terms from the new Congress that would be elected in the fall of 1866. During the summer months, Andrew Johnson spent an extended period of time campaigning in a number of the states, encouraging state voters to support his plan of Reconstruction and oppose that of Congress. However, in every state except Tennessee, Johnson's home state, Congressmen sympathetic to the so-called radical position were elected. As a result, the new Congress that convened in the fall of 1866 came to be known as the radical Congress. Two-thirds of the congressional membership were now devout opponents of the President's plan for Reconstruction, and with that majority they were in a position to override any veto the President had. By contrast, the Confederate states in the fall 1866 elections chose former Confederates, or at least the majority of Confederate sympathizers, to fill legislative seats. Republican and Unionist sympathizers in the state, upset by this new direction, sent a new delegation to Washington to confer with the leaders of Congress, asking the new Democrats and former Confederates from the legislature to send another delegation to make their report on conditions in Arkansas to both the President and Congress, and that the present government be upheld. Both requests were largely ignored. Congress had a bigger question —namely Reconstruction of all the Southern states—and in answer, in July 1867, proceeded to pass the first of three acts designed to organize the reconstruction process.

The first Reconstruction act became law in March 1867 following an override of Johnson's veto. The new

state official, and try offenders at either regular or military courts.

Additional legislation was later passed to give military governors authority to register voters. Males at least twenty-one years old who had not been disfranchised for rebellion or conviction of felony and who would take an ironclad oath of loyalty to the United States government were allowed to be registered. When the reg-

legislation stated that except for Tennessee, which had earlier approved the Fourteenth Amendment and had been accepted as a member in Congress, all the other state governments in the old Confederacy were declared to be illegal. The ten states were subdivided into five military districts. Arkansas was paired with Mississippi in the fourth district under the direction of General Alvin Gillam who headquartered in Little Rock. The government of Isaac Murphy was declared to be only a provisional government subject to the authority of the military governor, who had power to declare martial law, remove any

istration was complete an election was to be called to elect delegates to a special constitutional convention. The new constitution was required to approve the Thirteenth and Fourteenth amendments and allow for black suffrage. In Arkansas, as in many of the former Confederate states, white reaction to this new program was quite negative. Early efforts were made to intimidate blacks and prevent them from registering. Blacks were aided in their efforts to register by the Union League, which had been founded in 1862 to assist slaves in making transition to a free society. Whites then began boycotting the

Little Rock is pictured here in 1864, when representatives of twenty-four Arkansas counties met there for the purpose of gaining readmittance to the Union. Courtesy, Arkansas History Commission

Cherokee E.C. Boudinot presented this photograph to William E. Ashley, son of Chester Ashley, in January 1866. The Southern Cherokee delegation consisted of (left to right) John R. Ridge, Stand Watie, Rich Fields, E.C. Boudinot, and Colonel William P. Adair. Courtesy, Arkansas History Commission

registration booths and some began supporting the Ku Klux Klan, aimed at further intimidation of black voters. The registration continued throughout the summer, and the vote for the new constitution was set for the first Tuesday in November 1867.

When voting day arrived numerous irregularities began to appear in the voting pattern. Because most whites chose to boycott the convention altogether, as a result only about 50,000 voters turned out. Later, whites com-

plained that the registration process cost about $48,000 and the expense was simply too great. Despite the controversy, delegates were elected for the special constitutional election that met in Little Rock on January 7, 1868. The convention was dominated by whites even though several counties had black majorities. In all, nine blacks out of a total of seventy-one delegates were elected. Only one county, Chicot, was represented solely by a black. Twenty-three of the seventy-one delegates were considered carpetbaggers, that is, coming into the state after the Civil War started. Later the argument developed that the Constitution of 1868 was a carpetbag document thrust on Arkansas by outsiders. However, the makeup of the convention would hardly support that argument; thirty-nine of the seventy-one delegates were white Arkansans who had lived in the state prior to the Civil War.

The convention met for six weeks and developed Arkansas' fourth constitution since statehood. The new document denied the right of secession. It greatly expanded the executive power by lengthening the governor's term to four years and giving him extensive appointing powers. Other measures included strong provisions for public education, requiring a minimum of three months per year, extending suffrage as well as the right to bear arms to blacks, and also created new legislative districts for representation. The delegates provided two methods for the ratifying process. One was by special polls with commissioners representing the convention working at the polls. These supervisors were to be paid eight dollars per day and had authority to hire clerks and judges needed for the election. The other polls were controlled by the military authorities because of the Second Reconstruction Act of Congress. Voters had the option of voting either at the booths established by the convention or at the polls operated by the military officers. Democrats chose to boycott the polls. When the results began to come in there were two sets of returns: the Convention polls showed a total of 30,380 for and only forty-one against the Constitution, while the military polls showed 27,913 for and 36,597 against.

The wide discrepancy in the two sets of returns obviously caused citizens to doubt the validity of the election, and it soon became apparent that there were numerous irregularities in the voting process. Not only did white Democrats intimidate blacks but it became obvious that Republicans stuffed the ballot box at a number of polls. After Democrats protested, the military sent Captain J.E. Tourtelotte to investigate, who reported that the Constitution would have been accepted in a fair election. The Constitution was then forwarded to Washington for approval. Congress adopted it and after President Johnson vetoed the congressional act, Congress overrode his veto and Arkansas was officially readmitted into the Union on June 22, 1868.

Although it would appear that the

To help blacks adjust to their new status after the war, the Freedmen's Bureau was established in 1865. This building in Arkadelphia, Arkansas, housed the Bureau's office. Courtesy, Arkansas History Commission

readmission of Arkansas into the Union in 1868 would bring an end to the Reconstruction process, just the reverse was true. Unlike 1864 when the majority of state voters were willing to support Murphy and abandon the Confederate followers, white Democrats in 1868 had become so united against the actions taken by the special convention and the United States Congress that they were determined to oppose the new government.

Because the ratification process had also included provisions to elect state officials, Powell Clayton, formerly of Pennsylvania, a member of the federal army that had occupied Arkansas, was elected governor. Another Union member, J.M. Johnson, a colonel in the federal army, was elected lieutenant governor. The new legislature met on April 2, and in one of its first actions reasserted its support for the Fourteenth Amendment. Following the governor's inauguration, the state General Assembly moved quickly to enact legislation. Of the variety of bills passed, some were of particular significance. For example, a Bureau of Immigration was created and the legislation appointed a commissioner charged with the specific responsibility of recruiting farmers to come to Arkansas to work and develop the land. Legislators were particularly interested in attracting German immigrants, but in fact, were active in recruiting all who would come to the state to work. There was also an active effort made to recruit blacks. A Colored Immigration Aid Society was also formed and given the responsibility of recruiting blacks throughout the United States.

The legislature also spent considerable time dealing with the issue of internal improvements. The office of Commissioner of Public Works was created and given the special duty to look after the construction of levees in the Arkansas Delta. The Commission was authorized to issue swamp land warrants up to 38 percent of contract price to any railroad that would build a roadbed that would also serve as a levee. Considerable interest was given to railroads, and the assembly passed a special law for selling railroad bonds. The incentive for railroad construction stimulated by these bonds led to some eighty-six companies being organized in the state between 1868 and 1871. Collectively the state had issued more than nine million dollars in railroad bonds.

The legislature also paid particular attention to education, and as mandated by the Constitution, the assembly passed a law requiring every school district to provide for a minimum of three months of school per year. The legislature also chartered the state's first university—the Arkansas Industrial University—at Fayetteville in 1872. Other interest in education included moving the Arkansas School for the Blind and Deaf to Little Rock and increasing its budget, and chartering Arkansas Agricultural and Mechanical and Normal School in Pine Bluff for the specific purpose of educating blacks.

While there were many positive gains made by the so-called Republican Congress in 1868, there were numerous difficulties as well. One of the more pressing matters became the issue of corruption among the legislators. Almost from the first days of the session, problems began to develop. For example, the legislature appropriated $125,000 to reimburse landowners for property lost in the war. However, in order to make a claim for that property, the claimant

Arkansas' first university, the Arkansas Industrial University, was chartered in 1872 in Fayetteville. Its name was later changed to the University of Arkansas. Fayetteville photographer B.E. Grabill took this photograph of Old Main on the campus about forty years after the beginning of the college. Courtesy, Arkansas History Commission

had to come to Little Rock, prove his claim, and declare his loyalty to the United States government and the Constitution of 1868. The effect was to provide windfall profits for lawyers.

Public printing began to attract increased attention because of the amount of money spent—individuals received the state printing contract. For example, J.G. Price, who served as speaker of the house and editor of the *Daily Republican,* was also awarded the state printing contract in 1868. His successor, the private secretary of Governor Clayton and the governor's brother-in-law, succeeded Price as the state's printer. Between 1868 and 1871, the cost of state printing amounted to more than $200,000—more than all state government costs for a full year and any period before the war. These were all discrepancies that attracted the attention of the public. For example, it became evident that many of the railroad companies that received bond money from the state were not in the position to construct railroad right-of-ways. A number of the companies defaulted and were forced to turn back their bonds to the state. Even so, of the almost ten million dollars appropriated, about seven million dollars actually were spent by the railroads. But as late as 1873 the state could still show only 300 miles of railroad track throughout the state.

These financial disclosures began to attract the attention of the general public and create opposition within the Republican Party and against Governor Clayton. Clayton escalated his problems by announcing that there was a need for a new registration system for voters, scheduling registration to be held prior to the Presidential election in November 1868. The governor was motivated in part because of the increased activity of the Ku Klux Klan, which had intimidated numerous blacks in rural counties out of participating in the election process. The governor called the state military and placed sixteen of the counties under martial law, empowering the military officers to register voters and supervise elections. This method added to his opposition and the cost generated by mobilizing the military—$300,000—increased the criticism by those who were concerned about the expense of state government.

In the spring of 1869 the internal opposition in the Republican Party came to a head. On April 8 Lieutenant Governor James Johnson met with seventeen dissident Republicans in Little Rock and organized formal opposition to Clayton. As stated in a memo, their opposition was based in part on the governor's use of militia, the extensive aid to railroads, and government overspending. In some respects this group was a reflection of the national movement known as the Liberal Republicans, which opposed actions of the so-called Radical Republicans at the national level. Efforts by Johnson and his colleagues caused the Arkansas General Assembly to be in a state of turmoil throughout much of the 1869 session. The conflict spilled over to more than just a conflict within the assembly and in fact became an all-out struggle for control of the Republican Party in the state.

In an effort to counter the opposition, Clayton further liberalized the election laws, which allowed more Arkansans to be registered. Clayton was then able to control the election process and his supporters won control of the state elections in 1870. But the

effect was to split the party beyond repair.

The hostilities came to a head when one of the senators elected by the Republicans, Alexander McDonald, retired from his seat, and the Arkansas General Assembly moved to appoint Governor Clayton to that position. Clayton, although desiring to be a United States senator, nevertheless was concerned about losing his base of support in Arkansas while he was in Washington. Therefore, he worked behind the scenes to maneuver Lieutenant Governor Johnson out of position by convincing Johnson to accept an appointment as secretary of state and the Senate to approve loyal Clayton supporter Ozra A. Hadley to the office of lieutenant governor. With Clayton in the Senate, Hadley then became acting governor and Clayton still retained some measure of control over state politics. However, Clayton would soon learn that this was not the case. Clayton's absence from the state allowed new leadership to develop—the opposition against Clayton and the so-called Regular Republicans was deeper and better-organized than he had anticipated.

Although the former Lieutenant Governor Johnson had now been neutralized, a new leader by the name of

The McKay Iron and Locomotive Works of Jersey City, New Jersey, built the first locomotive on the Cairo and Fulton Railroad. It pulled the first passenger train on February 1, 1872, from Argenta to the Little Red River and back. The crew consisted of W.P. McNally, engineer; Charles Seymour, fireman; L.R. Brown, conductor; and H.S. Pratt and Ben Bowlin, brakemen. Courtesy, Arkansas History Commission

Joseph Brooks arose to maintain active Liberal opposition to the Clayton faction of the Republican Party. Brooks had been a member of the federal army from Iowa who came to the state during the course of the war and remained. Brooks watched the split with some interest and in 1872 decided the time was right to launch his own political career. He concluded that his best hope for office lay with the reform in the Republican Party and soon became an outspoken advocate of the Liberal Party in opposition to Governor Clayton. With the gubernatorial election approaching in 1872, Brooks decided to organize a separate party. He and his supporters held a convention in May 1872 and organized a platform decidedly different from the Regular Republicans. The platform called for universal suffrage, universal amnesty, and honest men for office. The group also took

the name Brindletails because Brooks, a Methodist minister of eloquent ability in public speaking, reminded one of the members of tail bull due to his loud booming voice. The Democrats who had boycotted the election prepared to re-enter the political arena in force, and chose to throw most of their support behind Joseph Brooks. The Regular Republicans, observing the action of the Brooks-Brindletail Party, moved ahead with their own plans. They held a regular convention and nominated Elisha Baxter, who resigned his seat on the bench to accept the nomination for governor.

The campaign of 1872 was one of the most bitter in the state's history. Brooks was a vocal and active campaigner, using the corruption of the Clayton machine as his platform. Baxter, in sharp contrast, ran a quiet, sincere campaign, promising to gov-

Pictured here is the Elisha Baxter steamboat Hallie, which was captured by the Joseph Brooks forces on the Arkansas River near the mouth of Palarm Creek on May 8, 1874, during the Brooks-Baxter War. Courtesy, Arkansas History Commission

ern for all the people and broaden the election base. His style caused many Democrats to switch their support to Baxter late in the campaign. Clayton returned from Washington to stump the state for Baxter, and acting Governor Hadley was instrumental in supporting the Regular Republicans as well. One of Hadley's actions was to void Clayton's 1871 registration law and revive the 1868 election law originally adopted by the Constitution of 1868. The effect of the 1868 election and the 1868 registration law was to limit the number of people who could vote and place the polls under the watchful eye of the militia. When the elections were held many of Brooks' supporters were turned away because they did not qualify under the 1868 law. They consequently set up their own polls and even went as far as voting in both polls. The official returns of the 1872 election gave Baxter a majority of some 3,000 votes out of a total of 80,000 cast, even though the unofficial count gave Brooks a majority of 1,500 votes. Despite the discrepancy Baxter was nevertheless certified as governor.

Two days before the new legislature opened in January 1873, Brooks and his supporters called a convention in Little Rock to discuss the disputed returns of the election. At that meeting Brooks determined to take the position that the election returns from the November election were fraudulent. However, nothing more was said at the time and the legislature opened on schedule and certified Baxter as governor.

As governor, Baxter made a major effort to fulfill his party pledge, appointing the best men he could to office regardless of political party. In a matter of months Baxter's policies began to create problems among his Regular Republicans, who feared he was too pro-Democrat and not supportive enough of the party. Baxter's difficulties with the individual party members were compounded in late spring when Brooks filed suit with the State Supreme Court charging that Baxter's election had been fraudulent. The court refused to hear Brooks' claim and the matter remained in dispute and unresolved through the summer of 1873. Baxter continued his policies of appointing men from all areas of the state and all political beliefs and called a special election to fill vacant positions in the legislature. The majority of those elected in the special election were Democrats and by the fall of 1873 the Arkansas General Assembly had turned decidedly Democrat, a significant shift from the Republican domination. As the officeholders became increasingly Democratic and as the legislature began to return to the pro-Democrats, Regular Republicans— particularly under the leadership of Powell Clayton— became disturbed with Baxter, and many of those who had previously supported Baxter against Brooks now deserted Baxter to support Brooks in his charge of election fraud.

The controversy reached a turning point in April 1874 when Brooks again petitioned the courts to declare Baxter's election illegal. The Pulaski County Circuit Court upheld Brooks on April 15 and he immediately took the oath of office for governor before John McClure, chief justice of the state supreme court. Aided by supporters in the state militia, Brooks then marched to the capitol and ousted Baxter from office. He also ordered seizure of the state armory and began fortifying the capitol grounds.

Baxter moved first to the campus of St. John's College in Little Rock, then set up headquarters at the Anthony House a few blocks east of the capitol. There he declared the state under martial law and called out the militia. Some 2,000 men responded to his order. Brooks had approximately 1,000 supporters and the two forces faced each other along Markham Street. Both "governors" appealed to President U.S. Grant for support. Most of the elected officials in the state continued to support Baxter.

Federal officials were reluctant to become involved in the dispute. Senator Clayton had considerable influence within the "regular" Republican party. However, his support of Brooks—so closely associated with the liberal faction of the party—caused some confusion. Meanwhile, conditions in Arkansas grew increasingly tense. Although most of the action was concentrated in Little Rock, there were Brooks and Baxter factions all over the state. The most significant confrontation between the two forces came in Jefferson County, at New Gascony, where a bloody engagement left twelve men dead. Brooks' forces also captured a steamboat, the *Hallie,* on Palarm Creek west of Little Rock as it attempted to bring supplies to Baxter supporters.

The mounting tension forced the Grant administration to act. The President ordered federal troops at the Little Rock arsenal to take up position between the two groups in Little Rock. He also sent a message to both parties, asking that the General Assembly be convened to settle the dispute. Baxter readily accepted Grant's suggestion; Brooks, however, insisted that the matter was a legal issue. Baxter also offered to disband his militia. His moderate approach

shifted opinions in Washington in his favor and on May 15 Grant officially recognized Baxter as governor. The General Assembly reconvened and quickly reiterated its support for Baxter. Brooks' forces rapidly dispersed, bringing an end to the state's Brooks-Baxter war.

Within days after order was reestablished, the Democratic-controlled assembly called for a consititutional convention to revise the 1868 Constitution. The convention met in Little Rock on July 14 and stayed in session until early September. Seventy of the ninety-one delegates were Democrats. The document they drafted differed radically from the one adopted by the Republicans. Many of the changes centered in the area of executive authority. The governor's term was reduced to two years, almost all of the office's former appointive power was removed, the office of lieutenant governor was eliminated entirely, and the other constitutional offices—secretary of state, attorney general, treasurer, auditor, and land commissioner—were to be elected rather than appointed by the governor.

Ratification of the new document and election of new officials were scheduled for October 13. Although Baxter had two years remaining in his term as governor he readily accepted the convention's action and vacated his office. Numerous Democrats encouraged him to run for governor on their ticket but he declined. The Constitution of 1874 was approved by the voters by a three-to-one margin, despite appeals by many Republican leaders to ignore the election. With a new Constitution and a new slate of elected officials, many Arkansans prepared to put Reconstruction behind them and prepare for a new era.

G.C. Widney's Settlement of Arkansas Post 1686 *appeared as a supplement to the* St. Louis Globe Democrat *February 16, 1902. Courtesy, University of Arkansas at Little Rock Archives and Special Collections.*

Arkansas' oldest newspaper, the Arkansas Gazette, was founded by William E. Woodruff at Arkansas Post in 1819, the year Arkansas Territory was created. Two years later Woodruff moved the paper to Little Rock, where it has continued. In 1919 the Gazette celebrated 100 years of publication in this commemorative issue. Courtesy, Arkansas History Commission

President Andrew Jackson appointed Kentuckian John Pope territorial governor of Arkansas in 1829. During his term of office, which lasted until 1835, he began construction on Arkansas' first statehouse. The building was not completed until 1840. Courtesy, Arkansas History Commission

Right: *Edward Payson Washburn (1831-1860), famous for his* Arkansas Traveler, *painted this self-portrait. Washburn was the son of Cephas Washburn, an early Protestant missionary to the Western Cherokees. Courtesy, Arkansas History Commission*

Facing page, top: *In 1870 Currier and Ives published Edward Payson Washburn's* Arkansas Traveler. *The publication brought fame to the painting, which represents Colonel Sandy Faulkner, composer of the fiddle tune "The Arkansas Traveler." Courtesy, Arkansas History Commission*

Facing page, bottom: *When Currier and Ives published Washburn's* Arkansas Traveler, *they also published this companion piece,* The Turn of the Tune. *Courtesy, Arkansas History Commission*

A Washington, Arkansas, blacksmith named James Black forged a knife for James Bowie in 1831, which became famous around the world as the "Bowie Knife." Bart Moore of Cucamonga, California, owns this knife, which is believed to be the original owned by Bowie. Courtesy, Bart Moore

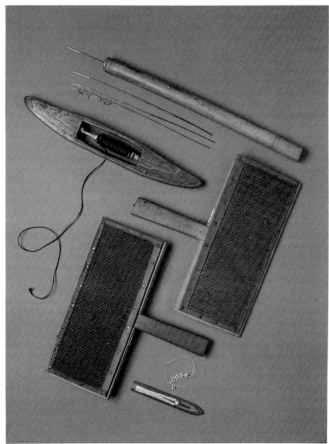

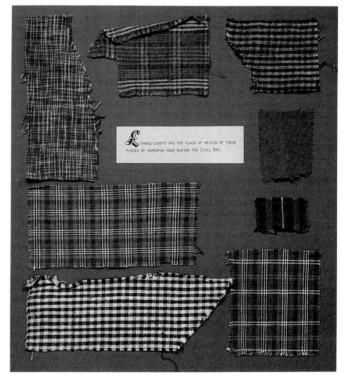

During the Civil War, when trade with the North was cut off, manufactured goods became scarce. As a result, Arkansas' women were forced to use skills from pioneer days in making clothing. Cotton cards, spinning wheels, looms, and needles, among other things, came back into demand. Courtesy, Arkansas History Commission

Lonoke County women produced these pieces of homespun during the Civil War. Although homespun was less attractive than manufactured cloth, the ladies were proud of their contribution to the war. "The Homespun Dress," a popular ballad by Carrie Belle Sinclair, gave three cheers "for the Homespun Dress, our Southern ladies wear!" Courtesy, Arkansas History Commission

The first battle Arkansas troops were involved in was at Wilson's Creek (also known as Oak Hills), Missouri, on August 10, 1861. Although the Confederates forced the enemy to retreat northward because of heavy losses, they did not follow up the victory. Courtesy, Arkansas History Commission

Patrick Cleburne of Helena rose from the ranks to become a Confederate major general. Known as the "Stonewall Jackson of the West," he was killed at the battle of Franklin, Tennessee, in 1864. Courtesy, Arkansas History Commission

Powell Clayton, who served as Union brigadier general in the Civil War, became a prominent Republican during Reconstruction, serving as governor from 1868 to 1871. He resigned in 1871 to accept a U.S. Senate seat, which he gave up in 1877. This portrait, commissioned by Clayton's great-nephew, John R. Le Bosquet, hangs in the state capitol. Courtesy, Arkansas History Commission

Frank Leslie's Illustrated
Newspaper *ran E. Jump's
sketch of Malvern Station
on the line of the St.
Louis and Iron Mountain
Railroad, the first rail-
road to cross the state.
The mid-1870s saw the
beginning of vast railroad
expansion. Courtesy, Uni-
versity of Arkansas at
Little Rock Archives and
Special Collections*

BIRD'S EYE VIEW OF THE CITY OF
LITTLE ROCK
THE CAPITOL 1871 ARKANSAS.

A. Ruger properly proportioned travel by rail and steamboats in his 1871 A Bird's-eye View of the City of Little Rock. *Although railroads were few in 1871, by the turn of the century nearly 3,000 miles of track would be laid. Steamboats, which reached their height of popularity before the Civil War, declined in the upcoming years because of increased railroad traffic. Courtesy, Arkansas History Commission*

Scenes of Pine Bluff featured in Harper's Weekly *March 8, 1879, covered law, education, and transportation, areas of importance to most towns at that date. These sketches are by H.J. Lewis. Courtesy, University of Arkansas at Little Rock Archives and Special Collections*

Above: *Augustus H. Garland was the first Arkansan to fill a cabinet position. From 1885 until 1889, Garland served as attorney general under President Grover Cleveland. He had earlier served as governor of Arkansas (1874-1877) and then U.S. senator (1877-1885). Garland is seen here with his wife Sarah Virginia Sanders Garland, and their child. Courtesy, Arkansas History Commission*

Right: *George W. Donaghey, governor of Arkansas from 1909 to 1913, is probably best known for his part in the building of Arkansas' present state capitol. During Donaghey's two terms most of the work on the building was completed. Courtesy, Arkansas History Commission*

Left: *Arkansas cities held fairs as early as 1875, when a mardi gras was held in Little Rock. Pine Bluff, Fort Smith, and other towns soon followed suit. Courtesy, University of Arkansas at Little Rock Archives and Special Collections*

Below: *Featured in the 1912 catalogue of the John Deere Plow Company was the Fort Smith wagon. Courtesy, University of Arkansas at Little Rock Archives and Special Collections*

Right: *The magnificent Hotel Eastman opened to guests on January 15, 1890. Erected in less than eight months, the five-story building contained 482 guest rooms. Other features included a bathhouse, several parlors, an observation tower, spacious verandas, elevators giving invalids easy passage, a complete kitchen, and furniture of oak and cherry. Courtesy, Arkansas History Commission*

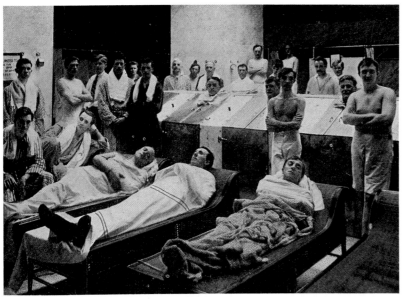

Left: *Hernando De Soto was reportedly the first white man to visit Hot Springs, where the Indians had long used the water for medicinal purposes. Since then, many of all ages have visited the popular resort and benefited from the hot baths, such as the men on this early twentieth-century postcard. Courtesy, Ray Hanley*

Right: *Prohibition came to Arkansas in 1915, when the Newberry Law was passed regulating liquor sales. This was followed by the Bone-Dry Law, which prohibited liquor sales entirely in 1917. Courtesy, Ray Hanley*

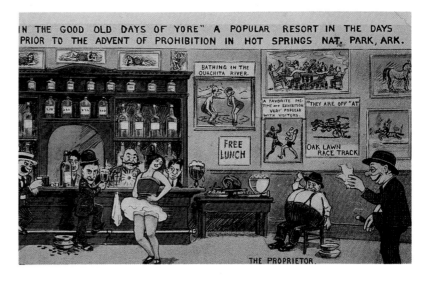

The largest red oak tree in the United States was located in Washington, Arkansas, until it was destroyed by fire in 1980. This photograph was taken after the roots had caught fire. Courtesy, Southwest Arkansas Regional Archives

Religion has played an important part in the lives of Arkansans through the years. Around the turn of the century gatherings similar to present-day retreats were called camp meetings. This one, titled "Sanctified," was held at Calamine in the summer of 1897. Courtesy, Arkansas History Commission

Arkansas in the Gilded Age

CHAPTER IV

Political Reconstruction in Arkansas ended in 1874 when the Democratic Party regained control of both houses of the General Assembly, the governor's office, and seats on the Supreme Court. But the party that came to power in 1874 was not the same group of leaders that dominated the state's political life in the years preceding the Civil War.

The old Democratic Party had been a party of kinship, a party built upon family, with issues centering primarily around agriculture and preserving the planter society in the days of the Old South. The new Democratic Party was a party with a more diverse interest and make-up in the membership. It included not only conservative businessmen but featured many leaders from the Confederacy—military heroes whose political careers were tied to their role and participation in the war. For the balance of the nineteenth century the war continued to dominate, if not as a direct then as an indirect issue, in all the major statewide elections. Former Whigs, who had been members of the loyal opposition before the war, never felt comfortable with the new Northern Republican Party and therefore chose to join the Democratic Party as a way to regain their political identity. While there was still some rural base to the Democratic Party, the power and control had noticeably shifted from the planters of old to the new conservative businessmen in the major cities and towns throughout the state. The new Democratic Party also had a new political agenda, featuring a program of industrialization and diversified agriculture, whereas the old party before the war had focused its attention primarily on cotton and limited interests. There was a noticeable shift in Democratic

Eight of the members of the 1885 House of Representatives were black. The six pictured here are, top, left to right: S.H. Scott of Jefferson County; J.B. Brooks of Lafayette County; and J.H. Bradford of Mississippi County. On the bottom, left to right, are: G.H. Jones of Chicot County; Thomas R. Kersh of Lincoln County; and I.G. Bailey of Desha County. Scott and Bradford were lawyers, the other four were ministers. Courtesy, Arkansas History Commission

economic thought that led them to move away from emphasizing an agrarian society to implement plans that would promote extensive industrialization. The Democrats believed as their Republican counterparts had that the quickest way to restore prosperity was to develop the state's natural resources, emphasizing its mild climate, to recruit additional investors in the state, point to the large pool of cheap and dependable labor, and to offer tax cuts to selected industries attracted to the state. The Democrats also promoted efficiency and economy in government, but the main thrust was a more diverse economy.

The Democrats were interested not only in changing their own image but also in undoing many of the things the Republicans had done before them. Led by the predominantly Democratic General Assembly, various attempts were made in the period after 1874 to curtail the appropriations for public school programs and social services, including the state penitentiary and mental hospital, and revise the tax laws that would benefit industry, particularly railroads. The Democrats' new philosophy, coupled with efforts to overturn what the Republicans had done, caused the Democrats to be labeled Redeemers. They were to redeem the state from the evils of Reconstruction and plan a new direction for the state's development. To redeem the state it was essential that the Democrats build a broader political base than they had had before the Civil War.

The Republican Party had made significant inroads in registering blacks to vote and in many parts of the state blacks had the power to determine the outcome of elections. Therefore, the new Democratic Party reached out to include blacks among its membership as well. This came to

Left: *Grapes were grown in both Altus and Tontitown. Here, the grapes from Tontitown vines are being loaded into refrigerated rail cars at Springdale, Arkansas. The grape culture was brought to Tontitown by Italian immigrants. Courtesy, the Shiloh Museum*

be referred to as the fusion principle—the idea of fusing black and white voters into an integrated party with an integrated ticket for statewide races. Fusion represented a merger of both black and white businessmen and large landowners, but all controlled by a Democratic central committee that determined the position on the ballots for the various statewide races. In most instances, what the fusion principle meant was that in almost every case blacks would be placed on the ticket in most political races between 1874 and 1890—a position that was usually reserved for the office of the superintendent of public instruction. All the other major offices, including the governor, the congressional and senate offices, and the secretary of state, were dominated by white officeholders. However, for a period of a little less than two decades the Democratic Party was integrated and sought to

attract attention from both black and white voters.

As the new Democratic Party prepared to rule in 1874 it did so with a number of problems. For example, the leadership faced the growing public debt that the state had been accumulating, particularly since the end of the Civil War. By 1874 the public debt had grown to an estimated seventeen million dollars. Part of the deficit was a carryover from the 1840s when two state banks, the state bank and the real estate bank, had gone bankrupt and the state defaulted on the bond payments. Never fully resolved, that debt continued to be reflected against the state's credit. But a larger segment of the debt was that accrued by the Republican administration during the Reconstruction period. A large part of that debt was built into bonds that had been voted and the money spent to build railroads. Unfortunately, in 1874 while some thirteen million dollars had been spent on railroad construction, there was less than 300 miles of track in the state and the lack of more tangible evidence of how the money had been spent led many of the Democratic Party leaders to charge, at least privately, that there must be graft and corruption within the Republican Party. The inability to clearly identify where the bond money had been spent caused many in the Democratic Party to discuss repudiating the debt.

This repudiation idea came to be an increasingly divisive concept within the party. There were those who felt that all the debt should be abolished since it was impossible to determine what was valid and what was not. There were others who felt that some effort must be made to identify the legitimate expense that had been incurred during the Reconstruction period, and that the state should stand good for that money. That which could not be accounted for should be repudiated. Others felt that the state must honor its debts regardless of whether it could account for the expenditures or not. This discussion on whether or not to repudiate the state debt raged back and forth for years in the state before being resolved.

Of additional interest to the Democratic Party was a plan to attract new immigrants to the state. With the abolition of slavery the labor force drastically changed, and many of the Democratic leaders felt that the state would benefit from immigrants from Europe settling large sections of the state that were undeveloped. So the state began an active recruitment effort to recruit immigrants from central and western Europe. Ironically enough, most of the Southern states were in the same game as Arkansas,

and recruiting immigrants became rather competitive. The Arkansas General Assembly created an Office of Immigration within the Department of Agriculture and authorized that office to spend public funds in an effort to recruit more settlers to the state. Unfortunately, the office was never properly funded. There was never enough money to allow the state to send recruiters abroad to directly recruit settlers, or even send a recruiter to the East Coast in an effort to meet the growing number of immigrants making their way into the nation. As a result, while the state did attract some immigrants, particularly Germans and Italians working on the railroads, it was never able to compete with other states. While Arkansas' population continued to increase during this period, it continued to mainly be the result of natural birth and immigration from the older Southern states.

One issue that the Democrats continued to remain conscious of was scandal. The party not only centered on mud-slinging toward the Republican Party, but made an effort to convince voters that the Democrats were the party of integrity and the party that would account for the expenditure of state funds. Given those priorities and the new outlook of the party, the state prepared to do business in 1874 in a way that it had not done before. The leader of the Democratic Party was Governor Augustus Garland, elected by a wide margin in the election of 1874. Garland had a long-term involvement with the party, was an active participant in the Confederate Congress during the Civil War, and was also a distinguished lawyer who had argued cases before the Supreme Court. In fact, one of the landmark cases Garland won in

the Supreme Court was that Confederate lawyers should not be disbarred because of their service in the Confederacy, and should be allowed to practice law and argue cases before the United States Supreme Court.

Garland inherited some of the lingering problems of Reconstruction, including the public debt. To remedy the problem of the large debt the General Assembly authorized the issuance of $2.5 million in bonds and hoped to get the state on a better credit system. The legislature also made strong concessions to industry by carrying out the redeemer promise to industrialize the state. Tax exemptions for a period of seven years were granted to all manufacturing concerns that would invest in cotton or woolen goods, farm implements, cottonseeds, or leather. A special campaign was

launched by the land commissioner of the Iron Mountain and Southern Railroad, J.M. Loughborough, and Little Rock real estate promoter T.B. Mills. They had a plan to invite the leading newspapermen of the region to Arkansas to demonstrate how the state had recovered from the war. In September 1875 more than seventy representatives from twelve states joined the tour on the St. Louis and Iron Mountain Railroad. They traveled through the state on tracks owned by the railroad, spent time in Little Rock, and were welcomed by both Democratic and Republican party leaders alike. The general impression received by the visitors was that the state was undergoing a vigorous, healthy economic growth, fully recovering from Reconstruction. The newspapermen returned to their re-

The first Arkansan to hold a presidential cabinet position was A.H. Garland (1832-1899). Garland, a former governor and U.S. senator, was chosen to be Grover Cleveland's attorney general in 1885. Courtesy, Arkansas History Commission

The Peter Van Winkle sawmill at War Eagle, Arkansas, was rated as the largest in size and output in the state during the 1870s. Courtesy, Arkansas History Commission

spective states and wrote articles about their Arkansas experience. Loughborough and Mills collected these and printed them in a book called *The New Arkansas Traveler.* Conscious effort was made to change the state's image from a natural environment of the "Bear State" to one that would express vigorous growth and development in the new South. Garland, with his leadership capabilities, was a stabilizing influence in the state's politics for the next four years. The unsettled conditions that had characterized much of Powell Clayton's regime were largely resolved and Garland governed during a period in which the state's prosperity began to return.

Rather than seek reelection as governor, Garland decided to accept the advice of his friends and run for the Senate seat held by Powell Clayton. In a spirited campaign he easily won the election and moved to Washington. Arkansas voters geared up to face a wide-open campaign among several candidates in the Democratic Party who sought the governor's nomination. The leaders included Grandison D. Royston, Thomas Fletcher, and William Miller. The campaign was primarily one of personalities, although the issue of state debt still hovered. Both Democrats and Republicans were divided on how to handle the debt issue. The Democrats developed a faction known as the "Statehouse Ring," which divided the party by supporting Miller. The Democratic convention met in Little Rock on June 14, 1876, and after a lengthy debate about the debt and the method of voting, the delegates

finally chose Miller as their candidate for governor.

The Republicans were split between supporters of Powell Clayton and a group known as "newdealers," who were predominantly black. The regulars were led by Ozra A. Hadley, who nominated Joseph Brooks for governor. The Republicans established their platform on a policy of equality, tax support for industry, education, and liquidation of the state debt. The newdealers refused to go along with Hadley and nominated A.W. Bishop as their candidate.

The election of 1876 saw both parties divided internally, split not only over party control but over the method of repaying the state debt. The Democrats had the most to gain from the election and pulled the party together with a warning that a division within the ranks might lead to the return of Republican rule. Miller won with a comfortable margin over Brooks. Following the election the executive committee of the state Democratic Party organized a Democratic club room over the Southern Express office in Little Rock and sent out a call for a party caucus to organize the legislature. The group made a strong appeal for party harmony and intimated that discipline would be applied for those who did not comply. This strong-arm tactic of the state Demo-

Arkansas participated in displays in New Orleans, Louisville, Chicago, and Atlanta as well as this 1894 St. Louis Exposition to advertise the state's products and resources. Courtesy, Arkansas History Commission

119

cratic Central Committee became a pattern for the future as Arkansas moved toward the political term of the "Solid South."

The new legislature had to face the persistent problem of the state debt—the chief issue during Miller's administration. The state finance board submitted a plan to adjust the debt and pay only the part that could be legitimately contracted. That plan came to be known as the Adams-Redfield Plan and gained support among many of the regular Democrats. The *Arkansas Gazette* supported the Adams-Redfield Plan and urged its support. The group opposing the Adams-Redfield Plan were known as the "Repudiationists," led by William Fishback, who argued for total debt abolition. The state Supreme Court joined the force by ruling that certain railroad bonds, amounting to five million dollars, were unconstitutional, as were the levee bonds. With that support the Repudiationists began to gain the upper hand. The *Arkansas Gazette* switched its position and pushed to repudiate all of the state

debt accumulated since the war. Although the Repudiationists' issue gained the most attention in the 1870s, there were other concerns to be addressed. For example, third parties offered a strong challenge and the black vote continued to be important to both Democratic and Republican parties.

Within the Democratic Party in the 1870s, many of the Whigs who had joined the party near the end of the Civil War became increasingly unhappy with the party and so party loyalists had a difficult time keeping them in line. There was a continuing concern within the Democratic Party of how to convince blacks to stay within the party and a fear that they would move back to the Republican camp. In addition to the internal strife and the emerging third party, there were also general issues of support for industry, plans to reduce cotton acreage, support for public education, and efforts to increase the number of railroads within the state. Within this framework of issues and internal structures the party came to

For a small town like Corning, Phipps and Arnold's in 1908 was a quality store that gave careful attention to merchandise and display. Courtesy, Special Collections, University of Arkansas Libraries, Fayetteville

Right: *Founder of the Unionist paper* The Unconditional Union, *attorney William Fishback was instrumental in the writing of the 1864 Constitution. He later represented Sebastian County at the 1874 Constitutional Convention and served in the legislature from 1871-1881. In 1893 he was elected governor. Courtesy, Arkansas History Commission*

Far right: *Following William Miller to the governor's seat in 1881 was Thomas J. Churchill (1824-1905). Raised in Kentucky, Churchill came to Little Rock in 1848 following service in the Mexican War. In 1849 he married Ann Sevier, daughter of Ambrose H. Sevier. During the Civil War he reached the rank of major general in the Confederate Army. Courtesy, Arkansas History Commission*

feel most comfortable with William Miller, and supported his renomination for a second term in 1878. However, as that campaign shaped up, the *Arkansas Gazette* began to urge the party to take a different approach to the issues. Strong editorials in the *Gazette* called for candidates in the 1878 election to speak out in favor of increased immigration, development of a common school system in the state, and an improved climate for railroad and manufacturing concerns.

Miller was the choice of the party professionals, but he was not without his detractors. A group of former Confederate Army officers led by Thomas Fletcher, S.B. Hughes, and B.T. Embry joined forces to block Miller's renomination at the state Democratic Party convention. The only hope the opponents had was for them to stand together consistently throughout the convention's voting process. After the fifteenth ballot was cast it was apparent that the opposition was not able to hold their support together and Miller was nominated for a second term. In conjunc-

tion with his nomination, the party adopted a platform calling for a constitutional amendment to repudiate the unjust debts of Reconstruction. The party also made a strong appeal to blacks to support the party and help them redeem the state from Republican corruption. Miller's easy victory in the election of 1878 caused a sense of optimism to prevail throughout the party. The party seemed to be on the verge of unification and an air of good feeling seemed to run throughout the state. But no sooner had the leadership begun discussing a unification movement than bickering broke out again regarding selection of the United States Senate seat. The state legislature cast seven ballots before they finally chose J.D. Walker to join Augustus Garland as the junior United States Senator.

Miller's second term as governor was largely uneventful primarily because he continued to face a divided General Assembly. In the new Assembly there was a strong group who believed that an amendment should be proposed to the state Constitution to

repudiate the debts accumulated during the Reconstruction period, particularly the Holford Bonds. After much debate, it was determined that a special question would be placed on the ballot in the next gubernatorial election to decide whether or not to refer the debate to voters. Beyond that, Miller was able to show little in his second administration. Although he wanted to seek a third term, the party professionals determined that it would not be wise to support him, particularly in light of the division within the party. The party turned instead to Thomas J. Churchill, another veteran of the Civil War, as its nominee in the election of 1880. In addition to serving in the Civil War, Churchill had been a plantation owner, the postmaster of Little Rock, and had been elected state treasurer in 1874. He was serving in that capacity when he was nominated for the gubernatorial race of 1880. By 1880 the Democrats had come to face not only problems within the party and the factionalism that had developed, but also growing opposition

from the rural areas of the state. And although the party had been successful in neutralizing the Republican Party it did not mean that it went unchallenged in other quarters. One of the groups that began to gain support in opposition to the Democrats was the Greenback Party. Organized nationally soon after the Civil War primarily for the purpose of trying to inflate the currency using "greenbacks," or paper money, the group sought to help rural America overcome its debt problems. In Arkansas the Greenback Party received active support in the southwest portion of the state as well as in the upper Arkansas River valley. Republicans, although not in sympathy with the issues of the Greenback Party, saw the opportunity to join it and perhaps defeat the Democrats.

With the Democratic Party divided, the twin force of the Greenbackers and the Republicans caused some concern among the Democrats. Nevertheless, in the gubernatorial race of 1880 the Democratic Party was able to elect Churchill, primarily by claiming the Greenback Party was nothing more than the Republican Party in disguise. The Democrats pointed out that the Republican Party was still the party of war, Reconstruction, debt, and scandal.

While the outcome of the election was never in doubt, the campaign did bring out certain issues that would continue to be a problem for the Democratic Party. A key campaign issue advocated by Democratic Party leadership was the repudiation of the Arkansas state debt. Democratic businessmen were generally opposed to repudiation, while the rural areas of the state strongly supported the idea and the party continued to be caught in the conflict between the two inter-

Arkansas' secretary of state from 1879 to 1885 was Jacob Frolich (1837-1890), who founded the White County Record in 1866. Courtesy, Arkansas History Commission

est groups.

The most ardent spokesman for repudiation was state legislator William Fishback from Fort Smith. Fishback had been active in the Union Army, had stayed in Arkansas after the Civil War, and had been elected to represent the Fort Smith area in the Arkansas General Assembly. The opposition to repudiation was led by Senator Augustus Garland, who tended to represent the business interests of the state.

When the final vote tallies were counted in 1880, the proposed amendment to the Constitution to repudi-

Before the days of Prohibition, liquor was distributed freely in Arkansas by dealers. The Green River and Mountain Dew Distillery of Owensboro, Kentucky, proudly advertised its Arkansas dealers through this promotional photograph. Courtesy, Arkansas History Commission

ate the debt also appeared to have passed. However, when Secretary of State Joseph Froblick attempted to certify the results of the election, a controversy developed about whether the amendment had really been approved. By Froblick's count 64,497 had voted for the amendment while 41,049 had voted against it. Froblick later determined that 132,985 votes had been cast and when he subtracted the 64,497 affirmative votes from the total vote figure that left a balance of 68,488. In other words, a majority had voted against the amendment. Froblick therefore certified in his official returns that the

proposed amendment had failed. Critics charged that Froblick should have taken one-half of 132,985 plus one to get his majority.

By the early 1880s the new Democratic Party appeared to be riding a wave of success, and the party seemed to be unified for the first time in four years. However, as the Democratic leadership was still boasting of its new gains, scandal was discovered in the governor's office. In March 1881 a routine audit of the Treasury showed a shortage of more than $50,000 in state scrip. The shortage appeared in the Permanent School Fund and apparently developed when new scrip had been burned along with old scrip that had been brought in to be retired. The auditing committee's recommendations were taken up by the Senate, which established a special committee to make an investigation. The Senate committee showed a shortage of a little less than $50,000.

Not to be outdone, the House of Representatives authorized a committee of its own to look into the matter. The House committee found the same discrepancies as the Senate but also discovered that an additional $50,000 belonging to the Permanent School Fund had been burned.

Reports began to circulate within the Statehouse about Governor Churchill, particularly because these shortages had occurred while Churchill was serving as state treasurer. Churchill, however, maintained his innocence, contending that the shortage was due to bookkeeping errors, not wrongdoings on his part. The investigations left the Democratic Party open to charges of corruption, especially since the Democrats promised to clean up the state and redeem Arkansas from the perils of Republican Party cor-

Harper's Weekly *pictured life continuing despite disaster in the 1882 Mississippi River flood. These Arkansas City ladies were sketched by Charles Upham using boats to carry on their shopping. Courtesy, Arkansas History Commission*

ruption during Reconstruction.

In an effort to clear up the matter, a joint committee was established between the House and Senate to investigate the treasurer's office. When the final report was concluded, it showed a shortage of $14,000. However, the General Assembly refused to accept the report and appointed still a new committee to investigate the matter again.

When the new committee reported that the shortage was approximately $233,000, a bill of impeachment was drawn up against Churchill. However, when an impeachment vote was taken, it failed by a margin of 36-17. A suit was then filed against Churchill in May 1883 in Chancery Court requiring him to repay the state for monies lost during the time that he was treasurer. The court appointed an independent auditor to investigate the issue and found the shortage to be about $80,522. Although Churchill continued to maintain his innocence, he ultimately agreed to pay that amount and to close the matter.

By the time the Democrats began preparing for the campaign of 1882, Churchill had run into deep trouble within the party leadership. Most of the leaders disassociated themselves from Churchill and could not afford to support him because of the need to maintain an image of honesty and integrity.

The campaign of 1882 gave all indications of being a heated and wide-open race for the nomination. Five men were announced as candidates. The best known was Federal Judge J.H. Berry, judge of the Fourth Circuit. The Churchill scandal figured to be an issue in the campaign but, fearing outside criticism, the Democratic leadership focused attention on resubmitting the debt repudiation to

the voters for approval. Also, the party recognized that if they remained divided, the Republicans and Greenbacks could unite and bring them defeat. Consequently, for the election itself, the party unified, nominated Berry, and drafted its platform for resubmission of the Fishback Amendment for repudiation of the state debt. The Fishback Amendment was the only major plank in the Democratic Party's platform.

The Greenback Party nominated Rufus K. Garland, brother of Augustus Garland, for governor and made a strong appeal to the voters, particularly in rural Arkansas, to support their party. They made a great deal out of the Churchill scandal and pointed out that the Democratic Party itself was guilty of misusing public funds. The Republicans, encouraged by the Churchill scandal and strongly opposed to the Fishback Amendment, decided to hold their own convention and nominate their own candidate. They nominated W.D. Slack, commissioner of the Little Rock and Fort Smith Railroad, and adopted a platform of opposition to repudiation, criticizing the Democratic Party for bad government.

The campaign was a strong three-way race. The final tally showed that almost 60,000 votes were cast against the Democratic Party nominee. In the previous election, a little more than 30,000 opposition votes had been cast. The Democrats had only increased their vote total by 3,500 votes over the previous election while the opposition had increased its vote total by more than 28,000. However, in the final analysis, neither the Churchill scandals, the disagreement over repudiation, nor the popularity of Rufus K. Garland were enough to overcome the Democratic Party's great strength.

The legislature under Berry spent most of its time continuing the investigation of the Churchill scandal. It also appointed a committee to investigate former Governor Miller. A majority report of that special committee said that the former governor owed the state $300 but a minority report exonerated him for many charges and Miller did not pay the state any funds.

Several newspapers became increasingly critical of the Assembly members for spending all of their time investigating scandals and not enough time attending to the business of the state. The Assembly did make a move to regulate the railroads by appointing a board of commissioners consisting of the governor, the secretary of state, and the auditor. The commission was given the responsibility to reappraise railroad property in Arkansas for taxation purposes. The St. Louis, Iron Mountain, and Southern Railroad filed suit in Chancery Court to stop the reassessment on the grounds that the appraisal violated their exemption rights by special legislation. They were soon joined by the Little Rock and Memphis Railroad as a partner to the suit. However, the Chancery Court ruled in favor of the state and agreed that the commission did have the authority to order reassessment. The railroads appealed to the state Supreme Court and then to the U.S. Supreme Court, but the ultimate decision was in favor of the state. The railroad commission moved to reassess railroad property and increase the assessment by more than six million dollars.

In other matters, a steady decline in agricultural conditions led farmers to a new sense of militancy in the 1880s. The price of cotton following the Civil War continued to decline and by 1882 the price had dropped to 8.5 cents per pound. Low prices, coupled with the increased problems of the crop-lien system and tenant farming, led many farmers to frustration and despair.

Many farmers felt compelled to organize and concentrate their energies on political solutions. Consequently a group met in Prairie County in 1882 and formed an organization called the "Agricultural Wheel." In the words of one of the organization's founders, "No machinery can run without one great drivewheel, so agriculture is the great wheel of power that controls the entire machinery of the world's industries. Who could live without the farmer?" The group also used the name "Brothers of Freedom."

For a time the Agricultural Wheel tried to work within the Democratic Party. But by the late 1880s it became increasingly apparent to many farmers that their interests were not the same as those of the Democratic business community; a decision was made to form a third party and challenge the Democrats in the upcoming gubernatorial election of 1888.

In the minds of the farmers, traditional Democrats, the Redeemers, reflected the priorities and interests of the few and were not particularly interested in the debt-ridden farmers. The farmers saw no solution in the Democratic Party.

To assist in their efforts to challenge the Democrats, the Agricultural Wheel members joined with another small group known as the "Union Labor Party" to build themselves as a grassroots organization determined to gain control of the political process in the state and reestablish the priorities of state government. It was not

The prices of the main cash crop, cotton, continued to fall following the Civil War, and farmers grew more discontented as their situation worsened. Courtesy, Arkansas History Commission

coincidental that the Republicans also chose to join with the Agricultural Wheel members in 1888 and the Democratic Party faced perhaps its most serious challenge since regaining control of government in 1874.

The Wheelers nominated physician C.M. Norwood, a one-legged Confederate veteran from Prescott, for governor in 1888. The Democrats countered by nominating longtime party faithful James M. Eagle. Eagle was an ordained Baptist minister and had gained considerable reputation in rural Arkansas because of his extraordinary efforts to travel throughout the state making speeches on behalf of the Arkansas Baptist Convention.

The campaign of 1888 was one of the most hotly contested campaigns in the post-Civil War period. Eagle received some 54 percent of the votes and Norwood polled about 46 percent but only 15,000 votes separated the two men. Many Arkansans felt that in an impartial election Norwood would have won. Norwood asked for a recount but his plea of fraud fell on deaf ears. Eagle and the Redeemers stayed in power and continued the Democratic Party's stronghold.

In retrospect, it seems that the major factor in the Wheeler's defeat was the fact that the party had also embraced the support of black voters, particularly black farmers. In an effort to muster as much support as possible against the Democrats, the Agricultural Wheel joined with a group known as the Agricultural Star, predominantly black farmers who organized in 1882. The union of these two parties led the Democrats to charge that the Wheelers were simply trying to follow the practice of the Republicans during the Reconstruction period, namely organizing black voters against white voters. In fact,

James P. Eagle (1837-1904), a farmer turned politician, served in the Arkansas legislature in 1873-1878, and 1885. He was elected governor and served from 1889-1893 but declined to seek a third term. Ordained to the ministry, Eagle served as president of the Baptist State Convention from 1880-1904 and was elected president of the Southern Baptist Convention in 1902. Courtesy, Arkansas History Commission

the Redeemers charged, the Agricultural Wheel was nothing more than the Republican Party with a new name.

The election of 1888 represented a turning point in the state's political history. Not only did it present the Redeemers with their greatest challenge, but it also led to a significant change in their tactics and strategy. The old approach of fusion (trying to unite black voters with the Democratic Party to keep their support away from the Republicans) now was over and the Democratic Party moved to establish guidelines to discourage black voters from participating in the election process.

Wheel leaders, however, were not discouraged. Their strong showing in the election of 1888 convinced many that they would soon successfully challenge the Democratic control of the state.

In the months following the gubernatorial election, Agricultural Wheel leaders met with farm groups in other

Arkansas' first streetcar system began operation in Hot Springs in January 1875. It was originally pulled by one horse over a two-mile track from the old Benton Road (Spring Street), north along Valley Street (Central Avenue) to Park Avenue where it ended at Mount Ida Street (near Arsenic Springs). Charles N. Rockafellow, whose drugstore is pictured here, was one of the major stockholders. In 1891 there would be efforts to pass a separate coach law segregating public transportation. Courtesy, Garland County Archives

Southern states and made plans to become a national party. In December 1888 a joint meeting was held in Meridian, Mississippi, and the Wheelers voted to join the Farm Labor Union. At the same time they voted to expel black members from the Agricultural Wheel organization. Black farmers were encouraged to form a separate Agricultural Wheel organization but were not a part of the mainstream of the Agricultural Wheel movement.

By early 1892 the Agricultural Wheel was in a position to join with other Southern farm parties and organize what came to be known as the "Peoples Party" or "Southern Alliance," also known as the "Populist Party." The Populists met in Little Rock in June 1892 and formed a convention to nominate a candidate to challenge the Democrats in the 1892 election. Fifty-two of the seventy-five counties were represented and the party seemed to have a broad base of support. The Wheelers adopted a platform with a specific appeal to farmers. Charging that the Democrats were the party of the few and not representative of the overall interests of the people, the Wheelers called for free textbooks in public schools, defeat of the poll tax, and abolition of the convict lease system. The party appealed to black voters for support by denouncing lynchings and promising that the party would help all of

Apple processing in preparation for canning was momentarily stopped for this group photograph. The great apple orchards, located in northwest Arkansas, began to decline in the 1920s. Courtesy, the Shiloh Museum

Rural Arkansans pushed for improved public schools in the 1890s. In some areas, private schools like the Hope Female Institute helped fill the educational need. These students posed in their Sunday best for this 1898 photograph. Courtesy, Southwest Arkansas Regional Archives

the downtrodden sons of toil, regardless of race.

This effort to win the black vote was significant, particularly in light of the fact that the national Populist Party had moved to exclude blacks from membership. But based on the Populist economic philosophy that farmers and workers were the creators of the nation's wealth and that both black and white farmers were exploited, the state Wheel leaders felt it was only appropriate to appeal to the black voters for support. In truth, the only way they could hope to defeat the Democrats was to pick up all the disenchanted votes among white voters as well as a significant portion of the black voters to offset the organizational strength of the Democratic Party. Racial attitudes, however, proved to be the undoing of the Populists in Arkansas. In the words of one of the local newspapers, "This is a white man's country and white men are going to rule it." When the third party opened its arms to blacks at its state convention, it invited certain death at the polls the next fall.

Among the continuing themes in Arkansas history were the relationships fostered in the black and white populations. M.W. Gibbs, a prominent black leader in Little Rock, wrote in his memoirs in 1902, a book titled *Shadow and Light,* "It can truly be said of Little Rock that the press and the leading citizens have been more just and liberal to her colored citizens than any other city." Blacks were admitted to the Board of Trade, the Real Estate Exchange, the bar, and professional and literary societies. A black newspaper reporter from Chicago visited Little Rock in the 1890s and reported seeing black doctors with white patients, black lawyers with white clients, and black

merchants with white customers. In 1898 a survey of the Little Rock business community revealed that nine black businessmen were listed as owners of restaurants and two were listed as hotel operators.

Generally, until the 1890s there were no restrictions on the use of public facilities. For example, the Ex-Slaves Association convention held in Little Rock in 1897 met at West End Park and was followed by the State Confederate Union the next week at the same place. The division in race relations was usually based on class rather than on race. The Capitol Theater in Little Rock, for example, had a parquet area reserved for whites only but the balcony was open for both races.

The changes in race relationships that began to occur in the late 1880s were brought on primarily by economic conditions. As farm prices declined and the crop-lien system became more acute, many black farmers turned to third parties in an effort to gain political relief. This led to the Democratic Party making a move to disassociate itself from black voters. What followed was a series of restrictive legislative enactments, known collectively as the Jim Crow laws, beginning in 1891 with the poll tax, followed in 1892 by the separate coach law. Then in 1896 the U.S. Supreme Court issued one of its most famous decisions, the *Plessy vs. Ferguson* case, which upheld the right of segregated facilities for the races. The crowning blow to race relations came in 1907 when the Democratic Party adopted its all-white primary and effectively read the black voters out of the Democratic Party.

The Democrats gave lip service to reform but most reform in the 1890s showed a definite division within the state's political system. On the one side was a group made up of small farmers, tenant farmers, small businessmen, and general laborers. On the other side were the conservative Democrats who were influenced to a great extent by railroad and insurance interests and by the larger business concerns.

To some degree the conflict within Arkansas was the same as that which was being expressed nationally. In the national picture many members of rural America had come to believe that their major problem lay in not having an adequate supply of money in the nation's monetary system.

Repeated attempts had been made since the end of the Civil War to develop a plan for inflating the economy, and by the 1890s a concentrated move had been organized to advocate inflating the currency by circulating additional silver coins. The basic plan called for increasing the minting ratio of silver to gold at a rate of sixteen silver coins for each gold coin minted. Advocates of inflation believed that if the economy were inflated, then prices for farm goods, for example, would improve, the debt picture would be reduced, and farmers and workers would be in a better position to compete in the economic sector.

In addition to the free silver issue, rural voters also advocated improved public roads, more stringent regulation of the railroads, and prison reform. Rural Arkansans were also in need of improved public schools and cheaper textbooks. Until the 1890s the Democrats' approach to the complaints of rural Arkansans was essentially to blame the economic problems on outside interests, especially bond holders and trusts of the national banks and the creditor class in general.

Despite the promises of the Demo-crats, farm prices did not measurably improve in the 1890s. Mortgages on farm land continued to mount and repayment of the debt had become a serious problem. The general belief was that the so-called common man was losing faith in the Democratic Party. The state came to be divided between two groups: one group represented the eastern planters and the larger towns; the other group represented the hill farmers of the west and the smaller towns. This split was best dramatized in the Democratic primaries of 1896.

Two candidates emerged in the 1896 primary campaign to seek the nomination for governor: James H. Harrod and Daniel W. Jones. Jones, sensing that voter attitude was turning toward inflation, asserted that he would not support the national ticket if it endorsed the gold standard. Harrod, on the other hand, said that the money question was an individual matter and not an issue for the party to be concerned with. The issue soon evolved into whether or not the candidates would support the national party. But in one of the campaign primaries Harrod said, "I am in favor of free silver at sixteen to one, but if the Rothschilds write the platform and the Devil is the nominee, I am for them," speaking in terms of the national Democratic Party. Jones emerged as the clear favorite and won the Democratic nomination in 1896.

The Republicans nominated Harmon L. Remmel, who took no position on the free silver issue. The Populists nominated A.W. Files, who took a strong position in favor of free silver as well as supporting a plan for initiative and referendum petitions.

The Democratic platform in 1896 called for free silver or at least a bimetal monetary system. It also supported the establishment of a railroad commission and an income tax, while it also opposed the government sales of interest-bearing bonds in times of peace. Despite the call for reform in the Democratic platform, there was no serious discussion of the issues and the Democrats won the election again fairly easily.

Perhaps the most significant point about the 1896 election was the small vote of the Populists. Files polled only 14,000 votes, a clear indication that the Democrats were maintaining control of the political process. Jones's election, however, indicated that the party was shifting from its conservative supporters to more of a reform

element within the party. The conservatives seemed to be losing their grip on the state and the rank and file voters were shifting more to the left.

The Legislature was even more radical than the governor and, beginning in 1896, the next decade was decidedly reformist in its legislation. Key factors passed in the 1896 election included plans to regulate the railroads—a railroad commission was created, and additional laws were passed to protect passengers against fraud, overcharges, and requiring the railroad to publish rate schedules.

In follow-up sessions additional legislation was passed to require reassessment of railroad property. Railroads were made liable for damages

The establishment of a railroad commission was demanded by Democrats in 1896. Pictured here are the 1899 Railroad Commission members. Courtesy, Arkansas History Commission

Facing page, top: *With heavy machinery available, railroad construction became easier and required fewer workers. Only three are seen working on this route from Marianna to Mena. Courtesy, Ray Hanley*

Facing page, bottom: *Lumber is one of Arkansas' most valuable natural resources. In the past, logs have been transported in different ways. One way is by train, such as this one used in 1903 by the G.F. Bethel sawmill in Mansfield. Courtesy, Arkansas History Commission*

Above: *Walter Nash (right) and two unidentified railroad employees pose with a passenger in the interior of a Rock Island railroad car in about 1905. Courtesy, Arkansas History Commission*

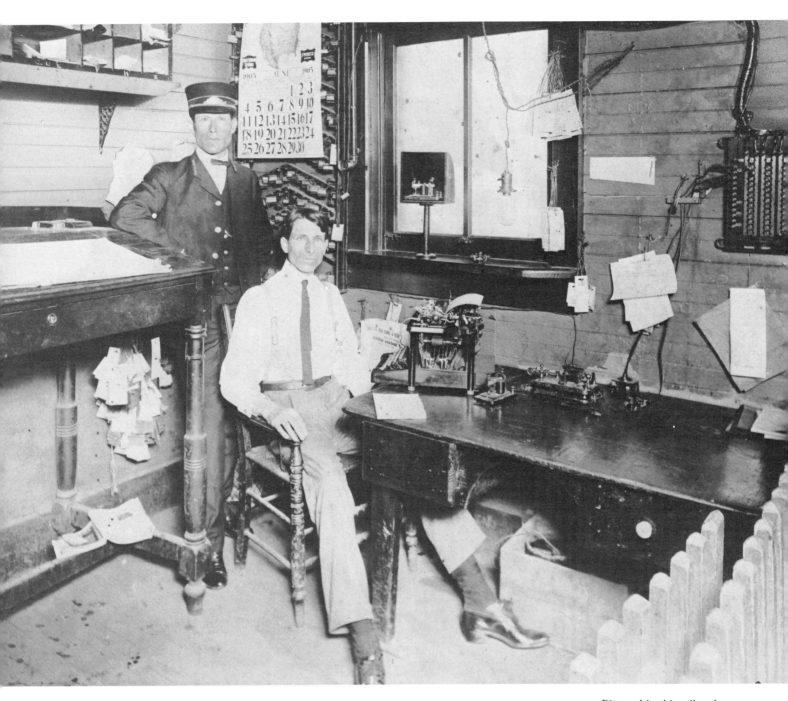

Pictured in this railroad office is Walter Nash, who worked at Bellville on the Little Rock and Fort Smith route of the Rock Island Railroad. The wall calendar behind Nash dates this photograph in June 1905. Courtesy, Arkansas History Commission

to baggage and livestock killed by their trains. Legislation was also passed requiring railroads to stop at more places, to construct depots, and to provide provisions for the comfort of the passengers. Finally, a law was passed to tax private cars operated on lines within the state.

Accompanying the railroad legislation was additional reform legislation aimed at corporations. In 1897 the legislature passed a mild antitrust law against combined influences of the railroad and insurance companies and against corporate wealth in general. But two years later the legislature passed a more stringent law known as the Rector Anti-trust Law that forbade pools, trusts, and other conspiracies in restraint of trade to control prices. It also had a special provision stipulating the conditions under which foreign corporations, that is, corporations with charters outside the state, could do business in the state. Finally, a special provision was included to regulate the issuance of fire insurance policies within the state.

In an effort to gain support among rural voters in Arkansas, the Democrats in the 1897 session passed legislation for regulating fencing levees and providing for quarantine districts among the livestock owners. They also passed a law regulating the weighing and marketing of cotton. Governor Jones was able to use his reform program to be renominated and reelected in 1898, although his margin of victory was smaller than in his first campaign.

Most of the action after 1898 and for the next decade focused on a new politician in the state, Jefferson Davis, who was elected attorney general in 1898 and soon attracted statewide attention. Davis was born in Little

River County and moved to Russellville with his family at an early age. Though his father was a lawyer, young Davis was not well educated, but he did pass the bar exam of the state at age nineteen. Within six months after being elected attorney general, he decided that his political career was best suited for the governor's office and he made plans to run for the governorship.

Davis' opponent in 1898 for attorney general had been a law professor from the University of Arkansas named F.M. Goar. Goar died within the course of the campaign and Davis won the election without any opposition. As attorney general, Davis began an active policy of enforcing the Rector Anti-trust Law passed by the previous General Assembly. Davis interpreted this to be a restriction against any company that had been charged with fixing prices anywhere in the world, and he began antitrust action against 126 companies, mostly insurance companies.

The widespread legal effort by Davis soon ran into trouble in the state Supreme Court. Arguing his first Supreme Court case, Davis was unable to make a convincing argument and lost. An issue that would later come to identify Davis more directly than any political issue was the controversy that developed between himself and the Supreme Court chief justice: when Davis wanted to take off his coat while arguing his case, the justice refused to allow him to do so. Davis charged that he lost the case primarily on personality and not on substance of the case. In retaliation, Davis then withdrew his charges against the remaining 125 companies. The antitrust issue was not the only area where Davis attracted statewide attention. He also strongly opposed a

Born in Jefferson County in 1846, Frederick T. Anderson painted Red Bluff 35 Years Ago *in 1907. The grandson of Antoine Barraque, a prominent early settler of Arkansas, Anderson was first recognized as an artist in an 1874 article in the* Memphis Daily Appeal. *The painting now belongs to Mr. and Mrs. Eugene Harris Adams. Courtesy, Southeast Arkansas Arts and Science Center Adams*

proposed plan to build a new state capitol and he objected forcefully to plans that were made by the General Assembly to acquire a site for the state penitentiary. Davis' opposition to these issues, as well as his performance before the state Supreme Court, brought him into conflict with many established Democratic leaders and even with Governor Jones. Because of that opposition, Davis made the decision to run for governor in the upcoming 1900 gubernatorial campaign, despite having held office as attorney general for less than six months.

The turn of the century offered Arkansans an opportunity to reflect on events of the four previous decades. They had entered the Civil War as frontiersmen, living in a region that was underpopulated, economically underdeveloped, and looking westward for future growth. They had emerged from the war and Reconstruction emotionally and politically tied to a region from which most of them had come—trying to revive a dying society.

For white, male Arkansans with an interest in business, the late nineteenth century offered an opportunity to grow—in railroads, in insurance, in politics, even in large-scale agriculture. But the vast majority of Arkansans, white and black, were forced to eke out an existence as sharecroppers, tenant farmers, or small subsistent landowners. Theirs was not an easy life and the economic pressures led to political agitation frequently expressed in third party movements.

Black Arkansans, almost overwhelmed by their freedom from slavery, found adjustment to the new social order a difficult process. Courted by both major parties for political support, blacks learned all too often that white politicians wanted their vote but not their talents. By the end of the century, attention for political support had faded and blacks were once again pushed into a segregated society.

Arkansas women in the late nineteenth century saw very little change in their circumstances. Some women did find an opportunity for growth in the reform movements of the period. The temperance campaign provided women with an occasion to talk strategy, to plan political objectives, and to work together for common goals. The *Woman's Chronicle,* a newspaper published in Little Rock for five years in the late 1880s and early 1890s, was an advocate of women's rights and voiced concerns. The paper, edited by Catherine Cuningham and Mary Burt Brooks, circulated throughout the South.

Regardless of their social or economic standing, Arkansans in all parts of the state could give testimony to change, either profound or miniscule, in their lifetime. The railroad was perhaps the most dominating influence in the lives of most people. Not only did it increase the speed of travel, but routes went all over the state and pulled settlement away from the rivers for the first time. Technological progress gave most Arkansans reason for hope as they faced the twentieth century.

Governor Charles Hillman Brough stands on the steps of Arkansas' new state capitol with women's suffrage supporters. The General Assembly allowed partial voting rights to women in 1917, but the law was amended in 1920, when the Nineteenth Amendment granted women the right to vote in national elections. Courtesy, Arkansas History Commission

The Progressive Era and Arkansas

CHAPTER V

Historians frequently refer to the first two decades of the twentieth century as the "Progressive Era." For most people "Progressive" meant change—for the better. Nationally, Progressive leaders were interested in eliminating graft and corruption in politics, making the economy competitive in the marketplace, and restoring a sense of morality in society. Arkansans shared these values, although the percentage of Progressive support in the state was smaller than the nation as a whole.

Lacking an industrial society, or even a large city, Arkansas did not have the same problems as states in the East. But this is not to say that the state was free from political corruption, monopoly, or intemperance. Indeed, most political observers knew about the misuse of funds and disputed elections of the nineteeth century. Railroads and insurance companies offered most Arkansans a glimpse of monopoly, and the temperance movement publicized not only the evils of liquor but also the problems that women and children had in coping with a male-dominated society.

Arkansas was still more than 80 percent rural in 1900 and for many of the citizens change would come in terms of better cotton prices, improved transportation, and lower taxes. In a sense they had always been interested in these issues, but the new century offered hope for a fresh start, a hope that many Arkansans placed in their political leaders.

In the gubernatorial campaign of 1900, Jefferson Davis' appeal was to the rural voters and his speeches had a standard pitch. He always opened with an explanation of his antitrust fight before the state Supreme Court and made a point of explaining how the court had refused to allow him to

Jefferson Davis, a Russellville lawyer, served three terms as governor (1901-1907) and then was elected U.S. senator (1907-1913). He was the only politician of the period who aroused a great factional division in the Democratic Party. Davis held the record for the most successive terms in the governor's office until it was broken by Orval Faubus. Courtesy, Arkansas History Commission

take off his coat. He then read a few of the bad things about himself that the city press had written and then attacked the newspaper editors, claiming they could be bought for a nickel. Davis also called for the people not to sacrifice themselves for the corporations and the money barons of the East and to show them who ruled Arkansas by electing him as governor.

Davis' style was also to be highly critical of his opponents. In 1900 he faced three opponents, John Gould Fletcher, a longtime member of the party, A.F. Vandiver, and Edgar S. Bryant. Davis' attacks were so fierce that Fletcher and Bryant dropped out of the race. Vandiver stayed in the race because, in his words, he was "determined not to let the party be carried away by the extremists." Davis also spent a considerable amount of his time critizing former Governor Jones, who was in an active race for United States senator against incumbent J.H. Berry.

Davis won the 1900 election handily, and in the next six years was reelected two additional times but was never able to hold together a permanent political coalition. Despite his personal fanfare, there were few major issues of any consequence in his administration as governor. The legislature did pass new antitrust legislation that the Supreme Court upheld but the impact of that legislation led two-thirds of the fire insurance companies in the state to pull out. They did not return until the legislature repealed the law in 1907.

Davis also pardoned a number of convicts, creating a great deal of controversy in the state, but Davis defended himself by saying that he paroled people while his opponents paroled the railroads. The governor was also involved in a dispute with the state Prison Board over the purchase of the 11,000-acre Cummins Farm, which was proposed as a site for a new prison. Davis opposed the purchase. He claimed that the land was flooded and overgrown with Johnson grass and was selected only because of the political connections that the owner had. He also said the price was exhorbitant. And so the controversy raged.

The prison problem had roots dating back to the Civil War. In an effort to deal with the lawless element in the Western states, the United States Congress had focused attention as early as the 1830s on strengthening the federal courts. Arkansas came in for its share of the attention, particularly after Indian territory was designated in the 1830s and the eastern tribes were removed to the area west of Arkansas' western border. To help control lawlessness, the United States government had created a district court headquartered at Little Rock. The court was initially charged with enforcing all federal statutes in the area extending west to the Rocky Mountains. In the period before the

Civil War this court had seen considerable action. Deputy United States marshalls were commissioned by federal judges to ride west to arrest and bring back to Little Rock individuals who were named on federal warrants. The deputies were paid a commission for each person arrested, plus their travel costs.

In the 1840s Congress moved to divide the western district in Arkansas and move the seat of justice closer to the scene of the crimes. That action became official in 1851 when the western district court was moved from Little Rock to Fort Smith. While the costs of transportation to and from the Rockies declined somewhat, the court was still under considerable attention because of the amount of money it cost to run its business—$250,000 in the 1850s.

By the end of Reconstruction in Arkansas, the federal court of the western district was receiving criticism from United States officials because of its costs. A congressional committee investigated the court's expenditures and held that Federal Judge William Story was guilty of

Next to his teacher in the front row of the 1902 graduating class of Little Rock High School is John Gould Fletcher, called "Don" by his classmates. Courtesy, Arkansas History Commission

Arkansas has been plagued by fires from early days to the present, with Hot Springs suffering in 1878, 1905, and 1913. As precautions, fire departments and fire insurance developed. Texarkana's pride in its fire equipment led to this postcard. Courtesy, Ron Hanley

questionable use of funds; he was asked to resign.

In Story's place was appointed a man who would come to be legendary, not only in Arkansas history but throughout the West: Isaac Parker, a native of Ohio, who was born in 1833. He trained in law and practiced in St. Louis before he was elected to the United States Congress in 1870 for one term. Parker had been appointed as territorial governor of Utah in March 1875, but upon the resignation of Story accepted an appointment as judge of the western district of Arkansas. Parker made his way to Fort Smith, arriving in May of 1875, and immediately set out to reestablish integrity in the federal court and to

bring law and order to the western district.

Fort Smith in 1875 was described by a contemporary as having some 2,500 people but no paved streets, no sidewalks, only a few lanterns for streetlights, no factories, no decent public schools or hotels, and streets that were filled with cowboys and Indians who supported thirty prosperous saloons. The jail, two rooms of cut stone, sometimes held as many as 150 prisoners. A single washbasin was placed in each room and two barrels served as bathtubs. There were few beds and, as one newspaper correspondent described, the place smelled of tobacco, sweat, and decayed food.

Parker had a special gallows con-

Later condemned as a fire trap, this Cummins Prison stockade was built in 1927. Courtesy, University of Arkansas at Little Rock Archives and Special Collections

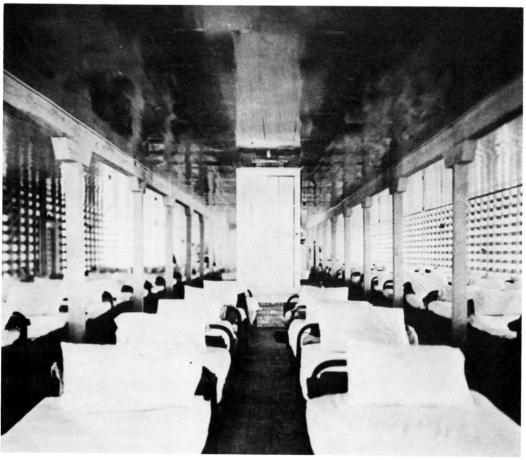

This Cummins Prison barracks housed large numbers of prisoners together, in contrast to more modern and improved prisons where inmates are celled in smaller groups. Courtesy, University of Arkansas at Little Rock Archives and Special Collections

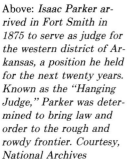

Above: *Isaac Parker arrived in Fort Smith in 1875 to serve as judge for the western district of Arkansas, a position he held for the next twenty years. Known as the "Hanging Judge," Parker was determined to bring law and order to the rough and rowdy frontier. Courtesy, National Archives*

Above: *Noted for their fearlessness were U.S. deputy marshals Coon Ratteree (left) and Heck Bruner. Under Judge Isaac Parker they brought in many dangerous outlaws, including the notorious Ned Christie, for whom they claimed the reward that had been offered. Courtesy, Arkansas History Commission*

Facing page, top: *When Isaac C. Parker was made judge of the Federal District Court for western Arkansas in 1875, he began to clean up the Indian Territory. Harper's Weekly captured a scene of prisoners en route to Fort Smith. Possibly they were among the seventy-nine (some say eighty-eight) hanged in Parker's term from 1875 to 1896. Courtesy, Arkansas History Commission*

Facing page, bottom: *More than 9,000 cases were tried in Isaac Parker's courtroom. The accused, knowing that a twenty-foot gallows stood outside the courthouse, probably wished Parker had a nickname other than the "Hanging Judge." Courtesy, University of Arkansas at Little Rock Archives and Special Collections*

structed that was twenty feet long with the capability of hanging twelve men at one time. Although the judge never sentenced twelve men to be hanged at the same time, the gallows served as a visible deterrent to the criminal element in the western district.

Parker opened the court almost immediately upon arrival. His first case was the murder trial of Daniel Evans, charged with killing a companion on a trip from Texas. The Evans trial was followed by a trial of a man convicted of stealing a horse and killing a pursuing deputy. By the end of the summer Parker had sentenced six men to be hanged and announced that the hangings would be open to the public. People came from as far as forty miles away to witness the event. Parker successfully created the image of a tough judge who would hand out harsh penalties to lawbreakers.

In the next twenty years Parker handled more than 9,000 cases and sentenced more than 160 individuals to be hanged. There is disagreement as to how many were actually executed. Some reports list seventy-nine, others report eighty-eight. The large volume of cases handled in the Parker court attracted attention and the public display of hanging also reached the attention of journalists throughout the nation. Parker's court was regularly reported in the newspapers, both by the Fort Smith paper and papers throughout the nation. Parker soon earned the reputation as the "Hanging Judge."

Parker was not alone in his efforts to bring law and order to the frontier. He was assisted for fourteen of his twenty years by United States Prosecutor Henry Harrison Clayton. Clayton had the reputation of being the best prosecutor in the southwest, but

like Parker frequently relied upon bullying tactics in the court to get a conviction. Parker and Clayton were opposed primarily by a single defense attorney, J. Warren Reed, who, in a period of seven years, defended 134 accused murderers, of which only two were convicted by Parker. Reed was described as being more intellectual than Parker and able to use the fine points of the law to gain an acquittal for his clients.

Parker's publicity, and perhaps his success, led him into trouble with the United States Supreme Court. After the 1880s the Supreme Court increasingly overturned Parker's convictions and Parker in turn responded with criticism of the Supreme Court as being too technical in its decisions. In 1896 the Indian territory was taken from his jurisdiction and Parker was left with a district comprised of only the western region of Arkansas. Much of Parker's reputation and interests had been built on rounding up the violators who had taken refuge in Indian territory and his court was never the same. Parker died of Bright's Disease less than three months after the loss of his jurisdiction. His death brought to a close one of the most notable periods in Arkansas history.

The law west of Fort Smith drew attention to a broader issue in Arkansas in the post-Civil War period, that of prison reform. The Arkansas State Penitentiary was the first state agency chartered in 1842. Although it was the oldest of the state's institutions, before the Civil War the state prison amounted to very little, primarily because there were so few inmates. As late as 1860, on the eve of the Civil War, the prison only had 107 inmates. The prison itself was abandoned entirely in 1863 when federal troops occupied the city of Little Rock.

In 1882 Frank Leslie's Illustrated Newspaper *depicted an incident at Fourche Creek in Arkansas, where escaped convicts were tracked with bloodhounds. Courtesy, Arkansas History Commission*

Following the war, state officials, led by Governor Isaac Murphy, made an attempt to revive the state penitentiary. In 1866 Murphy conducted an investigation of the facilities located five miles from downtown Little Rock and suggested that the buildings were not in a sufficient state of repair to house the inmates. He suggested that the state adopt a plan for short-term leases of inmates to private contractors, so the state could use the time to repair the buildings. The assembly, however, ignored the governor's recommenda-

The first state penitentiary was located in Little Rock on Robert Crutchfield's farm, the site of the present state capitol. Later the prison moved to a site off Roosevelt Road. Pictured here are the mess hall and "The Walls," in 1918, above; and "The Walls" in about 1927, at right. Courtesy, University of Arkansas at Little Rock Archives and Special Collections

tion. They adopted a plan to lease the convicts to private contractors, but continued to house them in the facilities of the state penitentiary.

Asa Hodges was the first individual to be granted a contract to lease convicts for private work. By terms of the contract, the individual was to pay the state a specified amount per inmate and in turn the individual could use the inmates for whatever work projects he desired. Hodges paid the state the equivalent of thirty-five

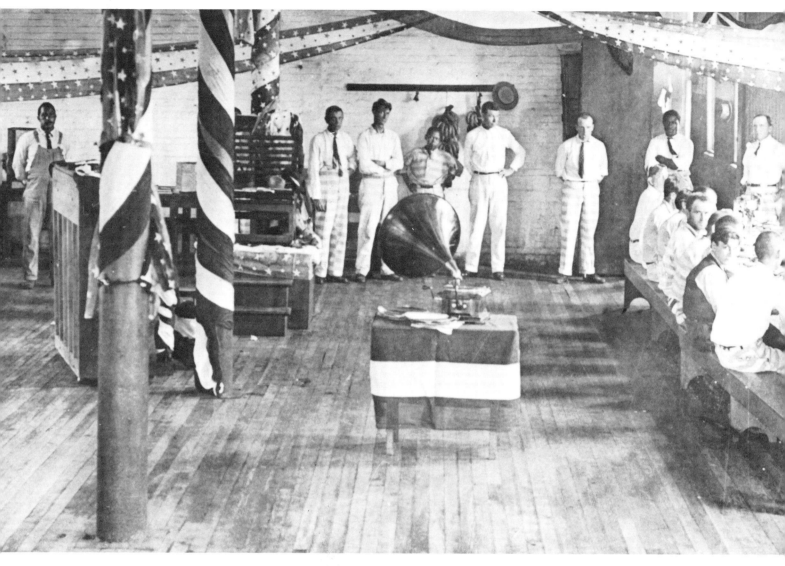

cents per day per inmate and frequently worked the inmates from dawn until sundown. He also provided very little health care for the inmates and his general abuse of the prisoners caused the Assembly to cancel his contract after seven years.

In 1873 the legislature issued a new policy to govern the convict-lease system. The new policy allowed the prison to be maintained under private control, but the lessees had to conform to certain provisions in the contract. For example, a contractor could not work inmates for more than ten hours per day and all work projects had to be under the supervision of the superintendent and inspector of the state penitentiary. Under the revised program, the first contract was issued to John Peck and then subsequently to Zeb Ward. Ward used the convict-lease system through much of the last half of the nineteenth century and accumulated what one journalist described as "a handsome fortune for all of his work."

The legislature also in 1875 passed a new law defining grand larceny. Prior to the Civil War larceny had been punishable by fines or whipping and was largely unenforced as it pertained to whites. But the 1875 law made stealing anything worth two dollars or more punishable by one to five years in the penitentiary. For

These prisoners in the Arkansas State Penitentiary were allowed to celebrate the nation's independence on July 4 in the early 1900s. Prison life, however, was not always this pleasant for inmates of "The Walls," located on the site of the present State Police Headquarters in Little Rock. Courtesy, M.J Lozano

153

The lessee of the Arkansas State Penitentiary from 1872 to 1882 was Zeb Ward (1822-1894). Ward was also owner and developer of the Little Rock waterworks system and president of the Little Rock and Mississippi Railroad. Courtesy, Arkansas History Commission

stealing items worth less than two dollars, the individual could be sentenced for up to one year in the county jail and a fine of up to $300.

A review of the prison inmate roster in the period after 1875 indicates that blacks were primarily the ones punished under the new larceny law. With this new law the inmate population tripled in less than a decade. In 1875 the population stood at 200; in 1876, the year after the law passed, it was 400; by 1882 the figure had reached 600. In 1881 the legislature revised the larceny law to increase the amount from two dollars to ten dollars but the penalty remained the same, from one to five years in the penitentiary.

The increase in prisoners led to more abuse among the state prison population. In 1875 the *Little Rock Evening Star,* a black newspaper, reported that prisoners were commonly mistreated, provided poor food and inadequate clothing, were overworked, and frequently beaten severely; in some cases to the point of death. Charges were leveled against Zeb Ward, who then held the contract with the state, and Ward demanded an investigation by the state Penitentiary Board. The board spent two weeks investigating the charges and reported that there was an occasional excess of force. In fact there had been at least one killing due to inhumane force. The board asked for a Grand Jury to investigate the matter further. The Grand Jury's investigation reported that in 1880, 25 percent of the state prison population died, and strongly suggested that abuse was a primary factor in their deaths. However, the Grand Jury did not hand down an indictment and Ward continued to hold the contract with the state.

The charges were sufficiently damaging for the legislature to cancel his contract in 1881. A new contract was issued to J.P. Townsend and L.A. Fitzpatrick of Helena. They agreed to pay the state the equivalent of $3.75 per month for each prisoner, which yielded a revenue of about $25,000 per year for the state.

Prisoners were used in the coal mining industry in the Arkansas Valley as that industry began to develop in the late 1800s. Conditions in the coal mines were extremely unsafe to a marked degree. The unsafe condi-

tions, coupled with poor food and general physical abuse, led to a riot among the workers in 1888 in the small community of Coal Hill in Johnson County. The prisoners went on strike and barricaded themselves in the mine demanding improved conditions, better food, and shorter working hours. The strike was brutally put down and a number of prisoners were killed. However, the incident did raise a considerable amount of attention about the plight of the prisoners and a growing number of opponents began speaking out against the

Most of the work done by prisoners was in public works. Shown here is a road construction gang. Courtesy, Arkansas History Commission

155

This coal mine was located near Hartman. Coal was first discovered in Johnson County during Archibald Yell's term as governor. In the late 1800s convict labor was used for mining. Poor conditions led to a riot in 1888 in Coal Hill. Courtesy, Arkansas History Commission

convict-lease system. Farmers in particular resented the use of convicts as laborers on the plantations and felt that convict labor gave an unfair advantage to the larger property holders. The system also took jobs that non-prisoners could have done. The combination of the public attention as a result of the Coal Hill incident and the opposition of farm organizations led to the state abandoning its convict-lease system and reasserting public control over the penitentiary.

In 1893 the legislature appropriated $30,000 per year to operate the state prison system and also began plans to acquire a farm onto which they could move the prisoners, thus abandoning the concept of keeping all the prisoners in a single area behind walls. The search for a farm outside of Little Rock was filled with a considerable amount of political maneuvering. A number of individuals had property they wanted to sell the state, but for one reason or another the choices were refused. By the turn of the century, the state Prison Board had decided on the Cummins Plantation, downstream from Little Rock on the Arkansas River, a plantation that had a large cotton acreage and would provide the prisoners with an opportunity to be involved in work while producing a crop that would pay part of the upkeep and maintenance of the prison system. Negotiations were entered into by the state prison board with the Cummins family and, despite the opposition of Governor Jefferson Davis, the land was acquired in 1907 for a price of $140,000. The inmate population was then moved to the Cummins Plantation, which is still the site of the state prison system.

The bankruptcy of Arkansas' first two banks in the 1840s did not prevent banking from flourishing in later years. This is the interior of the Farmers and Merchants Bank of Des Arc around 1900. Courtesy, Arkansas History Commission

Governor George W.
Donaghey and William
Jennings Bryan toured
Arkansas in a special
train in September 1910,
speaking for a proposed
initiative and referendum
amendment to the consti-
tution. The tour began
September 6 and ended
on September 9 in Cam-
den, where they were re-
ceived by Judge George W.
Hays and R.H. Terrell.
Courtesy, Arkansas His-
tory Commission

Another example of the governor's conflict with the lawmakers came early in his second session, 1903, when the assembly adjourned after passing more than 300 bills in the final days of the session. The governor only had twenty days to sign the bills before they became law. Davis sifted through the volume of bills, selected those he wanted to sign, placed the others in a wheelbarrow and, in a dramatic scene, wheeled the unsigned bills to the office of the secretary of state where they were deposited as a pocket veto, a veto later upheld by the state Supreme Court.

In his second term Davis vetoed supplemental appropriation for construction of the state capitol because it exceeded the construction allotment. It became apparent that the conservative element within the Democratic Party was disenchanted enough with Davis to counter some of his political actions. A legislative committee was set up to investigate charges of fraud in state government and the only charge that the committee brought back was regarding misuse of the governor's contingency fund.

In Davis' third term he developed a much lower profile. He had plans to seek the Senate seat in the United States Congress and did not want to alienate the legislature because he would need their support to be elected. Davis opened his third term with a plea for reconciliation and asked for a taxing schedule to be established for all corporate properties in the state. He asked that the schedule be set to be the same as the taxing rate for railroads. He asked for an insurance licensing law and called for further reform in prison management. He also suggested that the state Treasury was running a surplus and that there should be a rollback in taxes.

None of the major programs that Davis advocated were enacted because of strong opposition from lobbyists and special interests. Davis, however, because of his interest in the United States Senate seat, did not push for the measures with the same vigor that he had done in his previous two administrations. As a result no substantial legislation came out of his third term. He was, however, chosen for the United States Senate seat and served in that capacity until his death in 1913.

The decade following Davis' tenure as governor was characterized by one of gradual change and did not include the turbulence and controversy of the Davis years. State programs were gradually expanded even though it was difficult for many Arkansans to accept the new concept of state government as providing a broader range of services. It was also a period of growth and prosperity. The first decade of the twentieth century saw the state's population grow at a faster rate than it had grown at any time since the Civil War.

While progress was the general tone of the second decade, the period was not without its uncertainties. John S. Little succeeded Davis as governor. However, he suffered a mental breakdown within days after being sworn in and never effectively functioned as chief executive. The state spent much of the next two years with an acting governor; as a result, leadership in critical areas was lacking as the state waited to elect a new chief executive.

George Donaghey, a businessman from Conway, was elected to succeed Little. Donaghey was the first non-lawyer to be elected to the office of

Although the cornerstone was laid for the new capitol in 1900, building the new capitol proved troublesome and expensive. In 1908 George W. Donaghey, a contractor, was elected governor on a promise to finish the capitol, and a new start was made. Courtesy, Arkansas History Commission

governor since early in the nineteenth century. Donaghey's early career had been largely undistinguished. As a teenager he worked on a ranch in Texas before returning to Arkansas and taking up carpentry for a time. He also studied for a few months at the Arkansas Industrial University where he studied architecture and structural engineering. He dropped out of college to go into business for himself and got his first major break when he was awarded the contract to build the Faulkner County courthouse. He later received an additional contract for the courthouse in Washington County and constructed the buildings on the University of Arkansas campus.

A fire in 1886 destroyed much of the downtown business district in Conway, and Donaghey rebuilt a

number of buildings. In addition, he received contracts for buildings at Hendrix College and a number of railroad depots. By the time he ran for governor, he had distinguished himself as a successful businessman. He campaigned for governor primarily on his plan to complete the construction of the state capitol. In his inaugural address Donaghey outlined a three-point program that included increasing the number of high schools, particularly those that would emphasize teaching and training in agriculture, completing the state capitol, and reforming the state revenue system.

The legislature cooperated with Donaghey by passing a bill to create four regionally established high schools that would be designated to teach and train Arkansas young peo-

ple in agriculture. These schools were set up at Jonesboro, Magnolia, Monticello, and Russellville. The initial curriculum was two years. In addition to the regional high schools, the legislature also increased appropriations for education that allowed local school districts to employ more than 1,000 new teachers and to lengthen the school term by an average of almost one month. The common school fund was also increased by six million dollars. The legislature also agreed with Donaghey on revenue reform and created a special tax commission to oversee the assessment of property and tax collections in the state. The legislature levied a new

corporate tax that was designed to bring additional revenue into the state Treasury.

The attempts at revenue reform pointed up a nagging problem in the state's history. The debt issue of the nineteenth century had not gone away and by 1910 state revenue was in trouble. The legislature frequently appropriated more money than the state Treasury had and tax collecting was poor at best. The legislature had adopted a practice of passing appropriation bills whenever they were called up before the Assembly. Often the governor would sign a bill early in the session only to see the Treasury depleted before the session was over.

Governor Donaghey succeeded in completing the state capitol. On January 9, 1911, the General Assembly moved in, with the rest of state government following by 1914. Three years later the completely paid-for project was formally ended. Courtesy, Arkansas History Commission

The governor was forced to veto bills simply because of the lack of funds.

To complicate matters, former Governor Davis had altered the revenue records to make it appear that the state's income was greater than it actually was. When showing the surplus to the legislators, he persuaded them to cut taxes, a measure that was popular to the voters but of course did not help state government. The legislators were reluctant to change their traditional practice of passing any legislation on call. Donaghey was forced to enact very strict administra-

option of increasing the rate of taxation but chose instead to simply assess at full value, leaving the job of new assessment to the newly created tax commission. Beyond this, however, the legislators refused to make any further reforms in the revenue system. They did levy taxes on foreign corporations doing business in Arkansas and imposed a five dollar automobile license fee, but the revenue produced by those sources was limited at best.

Donaghey was unhappy with the legislators' refusal to reform the reve-

Originally called the Cardinals, the University of Arkansas football team was first referred to as the Razorbacks by Coach Hugo Bezdek in 1909. In this 1909 game Arkansas beat the University of Oklahoma 21-6. Courtesy, Special Collections, University of Arkansas Libraries, Fayetteville

tive management in an effort to make the state revenues cover the entire budget. He called the department heads together and obtained their mutual consent to limit spending in all of their areas.

Donaghey's success in his first term allowed him to be reelected in a very popular mandate. During his second term the legislature proved more cooperative concerning the revenue program. One of the first measures they passed after 1911 was a law requiring property to be assessed at full value. The average rate in 1911 was about 50 percent and some property was actually assessed at zero. In light of this, legislators also considered the

nue system and called them back into special session in May 1911. The purpose of the session was to revise the revenue laws to provide sufficient state revenues and to distribute the burden of taxation over a broader section of the population in an effort to reduce the overall tax structure.

Donaghey also asked the legislators to abolish the convict-lease system used in the state prison system and to reorganize the penitentiary system. The legislators refused to deal with the convict-lease system; Donaghey by executive order pardoned more than 300 convicts on the lease system and successfully destroyed the program. In the next session the General

Assembly moved to officially abolish the convict-lease system as a method of caring for prisoners in the state penitentiary system.

Donaghey sought a third term but was defeated by a young lawyer named Joe T. Robinson. Robinson would go on to become one of the state's more illustrious politicians; however, he was in office as governor only a short time. After Robinson was elected governor in November of 1912, Senator Jefferson Davis died. Donaghey appointed J.N. Heiskell, editor of the *Arkansas Gazette,* to fill Davis' unexpired term until the General Assembly met on January 14, 1913. W.M. Kavanough was named to serve out Davis' first term, replacing Heiskell. By the time Davis' new term was scheduled to begin on March 10, 1913, Robinson had taken over the office of governor from Donaghey. Robinson then resigned as governor and persuaded the state Senate to appoint him to fill Davis' seat. In the space of three months, Arkansas had four different senators and Joe T. Robinson held three different offices.

Robinson's resignation as governor left the office in the hands of the presi-

This float in a parade at Hope, Arkansas, around 1912 was sponsored by the Women's Christian Temperance Union. Included are: Johnnie Hereford, Margaret Brown, Frances Robinson, Rebecca Norton, Hazel Philips, Louise Ware, Vera Golston, Ella Lundy, Hortense Briant, Anne F. Duckett, Rene Acket, Mannie Bridewell, Florence McRae, Mary White, Annie J. Gibson, Mary Arnold, and Ethel Arnold. Courtesy, Southwest Arkansas Regional Archives

dent pro tempore of the Senate, W.K. Oldham, of Lonoke. However, three days before the General Assembly adjourned in 1913, they elected J.M. Futrell of Greene County to be the new president pro tempore. Oldham did not want to vacate the governor's office, saying that it had been Robinson's intention that Oldham would continue as governor, and he asked Attorney General William Moose for an opinion. Moose upheld Oldham but Futrell refused to accept the decision. When the legislature adjourned on March 13 he opened a second office in the capitol building. For the third time in its history the state had two chief executives. The question of who would be the official governor was referred to the state Supreme Court and both Oldham and Futrell agreed to abide by the court's decision. The court ruled in favor of Futrell and Oldham vacated the office. Futrell then issued a proclamation calling for a special election for governor to be held on July 23, 1913.

The announcement of the special election touched off a new round of political maneuvering within the Democratic and Republican parties. The Democrats were divided between the continuing followers of Davis and the favorite of the Davis group, George W. Hayes. Hayes was born in Ouachita County near Camden, attended Washington and Lee University in Virginia, and entered law practice in Camden upon graduation. The opponents of the Davis group were led by Stephen Brundredge of Searcy. Brundredge concentrated on the cities and towns for his support and Hayes relied upon Davis' connection with the rural vote. Hayes was declared the winner over Brundredge by a very narrow margin. Brundredge filed suit in Pulaski County Chancery Court to prohibit the certification of Hayes as the winner and appealed the Chancery Court's decision all the way to the state Supreme Court. However, the court moved in favor of Hayes, who was certified as the Democratic nominee. Hayes easily won in the general election against Republican Harry H. Myers.

When Hayes became governor in 1913 he faced one of the largest deficits since Reconstruction. The state Treasury showed a deficit of more than $400,000 and Hayes called for the strictest economy among his department heads in an effort to live within the state's budget. In addition, Hayes pushed a measure to have property reassessed. There was a tremendous gap between state expenses and incoming tax revenue. According to the United States Census, property in the state was worth $1.5 billion but the assessed valuation was only $450 million. Hayes contended that the tax rates were high enough if the property could be equitably assessed. However, his proposal before the General Assembly failed to be enacted and the state had to continue under its very limited budget. The Legislature did pass laws regulating the hours for the employment of women, extended suffrage to women, and authorized married women to own property as well as make contracts and carry on business in their own names. The state also followed the national lead and enacted a child labor law prohibiting employment of children under the age of sixteen for all but non-farm work. As a reflection of the time, the legislature passed a very strict law regulating the sale of alcohol. The Newberry Act, as it was known, provided for local option on liquor sale and was a prelude to what was referred to as the Bone-Dry Law,

With Prohibition came the moonshiner, who made illegal whiskey for himself and others. Law enforcement officials found this still in Hempstead County. Courtesy, Arkansas History Commission

which prohibited the sale of liquor in the state.

Hayes did not seek reelection and a spirited contest ensued in the Democratic primary between Charles Brough, a professor of law at the University of Arkansas, and Earl Hodge, the incumbent secretary of state. Brough won by a narrow margin.

Brough was born in Clinton, Mississippi, on July 9, 1876. His father was engaged in banking and mining and provided Brough with an excellent education. He graduated from Mississippi College at the age of seventeen and went on to do graduate work at Johns Hopkins University. He completed his Ph.D. in philosophy, political science, and economics at the age of twenty-one. He taught school for awhile in Mississippi and then came to the University of Arkansas as a professor of economics and sociology.

Brough made revision of the state

revenue his major issue and told the Arkansas General Assembly that the state's indebtedness was approaching $750,000. To remedy this, Brough proposed a short-term loan and revision of the property assessment and also proposed to create a budget system to regulate appropriations. Brough also persuaded the legislators to pass a millage tax to support state institutions of higher education. Under the millage tax bill of 1917, revenue more than doubled in support of higher education.

In addition to revenue reform, Brough also placed major emphasis on education. He called for the creation of the state Textbook Commission to adopt standardized textbooks throughout the state and for a uniform textbook system at the elementary school level. He also asked the legislature to pass a law making attendance compulsory for all children between the ages of seven and fifteen.

America was at war during Governor Charles H. Brough's administration. Many soldiers received their training at Camp Pike near North Little Rock. The base hospital was considered to have the latest equipment. Courtesy, Ray Hanley

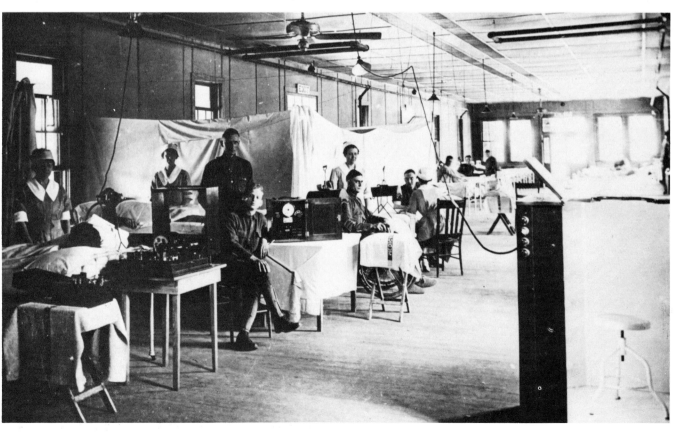

Related to the education issue was also Brough's concern for illiteracy in the state. With his urging, legislators passed a law creating an Illiteracy Commission aimed primarily at improving the literacy rate of adults. In 1900 the population aged ten and older was 20.4 percent illiterate. In 1920 the figure had dropped to 9.4 percent, thanks in large measure to the efforts of the Illiteracy Commission organized in the Brough administration. Among blacks the figure was even more dramatic. In 1900 the illiteracy rate among blacks ten years and older was 43 percent but in 1920 the figure had dropped to 21.8 percent.

Brough also pushed for a constitutional convention, which the legislature authorized. The elected delegates met in Little Rock in 1917 to draft a new document to replace the 1874 Constitution. Among the significant revisions in the proposed 1917 Constitution was to make the governor's term a four-year term without reelection, to increase women's suffrage, and to prohibit the sale of alcohol. The new document was submitted to the voters for approval and was defeated by more than 15,000 votes. A combination of bad weather and rural opposition to the proposed changes led to the new constitution's defeat.

One issue that attracted national attention in Brough's administration concerned the Elaine race riot that occurred in October 1919. The issues of the riot were filled with controversy and an exact reproduction of the situation may never be possible. However, it is possible to piece together the basic outline of what precipitated the riot itself.

On October 1, 1919, a group of blacks were holding a meeting in a church in Hoopspur, some ten miles outside the small town of Elaine. They became embroiled in a controversy with a white sheriff's deputy and exchanged gunfire. What followed was a week of conflict in which five whites and between seventy-five and two hundred blacks were killed. Twenty-five blacks were later arrested for murder and convicted, although most were eventually pardoned.

The blacks were meeting at the church at Hoopspur primarily in an effort to organize for improved prices for their cotton. The roots of the price conflict went back to 1916 when black sharecroppers led by Robert L. Hill organized as the Progressive Union Party and made plans to get better prices for their cotton. By 1919 several hundred black sharecroppers had joined the Progressive Union. In September the Progressive Union asked a Little Rock attorney, U.S. Bratton, to come to their community and represent them in getting a fair settlement for the price of their cotton.

Bratton sent his son, O.S. Bratton, to meet with the Progressive Union and arrange a plan to improve the price received for cotton. While Bratton was meeting with leaders of the Progressive Union movement, another group of blacks near Hoopspur heard of Bratton's arrival and decided to meet at the church to retain him. While they were at the church the conflict with the deputy sheriff began. When the deputy sheriff and a companion supposedly stopped on the road outside the church to fix a flat tire, gunshots were heard; the two men, in turn, returned fire, which led to a shooting spree.

During the week local authorities telegraphed Governor Brough for help and he ordered 400 troops under the command of Colonel Isaac C. Jenks to march to Elaine and help es-

In 1919 a race riot broke out when blacks organized to get a higher price for their cotton. Concerned white citizens met in front of the Elaine Mercantile Company. Courtesy, Arkansas History Commission

Left: *Governor Charles H. Brough ordered troops under the command of Colonel Isaac Jenks to establish order in Elaine. The town was placed under martial law and many blacks were taken into custody. Courtesy, Arkansas History Commission*

Below: *Following the Elaine riot, trials were held for the murders committed during the week of October 1, 1919. Twenty-five blacks were arrested and convicted on murder charges in short trials that followed. Most were eventually pardoned. Courtesy, Arkansas History Commission*

tablish order. Jenks placed the town under martial law, disarmed both blacks and whites, and took several hundred blacks into custody. Jenks then called upon the governor to investigate the causes of the riot and Brough appointed a committee of seven, all of whom were white.

The army withdrew on October 7 and the committee began its investigation. Many complaints were made involving the tactics used by the committee. Charges of death threats and torture, including use of the electric chair, being blindfolded and garroted by rope, were brought by the witnesses against the committee. In the course of its investigation the committee detained 143 blacks and ultimately discharged 21 of them, holding 122 more for criminal investigation by the Grand Jury.

The Grand Jury met for three days and ultimately indicted seventy-three of the individuals for their role in the race riot. Trial was scheduled for November 3. Six men were tried on the same day, including Frank Hicks, who was charged with killing the deputy. All pleaded innocent. The jury deliberated seven minutes and issued a guilty verdict for all six. At a subsequent hearing the jury found five others guilty of first degree murder for aiding and abetting, after deliberating only eight minutes. Five more were convicted on the next day within minutes after the jury had left the courtroom. The trials continued until November 18. During that time thirty-seven were convicted on charges of second degree murder. All the trials for these lasted a full day and the accused were given five to twenty-one year sentences. The last conviction came on November 18—a first degree murder charge. The trial lasted for two hours and five minutes and the jury deliberated for four minutes before finding the individual guilty. The National Association for the Advancement of Colored People vehemently opposed the decisions handed down by the court and appealed to the state Supreme Court. The death sentences were appealed to the United States Supreme Court and none of the twelve death sentences were ever carried out.

It was a bit ironic that the Elaine race riot overshadowed much of Brough's second administration. Of all the governors who had served Arkansas to that time, he was perhaps the most sensitive to issues concerning blacks. He had been a strong advocate of black civil rights and in his second gubernatorial campaign was criticized for being "pro black" by an opponent.

In some respects the riot also signaled an end, at least temporarily, to the reform movement in the state. However, the previous twenty years had seen important changes in Arkansas. Major gains were made in education, at all levels. New procedures were instituted in the state prison system and an improved taxation program developed. Women made significant social and legal progress and Arkansas became the first state in the South to grant women the right to vote in primary elections. Children received protection from certain hazardous jobs and the number of working hours per day was regulated. Specialized agencies, including the Tax Commission and the Highway Commission, were created to address specific problems in the state. The reform impulse may have been dying by the early 1920s, but even so Arkansas had established a substantial progressive record since the turn of the century.

U.S. Bratton, a lawyer appointed assistant U.S. Attorney for the eastern district of Arkansas in June 1897, was one of the Arkansas Gazette's Men of Affairs *caricatured in the 1908 publication of that name. Courtesy, Arkansas History Commission*

171

Factory employees line up after lunch to work at the Tuf-Nut Garment Manufacturing Company, makers of overalls, work clothing, shirts, and pants. Tuf-Nut's products sold in five adjoining states. Courtesy, Arkansas History Commission

Arkansas Between the World Wars

CHAPTER VI

The two decades between World War I and World War II could be almost evenly divided as a decade of relative prosperity and a decade of extreme economic depression. In the 1920s, Arkansans placed a great deal of emphasis on reorganizing and in many cases dismantling the state agencies that had been put in place by the progressive governors, Donaghey, Hayes, and Brough. They also searched for a tax program that would provide permanent funding for the state's school program and promote highway construction.

It was also a period of fairly significant social unrest as Arkansas began to mirror the national trend of movement from farm into city. While the migration pattern in Arkansas was at a much lower rate than the national average, nevertheless tensions between rural and urban Arkansans began to increase. This tension was best expressed by the activities of the Ku Klux Klan and also the efforts of the legislature to preserve the traditional values of the state's religious organizations by passing a law requiring Bible reading in public schools.

The first effort to reorganize the state government in the 1920s came from Thomas C. McRae who was elected governor in 1920. McRae, sixty-eight years old when he was elected, was the oldest man ever elected to the governor's office. He spent much of his time trying to abolish agencies set up during the Brough adminstration. McRae was particularly concerned about the Corporation Commission which in his view had become inordinately expensive. In the year prior to his election the Corporation Commission spent more than $60,000 and McRae felt that the commission should be abolished and replaced with the old Railroad Commission

Lawyer and former U.S. representative from Arkansas (1885-1903), Thomas C. McRae (1851-1929) was elected governor in 1920. Following a second term, McRae left office in 1925. Later he was appointed special chief justice of the Arkansas Supreme Court. Courtesy, Arkansas History Commission

which had spent only one-third as much during its brief tenure. The fact that the Corporation Commission was also asking for its budget to be doubled added to McRae's belief that the commission should be abolished. McRae was also concerned about the organization of the state Highway Department and believed that it too needed to be reexamined. The highway program had become increasingly controlled by special interests groups at the county level.

In addition to the Corporation Commission and state Highway Department, McRae also singled out the Tax Commission, the Board of Control, and the Penitentiary Commission as examples of agencies in the state that needed to be abolished or at least reorganized. The General Assembly was in the mood to comply with the governor's request. All but the Board of Control were abolished and the Railroad Commission was reconstituted and given powers that formerly belonged to the Corporation Commission.

McRae, in addition to reorganizing the agencies, wanted a more comprehensive highway program developed in the state. However, when he made his proposal to the General Assembly he found that the local county interest groups were successful in lobbying legislators and preventing any significant change in the state highway program.

McRae ran for reelection with only token opposition and in his second term focused primary attention on tax reform. He was particularly concerned about the state property tax and proposed that it be replaced with an income tax and an inheritance tax as well as a corporate tax on insurance and franchise taxes. McRae believed taxes should be based on profits rather than property and should be the basis for any tax program in the state. The increased revenues that McRae expected to gain from this tax reform were to be earmarked for education. He also proposed that public lands be transferred to the Permanent School Fund and revenues derived from the sale of those lands also earmarked for education.

When the General Assembly proved reluctant to go along with the plan for tax reform, McRae called a special session and placed tax reform as the single item on the agenda. After extended debate the legislators agreed to proposing a new tax program but did not accept McRae's plan for income and inheritance taxes. Instead, the legislators placed a tobacco tax in effect and earmarked the revenues generated from the sale of cigars and cigarettes for education.

In the special session McRae also suggested that the legislators increase the motor oil and gasoline tax and allocate the revenue for highway construction. Again, he advocated this plan on the basis that those who use the roads should pay for them. The Supreme Court, within weeks after the special session of the General Assembly had adjourned, declared the tobacco tax unconstitutional. Thus, McRae was still without significant tax reform and had no special funds for education. The governor then called another special session to revise the tobacco tax to make it constitutional. Legislators again complied, designating $150,000 for vocational education, and passed a bill that would allow veterans of World War I to enroll in college with free tuition.

Both special sessions cost the state more than $60,000. McRae's critics pointed out that his efforts to eliminate duplicative boards was offset by the costs of these special sessions.

In the second regular session in

Convicts are using steam-powered drills in construction of the road between Eureka Springs and Seligman. The use of convicts for road construction was allowed by the Harrelson Road Law. Courtesy, Arkansas History Commission

McRae's second term as governor, the legislators finally passed a comprehensive road bill. It was known as the Harrelson Road Law, passed in October 1923. The law renamed the Highway Commission the Commission of Lands, Highways, and Improvements and declared primary and secondary

organized in Arkansas in 1921 and by 1924 claimed to have a membership of at least 50,000. It was headed by the Grand Dragon of the Realm and Exalted Cleops, John A. Comer, with headquarters in Little Rock. Klan Number One in Little Rock was the major chapter in the statewide Klan

Many Arkansans joined the new Ku Klux Klan, which came to Arkansas in 1921. The Klan's political control peaked in 1924. Courtesy, Arkansas History Commission

BE A REAL CITIZEN!

Renew your Driver's License

Pay your POLL TAX

Join the U.S. Klans
Knights of the Ku Klux Klan

INCORPORATED
(A Chartered Organization)

Ask next man you meet or write: Box 1241, LITTLE ROCK

roads as well as which roads would be state highways. The legislature funded the new commission with a four-cent tax on gasoline and a ten-cent tax on oil, as well as providing for a graduated motor license fee. The Harrelson Road Law allowed for the use of convicts for road work.

The highway legislation was the primary gain that came out of McRae's second administration and he did not seek reelection in 1924. The 1924 gubernatorial campaign was a wide-open campaign with no less than six candidates seeking the office of governor. It also attracted particular attention because of the activity of the Ku Klux Klan. The Klan had been

organization. Comer sought candidates to endorse for governor in the 1924 campaign and the Klan had a special primary of its own prior to the Democratic primary. With Comer's support, the Klan endorsed Lee Cazort of Jackson County as its candidate. Cazort had been speaker of the House at the age of twenty-nine in 1917 and president pro tempore at age thirty-three in 1921. He was the youngest ever to hold both of those positions. He had retired from politics in 1921 until the Klan enlisted him to run for governor in 1924. He was only thirty-six at the time. The other candidates in the 1924 race included John E. Martineau, judge of

Pulaski County Chancery Court, an avowed critic of the Klan. In fact, Martineau pointed out in the course of the campaign that he was the only critic of the Klan and urged his fellow candidates to also speak out in opposition to Klan activities.

The leading candidate in the 1924 campaign was Tom J. Terral. Terral was serving as a salesman for a book publishing company at the time he entered the race. He was born in Louisiana and had moved with his family to Arkansas in 1907. He was elected secretary of state in 1916 and served in that capacity until 1920 when he ran for the governorship against McRae and was defeated. But in 1924 he ran with McRae's endorsement. Terral was quite interested in the Klan; in fact, he had applied for membership but had been rejected three times by the Little Rock Klan and once by the El Dorado Klan before finally being accepted by the Morehouse Parish, Louisiana, chapter. Comer, however, still denied that Terral was a member and did not recognize his membership in Arkansas.

Terral was elected and continued McRae's plan for efficiency in government with a particular eye toward reducing the number of government agencies. His first area of concentration was the Game and Fish Commission which in his mind was simply too expensive to maintain. The Game and Fish Commission had an annual budget of about $160,000. Terral proposed that the commission be abolished and that its funds go toward education. He pointed out that there were fifty-seven districts in the state that had no schools at all, which affected some 2,000 students. Another sixty-four districts which had 4,000 students had less than three months of school per year. The duties of the

Elected governor in 1924 was Thomas J. Terral (1882-1946), former secretary of state (1917-1921). During Terral's one term, the Board of Charities and Corrections and Arkansas' first state park, Petit Jean, were created. Terral practiced law in Little Rock after his 1926 defeat by John E. Martineau. Courtesy, Arkansas History Commission

Game and Fish Commission, he suggested, could be reassigned to county sheriffs and deputies.

In addition to abolishing the Game and Fish Commission, Terral also advocated abolishing eleven other honorary boards totaling sixty-three members. These individuals were not paid salaries; however, they met once a month and the state paid the expenses for their meetings. He even went so far as to suggest that the state abolish the Efficiency Committee which had been set up by McRae to study the needs for reforming state government.

In addition to the efficiency in government issue Terral also proposed additional aid to education. He par-

Top: *The Pine Grove school east of Garfield was a typical one-room schoolhouse. Courtesy, J.N. Heiskell Collection, University of Arkansas at Little Rock Archives and Special Collections*

Bottom: *Thomas J. Terral established a loan fund for needy students at the University of Arkansas. Monthly living costs in Ella Garnall Hall, a women's dormitory, were about sixteen dollars in 1910. Courtesy, Arkansas History Commission*

ticularly was interested in establishing a revolving loan fund for needy students at the University of Arkansas and proposed that the legislature issue an additional $650,000 in bonds for constructing two additional buildings on the University of Arkansas campus.

The move by Terral to reform government by abolishing a number of boards attracted opposition by those individuals affected. They promoted an active campaign with the General Assembly and with voters in various districts and Terral became quite unpopular as governor. When Terral an-

nounced his bid for reelection in 1926, John Martineau came out in strong opposition against Terral in the primary campaign and defeated Terral by about 14,000 votes. This was only the second time since Reconstruction that a Democratic candidate seeking reelection was defeated, at least in the primary.

Martineau campaigned on a plan for better roads and better schools, as did most Southern candidates in the 1920s. Martineau proposed to develop his road program by persuading the General Assembly to issue thirteen million dollars in additional bonds for road construction for a four-year period. In addition to beginning a major construction program for designated highways in the state, Martineau also proposed, and the legislature accepted, the idea of the state assuming the

indebtedness of all the local improvement districts that had been created in the early 1920s. The combination of the bond program and the assumption of the local improvement districts were embodied in the Martineau Road Law, which became the foundation for the state's highway program in 1927.

The Martineau Law set up a rational system for roads but also greatly increased the indebtedness of the state to over seventy million dollars. Martineau proposed to pay for the indebtedness by increasing the gasoline tax by one cent to five cents per gallon. The legislature made a commitment to the bond buyers that they would keep state revenues at $7.5 million per year as a minimum for the next five years.

In addition to road construction,

Education in Arkansas began to advance around the turn of the century. Although attendance became compulsory in 1909 and efforts were made to strengthen secondary school education, few schools were of the quality seen in this 1919 photograph of West Side Junior High School in Little Rock. Courtesy, Arkansas History Commission

This wounded soldier home from the front appealed for recruits in Forrest City on April 17, 1918, during World War I. Courtesy, Arkansas History Commission

the legislature adopted Martineau's plan for additional bond revenues of some fourteen million dollars to pay for Confederate pensions. Known as the Confederate Pension Law of 1927, this legislation provided retirement for those not covered under previous pension plans. The fourteen million dollar bond issue was expected to generate about three million dollars until 1933. An individual could claim a state pension by having a minimum of a one-year residence in the state. The generosity of the pension plan promoted a number of Confederates to move to the state. The previous law of 1915 specified that an individual must be a veteran or a widow of a veteran and must not own property in excess of $500 or have an income of more than $250 per year.

With a little more than his first year in office gone, Martineau accepted an appointment as a federal judge of the eastern district of Arkansas and resigned his position as governor. That brought to the governorship Harvey Parnell, the first lieutenant governor since Reconstruction. Parnell had been elected lieutenant governor in 1926 after the state Supreme Court revised its interpretation of the Constitution.

Parnell began his term by praising Martineau's road program and encouraging the state to assume an even greater responsibility for county road development. He also continued the general theme of government reform. With his support the legislature authorized the city manager form of government for cities with more than

Highway construction expanded greatly in the 1920s during the four-year term of Governor Harvey Parnell, who followed Governor John E. Martineau's footsteps in road advancement. Courtesy, Arkansas History Commission

Guerrillas operated on both sides during the Civil War. One of the most famous guerrilla leaders was William Quantrill, who was killed by Union troops. Quantrill's Raiders met annually until 1920, when the last annual reunion was held. Courtesy, Special Collections, University of Arkansas Libraries, Fayetteville

8,000 people. The legislature also authorized a policeman pension plan for cities of more than 50,000, and separated the state Highway Commission from the state Land Office and increased the size of the commission from three to five members.

The legislature also created the Commission on Business Law and Taxation. Rumor had persisted that industries were hindered from developing in Arkansas because of the unfavorable tax laws. The commission was charged with the responsibility of reviewing the laws and reporting on reorganization. The commission members took trips to Virginia and North Carolina to study their tax base and recommended a revision of the tax laws. The legislature passed a new tax bill called the Omnibus Bill which levied tax on net incomes and on occupations. The occupation tax drew a large protest and the legislature revised that part of the bill into what was called the Hall Bill, named for A.J. Hall, representative from Logan County.

The Hall Bill established a graduated tax of one percent on the first $3,000 of net income, 5 percent on all income above $25,000, and provided exemptions of $1,500 for single persons, $2,500 for heads of families, and an additional $400 additional exemption for each dependent under age eighteen. Business was taxed a flat 2 percent of its net income.

During the summer of 1928 the new Highway Commission came under increased criticism by county officials for absorbing and directing the new highway program. A number of lawsuits were filed against the Highway Commission to block their efforts to consolidate local roads into the state highway system. The governor called a special session of the legisla-

ture to address the issue of the lawsuits. After an extended debate, the General Assembly appropriated an additional $650,000 to be set aside for use by the Highway Commission in negotiating sales and takeover of land at the county level. The Highway Commission was also authorized to convert bridges in the counties to toll bridges and the assembly voted an additional $7.5 million to construct more toll bridges. Finally, the special session voted an additional eighteen million dollars for additional highway

During the 1920s much of the state's legislation dealt with roads. Improvements were funded by landowners through road improvement districts until 1923, when the Harrelson Road Act switched the responsibility to road users. Under Governor John E. Martineau the state assumed responsibility in 1927, marking the real beginning of Arkansas' highway system. Courtesy, Arkansas History Commission

construction.

The enormous amount of monies coming into the state's highway program plus the increased size of the commission led to charges of kickbacks and special favors being directed toward commissioners and road contractors. This became an issue in the 1930 campaign, but Parnell was able to defeat Brooks Hayes. By 1930 though, the Great Depression had begun to affect the state in a significant way and attention began to turn away from highway construction to the issues of a depressed economy and how best to deal with unemployment.

In reality the Depression in Arkansas began in 1927, two years prior to the stock market crash in 1929. A key factor in creating the Arkansas depression was a natural disaster known as the Great Flood of 1927. Heavy rains began in April and lasted into May in the lower Mississippi Valley. The Mississippi, White, and Arkansas rivers stayed at flood stage for almost a month. Almost half of the state's cropland, some two million acres, was under water. Thousands of miles of railroads, levees, highways, county roads, and bridges were also destroyed by the flood waters. The farmland remained flooded into May even after the rain stopped, too late to plant in many areas. There was also considerable loss of livestock and equipment.

While the flood was devastating, there were some positive things to come out of it. Because of the disaster, private relief agencies rushed in and Arkansas received help from the entire nation. The number of pellagra cases was reduced significantly as much of the population was provided balanced meals over an extended period of time by the Red Cross. The state began conservation efforts in some areas by planting alfalfa seeds provided by the federal government. The flood also led to the establishment of the first airmail service in the state between Little Rock and Batesville because flying was the only way to get mail over the flooded delta.

There was no official estimate of losses for the state, but the federal government, in assessing damages in six of the states in the lower Mississippi Valley, estimated that losses were as high as $135 million. The federal government provided about $75,000 in emergency funds while the Red Cross and U.S. Public Health Department provided $200,000 and the Rockefeller Foundation provided $20,000 to aid the flood victims.

In 1930 the flood was followed by a severe drought that was equally devastating on crops. During the summer of 1930 the weather bureau in Little Rock reported 100 consecutive days of no rain and the drought stretched into the spring of 1931. The principal crops of the state, corn and cotton, were withered in the field. The combination of the flood of 1929 and the drought of 1930-31 caused state revenues to decline significantly, a fact that was compounded significantly by the heavy indebtedness incurred in 1927 by the state's road and bond program.

With conditions deteriorating, in 1930 state officials appealed to the federal government for assistance, but the federal government under the leadership of President Herbert Hoover had developed a policy of relying upon private charity for supporting individuals hurt by natural disasters. By November 1930 the drought had affected not only Arkansas but had stretched through Tennessee, West Virginia, and into Virginia and Maryland. This prompted Hoover to appoint a national drought committee to investigate ways in which federal assistance could be provided. The committee recommended that the federal government reduce transportation rates on interstate carriers so that additional hay, feed, and water could be shipped into the drought areas. In some instances livestock could be shipped out of the areas to where there was a better supply of feed and water. The aid, however, was limited to those whose primary income was derived from farming and who could not pay the standard rate. County agents were empowered to make the determination of who was eligible to receive aid under the Drought Relief Program.

On the state level, Governor Parnell appointed a Drought Committee headed by Harvey Couch of Pine Bluff, the president of Arkansas Power and Light Company, to investigate the need of drought victims in the state. Couch presided over a statewide operation that had county committees to monitor local conditions and provide recommendations for relief. Unfortunately the state had no money for the drought victims.

By December of 1930 the situation was critical throughout the state, a condition that prompted T. Roy Reid, the assistant director of the state's Agricultural Extension Service, to predict that more than 100,000 families would be in dire need of food by the end of the year if relief was not provided. Crops in many areas were called a total loss. Judge A.T. Collins of Little River County reported to the drought committee that 500 families in his county "do not know where they will get food tomorrow." He went on to say that the matter would become even more criti-

In 1913 Harvey Couch organized what would become the Arkansas Power and Light Company. The need for electricity increased with World War I and the discovery of oil in southern Arkansas, so in 1924 Couch built Remmel Dam on the Ouachita River and in 1929 began Carpenter Dam. Courtesy, Mr. and Mrs. Pratt Remmel

cal in the next two to three months.

The extreme conditions increased tensions in many communities, in particular between black and white residents in the Delta region. Tensions reached the surface in Loneoke County when a group of blacks working on a road construction project were fired upon by a group of unemployed whites who resented the fact that blacks were employed when they were not. Parnell sent troops from Camp Pike to patrol the area and maintain order.

With little help coming from the drought committee, attention was turned to the Red Cross which ironically shared the same building as the drought committee. The Red Cross in Arkansas had a disaster budget of about five million dollars and indicated it could only give aid to those in the most desperate conditions. In spite of this, rumors spread throughout the state that the Red Cross would give food to all who requested it. How to determine need became difficult, as well as a political problem when in many counties, particularly in the eastern part of the state.

Tensions reached another peak in January 1931, when a group of farmers invaded the town of England, Arkansas, spurred by rumors that the Red Cross intended to provide food for all who requested it. Unfortunately, when the farmers arrived in town and did not find Red Cross officials available, they believed that they had been tricked. In truth, the system used by the Red Cross had temporarily broken down. The procedure called for individuals to file an application with the Red Cross indicating a statement of need and from that a determination of need was made. In the town of England the local chapter of the Red Cross had run out of its supply of applicant forms to fill out and had closed its doors momentarily. Upon learning that the Red Cross office was closed, however, the farmers turned into a mob with many openly stating that they would take food directly from the local merchants if the Red Cross did not provide assistance. What could have been potentially an explosive scene, reported in the national press as a food riot in England, was avoided when the local merchants opened their doors and allowed the farmers to receive food without the formal application process of the Red Cross. The "food riot" demonstrated that rural Arkansas, the food producing region of the state and one of the most prolific food producers in the entire nation, was in trouble and could not produce enough to supply the needs of its farmers. The problem was twofold: the first was getting through the winter with too few supplies and a second was having seed for spring planting. Harvey Couch estimated it would take a minimum of twelve million dollars to get the farmers on their feet again.

The state was in no position to meet the farmers' problems because of the tremendous debt that the Treasury was laboring under, incurred by the highway program. In fact the debt was one of the most profound problems that Arkansas faced throughout the 1930s. By 1932 payrolls in the state had fallen 45 percent below their 1929 level. Per capita income was $305 compared with the national average of more than $450.

Deposits for all Arkansas banks in 1929 were $137 million, but by 1932 they had declined to only sixty-two million dollars. Moreover, the banking infra-structure was weak. The major bank in the state, the Ameri-

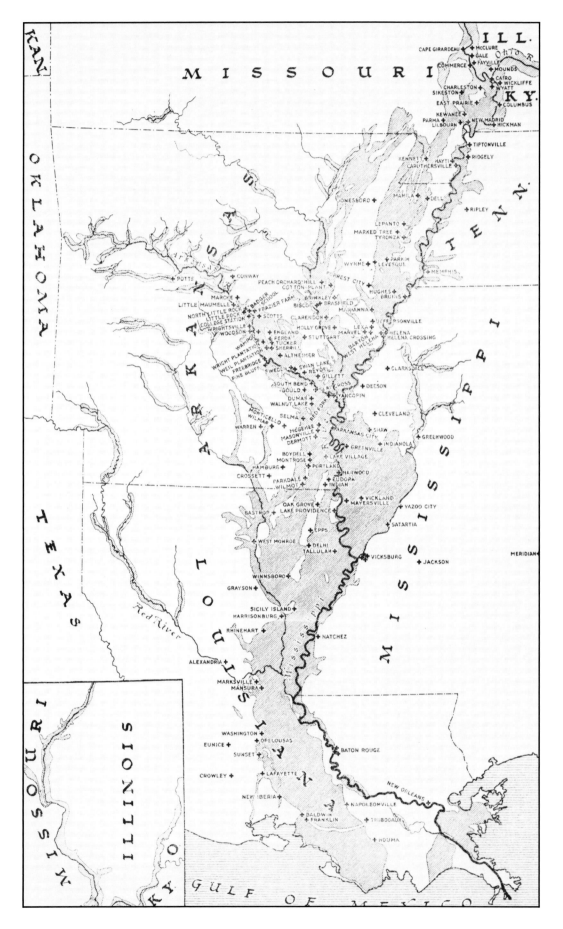

Arkansas, Louisiana, Mississippi, Tennessee, Kentucky, Illinois, and Missouri suffered severely as approximately 26,000 square miles were covered by floodwaters in 1927. Red Cross relief camps were set up throughout the area. Courtesy, Arkansas History Commission

Above: *Arkansas City was only one town in Arkansas affected by the flood of 1927, one of the greatest natural disasters the United States has ever faced. During this time many area residents were housed in tents provided by the Red Cross. Courtesy, Arkansas History Commission*

Right: *In addition to disaster relief, the American Red Cross has provided training for Arkansans, such as this nursing class held in Leslie during World War I. Courtesy, Arkansas History Commission*

Problems caused by drought drove farmers seeking relief to the Red Cross in Conway in 1930. Although these men were desperate for bread, the Federal Farm Board was appealing to farmers elsewhere to produce less wheat. Courtesy, Arkansas History Commission

Following flood and drought, farmers' situations worsened. England, Arkansas, narrowly averted a food riot in 1931. Courtesy, Arkansas History Commission

can Exchange and Trust Bank headed by A.B. Banks, had forty-five branches throughout the state. In 1930 the bank was forced to close its doors, which brought a chain reaction of bank closures throughout the state.

Related to the banking issue, 95,000 Arkansans were employed in nonagricultural work and with the bank shutdown many of them were now without jobs. Cotton was the chief source of revenue for the state and it had declined sharply as well. In 1929 the value of the cotton crop was put at $129,390,000 but in 1932 the cotton crop had declined in value to only $42,870,000. All agriculture revenue reflected a similar decline, dropping from $248,200,000 in 1929 to just $100 million in 1932. By 1932 Arkansas had the highest per capita debt in the nation. The average gross state revenues were about fourteen million dollars but the state debt was almost nine times greater than that.

The good roads movement of the 1920s was responsible for much of the state's indebtedness. The problems began in 1923 when the legislature passed the Harrellson Road Law. The Martineau Road Law in 1927 provided for a comprehensive road system and assumed the local indebtedness of the individual districts. The legislature made a four-year commitment of thirteen million dollars per year of highway bonds to finance the roads in the areas without improvement districts. Benjamen H. Ratchford wrote in a book on American state debts that, "Probably no state ever embarked upon a more ambitious

Cotton has always been an important crop in Arkansas. After it is picked, cotton is ginned and baled. These bales are being stacked in a warehouse on the Wilson Farm, once the largest cotton plantation in the world. Courtesy, Arkansas History Commission

borrowing program in relation to its resources than did Arkansas in 1927."

Another matter, not immediately apparent, was the plan used to market the bonds. A Little Rock firm, Halsey Stuart and Company, was employed to handle the bonds for the state. The company initially set the interest rate at 4.05 percent interest, later raised the rate to 4.75 percent interest, and then to 5 percent interest. But bond sales were slow, at least

lion payment by the state.

In 1931 the legislature approved $7,010,000 in new bonds, $1.5 million of which was to be earmarked for drought relief. The remainder was to be used for new construction at state colleges and state hospitals. In addition, local school districts issued a total of two million dollars in bonds which they had subscribed to pay teachers' salaries. On the state and local level, Arkansas was issuing

Expansion for the State Hospital was authorized and funded by the legislature in 1919 and 1931. Courtesy, Arkansas History Commission

in the early years. By 1929 sales had picked up somewhat but this was due largely to a misrepresentation of the state's assets by Halsey Stuart and Company which reported to buyers that property valuation in Arkansas in 1929 amounted to $1,219,441,326. The actual value was perhaps one-half of that and no effort was made to establish the real value. The legislature, rather than correcting the estimated value, removed all limitations on bond indebtedness except that the amount should not exceed an amount that could be serviced by a $7.5 mil-

bonds to cover day-to-day operating expenses. Bonds that had been issued in times of prosperity came due when the state and national hardships were so acute that the state simply could not meet the payments.

Added to the debt problem was the growing realization that there was serious mismanagement in the state highway program. In March 1931, in response to rumors of mismanagement, the General Assembly created an Audit Commission. Julius Marion Futrell of Paragould was named commission chairman and six other members were appointed, one from each of the state's congressional districts. The Audit Commission debated on how to proceed with the investigation but the fact that the state's indebtedness had increased from almost nothing in 1926 to $160,298,000 in 1932 with little to show for it called for some action. The commission was given $100,000 from the highway fund for operating expenses, but it did not have the power to subpoena witnesses or to summon engineers or contractors. Futrell resigned in disgust upon learning of the weakness of the commission, charging that it was a political ruse.

The General Assembly then debated ways to make the Audit Commission stronger. Controversy arose when two members of the House of Representatives indicated that they had been offered bribes to vote for adjournment without considering any revision to the commission bill. The bribe was allegedly made by Dwight Blackwood, new chairman of the state Highway Department, who denied the charges. A new bill was passed, making the Audit Commission stronger by giving it the power to subpoena witnesses.

Within the first few weeks the commission learned that the Highway Department had paid the Hogan Construction Company $71,500 as a rental fee for unused construction machinery. In addition, the Hogan Company and the C.S. Constant Company were guaranteed a 15 percent profit on their highway construction work. The investigation also showed that two companies were overpaid by as much as $80,000. The

Before being elected to two successive terms in the governor's office, J.M. Futrell, seated second from the left in the first row, had served in the Arkansas State Council of Defense from 1917-1919. Courtesy, Arkansas History Commission

"cost plus contracts," as these contracts came to be known, came to be the focus of the controversy.

Justin Matthews, a Little Rock real estate developer appointed to the Highway Commission by Tom McRae in the early 1920s, denied that any cost plus contracts had been made. Three other members of the Highway Commission said they knew nothing of the contracts. However, Dwight Blackwood, the Highway Commission chairman, said that he would not take the blame alone because the other commissioners had authorized him to make the contracts.

More confusion developed when Charles S. Christian, chief highway engineer, told the Audit Commission that authorization for the contracts had come from Attorney General Hal L. Norwood. Norwood denied the charge. To clear up the matter the commission recalled R.H. Hogan, secretary and manager of the Hogan Construction Company, to testify.

With the controversy surrounding the cost-plus issue, Governor Parnell called another special session of the legislature to deal with the highway problem. The Audit Commission had exhausted its $100,000 operating expenses and needed additional funds to continue. The state was also near default in its own revenues.

In the session the legislature first attempted to deal with the debt and proposed a new bond issue of forty-seven million dollars to mature in ten years at a 4.5 percent interest rate. Another $100,000 was provided for the Audit Commission to continue its investigation.

In the continuing investigation the Audit Commission found that Dwight Blackwood, beginning in 1927 at a salary of $5,000 per year, had deposited $105,000 in various banks throughout the state over the next three years. Blackwood explained that he had earned the money while sheriff of Mississippi County and from his farm. As sheriff and collector for Mississippi County, he said he made $35,000 per year and received a percentage for fees he collected in the arrests he made. When the commissioners asked why he left that job for the Highway Commission which paid only $5,000, Blackwood was unable to offer an explanation. Albert S. Manning, engineer in District Two with headquarters in Pine Bluff, deposited $33,000 in the Merchants and Planters Trust Company of Pine Bluff but said it came from liberty bonds he had bought during World War I, plus his salary and money he had borrowed. Unfortunately, the bank closed three days after he had deposited his funds and he lost all of it.

Legislators, in view of the pressure brought by these revelations, moved to oust all of the Highway Commission members, but that item was not on the agenda for the special session and the General Assembly could not act. The only item they could take action on was refunding the bonds, which they agreed to do.

Parnell then ordered the special session dissolved, but sixty-eight of the 100 members of the House refused to go home. The governor called them a collection of "wild jackasses" and said they were playing power politics. It took an action by the state Supreme Court to dissolve the legislature, but even after the legislators left the capitol, many of them held a mass meeting in Little Rock. More than 1,000 supporters of the General Assembly showed up and demanded a new session. Parnell refused to call a new session and many

The Woodsmall Brothers used equipment typical of the early 1900s on this road across the White River at De Valls Bluff, in about 1915. Courtesy, Arkansas History Commission

Builder Justin Matthews produced this Art Deco sensation in 1929. Area merchants supplied furnishings for this "Modernistic Home for the Modernistic Family." The unusual house created traffic jams. Courtesy, Mr. and Mrs. Charley Baxter

people charged that he also was involved in the improprieties of the Highway Commission. However, no evidence was ever discovered that connected the governor directly with the cost plus contracts.

Armed with its new findings, the Audit Commission asked the Arkansas Supreme Court for an interpretation of whether the contracts were valid. The court ruled that all cost plus contracts of more than $1,000 were illegal. Attorney General Hal Norwood then filed 655 claims against various contractors for overpayment amounting to more than three million dollars and the state stopped pay-

ment on the existing cost plus contracts that had not been completed.

Attorney General Norwood and Pulaski County Prosecuting Attorney Carl Bailey also filed suit against all five members of the Highway Commission to recover almost two million dollars in overpayment. Their basic charge was that the Highway Commission had not held competitive bids or awarded contracts to the lowest bidders. The highway commissioners argued that Assistant Attorney General Claude Duty had held that the cost plus contracts were legal and therefore they could not be prosecuted. Duty, in fact, had performed service for the Highway Commission while assistant attorney general and had received $5,000 as a retainer fee in addition to his regular salary. Duty later returned the $5,000 at the request of the Audit Commission.

The state lost its case against the Highway Commission. Judge Mann of the Second Division Circuit Court ruled that the state must show fraudulent intent and the decision was upheld by the Arkansas Supreme Court. None of the commission members or any department employee were ever convicted on any charge. But A.S. Matting, the district engineer of Pine Bluff, committed suicide rather than face questioning by the Audit Commission. Dwight Blackwood ran as the Democratic nominee for governor in August 1932. Most of the other members, while resigning from the commission, remained active in state affairs.

In the Audit Commission's final report filed in January 1933, it itemized expenses as follows: $77,567,145 was spent for highway construction since the Martineau Road Law of 1927. Of this, $8,869,009.71, or approximately 11.43 percent, was spent illegally; $268,694.31 was spent for legal services, despite the fact that the assistant attorney general was on the payroll. The commission also estimated that it would cost seven million dollars to restore the state's gravel roads to the condition for completion before they could be incorporated into the state's highway system.

The highway program was not the only issue facing the state in the 1930s. In Arkansas the New Deal represented an attempt by the federal government to revive the state's economy without disturbing its underlying social structure. Nationally, the New Deal focused on relief, recovery, and

reform; in Arkansas, most of the emphasis was on relief. Public relief was the most difficult problem faced by Arkansans in the 1930s. Traditionally, assistance for the indigent had been regarded as the responsibility of churches and community agencies. However, by 1933 there was a pervasive feeling of helplessness sweeping through the state as voluntary agencies simply could not accommodate those in need of food, clothing, and shelter.

Herbert Hoover tried to break the relief problems by organizing the Reconstruction Finance Corporation designed to grant loans to large corporations, particularly banks and insurance companies. These companies were charged with the responsibility of loaning the money to individual companies, which in turn used the money to employ workers. This "trickle-down theory" held that money made available to the top levels of the economy would trickle down to the lower levels.

The reconstruction funds were granted to the states and distributed by counties. The funds were to be used for road and levee construction and other similar projects. Each county set up a three-member screening committee which was charged with the responsibility of investigating the individual project applications to see if they truly were needed. The county screening committees were too often concerned about the applicants' standing in the community and those who were labeled lazy or shiftless often found it difficult to secure assistance.

The Reconstruction Finance Corporation had little impact on Arkansas' relief problems and was the major reason why voters turned to the Democratic candidate for president in

1932, Franklin D. Roosevelt, in record numbers. Roosevelt won election by one of the widest margins in history and in his first 100 days as President turned his attention toward relief as the most pressing problem in the nation.

The United States Congress created the Federal Emergency Relief Administration headed by Harry Hopkins and charged it with the responsibility of dealing with relief problems in the various states. The FERA was to provide matching grants and direct grants to states for relief. States were requested to create their own state relief agencies and to disperse the funds.

In Arkansas, Governor J.M. Futrell appointed E.I. McKinley, who was also secretary of Commerce and Labor, to head Arkansas' Relief Commission. Hopkins in turn assigned Aubrey Williams, a social worker from Alabama, to organize the federal relief program in Arkansas. Conflict developed almost immediately between state officials and the new federal officials. Governor Futrell complained that outsiders were trying to take over and run the state and Williams, upon his arrival in Arkansas, called for a full-time administrator to run the state's relief agency. McKinley, as director of another state agency, was unable to fully devote his time to relief issues.

Ironically, on the day Williams arrived in Little Rock, a riot occurred outside the post office when relief applicants were denied admission to the relief office to file for relief payments. Williams considered the local officials incompetent at handling the problem and charged that McKinley had utilized political patronage to promote the relief program in Arkansas. Williams went on to say that Governor Futrell was a tobacco-chewing, conservative politician who was hostile to the basic goals of the New Deal. Futrell responded in kind by charging that Williams was an idealist who wanted to flood Arkansas with foreign-born social workers.

The basic issue was political conflict over patronage. Futrell complained loudly to Senator Joe T. Robinson about Williams' actions and said that the social workers and outsiders would undermine the state's work force, particularly the field workers in the delta. In spite of the conflict between the two men, both were able to agree on a full-time director for the state's relief program: William R. Dyess, a planter from Oseola.

Dyess, a native of Mississippi, moved to Arkansas in 1926 and supported Futrell in the 1932 governor's race. Williams considered Dyess a bright, articulate, sympathetic social worker and a good administrator. The full-time director made relief possible in the state. Dyess' staff included Floyd Sharp, executive secretary for the FERA in Arkansas; and W.A. Rooksbery, who was appointed reemployment director. Senator Robinson complained that Arkansas was not getting its share of relief payments and President Roosevelt asked Hopkins to investigate. Hopkins reported, "The setup in Arkansas has been the worst in the country. It looks as if we are going to have to pay practically all the bills"—a prophecy that proved correct.

The initial relief from the New Deal programs came in two ways: direct relief payments and a public works project called the Civil Works Administration. The CWA was an emergency relief measure for the winter and spring of 1933-34 and was

When government control programs reduced crop acreage during the Great Depression, many tenant farmers could no longer find work. To help these people, the federal government began resettlement projects in eastern Arkansas like Dyess Colony and Lake Dick. Through cooperatives, many were able to become independent landowners. Courtesy, Arkansas History Commission

During World War II Camp Pike was renamed Camp Robinson. President Franklin D. Roosevelt, in the front seat of the Packard, visited the camp in 1943. Courtesy, Arkansas History Commission

headed by R.C. Limerick, former chief engineer of the Arkansas Highway Department. By the end of 1933 CWA had reviewed 270,215 Arkansans who had registered for relief, but employed only 58,000 of those applicants. Federal officials constantly were concerned that individuals were receiving aid when they should not be. In Pulaski County, for example, one person in three was securing relief payments by 1934. By the end of 1933, the federal government had spent $8,424,053 on relief, exclusive of public works projects. The CWA had spent an additional three million dollars in 1933 but was terminated in April 1934.

By the end of Roosevelt's first term, the federal government had spent over sixty-one million dollars, excluding the Works Progress Administration funds. The WPA spent an additional $19,114,185, making a total of federal relief payments in the state $80,667,458 between 1933 and 1936. With the huge inpouring of federal dollars, it was inevitable that complaints began to develop about the process and the way funds were used. Both federal and state officials were concerned about the long-term problem of unemployment and there was a general fear by most officials that continued unemployment would lead to a permanent dependency on the public payroll.

In 1934 Williams sent Gertrude Gates, who was educated at the University of Chicago School of Social Work, to assist Dyess in determining relief needs. Gates requested that trained social workers be sent to aid in relief efforts and that each county have a social service supervisor headed by a social worker. This request again touched off a controversy over foreigners taking control over the state's re-

lief efforts. Senator Hattie Carraway asked President Roosevelt to replace Gates and she was removed in July 1934.

There were other controversies. The Bureau of Agriculture Economics reported that its acceptance rates for rural rehabilitation loans reflected a pattern of discrimination in the state. White applicants were granted loans at the rate of three times greater than black applicants. Committees were organized in each of the counties to review the requests for rural rehabilitation and these committees defended their actions on the basis of

Floyd Sharp (center) was the Arkansas state administrator for the Works Progress Administration. Courtesy, Arkansas History Commission

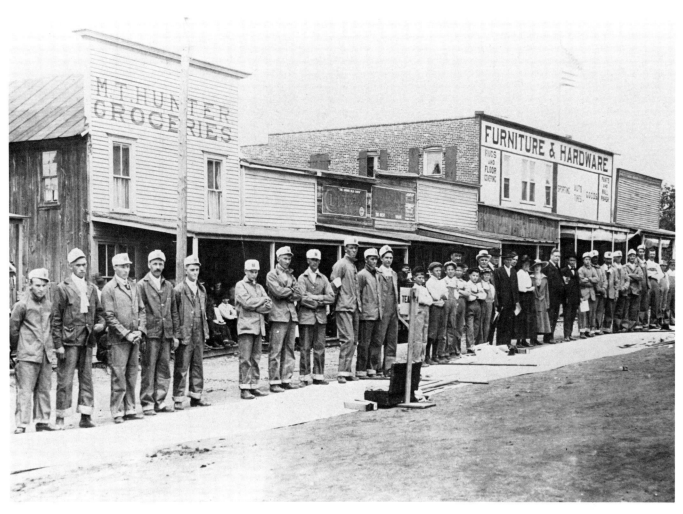

Facing page, top: *Arkansas has been a major supplier of bauxite, an ore used to make aluminum. The open-pit and strip-mining methods were more common than the underground mining operation, pictured here. The center man, known as a roof-trimmer, is checking for safety. Courtesy, Arkansas History Commission*

Facing page, bottom: *Snow Mountain Diamond Cave near Jasper is one of the lesser-known diamond caves in Arkansas. Blanchard Springs Caverns are the best known. Courtesy, Ray Hanley*

Above: *Mining was a risky business, and miners organized to improve conditions. The United Mine Workers were in existence in Huntington around 1912. Courtesy, Special Collections, University of Arkansas Libraries, Fayetteville*

These students attended Commonwealth College at Mena in 1925. The school, which had a reputation for getting actively involved in social issues, was closed in 1940. Courtesy, Special Collections, University of Arkansas Libraries, Fayetteville

the repayment record for loans made for rehabilitation. Most of the loans went to property holders rather than the unemployed.

These individual complaints led to organized protests by the summer of 1934. One of the first groups to organize was known as the Working Men's Union of the World, organized in Fort Smith by Ben M. Vick and John Eakins, both former members of the Progressive Labor Party. Vick and Eakins traveled through the coal mining district of the Arkansas River valley and organized miners. They concentrated on those who were trying to get relief payments and complained that Arkansas payments

were lower than those in neighboring states, particularly in Oklahoma. For example, Arkansas' rate of pay per week was seven dollars while in Oklahoma the rate was ten dollars per week. The general complaint of inequity in the relief system was heard throughout the various protest groups.

Vick and Eakins called for a strike in the fall of 1934, insisting that the workers be paid on the same scale as the neighboring states and protested the treatment that many of the relief applicants had received at the Fort Smith relief office. The union got more support in February 1935 when students from Commonwealth College near Mena joined in the strike. Sebastian County officials appealed to Dyess for assistance and he responded by suspending all federal assistance to the county. The protestors then staged a hunger strike. Local officials responded by arresting the student leader, Horace Bryan, and Claude Williams, an activist Presbyterian minister who had come into the state to assist in the protest movement.

Perhaps in partial response to the national protest of inequities the Roosevelt Administration decided to redirect its relief efforts in 1935. The FERA was continued but a new agency, the Works Progress Administration, was created to assist in additional relief efforts. The new concept was to shift policy from what was called the "dole" to work relief. States were required to support the infirm and those unable to work and also create a Bureau of Public Welfare. State officials were somewhat reluctant to add another agency but Hopkins forced the decision by cutting off all relief payments to Arkansas until the agency was created. The FERA in 1935 was supporting about 400,000 people. Hopkins promised to release funds, however, if the state would move toward creating the Bureau of Public Works and commit to the WPA project. It was estimated that 41,000 jobs would be dependent upon Works Progress Administration projects.

The state finally complied and created the Public Welfare Commission and authorized a sales tax of 2 percent, exempt on some foods and medicines. It then earmarked $500,000 dollars for the operation of the Public Welfare Commission and the money was to be distributed by population. Hopkins, however, opposed the method of fund distribution, saying that it must be made on need and not sim-

ply by population per county. State officials then revised the policy based on need and the distribution averaged about six dollars per month for indigent people. State officials also agreed to match federal payments for those on federal relief roles. Hopkins then released $1,528,415 which served as transition money from March to August 1935. Arkansas was the only state in the nation to get such funds.

No sooner had the disagreement over how the agency should be created was settled than a new dispute broke out over how to use the relief funds. A class action suit was filed in April 1935 in Pulaski Chancery Court to test the constitutionality of the sales tax. Merchants in Pulaski County and Stuttgart and Malvern stopped collecting the tax. But in June the Arkansas Supreme Court ruled that the tax was constitutional and should be collected in all cities and counties throughout the state. However, Attorney General Carl Bailey then confused the issue by stating that only $150,000 of the sales tax could be used for relief.

A new group known as the Arkansas Sales Tax Repeal Association, organized in Little Rock in the summer of 1935, began lobbying members of the General Assembly to have the sales tax repealed. In the midst of the controversy, Bailey reversed himself and ruled that $150 million of matching funds from sales tax should come from the general welfare fund. Governor Futrell then designated that sales tax revenue should be divided 35 percent for unemployment and 65 percent for education. Prewitt publicly complained about the allocation and was replaced in his office. A feud also developed between Futrell and Bailey over how the funds should be allocated. The matter was not resolved and the

state simply polarized into two political factions— those state officials who supported Futrell and the federal officials who supported Bailey.

In spite of the controversy, federal relief work did go on, particularly through the efforts of the WPA. By late 1935 the WPA was beginning to make an impact on the state. The original allocation of $4.8 billion dollars that Congress authorized to finance the program began to be translated directly into jobs in Arkansas and other states.

The concept of the WPA, a dual role of work plus a dole, caused some adjustment in the administration of the program in Arkansas. Floyd Sharp was placed in charge of the WPA program in the state and Dyess continued to serve as the state director of the relief work. By the summer of 1935 Dyess had become a quite popular figure throughout the state. Not only did he have high visibility, but the Dyess colony in eastern Arkansas had become a model for New Deal programs. Dyess was generally rumored to be a candidate for governor in 1936 and had many supporters, particularly among those involved with the federal relief programs. He was not without controversy, however, particularly with the county judges, many of whom saw the federal relief funds as a direct challenge to their political leadership. Many of them wanted to see the federal relief funds phased out.

Having to divide the state's sales tax revenue between unemployment relief and education proved difficult in the first few months the system was in operation. The unemployed found it particularly difficult to make ends meet and education suffered from the loss of federal money. Several schools were forced to close in

November. Pulaski County schools continued until January 1936. Craighead County was forced to close its jail and there were other examples of hardships at the county level because of the reduced income. Dyess flew to Washington to plead Arkansas's case and ask for additional funds to help make up the difference in the lost revenues. Through the intervention of Senator Joe T. Robinson, Dyess was able to get a special grant of $300,000 for the welfare commission. Tragically, on the return flight to Arkansas, Dyess and thirty-seven other people were killed when the plane crashed in St. Francis County. Floyd Sharp was then made the state director of the relief programs.

After 1935 the WPA proved to be the focus of attention for federal relief work in the state. In its first functional year, 1935-36, it employed some 32,480 people and provided a per capita income of $247 per person in the state. But by 1936 the national WPA program was beginning to be cut back and individuals employed in Arkansas were reduced from 32,000 to 18,000. The Welfare Commission only had enough money to support 6,000 people and the state's economy began to go into recession again.

Despite its popular appeal, the WPA was not above criticism in Arkansas. There was a continued complaint about political patronage being doled out to those who were special favorites of the governor and other state officials. Blacks also had a difficult time in getting employment, even with the WPA programs. The agency adopted a policy of having "seasonal placement of workers" who were adjusted to provide adequate manpower during the planting and harvesting seasons. Critics frequency complained that this was

Facing page: *This traveling grocery store serviced Forrest City in September 1938. Courtesy, Arkansas History Commission*

207

simply a manner of manipulation. Labor unions in particular were concerned about this aspect of the agency's work.

Even so, the WPA had a major impact on the state. For example, during its tenure WPA projects built 11,417 miles of roads, 467 new schools, and forty-four new parks. The major projects in Little Rock included a stadium, the War Memorial Park, and the public library. As late as 1941, the WPA was still the largest employer in the state with over 33,000 people on the payroll. By that time the WPA had spent $161 million.

There were other aspects of the New Deal that were concerned with

Effigene Locke Wingo (1883-1962) was elected to a full term in the U.S. House of Representatives after filling the remainder of the term of her late husband, Otis Theodore Wingo. After retiring from Congress, Wingo founded the National Institute of Public Affairs in Washington, D.C., in 1934. Courtesy, Southwest Arkansas Regional Archives

The Joseph Taylor Robinson Memorial Auditorium at Markham and Broadway in Little Rock was completed in 1940. Courtesy, Arkansas History Commission

more than relief. Much of the reform in the late 1930s centered in a new agency known as the Social Security Administration. The Social Security system had been established in 1935 by legislation of the United States Congress. The concept was opposed by the Arkansas congressional delegation who were concerned about the matching funds provision of the bill. Despite Arkansas' delegation opposition, a large percentage of the older population in Arkansas supported the program and lobbied actively for it. They joined the national Townsend Club Movement.

Charles Townsend, a political activist from Michigan, had organized an advocacy group for older Americans. The Townsend Clubs promoted his philosophy of providing individuals over the age of sixty with $200 per month provided they spent all of that money within thirty days. In Arkansas Dr. C.L. Orgon was the state coordinator for the Townsend Clubs and he identified thirty-six clubs with an estimated membership of 100,000 people actively campaigning for the Social Security program.

When the Social Security measure passed the United States Congress,

Little Rock attorney A.L. Rottenberry prepared a bill for the legislature which would allocate a portion of the state's sales tax to provide a pension for the Social Security recipients. The stipend would be fifty dollars per month to those older than age sixty and who did not own more than $500 in personal property. Rottenberry's proposal was strongly opposed by leaders of education in the state because they saw it as a potential rival for education program funds. Despite this opposition, Rottenberry filed the bill as an initiated petition after receiving more than 30,000 signatures, enough to allow the bill to be placed on the ballot during the general election. However, Rottenberry and his supporters' plans ran aground when the Arkansas Supreme Court ruled that the language of the bill was misleading and too vague to be constitutional.

When the bill was pulled off the ballot in the general election, Rottenberry then adopted a new strategy. He proposed a new organization known as the Social Security League which also actively supported a new initiative. In the 1938 election he again had sufficient signatures to have the measure brought before the voters. This proposed bill was struck down when the court again ruled that there were fraudulent signatures on the petition itself.

Following these efforts, the Arkansas General Assembly passed a bill prepared by W.H. Abington of White County which would provide for state participation in the Social Security program. The Abington proposal called for public assistance of three to nine dollars per month for the indigent, with the funds distributed to the counties. Eligibility for receiving the funds would be determined by county relief boards. This measure was passed by the Arkansas General Assembly. However, upon passage the Federal Social Security Board notified Arkansas that the proposal was not in compliance with federal regulations because it constituted public assistance rather than the pension fund which the Social Security System was intended to provide. Governor Carl Bailey then suspended the Abington bill and the state moved to meet the federal Social Security matching funds with a direct pension program supported by the state.

Even though some New Deal programs continued into the World War II era, many of the relief programs began to close by 1938. In that year the war that broke out in Europe altered the country's economic situation. In the five-year period in which New Deal relief efforts in Arkansas were at their peak, the federal government provided massive relief funds to assist the state economy.

From 1933 to 1938, the Federal Emergency Relief Administration spent more than forty million dollars in Arkansas. Likewise, the Agricultural Adjustment Administration spent $72,946,064. The Farm Security Administration spent $7,973,005 and the WPA spent $22,109,000 in the state. Altogether, the federal government contributed $279,143,021 in state relief and recovery support through March 1938.

By comparison other Southern states did not fare so well. Alabama, which had a population of more than 2.7 million, received $275,451,000 in support and Georgia received $292,448,609. The fact that Arkansas was able to receive federal assistance far in excess of its population may be attributed in part to the state's leadership and to the close friendship be-

The Boston Store at Earle, owned by David Schwartz, sold men's and women's clothing. Merchandise and prices were in plain view for customers in this farming area. Courtesy, University of Arkansas at Little Rock Archives and Special Collections

tween Senator Joe T. Robinson and President Roosevelt. But it was also due in part to the massive debt the state had before the beginning of the Depression. The state simply did not have the means as it entered the Depression to generate its own recovery.

During the 1930s Arkansas gained in population. Population in 1930 was 1,752,204. By 1940 the figure had increased to 1,949,387, an increase of slightly more than 5 percent. The national average during that period was slightly higher than 7 percent but many states, including the neighboring state of Oklahoma, lost population during the 1930s.

The war in Europe broke the Depression in the nation and in Arkansas. By 1939 the activity being generated to support the war effort began to have its effect. Manufacturing came to replace the federal relief programs and the economy began to be geared more to the private sector.

The two decades between the end of World War I and the outbreak of World War II presented a study in contrast. The first decade was fairly prosperous and offered a degree of social mobility for many people. The fiscal restraint and efficient budget policies initiated by Donaghey and Brough, together with the large infusion of federal dollars during World War I, allowed the state to enter the 1920s largely debt free. Discovery of oil in southern Arkansas and the limited mining of bauxite complemented the state's timber resources and cotton production and added to the state's revenue.

The state's lawmakers were so confident that prosperity would be permanent that they adopted "The Wonder State" as Arkansas' official nickname. Former governor Brough in his new role as chautauqua speaker and defender of the state's reputation told an audience that Arkansas had all the resources it needed to be self-sufficient and would prosper even if a fence was built around its borders.

Ironically, after hardly a decade, prosperity began to decline into an economic depression. State finances were upset when, in one year, the treasury went from a small surplus to its largest debt in history—a debt that it carried for more than a decade. Overproduction in cotton destroyed farm prices and hurt land values. A national recession in the housing market reduced demands for timber products and new oil discoveries in Texas and Oklahoma produced more competition.

Debt and economic depression forced many in Arkansas to become dependent on the federal government. The Wonder State was referred to in some circles in Washington as the Guinea Pig State because of the many experimental programs started there. But even in the midst of this new crisis there were positive gains. The state retained its population and its political influence. Not only did Arkansas elect the first woman, Hattie Carraway, to the U.S. Senate, but other Arkansans, Pearl Peden Oldfield and Effiegene Wingo served in the House of Representatives. Joe T. Robinson, after running unsuccessfully for vice president of the United States in 1928, served as majority leader of the Senate during Roosevelt's first, and part of his second, administration.

The highway bonds, responsible for so much of the state's internal debt, were finally paid off and state officials could finally deal with state finances on a more more manageable scale. After a decade of depression Arkansans once again looked forward to better times.

*Vast fields of thriving
crops add color to the
"Land of Opportunity."
Photo by Matt Bradley*

The Land of Opportunity

CHAPTER VII

World War II had a profound impact on Arkansas. About 200,000 men, some 10 percent of the population, served in the armed forces, and military defense spending began to reach every section of the state, just as the New Deal relief programs had done in the 1930s. Military bases were established at Camp Robinson, outside of North Little Rock, and Fort Chaffee, outside of Fort Smith, with bases also established at Blythesville, Newport, Stuttgart, and Walnut Ridge.

A prisoner of war camp was established at Dermott and two of ten national relocation centers for Japanese Americans were established in Arkansas, one in Rohwer and the other in Jerome, both of which opened in 1942. The Rohwer camp at its height had a population of more than 8,000 Japanese Americans and was closed in 1944. The Jerome camp in Chicot County closed in 1945. Ordnance plants were built in Camden, Jacksonville, and Pine Bluff; an artillery testing ground at Hope; a puric acid plant at Marche; and an ammonia plant at El Dorado. Altogether the total value of military spending in the state was $400 million.

The war's impact on the state was seen in ways other than direct defense spending. For example, private business also benefited significantly from federal support. Bauxite mining increased twelve times between 1940 and 1943. Two processing plants were built at Jones Mill and Hurricane Creek, leased to Alcoa Company, and later sold to Reynolds after the war. Between 1940 and 1950 the number of women in the state's workforce increased by more than 35,000 while the number of men declined by 14,000. The total labor force in 1940 was 634,300 and in 1950 it was 655,300, with women representing a significant part of that increase.

Perhaps the greatest impact was felt after the war was over. Out-migration, a trend that began with the outbreak of war, continued after the war was over. An increasing number of blacks and young wage earners left the state to seek employment in the large industrial cities of the Midwest and West. Though there was an increase in the older population, between 1940 and 1960 the state lost about 9 percent of its population. By 1960 the total population had dropped to 1,786,272 people.

Another impact of the war was the increased urbanization of the state. In 1940, before the war broke out, four out of five Arkansans lived on farms. By 1950 the figure had dropped to one out of two. Urbanization created a new set of financial problems for the state, due to more demands for services by the new city residents.

In agriculture, also profoundly impacted by World War II, there was a sharp decline in sharecropping and tenancy. In 1935 farm tenancy represented 65 percent of the state's farming population. In some counties in the Delta the figure was 70 percent to 90 percent. By 1945 the number of sharecroppers had declined to 45 percent of the farm population and in 1960 the figure was 24 percent. Agricultural workers represented 52 percent of the workforce in 1940, but by 1955 the figure had dropped to 35 percent. The total farm population in 1940 was 1,113,000, but declined to 595,000 in 1955. By 1959 the number of people on farms was only 95,000, about the same number the state had in 1887.

This decline was due primarily to farm mechanization. The perfected mechanical cotton harvester replaced hand labor and in turn led to many workers losing their jobs. Mechanization also reduced the number of farm units. In 1935, at its peak, the state had 235,000 farms; by 1940 that figure had dropped to 217,000 and by 1950 the figure was down to 145,000. By the same token, the average number of acres per farm began to increase. In 1940 the average number was eighty-three. Fifteen years later the figure had increased to 124.

Another change in agriculture was diversification. Soybeans, cattle, poultry, and food processing, particularly canning and freezing, began to replace cotton, which had dominated the agricultural economy since the

Two World War II relocation centers for Japanese Americans were located in Arkansas. The camp at Jerome was operated under the supervision of former missionary Joseph Boone Hunter. The inhabitants participated in various aspects of camp affairs. These two men in the cabinet shop are constructing furniture for a school and office. Courtesy, Arkansas History Commission

The increase in bauxite mining in the early 1940s led to the expansion of the industry. In addition to these drying kilns in Benton, Alcoa Aluminum had processing plants in Jones Mill and Hurricane Creek. Courtesy, Special Collections, University of Arkansas Libraries, Fayetteville

This photograph, taken in northwest Arkansas, shows how chickens were raised in 1952. The poultry industry continues to be successful. In fact, Tyson Foods, a poultry producer, is so successful it ranked 364th in the 1984 Fortune 500 list of the largest U.S. Industrial Corporations and ranked highest in total return to investors. Courtesy, the Shiloh Museum

beginning of statehood.

The state's timber industry was also influenced by the war. The returning soldiers needed housing, which resulted in a construction boom. Arkansas' lumber industry reflected the demands that were being made across the nation. Clear cutting, a system of replacing hardwood with fast-growing pine trees, began to dominate the timberlands in many sections of the state. Small sawmills gave way to interstate corporations which marketed Arkansas timber products on a national and international scale. The products shifted from hardwood, flooring, and finished products to pulpwood, plywood, insulating materials, and paper.

State politics were also affected by the war. Political candidates relied more upon radio—which was developing national networks—to get their

message across. Campaigns became more costly but one thing did not change: Democrats continued to hold the support of the state's voters without serious rival from the Republican Party.

An example of the Democratic party's strength can be seen in the gubernatorial election of 1944. Ben Laney, a businessman from Camden, faced Republican H.C. Stump in the general election. Laney's platform was the promise to run the state on businesslike principles. He won the election by an overwhelming margin: 186,000 to 30,000.

The 1944 elections were dominated by the United States Senate race between former Governor Henry Adkins and congressional Representative J. William Fulbright. A strong rivalry existed between the two, dating back to 1940 when Adkins—after pres-

Left: *Magazine Mountain, covered with a lush forest of trees, offers a splendid example of Arkansas' scenic beauty. Photo by Dick Dietrich*

Below: *Following World War II, the demand for Arkansas' wood products increased locally and nationally. The Southern Lumber Company of Warren has helped meet lumber needs. Courtesy, Special Collections, University of Arkansas Libraries, Fayetteville*

Before he was elected to the U.S. Senate, J.W. Fulbright served one term in the U.S. House of Representatives, where he was instrumental in getting the United States to commit to the United Nations. Fulbright's political career in Washington lasted more than thirty years. Courtesy, Arkansas History Commission

suring the board of trustees to fire Fulbright—replaced him as president of the University of Arkansas. Fulbright emerged as the victor in the 1944 campaign and went on to represent the state for more than thirty years in the United States Senate.

Within the state, attention focused on Ben Laney as he moved to bring efficiency and reform to the state's economy. Laney worked to establish a systematic way to finance state government. With his support, one of the first actions of the General Assembly in 1945 was to establish a revenue stabilization program. Prior to this act, the state treasurer administered 126 separate accounts and funds. The stabilization act sought to control revenue and disperse it on a consistent basis throughout the state. It also significantly improved the state's credit.

Another of Laney's major accomplishments was to consolidate the state's many boards and agencies. A result was the creation of new types of agencies. The Public Service Commission was appointed to direct the Corporation and Utility Commission. An Arkansas Resources and Development Commission, later the Arkansas Industrial Development Commission, was established to recruit industry into the state. To consolidate the state's many school districts, the Initiated Act I, proposed in 1945, merged all school districts with less than 350 students and required every district to have a high school. The act reduced the number of districts from 1,500 to 500.

The keystone to Laney's programs in the post-World War II period was an industrialization plan that called for cooperation between private industry and state government. C. Hamilton Moses, president of Arkansas Power and Light Company, led the private sector in establishing what he called the "Arkansas Plan" which helped develop the state's industrial base.

Left: *Arkansas Power and Light president C. Hamilton Moses was instrumental in developing the "Arkansas Plan," which helped build industry in Arkansas after World War II. Courtesy, Special Collections, University of Arkansas Libraries, Fayetteville*

Below: *To supply Arkansas with more electricity, Harvey Couch of AP&L built hydroelectric power-producing plants on the Ouachita River, creating lakes Catherine, Hamilton, and Ouachita. This early steam engine station is on Lake Catherine near Hot Springs. Courtesy, Special Collections, History of Arkansas Libraries, Fayetteville*

The Arkansas plan, designed to check the state's declining population, was built around the idea of preserving rural Arkansas by combining small manufacturing plants with a more diversified agriculture. Rather than being dependent upon one cash crop, cotton, rural Arkansans were encouraged to diversify their farming operations while earning additional revenue, at least part of the year, as day laborers. As the manufacturing-industrial base increased, some economic planners saw the opportunity for farmers to leave agriculture and become wage earners while still "living on the land."

Much of the creativity for the Arkansas plan was credited to Hamilton Moses, president of Arkansas Power and Light Company. Moses was motivated by both an altruistic concern for his fellow Arkansans as well as seeing an opportunity to expand his company's operation. He was joined by several business friends and officials from the state chamber of commerce. Together they formed the Arkansas Resources and Development Commission and began a public campaign to promote the state.

Members of the General Assembly, extending over several sessions, joined in the campaign. Additional funds were appropriated for research at the University of Arkansas, four regional community colleges were expanded to four-year institutions, and an Institute for Science and Research was chartered. Somewhat later, the legislature authorized the university to establish a Graduate Institute of Technology to be located in Little Rock.

Perhaps the crowning piece of the Assembly's actions came in 1953 when lawmakers adopted a new nickname, "The Land of Opportunity," for the state. This slogan began appearing on automobile license plates in the 1940s

The sparkling beauty of man-made Lake Ouachita is captured at sunset in this Dick Dietrich photograph.

and with the legislature's official action became an integral part of the state's identity.

Despite a successful governorship, Laney did not seek a third term in 1948. Instead, he turned his attention to national politics and became actively involved in the "Dixiecrat" movement, a conservative revolt within the Democratic Party in reaction to the liberal policies of President Harry S Truman. Truman had ordered the integration of the U.S. Armed Forces and also proposed a stronger civil rights law that would protect the rights of blacks in particular. That action by Truman, among others, led to a split in the Democratic Party and the beginning of the Dixiecrat Party in 1948. Laney ran for vice president on the national Dixiecrat ticket.

With Laney's temporary retirement from Arkansas politics, there was an open field for candidates in 1948. Of

the nine men who paid filing fees, only four were considered serious candidates. These included James McRael, a radio evangelist, fondly referred to by his followers as "Uncle Mac;" Jack Holt, former attorney general; Horace Tompson, collector for Internal Revenue; and Sid McMath, prosecuting attorney from Garland County who had earned a statewide reputation for his efforts to "clean up Hot Springs" from the gambling interests. McMath had also achieved recognition as leader of the so-called G.I. movement following the return of the many World War II veterans.

There were no real issues of substance in the campaign of 1948. McMath was viewed as the frontrunner although he was criticized by some as being too liberal since he was closely associated with Truman's civil rights program. But McMath countered his critics by pointing out his strong opposition to boss rule and by detailing his plan for improving the state's highway and education systems. In the primary, McMath won in a runoff against Jack Holt. In the general election, McMath defeated Republican C.R. Black by an overwhelming margin. Black received only 26,500 votes.

As governor, McMath focused major attention on changing the state's image. Soon after assuming office he appeared on national radio on the Arthur Godfrey Show and talked about the need to improve the state's highway program, industrial base, and educational systems.

Back at home, McMath worked actively with the General Assembly to promote a highway program. He persuaded the legislature to authorize twenty-eight million dollars in highway bonds, on the condition that the voters approve the proposal. The bond program was placed on the gen-

Chester Lauck and Norris Goff, the "Lum and Abner" of radio and movie fame, put Pine Ridge in Montgomery County on the map. The team's radio humor was centered around the "Jot 'Em Down" store. Courtesy, University of Arkansas at Little Rock Archives and Special Collections

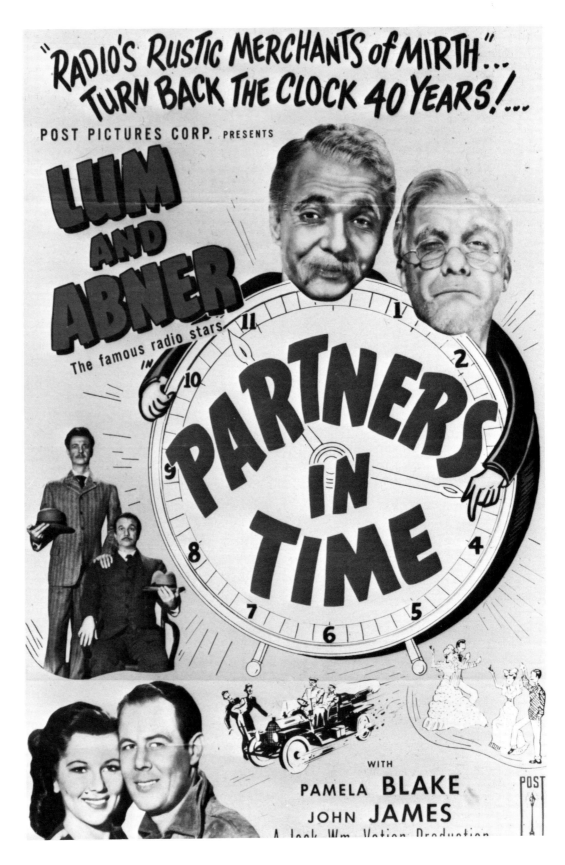

Governor Carl E. Bailey (right) enjoys a tune with fellow Arkansans Dick Powell (left) and Bob Burns. Courtesy, University of Arkansas at Little Rock Archives and Special Collections

Governor Carl E. Bailey (right) shares a bench with celebrities Chester Lauck and Norris Goff, better known as "Lum and Abner," at the October 1938 University of Arkansas vs. Santa Clara University football game. The three obviously were not pleased with the way things were going for the Razorbacks. Courtesy, University of Arkansas at Little Rock Archives and Special Collections

226

eral ballot and approved by a four to one margin. Much of the support for a new highway program was generated by adverse publicity from an out-of-state automobile company which advertised its cars' ability to pass the "Arkansas mud test."

The bond program stimulated the state's highway development and in McMath's administration more than 2,295 miles of roads were built. There was also a general improvement in road appearance: new highway signs were put up; strips were painted to mark the highway lanes; and a number of roadside parks were developed. The minimum age to get a driver's license was increased from fourteen to sixteen and in 1950 the National Highway Safety Council named Arkansas as having the best safety record of all the southern states.

With his highway program underway, McMath turned his attention to attracting industry. He proposed, and the legislature accepted, a package to establish tax incentives for any industry which would locate in the state.

The proposal included providing free plant sites, special training programs when needed, and highways and rail spurs to plant sites. The government's efforts to attract industry, coupled with the planning of Hamilton Moses and others, led to many companies locating in Arkansas.

In the area of education, the governor organized a series of caravans that traveled statewide with important public figures who spoke with school officials and community leaders. He appointed A.D. Bonds as commissioner of education and used Bonds—who was a member of the Atomic Energy Commission—as an example of the importance of education in the state's, and nation's, future. He received support from the legislature to increase financing of local schools and tried to improve education for blacks in the state.

As a final measure in McMath's first term as governor, he actively promoted election law reform. Remembering his days as prosecuting attorney in Garland County, he spon-

Facing page, top: *Former prosecuting attorney from Garland County Sid McMath won the governor's seat in 1948 and re-election in 1950. McMath had received statewide recognition when he successfully led the 1946 G.I. revolt in Hot Springs that ended the Leo McLaughlin political machine. Courtesy, Arkansas History Commission*

Below: *Sid McMath stressed general highway improvement, which has continued. This photograph shows North Little Rock before the current interstates 30 and 40 were laid. Courtesy, Arkansas History Commission*

Mrs. R.S. Warnock, Jr. (right), of the Arkansas State Pioneers Association presented the display cases housing the inaugural gowns of Arkansas' first ladies at the Old State House on February 8, 1955. Present to accept the cases were (from left) Ewilda Gertrude Miller Robinson, Ida Virginia Yarborough Hayes, Anne Wade Roark Brough, Mabel Winston Parnell, Lucille Kirtley Laney, Sara Anne Phillips McMath, and Celia Alta Haskins Faubus. Courtesy, Arkansas Gazette

sored, and the legislature passed, a proposal to prohibit block buying of poll tax votes. The poll tax, a part of the state's political system since the 1890s, was a means of abuse by political bosses who bought blocks of the poll taxes to vote en masse for a particular candidate. Further reforms made election violations a felony.

McMath won considerable support for his programs and actively sought a second term. He was challenged by former Governor Ben Laney who, fresh from his campaigns within the Dixiecrat movement, wanted to stop the "liberal reforms" of the McMath administration. The 1950 campaign was essentially between a conservative businessman and a reformer. Laney accused McMath of using the black vote, of supporting the "socialism" of the Truman administration, and of skimming highway monies. McMath countered by accusing Laney

of being a tool of the business interests and a non-Democrat because of his Dixiecrat involvement. He also pointed out that Laney failed to support the new medical center for the University of Arkansas even though funds had been made available in 1946 to construct new facilities in Little Rock.

In the election that followed, McMath won sixty-six of the seventy-five counties. His victory put him in the position to challenge the state's senior senator, John L. McClellan, who was up for reelection in 1954. But McMath's advisors felt the best way to maintain his statewide profile was to run for a third term even though, in the state's history, only Jefferson Davis had served more than two terms. Meanwhile, McMath began to face internal problems that clouded his political future.

Reports, first issued during Laney's

campaign, continued to point to problems within the state highway program. Remembering the 1930s problems, the General Assembly appointed a Highway Audit Commission in 1951 to investigate the charges of collusion between the Highway Department and the contractors and state politicians. As a part of its investigation the commission requested McMath's campaign contribution list to determine whether he had received undue support from highway contractors. McMath's campaign director, Henry Woods, refused to turn over the campaign files, later saying that such exposure would reveal the McMath campaign had received several contributions from the liquor interest—a disclosure that would be considerably embarrassing.

The highway audit cast a cloud over McMath's image as a liberal reformer. That, coupled with an unfortunate domestic problem involving a shooting in his family, brought added political problems. In spite of the difficulties, McMath sought a third term in 1952. His major opposition came from Francis Cherry, Chancery judge for eastern Arkansas who campaigned

The first gusher in Arkansas blew in at El Dorado in 1921. Oil in Smackover was discovered shortly after. Some oil is still produced in Arkansas and has been refined and stored in El Dorado, as seen here. Courtesy, Special Collections, University of Arkansas Libraries, Fayetteville

Above: *Incumbent Ben T. Laney, of Dixiecrat fame, was easily defeated by Sid McMath in 1950. Here, Laney looks like an old hand at breaking ground. Courtesy, Arkansas History Commission*

Above right: *U.S. Senator John L. McClellan, first elected to office in 1943, poses with Crip Hall, Arkansas' secretary of state from 1937-1961. Courtesy, Arkansas History Commission*

on a program of economy in government. In that primary campaign McMath was defeated overwhelmingly, winning only nine counties and receiving slightly more than 100,000 popular votes to Cherry's more than 200,000.

Cherry entered office with a great deal of good will but lost most of it within eighteen months. His ineffective personal relationships and poor leadership in dealing with legislators led to problems. He was also opposed for criticizing the welfare program and supporting the Arkansas Power and Light Company's rate-increase request. The summer following the rate increase was one of the hottest summers in the state's history and many people associated Cherry's approval of the increase with their high electric bills. The combination of the AP&L and welfare issues led to Cherry's growing unpopularity. Opposition developed quite early in his bid for a second term. His major opponent was Orval Faubus, a highway director appointed by McMath and publisher of a Madison County newspaper. Another potential opponent was Guy "Mutt" Jones, a legislator from Conway.

The basic issues in the primary campaign were the AP&L increase, Cherry's welfare cutbacks, and his

call for a 100 percent property tax assessment for real estate in the state. Even though journalists contended that voters that year were more interested in staying home with their air conditioners and televisions than they were in voting, Faubus was able to force the governor into a runoff.

Faubus was aided greatly in his campaign by support from McMath. The runoff between Faubus and Cherry in 1954 became one of the more historic events in Arkansas political history. Early in the runoff, Cherry criticized Faubus for attending Commonwealth College at Mena and taking an active role in student affairs. Commonwealth College, founded in the early 1930s, had a strong labor movement affiliation and

was suspected of being Communistic—a strong charge in 1954, a year tainted with McCarthyism. In fact it had been closed by local law enforcement officers upon investigating the college's operations.

Faubus' first approach was to deny that he had attended the college. Initially shaken by the charge, Faubus, after a few days of reflection, responded to Cherry's charge by admitting that he *had* attended the college, only because it was the only school he could afford with his limited income. However, he had left when he saw what the school's principles were.

Faubus' frank, forthright explanation created sympathy among voters and he beat Cherry by some 7,000 votes.

After defeating Sid McMath in 1952, Governor Francis Cherry supported an AP&L rate increase before unusually hot summers, making himself unpopular and bringing defeat by Orval Faubus in a bitter 1954 campaign. Here Cherry speaks at his 1953 inauguration. Courtesy, Arkansas History Commission

231

Orval E. Faubus, governor of Arkansas from 1955-1967, received national attention during the Little Rock school crisis. Faubus, called "the master campaigner," lost this 1974 campaign for reelection as well as an earlier attempt in 1970. Courtesy, Arkansas History Commission

In the general election of 1954 the Republicans thought they had their best chance of winning since the beginning of the twentieth century. The division between Cherry and Faubus had created sharp differences within the Democratic Party, particularly between the eastern and western sectors of the party. The Republicans nominated Pratt Remmel, the former mayor of Little Rock, who had a reputation of bringing reform, progress, and industry to the city. Cherry did not publicly endorse Remmel in the campaign but did give him private support; a number of Democrats openly deserted the party to vote for Remmel.

In the campaign, Remmel told voters to elect the man, not the party. He was careful to avoid the Commonwealth College issue. Married to the daughter of Harvey Couch, the founder of AP&L, Remmel was also careful to avoid speaking of the rate increase approved the previous year.

Despite the potential for division within the Democratic Party, Faubus won 200,000 votes whereas Remmel polled a little over 100,000.

That same year, McMath ran against McClellan in the senate race. Though McMath proposed a public debate, McClellan refused and ran on his experience and seniority, contending that McMath could not help Arkansas as much as he could. The voters apparently listened: McClellan won by 38,000 votes.

The decade following World War II was a difficult one for Arkansas. The decline in population became a source of embarrassment for many state leaders. Despite the best efforts of both public and private officials, the outmigration continued. Arkansas lost one seat in the House of Representatives in 1950 and gave up two more positions before the outflow was finally stopped in 1960.

The period between 1945 and 1954 was also one of transition. Agriculture, based on hand labor and a single cash crop in much of the state for more than a century, began to diversify. Cotton yielded to soybeans, and later to rice, in economic importance and poultry became a new enterprise for many rural Arkansans. By the 1950s Arkansas led the nation in broiler chicken production.

Work habits were also changing. More and more women were entering the work force and thousands of blacks left the state entirely to seek better paying jobs in the industrial cities. Between 1940 and 1960 the state's black population declined by 19.4 percent.

But while the short-term picture may have appeared bleak, the investments made in the Arkansas plan ultimately paid off. The Resources and Development Commission was replaced by a state-chartered Arkansas Industrial Development Commission in 1955. Within the next decade new jobs increased 57 percent, industrial wages were up 88 percent, and the state's per capita income grew 65 percent. For many, Arkansas was becoming the land of opportunity.

Autumn creates a symphony of color near Eureka Springs. Photo by Matt Bradley

Below: *Fort Smith had an important role during the Civil War and in the taming of the state's western frontier. Courtesy, Arkansas Department of Parks and Tourism*

Below: *This Civil War monument at Pea Ridge, located outside Elkhorn Tavern, honors the men who fought there in 1862. Courtesy, Arkansas Department of Parks and Tourism*

Below: *The Allin House in Helena testifies to Arkansas' Southern heritage. Courtesy, Arkansas Department of Parks and Tourism*

Facing page, top left: *Bathhouse Row is a popular tourist attraction in Hot Springs. Courtesy, Arkansas Department of Parks and Tourism*

Facing page, top right: *Historical markers, such as this one commemorating the United States surveying the Louisiana Purchase, remind Arkansans of their state's colorful history. Photo by Robyn Horn*

Facing page, bottom: *The Arkansas County Agriculture Museum preserves the tractors and other farm implements that helped make agriculture essential to the state's economy. Photo by Robyn Horn*

Facing page, top left: *By taking time to teach others, artisans Gerry and Sheri Phillips-Chisholm preserve the state's unique heritage. Photo by Matt Bradley*

Facing page, top right: *Attention to detail gives life to these wood carvings and shows the pride Gerry and Sheri Phillips-Chisholm take in their work. Photo by Matt Bradley*

Facing page, bottom: *This restored village looks just as it did in the 1890s, when Arkansans were looking forward to a new century. Courtesy, Arkansas Department of Parks and Tourism*

Left: *A young spinner is shown a new skill at the Ozark Folk Center, where traditions are shared and passed on. Photo by Matt Bradley*

Below: *As they swing their partners and do-si-do, square dancers raise some dust at Yellville. Photo by Matt Bradley*

Top: *Wild Azaleas thrive among the flora near the Buffalo National River. Photo by Matt Bradley*

Bottom: *Red Columbines grow along many Ozark streams. Photo by Matt Bradley*

Left: *This road winds its way through the beauty of Magazine Mountain. Photo by Dick Dietrich*

Above: *Cool, green havens
of Maidenhair ferns re-
fresh visitors to the Buffalo National River.
Photo by Matt Bradley*

Right: *The simplicity of
nature's designs only add
to their beauty. Photo by
Matt Bradley*

Top left: *Workers at the Atkins Pickle Company prepare fresh cucumbers for curing. Photo by Matt Bradley*

Top right: *The racehorse Gas-a-Gas seeks reassurance from his stablemate. Photo by Matt Bradley*

Left: *These Grand Prairie grain elevators were caught on film by Matt Bradley.*

Facing page: *Tending acres of meandering rows, a lonely tractor symbolizes the challenges and hard work facing Arkansas' farmers. Photo by Dick Dietrich*

241

Right: *This candler is shown grading eggs, assuring only the best quality goes to market. Photo by Matt Bradley*

Below: *Caring for livestock is an important part of the Arkansas farmer's job, as Billy Higgins demonstrates as he treats a calf for pinkeye. Photo by Matt Bradley*

Bottom: *City dwellers find needed relaxation in the quiet solitude of the Arkansas countryside. Photo by John McDermott*

Left: *This young fisherman displays the day's catch at a bass fishing tournament in Lake Ouachita. A fish feast awarded all participants. Photo by Matt Bradley*

Below: *Raymond Schroeder's catfish farm near Carlisle is seen here. Photo by Matt Bradley*

Bottom: *The state's rivers and lakes are full of fish, and this enterprising Arkansan plans to catch a few. Photo by John McDermott*

Right: *Families find a colorful autumn retreat in the Ouachita Mountains. Photo by Robyn Horn*

Right, center: *The nooks and crannies of Devil's Den State Park arouse the curiosity of many visitors. Courtesy, Arkansas Department of Parks and Tourism*

Right, bottom: *New friends come in all shapes and sizes at Jim Gaston's White River Resort. Courtesy, Arkansas Department of Parks and Tourism*

Above: *At Dogpatch-USA, kids of all ages can have a day of fun. Courtesy, Arkansas Department of Parks and Tourism*

Right: *The afternoon sun backlights these sailors at Lake Maumelle near Little Rock. Photo by Matt Bradley*

Facing page, top left: *Canoeists on the Buffalo National River drift through canyons of lush green foliage. Photo by Matt Bradley*

Facing page, top right: *The pace changes as the water becomes rough on a trip down the Buffalo National River below Ponca. Photo by Matt Bradley*

Facing page, bottom: *Boaters enjoy the clear smooth waters of Blue Mountain Lake. Photo by Dick Dietrich*

Muzzled competitors head for the starting gate at Southland Greyhound Park. Courtesy, Arkansas Department of Parks and Tourism

Jockeys battle for the inside position as they round the turn at the Oaklawn Jockey Club. Photo by Matt Bradley

Above: *Known as the Bat House or Skull Bluff, this water-eroded limestone along the Buffalo National River beckons to be explored. Photo by Matt Bradley*

Right: *These hunting enthusiasts find plenty of game to pursue in the wilds of Arkansas near Rose Bud. Photo by Matt Bradley*

249

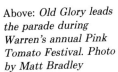

Above: *Old Glory leads the parade during Warren's annual Pink Tomato Festival. Photo by Matt Bradley*

Right, top: *Arkansans will suffer just about anything—even biting cold—to support the Razorbacks, the state's favorite team. Photo by Matt Bradley*

Right: *The Dancing Razorback takes a breather, gathering strength to cheer the Razorbacks to victory. Photo by Matt Bradley*

The University of Arkansas at Fayetteville testifies to the state's dedication to higher education. Courtesy, Arkansas Department of Parks and Tourism

The Razorback symbolizes the winning spirit that has propelled the state to the forefront of college football. Photo by Matt Bradley

Right: *Visitors to the Blanchard Springs Caverns are awed by the Giant Column on Dripstone Trail. Photo by Matt Bradley*

Facing page, top left: *Day breaks pink and tender on Lake Ouachita. Photo by Dick Dietrich*

Facing page, top right: *Sheltering leaves diffuse the strength of a hot summer sun in Hemmed-in-Hollow along the Buffalo National River. Photo by Matt Bradley*

Facing page, bottom: *Autumn in the Ozarks will soon slip into the stark beauty of winter. Courtesy, Arkansas Department of Parks and Tourism*

As the sun sets on the "Land of Opportunity," these Arkansas River canoeists are highlighted in shimmering orange. Photo by Matt Bradley

255

Little Rock comes alive with light as the sun sets over Arkansas' capital city. Photo by Matt Bradley

Contemporary Arkansas

CHAPTER VIII

McMath's defeat in 1954 helped Faubus take over the state Democratic organization. In the next twelve years he showed great political astuteness by choosing men to head state agencies and departments who would strengthen his organization. The key example of this was his appointment of Winthrop Rockefeller, a confessed Republican and new arrival from New York, to head the Arkansas Industrial Development Commission. Faubus was also careful to avoid scandal and took a very pragmatic approach toward government. He made no effort to interfere with the special interest groups at the county level and pictured himself as an Andrew Johnson who had come up the hard way.

In his first administration, Faubus emphasized education as a key to his political program. With his support the General Assembly approved a twenty-two-million-dollar tax increase earmarked for education and made a significant impact on improving the system's funding level. With legislative support he also advocated the establishment of a children's colony which became a model institution for the mentally retarded. Faubus carried out his campaign promise of improving welfare assistance to the aged, promoted improvement of rural roads, and expanded the state Democratic Central Committee to include six blacks. He was also the first governor in the state to use public opinion research to develop programs.

With a good record established in his first administration he filed for reelection in 1956. Only two serious candidates opposed Faubus in the Democratic primary: Jim Snoddy, a businessman from western Arkansas; and Jim Johnson, a former state senator from southern Arkansas. The

Orval E. Faubus campaigns at the Faulkner County Courthouse at Conway during the 1962 campaign. Faubus beat two Democratic challengers, former Governor Sid McMath and former Congressman Dale Alford, for another term in office. Courtesy, Arkansas History Commission

chief issue in the campaign centered around integration of public schools. In 1954, the year Faubus was first elected, the U.S. Supreme Court handed down its *Brown* decision which overturned the historic *Plessy vs. Ferguson* integration issue. According to the *Brown* decision, separate educational facilities were inherently unequal and should be integrated with all deliberate speed.

By 1956 the integration issue was becoming a matter of concern in many southern states. Johnson, an outspoken critic of the Supreme Court decision, headed efforts to prevent it from being implemented in the state. The *Arkansas Gazette*

called Johnson a "mishmash of distortions, half truths, deliberate lies, served up to the voters against the background of stringed music, pious exhortations on behalf of the bedraggled revenue producing crusade of the White's Citizens Council. It was demogoguery with the addition of racial overtones." Faubus ran on his record. He said he needed the second term to continue the programs he had started and the voters agreed by easily reelecting him with 58 percent of the vote. Johnson won in only two counties and Snoddy did not carry a single county.

During Faubus' second term, school integration became a reality. The process had begun first at the University of Arkansas soon after World War II. By 1955 all public schools in the state had desegregated, as had five of the six state-supported colleges.

In the state school board elections of March 1957, two moderates won over two segregationists. During the summer, school officials made plans to desegregate the high schools. When school opened in September a crowd of whites gathered outside Little Rock Central High School to oppose the enrollment of nine blacks. Faubus called out the National Guard to preserve peace and so began a series of events that was soon to be known around the world. Why did Faubus react as he did? Rockefeller, who spent two-and-one-half hours with Faubus just prior to the decision to call out the National Guard, said, "I reasoned with him, argued with him, almost pleaded with him not to interfere, telling him that the local situation was none of his business. I am sorry, Faubus said, but I am already committed. I am going to run for a third term and if I don't do this Jim Johnson and Bruce Bennett will tear me to shreds."

For his part in the school crisis, Faubus blamed federal authorities. He said, "They can sit back and issue a court order that was going to cause literally hell and destroy many people economically and politically and they can just sit back and fold their hands and let somebody else reap the storm. Well, hell, this was the storm." He also called the federal authorities cowards "for not coming in at the beginning and saying, 'This is a federal court order. We are going to have federal authority here to see to it that it is obeyed and enforced.' Then I wouldn't have had to have been involved."

Faubus' action led to a confrontation between the state and national governments. Congressman Brooks Hayes, who represented Little Rock in the Second District, arranged for a meeting between President Dwight D. Eisenhower and Faubus, but the meeting produced no results. On September 20 the federal court ordered Faubus to end resistance to integration. The guard was withdrawn and when crowds gathered again threatening violence President Eisenhower nationalized the National Guard and also sent in troops from the 101st Airborne Division to maintain order at the school.

For the balance of the 1957-1958 school year, Army troops patrolled the hallways of Central High and maintained order. Faubus' reelection bid for his third term in 1958 carried with it the integration issue as he had anticipated. By that time, however, Faubus had become an underdog in the confrontation with the federal government and was receiving increasing support from voters. Faubus won 69 percent of the vote in the Democratic primary and in the general election he carried all the counties.

Following his election Faubus called a special session of the legislature in the summer of 1958 and won support to close schools in the state upon threat of violence, a position that was later supported by a public referendum. Armed with that authority, Faubus then closed the schools in Little Rock for the year 1958-1959.

By the end of 1958, thanks to his school integration policies, Faubus was one of the ten most admired men in the world, according to a Gallup Poll. Jim Johnson complained, "Faubus used my nickel and hit the jackpot."

Faubus encountered a growing resistance in the 1960s. In addition to

Right: *Thurgood Marshall, left, Daisy Bates, foreground, and two of the nine black students who fought to attend Little Rock Central High leave the federal courtroom in September 1957. Courtesy, Arkansas History Commission*

Below: *After nine black students were refused admittance to Little Rock Central High School in September 1957, President Dwight D. Eisenhower sent federal troops to ensure their entrance. The troops remained until the close of the school year. Courtesy, Arkansas History Commission*

In 1963, shortly before his death, President John F. Kennedy dedicated Greers Ferry Dam, which was built by the Army Corps of Engineers. Congressman Wilbur D. Mills is directly behind Kennedy. Congressmen Oren Harris, E.C. Gathings, and J.W. Trimble are in the front row on the right. Courtesy, Arkansas History Commission

the revival of the Republican Party there was a growing organization among black voters. In 1958 only 63,000 black voters were registered, but by 1966 the figure had increased to 100,000 out of a total of 640,609 registered voters.

The state's growing urbanization and the length of time Faubus was in office also worked against his political career. Though he was reelected, in 1962 Faubus won only 51 percent of the vote in the Democratic primary including 104 percent of the registered voters from his home county of Madison. Ironically, his former mentor, Sid McMath, was his chief opponent and came within 6,500 votes of forcing Faubus into a runoff.

The next serious challenge to Faubus came in 1964 when Rockefeller announced his intention to run for governor on the Republican ticket. Rockefeller estimated that he had spent ten million dollars in building

the Republican Party in the 1960s and in the campaign focused on his accomplishments as chairman of the Arkansas Industrial Development Commission. As Rockefeller noted, more than 600 new industries had come to Arkansas during the period he served as chairman, and the state had reversed its population loss. Altogether Rockefeller estimated that he had spent thirty-five million dollars in the state, including five million dollars for philanthropic causes.

In the campaign against Faubus, Rockefeller talked about the need for change and Faubus countered by arguing that outside money was trying to buy Arkansas. It was a bad year for Republicans nationally as President Lyndon Johnson defeated Barry Goldwater in a landslide victory. Faubus gave strong endorsement to the Democratic ticket and that, coupled with the fact that Rockefeller balked at the 1964 Civil Rights Act,

On the campaign trail, Winthrop Rockefeller had the attention of young and old alike at this small town store. Courtesy, University of Arkansas at Little Rock Archives and Special Collections

costing him some votes in the black community, led to Faubus easily winning reelection. Faubus won his sixth term with 84 percent of the black vote in the state and 57 percent of the overall vote. Rockefeller's support was primarily in the northern and western parts of the state.

Despite his poor showing, Rockefeller was determined to improve his position in the state's political circles and between 1964 and 1966 worked actively within the Republican Party. Faubus did not seek reelection in 1966 and ended a twelve-year career, the longest in Arkansas political history. The Democratic primary became an all out fight between Jim Johnson, Dale Alford, Frank Holt, and Brooks Hayes. In a very bitter primary campaign Johnson and Holt

won and in the runoff Johnson defeated Holt by a narrow margin to face Rockefeller in the general election of 1966.

By the time the general election approached the Democratic Party was the most divided it had been since the late nineteenth century. Johnson's criticism of Faubus had alienated the Faubus wing in the party and a newly formed Election and Research Council had actively publicized election irregularities that occurred in the Democratic primaries. The Republican Party was well organized, well staffed, and had an element of reform in their campaign promises. A number of Democratic organizations organized to support Rockefeller, including Women Democrats for Rockefeller and Independent

PILKINTON "JUSTICE" Old Tyme POLITICAL RALLY EVY DAY A.A.A. ALUMINUM Co Sponsored by... Levy Builders

Democrats for Rockefeller. All were signs of trouble for the general Democratic Party.

In his campaign Johnson focused on Rockefeller being an outsider and referred to him as a "prissy sissy, a phony cowboy and a rich man trying to buy the governorship." But Rockefeller chose to ignore Johnson's rhetoric and won by a very convincing vote. Rockefeller polled 300,000 votes compared to Johnson's 250,000. The victory was due in part to the urban vote, the black vote, and the dissident Democrats, as well as strong support from voters with above-average incomes. In all he carried thirty-five counties and 54 percent of the vote. Perhaps as a sign of interest in the campaign, 76 percent of the registered voters participated.

As governor, Rockefeller pushed for reform. He created the Department of Administration and established a management-by-objective system of operations to administer state government. He pressured the General Assembly to reorganize the state agencies (numbering more than 100) into thirteen cabinet-level departments. He advocated tighter regulation in the sale of bonds and securities in the state.

Rockefeller also closed down gambling operations in Hot Springs and pushed for prison reform. He appointed a Constitutional Revision Study Commission to draft ideas for proposed changes to the 1874 Constitution and pushed for tax reform to increase state revenue.

However, as Rockefeller was to

After twelve years in office, Orval E. Faubus decided not to seek another term. The Democratic Party saw a bitter fight between candidate hopefuls Jim Johnson, Dale Alford, Frank Holt, and Brooks Hayes. The candidates seem calm at this 1966 Levy Day celebration. Courtesy, Arkansas History Commission

263

Winthrop Rockefeller, a New York millionaire who moved to Arkansas in 1953, first served his new state as chairman of the newly created Arkansas Industrial Development Commission (AIDC) in 1955. Under his ten years of leadership AIDC brought new industry to Arkansas and helped existing plants to expand. In 1966 Rockefeller defeated Justice Jim Johnson, becoming the first Republican governor since 1872. Courtesy, Arkansas History Commission

learn, programs were not always easy to implement. From the beginning he had problems with the General Assembly. There were never more than five Republicans in the General Assembly and he had trouble getting major ideas pushed through the committee structure. Moreover, Rockefeller never really understood the problems that rural legislators faced and had difficulty communicating with them.

To develop better communication with the legislators he invited the entire General Assembly to his farm, Winrock Farms, for an overnight visit and retreat. But as Rockefeller was to say later, he couldn't tell whether it had any impact. When the legislators left they took with them $3,000 in souvenirs, including a Steuben glass egg. Despite the lack of cooperation and support from the legislature, Rockefeller won reelection in 1968. His major opponents in the primary were Virginia Johnson, wife of Jim Johnson, and Marion Crank.

More attention in 1968 politics was centered on the Senate race between Jim Johnson and William Fulbright. Fulbright's outspoken opposition to the Vietnam War had caused concern within the state and Johnson led a movement to try to oust him. He called Fulbright "the pinup boy of Hanoi, an arrogant intellectual who was out of touch with the people and interests and needs of Arkansas." Despite Johnson's colorful campaign Fulbright won 53 percent of the vote and carried forty-one of the seventy-five counties. One of the anomalies of the 1968 election in Arkansas was that Rockefeller, a moderate Republican, defeated his challenger, Virginia Johnson, while William Fulbright, a liberal Democrat, defeated conservative Jim Johnson. Yet the state in

Relying heavily on television in his 1970 campaign for governor, Dale Bumpers was able to block Winthrop Rockefeller's attempt at a third term. In 1974 Bumpers chose to challenge long-term Senator J. William Fulbright and won. Courtesy, Arkansas History Commission

the presidential campaign gave the majority of its support to George Wallace, a conservative independent.

In his second term, Rockefeller continued to push for the same reforms that he had introduced in his first term with the same lack of success. He ran for a third term in 1970 but was defeated by Democrat Dale Bumpers. Bumpers had won in a runoff in the Democratic primary against Orval Faubus.

Bumpers' style was to use a television blitz which has generally been credited to the influence of his campaign advisor, DeLois Walker. Bumpers also benefited from the new Democratic Party which had been reorganized and restructured since the Faubus days. Losing to the Republicans had caused the Democratic Central Committee to reevaluate its position and to shift from a less conservative to a more moderate operation.

Despite being accused of being wishy-washy (to which Bumpers replied, "Maybe I am and maybe I am

not"), Bumpers was able to use his television exposure effectively and won seventy-three of the seventy-five counties, outpolling Rockefeller by almost 200,000 votes. Rockefeller received 88 percent of the black vote but this was not enough to offset the gains made by Bumpers. One of the ironies of the campaign was that William Fulbright raised $10,000 for the Bumpers campaign and worked actively within the central committee to return the state to Democratic rule.

Other than being elected to the school board in Charleston, his home town, Bumpers had not served in public office. However, lack of political experience did not prevent his organizing an ambitious program. In his inaugural address he spoke about "a new awakening of our people" and urged the legislators to join him in guiding that awareness.

Bumpers represented a new order in state politics. Not only did he replace a Republican governor who had been unpopular with legislators, but

David Pryor gave his inaugural address at the Old State House after beating Republican Ken Coon in November 1974 to become the thirtyninth elected governor of Arkansas. Following a second term, Pryor successfully ran for the U.S. Senate in 1978. Courtesy, Arkansas History Commission

also 30 percent of the General Assembly's membership was new in 1971 and most had been elected from new urban-oriented districts. That, coupled with Bumpers' personal charisma and the fact that he had been elected without any identifiable ties to the state's traditional special interest groups, promised to bring a productive legislative session.

Bumpers chose tax reform as one of the major priorities in his first term. The plan he outlined called for an overall increase from 5 to 7 percent. However, rates for low-income families were reduced and a five-cent increase was placed on cigarettes. Since there was no general increase in sales tax and since much of the tax revenue was earmarked for teachers' salaries, the General Assembly—by a three-fourths majority—quickly approved the reform.

Education was another item high on Bumpers' agenda. In addition to increasing teachers' salaries, he also sponsored programs for state public kindergarten and free textbooks for high school students. He increased the number of community colleges in Arkansas and endorsed major construction projects at most of the state's public colleges and universities.

Bumpers was also active in social issues. He supported the new "consumer protection" division in the Attorney General's office and increased funding for services to the elderly, handicapped, and mentally retarded. He gave attention to the state prison system which had been declared unconstitutional by Federal District Judge J. Smith Henley, just months prior to Bumpers taking office. Bumpers eliminated using "trustee inmates" for guards and recruited Terral Don Hutto from Texas to be the new director for the prison system. Though other internal changes were made, the prison still remained under court order during the Bumpers' administration.

The Bumpers' program, coupled with a surging national economy, fueled in part by inflation, led to a growing surplus in the state treasury. Before the end of Bumpers' second administration the increase had surpassed $100 million. Bumpers found strong pressure from a number of special interest groups, including a coalition of city and county administrators, to spend the surplus. The city-county lobby persuaded the General Assembly to earmark 7 percent of state revenues for their purposes. Bumpers vetoed the bill on the basis that such an approach would destroy the state budgeting system.

Bumpers' early success led many political analysts to conclude that he was "unbeatable" if he sought reelection. Four candidates challenged him in the Democratic primary. Bumpers polled 65 percent of the vote to win without a runoff and then defeated Len Blaylock, former administrator in the Rockefeller administration, by winning over 75 percent of the vote in the general election.

In his second administration Bumpers continued to be an activist governor and placed more attention on administrative reform. During his first term he had made minor revisions in the Executive Reorganization Plan, initially proposed by Rockefeller, and got it approved by the Assembly. The reorganization consolidated some sixty departments into thirteen cabinet-level divisions. He also created a central personnel agency to recruit state employees and gave strong support to affirmative action programs. The latter point was the source of some criticism for Bumpers throughout his tenure as governor. Unlike Rockefeller, he did not attract a large number of blacks to his administration and no blacks were in his "inner circle" of advisors.

The period of prosperity continued in Bumpers' second term and so did his popularity rating. Doug Smith, a political analyst for the *Arkansas Gazette,* wrote that "more substantive, progressive legislation" had been created during Bumpers' terms than "any four year period in the state's history." Other newspapers columnists wrote about Bumpers' style, calling him a "secular evangelist," a "civil religionists," and a "moral populist." All noted his effectiveness as a politician.

There were some detractors to the Bumpers' regime. Critics pointed out that he often "temporized" over big decisions and that he was frequently noncommital in his public statements. He was also blamed for not doing more to shape public opinion on controversial issues. But, if opinion polls were any indication, Bumpers' detractors were grasping at shadows. By the end of his second term he had an approval rating of 90 percent.

Bumpers used that popularity to challenge J. William Fulbright for his U.S. Senate seat in 1974. Fulbright, along with Senator John L. McClellan and Representative Wilbur Mills, provided Arkansas with the most powerful congressional delegation in Washington. But he had grown increasingly out of touch with Arkansas voters by his outspoken opposition to the Vietnam War. The campaign was almost solely based on personality and Bumpers won 65 percent of the vote. In the space of five years Bumpers had soundly defeated Rockefeller, Faubus, and Fulbright—three of the most powerful politicians in the state's history.

The Bumpers-Fulbright campaign overshadowed to some extent the 1974 gubernatorial campaign. In that contest Orval Faubus came out of retirement to seek a seventh term. He was challenged by former Fourth District Congressman David Pryor and incumbent Lieutenant Governor Bob Riley. Faubus, responding to the "politics of moderation" popularized by Bumpers, said that he would appoint blacks, women, and young people to key positions in state government. He also pointed out that during the Little Rock school crisis, in comparison to the national racial strife of the 1960s, he had maintained a high degree of order and no lives were lost.

The most attention, however, was on David Pryor. The three-term congressman, and former state legislator from south Arkansas, had earned a reputation in some circles as being a liberal. In 1968, at the Democratic Party's national convention, Pryor served on the Credentials Committee and voted against seating the all-white delegation from Mississippi. He also received national attention by his investigation of nursing homes in the Washington, D.C., area. Disguising himself as an orderly, he worked weekends in nursing homes and got an inside look at how the elderly were treated. Using that experience he formed a special committee and held hearings in a rented trailer on Capitol Hill. The hearings produced a great deal of evidence on mismanagement and mistreatment of the elderly and led to federal legislation to regulate health care in nursing homes.

In 1972 Pryor gave up his congressional seat and challenged John L. McClellan for the U.S. Senate. McClellan, first elected to the Senate in

1942, had built a powerful political base, investigating racketeering in organized labor, publicly speaking out against the tactics of Senator Joseph McCarthy, and serving as chairman of the Appropriations Committee.

Two other candidates joined the campaign but the real contest was between McClellan and Pryor. The senator pointed out that Pryor, while he was in Congress, had a 100 percent pro-labor voting record. He also suggested that the congressman had been pushed into the race in retaliation for McClellan's work in exposing the misuse of pension funds by labor leaders. Pryor denied the allegation and pointed out McClellan's close association with the banking industry.

Pryor forced McClellan into a runoff. In the state's political tradition, no incumbent in the twentieth century had won reelection in a runoff. A turning point in the campaign came when McClellan accepted Pryor's challenge for a debate which was televised, live, to a statewide audience. In the course of the debate McClellan produced figures to show that Pryor had received several thousand dollars in campaign contributions from labor groups outside the state. Most political analysts credit that issue as being the deciding factor in McClellan's reelection. He won by some 18,000 votes.

Pryor, having served six years as a state legislator and six years as a U.S. congressman, now found himself as a private citizen at age thirty-eight. After the campaign he opened a law practice in Little Rock and commuted to Fayetteville to teach a political science course at the University of Arkansas. From that base he entered the race for governor in 1974.

Faubus revived the issue of Pryor's "liberal" record and charged that the former congressman was sympathetic to Vietnam draft evaders and that he supported gun control legislation. Pryor largely ignored the charges, and concentrated on winning support from education, black, and labor organizations. Many of Faubus' longtime supporters endorsed Pryor and the former governor found himself on the outside of his once powerful political organization. Pryor won without a runoff by polling 51 percent of the vote. He went on to defeat Republican Ken Coon, an administrator with the state chamber of commerce, in the general election, winning 66 percent of the vote.

Many in the business community had some misgivings about Pryor as governor, fearing that his reputation as a crusader and reformer would carry over to the statehouse. However, those apprehensions were quickly mitigated. In his inaugural address Pryor said, "We shall be judged, not by the addition of new state programs, but by the efficiency with which we have met our present needs." His words were prophetic. By 1975 the boom in the national economy was over. The surplus of the Bumpers' years began to shrink rapidly and Pryor was forced into a policy of fiscal restraint almost from the beginning of his administration.

Aside from his concern about the budget, Pryor made constitutional reform a matter of priority. Soon after taking office he appointed a special committee, endorsed by the General Assembly, to revise the 1874 Constitution. The state supreme court declared the method of reform unconstitutional because the general population had not had an opportunity to choose the committee. Pryor then supported an initiative petition to place the issue on the ballot at the next general election. The petition drive was successful and voters approved the concept of a new constitutional convention. The convention had not completed its work before Pryor left office.

In other matters Pryor made minor organizational adjustments for the executive branch. He created a Department of Local Service, and a Department of Natural and Cultural Heritage, and opened an overseas office for the Arkansas Industrial Development Commission in Brussels, Belgium. Little Rock businessman Frank White was appointed to administer the office.

In 1975 federal officials designated Fort Chaffee as a relocation site for refugees of the Vietnam War. Within weeks thousands of Vietnamese began arriving and state officials made hasty preparations to receive them. Pryor led in the planning and encouraged Arkansans to sponsor individual refugees in an effort to assimilate them into society. He also sponsored a bill in the General Assembly to grant state residency status for any Vietnamese enrolled in the state's colleges or universities.

Perhaps the thing for which Pryor received the most praise was the appointments he made to the various state boards and agencies. He appointed the first woman, Elsiejane Roy, and the first black, George Howard, to the state supreme court. He appointed the first woman, Anne Bartley, to the cabinet; the first woman, Patsy Thomasson, to the Highway Commission; and the first woman, Helen McLarty, to the AIDC. Consumer advocates John Pickett and Scott Stafford were appointed to the Public Service Commission and Pryor appointed women and blacks to all the boards of the state's colleges and universities. He also received high compliments for appointing Kaneaster Hodges of Newport to fill the unexpired term of John McClellan when the senator died in 1977.

Pryor's moderate, almost low-key, style offended few people and all but assured his reelection to a second term. Some elements in the state education association expressed concern that support for education had not kept pace with previous years. And some labor leaders expressed resentment over Pryor's use of the National Guard to break a strike by firemen in Pine Bluff. Otherwise, opposition was limited and even though Pryor faced three challengers, the most serious being Jim Lindsey, a former football star for the University of Arkansas, he won over 59 percent of the vote in the primary. In the general election he defeated Republican Leon Griffith by almost a six-to-one margin and polled 85 percent of the vote.

As Pryor began his second term, the economic slump was deepening. In an effort to rejuvenate the state's economy the governor proposed a sweeping plan to revise the tax and revenue system. The plan caught most members of the General Assembly by surprise and became the object of heated controversy throughout the session. Pryor's "Arkansas Plan" called for a 25 percent reduction in the state income tax and an incentive for counties and communities to increase local assessment. The plan received strong opposition from almost every special interest group in the state including educators, organized labor, and city and county officials. Legislators soon felt the pressure from these groups and the Arkansas Plan consumed almost the entire session of the Seventy-first Assembly. In an attempt to gain support, Pryor

held a series of town meetings throughout the state. But his presentations were not persuasive and he ultimately had to withdraw the plan from consideration.

The legislators spent so much time on the governor's proposal they failed to give adequate consideration to other measures and much of their work had to be redone in a special session. For example, a bill to fund kindergartens was based on incorrect enrollment figures and the program was seriously underfunded. An anti-litter tax bill was passed which did not include authorization to spend the money collected. The language in a bill mandating a general election referendum on the proposed constitutional convention was unclear and Pryor vetoed it. All of these measures were corrected in a special session.

The Arkansas Plan did some damage to Pryor's popularity. But even after dropping a few points in the opinion polls he still maintained a positive rating. His money-saving efforts, including a freeze on state employee salaries, earned him respect in the business community. His ability to guide the state through the national recession without cutting services or raising taxes was also viewed by most citizens as an accomplishment. In the words of one journalist, "much to the pleasant surprise of many, the 'old liberal, David Pryor' turned out to be a true fiscal conservative."

Pryor used his base as governor to prepare for the senate seat left vacant by McClellan's death. Shortly after making his announcement to run for the Senate, Second District Congressman Jim Guy Tucker and Fourth District Congressman Ray Thornton also announced for the seat. The early polls showed Tucker to be the leader.

However, a strong surge by Pryor in the last weeks of the campaign allowed him to finish in front in the primary. The race was one of the closest in the state's history—less than one vote per precinct separated the three candidates. Pryor then defeated Tucker in the runoff.

Bill Clinton had no serious opposition, either in the Democratic primary or in the general election, in the gubernatorial race. At thirty-two, the youngest governor in the nation, Clinton was an attorney, a Rhodes scholar, and a former law professor. He had run an unsuccessful race against Hammerschmidt in 1974, but was elected state attorney general in 1976. He had an air of progressivism, enhanced by his active wife, an attorney who preferred to go by her maiden name, Hillary Rodham.

Clinton had an ambitious legislative program, encompassing increased state funding for public schools, accelerated highway construction and repair, and improved health care services in rural areas. He also increased the administrative scope and power of the agencies responsible for energy matters and for economic development. Both were made cabinet-level departments.

As the national business recession began to cut deeply into Arkansas, unemployment increased and state revenues fell below projections. Frustrated by continuing inflation, many Arkansans resented any new taxation, especially the increase in automobile license fees that had been intended to pay for highway improvements.

Fort Chaffee became a center of controversy when the federal government decided to house Cuban refugees there in 1980. Frank White took advantage of public alarm over the situation in his campaign against Bill Clinton that year. Courtesy, Special Collections, University of Arkansas Libraries, Fayetteville

Above: *To the amazement of many, businessman and former Arkansas Industrial Development Commission director Frank White defeated Bill Clinton in 1980 after Arkansas became disgruntled over "Cubans and car tags." But 1982 voters put Clinton back in the driver's seat of Arkansas state government. Courtesy, Thomas Harding Photographs, Arkansas History Commission*

Right, top: *Bill Clinton, who had served as attorney general from 1977-1979, became governor at the age of thirty-two. Courtesy, Arkansas History Commission*

Right, bottom: *A higher quality of life for inmates of Cummins Prison can be seen in the religious and recreational opportunities offered. Courtesy, University of Arkansas at Little Rock Archives and Special Collections*

There were other problems as well. In the spring of 1980, federal officials, faced with a sudden influx of nearly 25,000 Cuban refugees, sent them to Fort Chaffee for housing and processing. Several thousand tried to escape, heightening fears among the population.

The atmosphere of unrest and economic discontent rebounded against the Clinton administration. Although the governor had no serious opposition in the Democratic primary, a

candidate, Monroe Schwartzlose, got more than 30 percent of the primary vote, in what many regarded as a message to Clinton. Then, in the general election, Republican Frank White, to the surprise of nearly everyone, won the governorship with 52 percent of the vote. Most political observers agreed that Clinton had contributed to his own defeat, but White had also run an effective campaign. His slogan of "Cubans and Car Tags" and his promise that state government would be "run like a business," matched the voters' mood. Republican presidential candidate Ronald Reagan, who had a similar message, won the state's electoral votes by a slight margin over Jimmy Carter.

White, a graduate of the Naval Academy with service in the U.S. Air Force, had spent most of his professional career as an executive with various financial institutions in the state. He served as director of the Arkansas Industrial Development Commission from 1975-76, but the governorship was his first major elected office. Personally devout, he suggested that at least part of the credit for his victory belonged to God.

White proposed a restricted and "realistic" legislative program emphasizing consolidation rather than innovation. No major new taxes were proposed or enacted. Car license fees were lowered, additional exemptions to benefit business were added to the state sales tax, and most state agencies were budgeted at a level that, considering inflation, represented a slight reduction.

White also reduced the number of state employees, put additional emphasis on vocational education and economic development, and continued efforts to improve the prisons. As

one legislator noted, "He did essentially what voters in November mandated; no new taxes, no new programs, lean budgeting." The General Assembly in 1981 did authorize cities and counties to add one cent to the sales tax, by popular vote.

During the early 1980s Arkansans, like other Americans, dealt with several emotionally charged moral issues. The legislature repeatedly refused to ratify the Equal Rights Amendment to the U.S. Constitution, although

Elena Hanggi (left) and Reba Whipple announce ACORN's political endorsements in May 1984. Among candidates endorsed were, from left, Thedford Collins and Nathan Dendy. Bill Clinton is represented by Rodney Slater, deputy campaign manager (right). Courtesy, Arkansas Democrat

273

Added to the capitol mall west of the Arkansas State Capitol is one of the state government's newest buildings. Called "Big Mac," short for Multi-agency Complex, the building houses the Arkansas History Commission, the State Library, the Department of Parks and Tourism, Computer Services, and the Arkansas Industrial Development Commission, among others. Courtesy, Arkansas Department of Parks and Tourism

some quiet progress was made in removing sexual discrimination from statute law. With little debate the 1981 General Assembly approved, and Governor White endorsed, a law requiring schools in the state when teaching biological evolution to give "balanced treatment" to the concept of scientific creation. After a federal court case that drew national attention, a judge ruled that the law was unconstitutional, because "the evidence is overwhelming that both the purpose and effect ... is the advancement of religion in the public schools."

Arkansans also continued to be concerned about crime and punishment. Early in 1969 a federal judge examined the "dark and evil world" of the state's prisons and declared

the entire system "cruel and unusual punishment" and therefore unconstitutional. However, in August 1982 another federal judge reviewed the state's years of effort and declared that the prison system met constitutional standards. It was a measure of accomplishment that in 1969 the prison system had eight guards and was practically run by the inmates, while in 1982 it had thousands of employees including hundreds of professional guards.

The 1982 gubernatorial race started with a bruising Democratic primary contest between Clinton, Tucker, and Joe Purcell. Clinton beat Purcell in the runoff to face a rematch with Frank White in the general election. This time Clinton started by apologizing for the mistakes of his first

First planted on the Grand Prairie in 1904 by W.H. Fuller, rice continues to be an important crop for Arkansas. This crop is particularly suited to the state's climate. This Riceland rice dryer is located at Hazen. Courtesy, Special Collections, University of Arkansas Libraries, Fayetteville

term, ran a smooth campaign operation, appeared more conservative, and got more than 54 percent of the vote.

In some respects Bill Clinton's "come back" symbolizes the spirit of Arkansas—the Land of Opportunity. Few, if any, states have had to overcome so many obstacles. Yet the state has managed to persevere. Debt (or, in more recent times, fear of deficits) has been an almost constant companion to public officials. The social and economic image associated with being poor have reached deep into the state's psyche. And the sense of being isolated from the main line of growth

and development has contributed to a strong sense of independence.

But while history may highlight the problems of the state budget and the struggles to meet bond payments, there have been many individual success stories. In the sesquicentennial of its birth as a state, Arkansas can boast of the wealthiest person in the nation—Sam Walton of Bentonville. It has the largest investment banking firm off Wall Street—Stephens, Incorporated, of Little Rock.

The Land of Opportunity has not only held the risk of failure, but also the potential to succeed.

The beautiful Arkansas State Capitol, framed by sparkling blue skies, is a solid reminder of Arkansas' heritage. Photo by Dick Dietrich

Partners in Progress
by Starr Mitchell

CHAPTER
IX

Arkansas business histories, because they are human histories, breathe life into the history of our state.

On the following pages you will meet young William Woodruff, who ended a six-week river trip from Nashville, Tennessee, in the fall of 1819 to set up a print shop in Arkansas Post and give the new territory a newspaper—the *Arkansas Gazette;* Eleithet Coleman, a dairy farmer whose great-great-grandchildren now run the dairy that he founded; and five Sisters of Charity, who converted an old house into a hospital in the 1880s, then boiled towels through the night for the first operation they assisted, all in the name of their patron, Saint Vincent.

Arkansas was a place for these men and women to use their talents, respond to the needs and opportunities of the times, and build a business. Because of the foundations they laid in the nineteenth century, their organizations, and the others represented on the following pages, are now making goals for the twenty-first century.

In these histories you will meet creative, energetic Arkansans who have built international markets for their inventions. Deciding on a use for a motorized auger, Pete Stoltz launched the glass-front vending industry in the 1960s from Polyvend, his plant in Conway. By "messing with chemicals," Ernest Joshua, Jr., developed a minority hair-care product, Isoplus, which he sells in forty-eight states, Canada, France, Africa, and the Caribbean.

We are constantly reminded of Arkansas' international connections, historical and current, in these business histories. The 1880s brought thousands of German immigrants to the Arkansas River Valley to work on the railroad, and Carl Bemberg was among them. His great-grandsons practice his trade today, at the iron works company he founded in 1885. Today's unusual international economy creates clients for Arkansas Modification Center, which puts gold trim on British-made jets for Saudi Arabian businessmen.

Eras of world history have personal meaning when translated through these stories of Arkansas' businesses. Assets at Twin City Bank, for example, swelled in the early 1920s because World War I had prompted construction of Camp Pike near North Little Rock, and triggered new economic activity.

The Great Depression in Arkansas, these corporate profiles show, produced occasional exceptions to hardship. John Cline enjoyed one of his most profitable periods during the Depression. He had invented a machine to make barrel staves for bourbon and beer kegs, and, when Prohibition ended, he was in the process of expanding his shop and hiring thirty-nine men to fill the orders coming to

Clarksville Machine Works. Crow-Burlingame, an auto parts dealership, boomed; everyone had to buy parts for the car they had—they couldn't afford to replace it. In 1933 Conlee Jackson put a $1,000 recipe to work, made a twenty-five dollar down payment for a secondhand stove, started to bake vanilla wafers, and found plenty of customers.

The next World War was hard on some Arkansas businesses. Bale Chevrolet sold one new car in four years. Then again World War II prompted the birth of Central Flying Service, one of the oldest and largest air charter businesses in the nation, founded to train pilots for the war. Guy Cameron was prohibited by the government from going to war; staying with the family feed mill was essential to the war effort. Frank Snell's profession was profoundly affected by World War II. The Veterans Administration pioneered research in orthotics and prosthetics for the sake of its injured soldiers.

These histories show that Arkansas' natural resources were considered an asset even before the territory was carved from the Louisiana Purchase. By 1832 congress declared four sections of land, with the Ouachita Mountains' hot springs in the middle, the first federally held and protected recreation area in the nation. A city grew around it for people lured by the waters. Further north, the Ozark Mountains are the natural backdrop to a newer community, Fairfield Bay. It was the first of many communities created by one of the nation's largest resort developers. Other of our resources, unseen, are extracted for industrial use. Arkla Gas drills and markets Arkansas' natural gas. 3M mines syenite from the world's largest granite quarry in order to make roofing granules. Dow Chemical Corporation and the Ethyl Corporation were drawn to Arkansas because of its rich bromine reserves beneath the south Arkansas soil.

One by one the business histories that follow describe a state coming of age, developing its services—hospitals, colleges, hotels, utilities, banks, real estate, insurance, and abstract companies; its professions—architects, attorneys, accountants, and engineers; its transportation; its media; and its construction trade. The stories cover the state's period of growing sophistication in marketing itself to manufacturers, and we will meet national companies who have chosen Arkansas as their home.

Many are stories of one person's dream, some are of people banding together for cooperative buying or marketing. They are family stories, corporate stories, and together they are Arkansas' story. If their beginnings are quaint, their transformation to maturity in a technological age is extremely impressive, and is documented in each article. The organizations whose stories are detailed on the following pages have chosen to support this important literary and civic project.

Eastern Arkansas is known for its richly productive farmland, where soybeans and cotton flourish. This crop duster helps ensure a good harvest. Courtesy, Arkansas Department of Parks and Tourism

ARKANSAS STATE CAPITOL ASSOCIATION

In 1899, sitting in chambers of the Old State House that overlook the Arkansas River, the Arkansas General Assembly members levied a special property tax for a new state capitol. They well knew the need for larger space for their growing state government and appropriated one million dollars for the building. The act created a commission to procure plans and specifications, and appropriated money to clear the selected building site.

Had Jeff Davis not been attorney general at the time, with an eye on the governor's seat, the early history of the state capitol would be different. His speeches pitted backwoods audiences against Little Rock's "high-collared roosters" and "silk stocking crowd," declaring the new capitol evidence of Little Rock's intention "to impose taxes upon the sons of toil for generations."

As long as Davis was just campaigning, plans for the building moved apace. George R. Mann, an outstanding Little Rock architect, was chosen to design the structure. A high knoll west of Little Rock was cleared of the state penitentiary, and the cornerstone was laid Thanksgiving Day, 1900.

When Jeff Davis became governor, however, he actually stopped the work. It resumed again in 1903 because, according to John Gould Fletcher in his writing of *Arkansas,* the state's residents showed "themselves too much in favor of" the capitol. Nonetheless, progress was slow. In 1907 the capitol was still an issue—this time in gubernatorial candidate George W. Donaghey's promise to have it completed. He was elected and, in 1909, appointed a new commission and hired Cass Gilbert, one of the foremost architects in America, to take over the work of planning and building the upper part of the structure.

The General Assembly of 1911 was the first to sit in the new building, but it was not completed

until 1915, 16 years after the groundbreaking. Its final cost was $2.2 million.

Today, the grandeur of the Arkansas State Capitol erases memories of early controversies. Since 1911 it has elegantly served its purpose, housing the affairs of Arkansas' state government, and in 1954 was voted "America's Most Beautiful State Capitol" by the National Association of Secretaries of State. With a floor plan based on that of the nation's capitol, the building rises 230 feet from ground level to the top of the dome, which has 26-carat gold on the lantern roof. Its exterior is made of limestone quarried near Batesville, punctuated by six brass front doors on the east—made by Tiffany's of New York. Marble from Vermont was used on the inside halls, and the columns are Colorado Ute marble. Wood trim of quarter-sawed oak gives warmth to the interior elegance.

The maintenance of the capitol

An aerial view of the Arkansas State Capitol Complex. In 1954 the National Association of Secretaries of State voted it "America's Most Beautiful State Capitol."

and grounds falls under the jurisdiction of the secretary of state. In 1982 that office, seeking a way to more actively engage people around the state in caring for the building, created the Arkansas State Capitol Association. Activities of the association involve both fund-raising and educational efforts. Its largest publication project is the special sesquicentennial book, *Arkansas: An Illustrated History of the Land of Opportunity.*

Members of the association, under the leadership of secretary of state W.J. "Bill" McCuen, are richly rewarded by their involvement to preserve a rich heritage.

The Capitol during construction in February 1910. The Legislature of 1911 was the first to sit in the new building.

CAPITAL HOTEL

At one time the Capital Hotel had to grasp from its past for proof of its importance, pulling famous names from its guest list that included Ulysses S. Grant and Sarah Bernhardt. It relied on esoteric groups such as Friends of Cast Iron Architecture to tout its architectural rarity.

The hostelry stood with cracked windows and peeling columns on Markham Street, an echo of what that street had housed in the Victorian era. And it haunted the dreams of a local Little Rock architect, Ed Cromwell, who knew what it could become again.

Cromwell steered the dream of reopening the Capital Hotel through years of a financial maze until it was properly packaged in the early 1980s—with Lincoln Hotels of Dallas as developers and the Arkansas Historic Preservation Program and Cromwell's firm as conscience for accurate preservation. Just under $10 million later, it stands a "little jewel box," as manager Charles Stoermer calls it, an intimate hotel that ranks with Chicago's Drake, New York's Plaza, San Francisco's Fairmont, and the Memphis Peabody. Travelers go out of their way to stay at the Capital Hotel; first-time visitors have flowers in their room, and returning visitors receive a welcome-back fruit basket and are greeted by name—the staff excels in remembering names.

The Capital's grand opening, or reopening, was in December 1983. It was, in fact, its third grand opening as a hotel—in a history that goes back to 1872 when the building was three stories high and home to six retail establishments. It became a hotel, with accommodations for 80 persons, in 1877. The renovated structure was named by Mrs. Morehead Wright, who explained, "I can think of no name more appropriate than 'Capital Hotel,' as it is a capital enterprise located in a capital building, which will do honor to

the capital of the state and I trust prove a capital success."

The hotel was across the street and down the block from the State House, and the lore is that more political decisions were made at the Capital than at the State House itself.

The local papers have always covered the Capital's openings. In the beginning fine details were noted—gas lights, magnetized annunciators, and rooms "carpeted . . . with superior English-body Brussels, containing in the pattern such daintily contrived figures that it looks as though it were a pity to walk on them." In 1908, when the facility closed long enough for an interior redecoration, the paper advertised it as having, at 50 by 100 feet, "the largest hotel lobby in the South."

Times changed. Modern hotels were erected across the street, and only the efforts of its owners, Amelia and Elizabeth Cassinelli, kept the building standing. It closed as a hotel in 1977. An irony of its 1983 reopening is the fact that having an up-to-date hotel across the street, the Excelsior, was advantageous in pulling the restoration funding together.

The restoration involved adding 45 rooms, in a new section that accurately replicates the rest of the building, to provide a total of 123

With Lincoln Hotels of Dallas as developer and the assistance of the Arkansas Historic Preservation Program, Little Rock architect Ed Cromwell realized his dream for the restoration of the Capital Hotel when it reopened in December 1983.

rooms. The amenities include the 84-seat "tablecloth service" Ashley Restaurant, an 85-seat bar, a mezzanine and lobby of particular charm, and five private meeting rooms. There is valet parking as well as travel and secretarial assistance on request.

The hotel caters, states Stoermer, to "the individual traveler who appreciates beauty and quality, friendly service, and good food and beverage away from home." Since its reestablishment the Capital has added to its guest list of famous people—Vice-President George Bush, entertainers Bob Hope and Tony Bennett, and author Alex Haley. Little Rock residents use the facility for receptions, dinners, and weddings.

The Capital Hotel is a rare part of Arkansas history accessible to everyone, and when it reopened the papers again were careful to note its details: Marbleized columns, 14-foot ceilings, and "turn-of-the-century carbon filament bulbs . . . reproduced to give a golden glow around the lobby's stained glass dome"—just like an illuminated little jewel box.

TWIN CITY BANK

The history of Twin City Bank is intimately tied with the history of its host city, North Little Rock. A loan from Twin City Bank (TCB), in fact, was the first money that the city had for paying its bills. That was in 1904; but the history that ties them together starts 19 years earlier, when brothers William C. and James P. Faucette moved to the community.

The young men were 20 and 18 years old in 1885 when they came to work on the railroad in Argenta, as North Little Rock was known then. Soon they had leased the Arlington Hotel on Magnolia Street, prospered, and began to build—an ice factory, an electric generating plant, and the city's third commercial building. By 1901 they had opened a private bank, Faucette Brothers.

The institution, though on the north side of the Arkansas River, was technically within Little Rock's city limits. It was not the wish of Argenta, nor the Faucette brothers, to be part of Little Rock. In 1890 they and other Argenta businessmen had tried to incorporate their town. However, this had alarmed the capital city, which stood to lose tax money, and Little Rock's legislators created enabling legislation that they used to annex Argenta as Little Rock's Eighth Ward.

In 1904, the year Twin City Bank was granted a state charter, it was located in this building.

William Faucette became the Eighth Ward alderman. He also won a seat in the state legislature, quietly created new legislation, and helped to recover the Eighth Ward for the north side. North Little Rock—population 6,500—became a city of the first class in 1904, electing, on April 1, the alderman as its mayor. Unfortunately, independence was costly: Little Rock had been collecting taxes from the area, and state turnback funds were not available for another year.

During this same time the Faucette brothers had applied for a state charter for their bank, which they planned to rename Twin City Bank. The charter was granted on April 23, 1904, and James Faucette became president. So it was his brother that Mayor William Faucette approached in search of a loan. The institution awarded the loan, and the new city began operation.

Sharing the same founding fathers and the same year of incorporation, and with a significant financial transaction to link their beginnings, TCB and North Little Rock have a historical kinship.

The economic boost that the community experienced, by becoming incorporated, was reflected in TCB's move in 1906 to a new two-story brick building at 201 Main Street. Later, when World War I brought the construction of Camp Pike to the outskirts of North Little Rock, economic activity bur-

James P. Faucette, founder and first president of Twin City Bank.

geoned in the area; as a result, TCB's assets increased by more than one million dollars between 1920 and 1926. Then, when the Great Depression hit the town and nation, the institution obeyed the President's orders and closed its doors with the rest of the country's banks on March 6, 1933. It reopened on May 1, as Twin City Savings Bank.

Now the largest state-chartered bank in Arkansas, with assets of $380 million, the institution has 180 employees working at 11 different branches who also donate volunteer service to numerous organizations in the community. They additionally participate in cultural, educational, and recreational programs that the bank itself has initiated; the acclaimed Arkansas Art Exhibition, featuring the state's artists; annual education grants distributed by the TCB student board of directors; and services, including complimentary dances and picnics, for senior citizens. Emulating the men who founded both Twin City Bank and North Little Rock, today's TCB officers and employees take an active interest in the community they serve—maintaining the tradition and the history the institution shares with its city.

JACKSON COOKIE COMPANY

The sweet aroma of freshly baked cookies and a cold glass of milk captivate the appetites of snack seekers of all ages, and at Jackson Cookie Company in North Little Rock, cookies abound with enough different flavors to satisfy every sweet tooth.

Jackson Cookie Company was originated in the 1930s, after J. Conlee Jackson determined that the crippled economy made his insurance sales a hopeless venture. He decided to try something with more palatable appeal, and the cookie business proved to be his first opportunity.

By traveling across the South selling packaged cookies from a vending truck, Jackson finally raised sufficient capital to open his own cookie factory on West Seventh Street in Little Rock in 1933. It was then that the young man devised his secret recipe and created the firm's delicious brand of vanilla wafers.

In its early days the company was a one-man operation. Jackson baked the cookies at night in a small three-shelf oven; and, once they had cooled, he hand counted and packaged each batch of wafers in bright-colored cellophane bags. His days were spent traveling throughout central Arkansas selling his product for 10 cents per pound.

The enterprise moved to its North Little Rock location in 1936.

The printing on this completely restored vehicle proclaims, "This 1933 Ford truck is one of the first trucks to deliver Jackson Cookies."

The building it occupied was destroyed by fire in 1943 and was rebuilt—the only commercial structure to be erected in Pulaski County during the World War II years. Symbolically standing in front of Jackson's main office is a beautifully restored replica of one of its first trucks: a 1933 Ford that is still in running condition. The vehicle was discovered in Texarkana, brought to North Little Rock, completely restored, and has been used in parades and various company promotions.

Today the firm produces more than three million cookies in a single day. After five decades Jackson's complete line of products numbers close to 100, and includes its longtime favorite, Lemon Jumble, as well as sandwich cremes, oatmeal, chocolate chip, peanut butter, saltines, graham crackers, and snack crackers. Although its line has expanded tenfold, the organization's original vanilla wafer still comprises a large portion of the products sold, and is considered by many to be among the best wafers in the country. Jackson

has on several occasions turned down requests to make this premium wafer for major national operations.

Jackson Cookie Company markets its products in 26 states. The firm has more than 100 full-time employees, and has another 100 independent distributors who own their own routes and distribute the complete line of Jackson products throughout the Sunbelt states.

In other outlying areas—including New York, California, Florida, and Chicago—Jackson products are sold through wholesalers and brokers.

Even today, after 53 years of continued service, the organization continues to use the old-fashioned cookie jars placed near cash registers in many rural and small stores. It still caters to children as its best customer for the penny cookies and does not wish to break this long-established tradition.

While the Jackson family retired in 1981 and sold the company, they left it in good hands. It was sold to the Fanelli family, whose heritage is rich in bakery tradition. Robert G. Fanelli, whose wife is a native of Memphis, Tennessee, has been in the wholesale bakery business for over 40 years. Although the ownership of the firm has changed, the quality of its products has not.

Jackson Cookie Company today continues with the same fine ingredients and techniques that have been in use throughout its history. It appears that future generations will be able to have the memorable experience of enjoying Jackson cookies as did their parents and grandparents before them.

The red, white, and blue Jackson Cookie trucks ply the highways of the Sunbelt states delivering cookies to independent distributors.

283

SNELL PROSTHETIC & ORTHOTIC LABORATORY

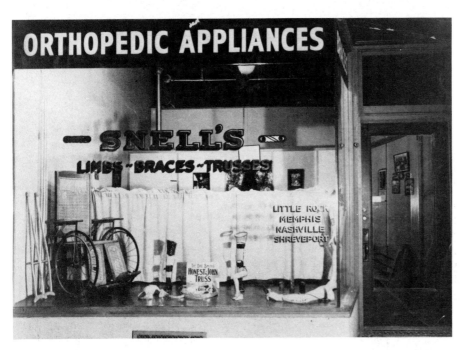

Snell Artificial Limbs opened in 1933 at 209 West Sixth Street in the old Arcade Building.

To begin work in the artificial limb business in 1911, Ralph W. "Pop" Snell had no one asking for his certification. He stocked up on red willow wood, rawhide, and tools, hung out his shingle, and with the help of salesmen went door to door to search out customers.

His grandnephew Frank, on the other hand, is conversant in thermo-plastics, studied a two-year course in prosthetics and orthotics, had to pass two board exams, and only treats patients who come to him on referral from a physician, with a prescription.

The world of the artificial limb business has transformed to the profession of prosthetics and orthotics, and Ed Snell, who is Pop Snell's nephew and Frank Snell's father, is the link between the worlds.

Ed Snell was at work in a handle factory in Nashville, Tennessee, when his uncle contacted him about going to Little Rock to take over a branch of Snell Artificial Limbs. It was 1945. Pop was based in Memphis and wanted a trustworthy family member in the Little Rock store. His son Jim had left that operation in 1938 to open an office in Shreveport, Louisiana.

Another son, Ralph, was in the same business in Nashville.

Ed professed to know nothing about the business, but was confident about his woodcarving skills. He agreed to go to Little Rock after a year's apprenticeship with his cousin in Shreveport.

The year was shortened to six weeks. Pop had become desperate. So, in January 1946, Ed moved to Little Rock and took over ownership of Snell Artificial Limbs, at 405 West Seventh Street. He had carved six artificial legs in his six weeks in Louisiana, and had stayed up nights talking about the business that now was his.

The office had been in Little Rock since 1933, originally at 209 West Sixth Street. Ed was coming into the trade at a critical transition point. Some of Pop's ways were still typical of the business—having a clipping service, for instance, that saved newspaper stories concerning traumatic amputations. Those injured were prospective customers.

At the same time the federal

government was effecting changes in the industry. Its influence had begun in the 1930s through new programs of President Roosevelt's administration. Vocational rehabilitation and Crippled Children's Services began making client referrals to artificial limb companies. By 1946 the Veteran's Administration had a colossal need for their services, with injured soldiers returning from World War II. To ensure the best care possible for its clients, the VA started subsidizing development and improvement of the construction and fitting of artificial limbs.

As Ed Snell describes the impetus for the trade to change, "We did a tremendous business with the VA. They set up standards we had to meet. There was nothing for us to do *but* meet the standards."

Ed more than kept up with the changes. When, in 1948, the Board for Certification in Orthotics and Prosthetics required certification of all people in his profession, he was the 117th in the country to be approved. When the VA set up continuing education seminars at three selected universities in the country, he was there. In his Little Rock laboratory he tested new parts and designs from the VA, reporting results as he collected his patients' responses.

"Knowledge is more important now than actual handwork," Snell says, describing a basic difference that the use of plastics, rather than wood, has brought to the industry. He has thrived on the changes. "We are constantly on the lookout for new ways of doing things," states the chairman of Arkansas' largest and oldest prosthetics and orthotics laboratory.

Snell's company, with 12 employees on its payroll, does in a week the dollar amount of business that it once grossed in a year. That is one measure of the changes. "It used to take the equivalent time of one man's entire week's work to

The new home of Snell Prosthetic & Orthotic Laboratory, on North University at F Street, was completed in November 1986.

fabricate one prosthesis. Now the time is somewhat less due to superior, commercially available component parts, which once had to all be made by hand."

To clarify the work at Snell, prosthetics is the science of design and replacement of absent portions of the body. While it refers to the whole body, Snell's expertise is in congenital or acquired amputation of the upper or lower limbs, or any part of that limb. Orthotics, a separate science that not all companies combine with prosthetic services, deals with reinforcement of a weakened or injured portion of the body. Snell concentrates on the lower limb and foot, the upper limb and hand, and the entire spine. The firm, whose entire work involves custom fitting for the patient, also offers prescription footwear.

The medical profession and the artificial limb business were not always aligned as they are today. Snell explains, "In the old days, the challenge to the doctors was in saving lives from trauma or disease. Amputation was a lifesaving procedure and after surgery their goal was basically accomplished. Presently, doctors are more involved in the proper fitting of a prosthetic device."

Today prosthetists and physicians meet together regularly. They are part of a clinic team, another result of VA involvement.

The Snell laboratory is Arkansas' oldest and largest in the profession.

Also on the team are a physical therapist, a nurse coordinator, a representative from a referral agency—and the patient.

Frank Snell, Ed's son and president of the company since 1984, attends 12 of those clinics per month. It is the typical way a prosthetist or orthotist spends a large part of his professional time. Yet even today, Frank, who started work at the firm at age 14—by "pushing the broom," as he recalls—is not finding himself exempt from changes.

While he spent two years studying upper-level business courses and two years studying orthotics and prosthetics, Frank describes the board exams required now as more extensive than the ones he took in the early 1970s. He knows, because he is one of four members of the Prosthetic Examination Committee, an arm of the American Board for Certification for Or-

thotists and Prosthetists. The quantity of information in the field is increasing exponentially, he explains.

And Frank, like his father, is watching new technology change the possibilities for prosthetic devices. While plastic provided better-fitting, longer-lasting, and more realistic-looking limbs, the innovative myoelectric devices are almost a revolution. They operate on batteries with electrical signals that simulate a muscle's communication with the brain. Still brand-new, they extensively broaden the possibilities for patients' use of substitute limbs.

If the past can be used to predict the future, Snell Prosthetic & Orthotic Laboratory—with the third generation at its helm—will keep pace with the changes. Its new building, Snell's fifth address in Little Rock, was constructed in 1986 to enlarge and improve its space for patient care. It is a physical indication of the company's commitment to continuing care.

FAIRFIELD COMMUNITIES, INC.

As isolated as the Arkansas Ozarks seem, they are becoming less so. The latest influx of settlers to the hills began in the 1960s. Some who came were young—the back-to-the-landers, coming to rough it. Some were retirees wanting to get away, but with amenities.

Besides the charm and mild weather of the Arkansas hills, many of the older people were drawn by a flyer in their mail box. It offered them bargain-priced wooded lots for sale and, later, the incentive of a four-day, three-night vacation for the price of looking at the property.

In Van Buren County, 80 miles north of Little Rock, the group making this offer was Fairfield

On Greers Ferry Lake in Van Buren County, Fairfield Bay is the second largest of the 28 communities that Fairfield Communities owns and operates in 10 Sunbelt states and the Virgin Islands.

Bay, Inc. It had taken its cue from similar successful ventures in the state. In the mid-1960s Randolph Warner, one of the original Fairfield partners, had visited, and been amazed by buyers' interest in, a development outside of Harrison. It had only a remote lake and hills to allure them.

An attorney in Fort Smith at the time, now president and chairman of the board of Fairfield Communities, Warner had "dabbled in real estate." He also had two clients who were home builders in

New corporate headquarters in Little Rock, occupied in 1986, reflect the astounding two-decade growth of Fairfield Communities, Inc., one of six Arkansas corporations listed on the New York Stock Exchange.

real estate development, George Jacobus and Neal Simonson. Each of these men knew well the "vagaries of a local economy," as Warner describes it, and were convinced of the feasibility of a community development that attracted a widespread market. Another significant factor was that the developers were responsible for providing all the amenities and most of the contractor services, thereby allowing economic control.

Thus, a partnership was formed. Acquiring 4,300 acres adjacent to the recently built Greers Ferry Lake, in one of the state's poorest counties, the enterprise in 1966 began to sell lots and build a retirement resort. Warner laughingly recalls George Jacobus, his predecessor as president, on a bulldozer when he was not showing lots or tending shop in a converted country gas service station near Shirley, Arkansas, with one employee, Allene Meadors, a longtime associate who did a little of everything in the early days.

Today, operating from a five-story corporate headquarters in Little Rock, Fairfield Communities is a corporation that in fiscal 1986 achieved $338 million in revenues and a net income of $8.8 million. It employs 4,000 people. A member of the American Stock Exchange

in February 1981, the firm is now one of only six Arkansas corporations listed on the New York Stock Exchange, a listing acquired May 31, 1983. In 1984 it was the 27th-largest home builder in the country. And 83,000 people own property in its 28 projects, both resort and residential, that cover 70,000 acres of land.

Something obviously clicked in the past two decades. Warner talks about effective marketing techniques—the firm still relies on direct mail pieces, by the millions—and well-run projects—satisfied owners, in significant numbers, "sell" their friends on joining them. However, he primarily stresses the financing that has successfully fallen together over the years.

The partners originally sold 400,000 shares of common stock and borrowed from Arkansas banks to finance their development, which by the close of 1968 had sold about 1,800 lots to people from 24 states, with 68 occupying homes there. In 1969 more stock was issued, and so were 30,000 shares of subordinated seven-year-notes (securities whose holders, in the event of a dissolution, can claim no part of the asset until bank and insurance debts are paid).

The securities were placed privately by the New York investment firm of Lombard, Vitalis, Paganucci and Nelson, Inc. This was not a haphazard choice; Jacobus knew Paganucci—they were both in the Dartmouth College class of 1953. The intention, with the private placement, was to get Fairfield in position to go public. That finally happened in 1971, following mergers with a public shell corporation and with a computer leasing operation that was also a public company. Again, the choice was not random: Robert Calender, the leasing firm's president, was another 1953 Dartmouth graduate. He became the chief financial officer for Fairfield Communities. By this time a phrase was coined among the executives that has stuck with the Fairfield story—"The Dartmouth Mafia."

The year it went public Fairfield owned just two communities, one in Arkansas and a second in Tennessee. Warner recalls that no one envisioned how the venture was

going to grow. "Our objective was always to build a company in the retirement/recreation business in remote communities. As we grew, we took advantage of opportunities," he says simply.

In 1972 the organization acquired Green Valley, a retirement community in the desert 20 miles south of Tucson. "That's when we began to see a national scope to the company," notes Warner—who the next year, upon Jacobus' retirement, was persuaded to leave his law practice and assume the presidency. "Then came the depression of 1974-1975," he recalls. "Nothing much happened but survival."

Fairfield began to buy again in 1976 and has continued to add communities, which it now operates in 10 Sunbelt states and the Virgin Islands. In 1979 the corporation began building and offering for sale, at its resort communities, specially designed and furnished

---

Fairfield Bay is home to 2,500 permanent residents, but another 65,000 people visit annually. Some are in workshops at the 400-person-capacity conference center. All have access to the award-winning golf courses and tennis courts, as well as the other recreational highlights afforded by the lake and hills.

vacation homes on a time-share basis. The company has become the world's largest operation in that industry. (A purchaser of a time-share interval is entitled to the exclusive use of the unit and access to community amenities for the particular week or weeks purchased.)

Fairfield time-share owners are part of the Fairshare Exchange, or FAX, and can exchange their week on a space-available basis for one at any other Fairfield community where time-share exists. The firm also has exchanges with other resorts, allowing Fairshare owners access to 700 resorts worldwide.

Condos on the Riviera seem far removed from wooded lots on Greers Ferry Lake, but access to those condos—for Fairshare owners—had its genesis right there in the Ozarks. Fairfield Bay, the second largest of the Fairfield Community resorts, is the permanent home of 2,500 people. Another 65,000 visit there annually. The original 4,300 acres have expanded to 14,300, with 7,000 of them still undeveloped. Taking advantage of its 40,000-acre lake, the community has a 180-slip marina, equipped for boating and fishing, and two private lake beaches. There are two outdoor pools, two 18-hole championship golf courses, a lighted tennis-court complex (selected as one of the top 50 tennis resorts in the United States by *Tennis Magazine*), four restaurants, seasonal horseback riding, a 100,000-foot shopping center and office complex, and a 400-person-capacity conference center. Its 1985 Four-Star listing in the *Mobil Travel Guide* was the fourth time for the honor, and it was the only Arkansas resort with that rating.

It is apparent that Fairfield Bay and Fairfield Communities, in developing a regional and now national marketing strategy to escape a fickle local economy, have contributed heartily to the economy of their host county and state.

CENTRAL FLYING SERVICE

In the golden age of aviation—when barnstormers hopped from field to pasture, Charles Lindbergh cleared the Atlantic Ocean, and Amelia Earhart disappeared—Claud Holbert, of Little Rock, was learning to fly.

Holbert was 16 when he soloed in 1926, a young member of the Arkansas Air National Guard. Over the next 13 years, with piloting and flight instruction jobs, he recorded 3,500 hours in the air. That was the last time he logged his flight time, although for the next 44 years he was constantly in the air. According to his son Dick, the pilot may have totaled a national record for time spent flying, something over 50,000 hours; but keeping up with statistics was not important to the senior Holbert—flying was.

Holbert flew crop dusters, flight trainers, and jet charters. He delivered the U.S. mail, piloted Winthrop Rockefeller, and mapped the Arkansas River six times—from its mouth to Tulsa. He trained pilots for war and took weekend passengers, in the days when it was profitable, on one-dollar rides. He did this while building a company of aircraft sales and charter flights, with their accompanying services, that ranks with the largest, safest, and oldest in the country.

Central Flying Service, like its founder's career, is a microcosm of Little Rock's aviation history since 1939. The enterprise began that

Central's Ford Tri-Motor was the first private commercial multi-engine charter service in the state. On weekends the company flew passengers on one-dollar rides.

year when Holbert and Edward Garbacz contracted with Little Rock Junior College to train pilots for the government-financed Civilian Pilot Training program (CPT). The government provided Central with seven Beech Staggerwing aircraft to start the program. When the United States entered World War II, CPT converted to the War Pilot Training program. At the height of the training, Central had 65 aircraft and 30 instructors. It produced several thousand graduates.

Flight training remained Central's primary source of business after the war. One new difference was the competition. With the end of the war, some 15 to 20 new companies set up operations around Adams Field—all headed by former war pilots. By 1950 all but Central had gone out of business.

The firm was engaged in other enterprises as well. One of its services was to operate the city's hangar. The Little Rock municipal government had decided in the

1940s to lease its hangar as a concession, and Central had won the lease. Still the first hangar one sees upon driving toward Central, it has its own place in history. The hangar was built in Waynoka, Oklahoma, for Trans International Airways—now TWA. Because Waynoka was in the middle of the nation, aircraft—in the days when there was no night flying—could reach it from either coast within daylight hours. Planes flew there to deposit their passengers, who then boarded trains to continue traveling overnight.

By 1936 Waynoka was no longer an essential stop, and the hangar was offered for sale. The City of Little Rock purchased, dismantled, moved, and rebuilt it at Adams Field, using WPA labor, all for $10,000.

Central added on to the Waynoka hangar in 1958, when it constructed a brick executive terminal building on its east side. The company had never considered a significant capital investment before then because the city had offered only a one-year lease. Now Central had a 10-year lease. The investment was symbolic for the 1950s,

Central Flying Service, at Adams Field, began as a pilot training program just before World War II.

the decade when aviation was undergoing a transition from a daredevil enterprise to an accepted business.

Central's physical growth did not stop with the 1958 expansion. By 1984 the firm had another new terminal building—with the Flight Deck restaurant, six hangars, and 23 acres of ramp space. It is one of the nation's largest fixed-base operations (FBO)—a term coined in the days when, in contrast to Holbert's operation at Adams Field, some pilots worked from their airplanes and had no permanent, or fixed, base of operation.

It is the organization's business growth that prompted its physical growth. Part of that growth has been in aircraft sales. Central began in 1939 as a Taylorcraft distributor, after Holbert purchased a Taylorcraft with $1,241 that he borrowed. In 1948 the company became a Beechcraft dealer; it continues to be, selling new and used planes. In 1964 Central was the first Beechcraft dealer in the country to reach a million dollars in sales. By 1980, of the 140 or so independent Beechcraft dealers, it was the first to exceed one million dollars in parts sales. When singling out individuals Beech has recognized Tom Smith, Central's director of maintenance and twice an Arkansas Aviation Mechanic of the Year, as its Beech Aircraft's Maintenance Man of the Year.

In addition to sales and sales services, the firm has a flight department with charter and rental services and a flight school. Central's charter service goes back to its first year of operation. The Ford Tri-Motor it purchased in 1940 offered the first private commercial multi-engine charter service in the state. In 1972 it had the first turboprop charter service, and in 1976 the first jet and jet helicopter service. The charter business was slow to develop in the first few decades, but revenues doubled when the Arab oil em-

bargo of the early 1970s caused customers to value the fuel and time efficiency of chartering planes.

In connection with Central's flight services, the National Business Aircraft Association has frequently given the company awards for safety in commercial flying and in its maintenance department. A Central pilot, Forrest Stolzer, won the Federal Aviation Administration's (FAA) National Aviation Mechanics Safety Award in 1968.

Training, Central's original business, continues. The expense of learning to fly and the lack of VA funding for pilot training has narrowed the students to those who need to fly for business purposes, or to pilots who need to upgrade their levels. College students use the company's flight training services in Arkadelphia at Henderson State University, where there is an aviation degree program. As part of the arrangement to work with HSU, Central also operates Arkadelphia's airport.

In addition to these areas the firm created Airport Services, Inc., in 1972, and since then has provided fueling to all of the airlines that come to the gates of the Little Rock airport.

Claud Holbert guided Central through this growth. He and Garbacz had dissolved their partnership in 1956, at which time Holbert became sole stockholder. In 1975 he retired as president and became chairman of the board. His son Don succeeded him as president of the company, and son Dick was named executive vice-president.

Central Flying Service is among the largest and oldest charter service and flight training operations in the country. It is located at Adams Field in Little Rock.

On the founder's 1981 retirement as board chairman, Don assumed the position; Dick became president at that time.

The founder's sons, not surprisingly, had grown up in airplanes. Both were members of the Armed Forces. As a helicopter pilot in Vietnam, Don won the Distinguished Flying Cross for valor and 32 Air Medals. He returned to Little Rock and Central in 1968. Dick, who like his father soloed at 16, had his tour of duty in Germany. He returned home and to the family operation in 1972.

Spread upon the airfield that once was farmland, then was an Army depot airfield, then was deeded to the city in the 1920s, Central Flying Service is literally built upon history. With his career and company, Holbert created more history for the airfield. He and his sons, appropriately, helped to found the Arkansas Aviation Historical Society in 1979. Dick has been the president since its inception.

Holbert, although retired, continued to be active in piloting planes after 1981. The following year he was inducted into the Arkansas Aviation Hall of Fame. He died in 1983, leaving his sons in leadership of a company with 46 of its own aircraft, 150 employees, and by most standards of measure one of the finest of its kind in the nation.

J.M. PRODUCTS, INC.

"When I won that, people here didn't know I existed. I never liked public life." Ernest P. Joshua, Sr., pointed to the plaque on the wall and the picture of the ceremony honoring him as the Arkansas Minority Small Businessman of 1984. That same year he was runner-up for the national award.

"I'm a quiet guy. I love the wilderness," he says, nodding to the mounted pheasants, squirrels, and bass in his office. "I like loneliness. That's when I can think. They'll get here in the morning and see lights on. I'll be back in the lab, mucking around with an idea. I'll get it, test it out on my hair, try it out on friends . . . . I do it the old way. I can look at it, I can feel a product, and know if it will sell."

What Joshua sells is Isoplus, formerly known as StyleCrest, a line of 56 cosmetic hair-care items. Among the nationally marketed minority hair-care products, it ranked fifth in 1985 sales among the top 13 manufacturers. From headquarters in Little Rock, his company, J.M. Products, ships Isoplus nationwide and to Canada, England, France, Africa, and the Caribbean.

Ernest Joshua is a man doing what he loves to do. His father taught him to love the out-of-doors. Courses he took in the Army opened his fascination with chemistry. After the service he put the fascination to work, "mixing up chemicals in my basement," and creating an "on-the-side" exterminating operation. That was in 1949. He was living in Chicago, newly married to his wife, Thelma, and driving a bus for the Chicago Transit Authority.

In a chance, early-morning meeting at a coffee shop, after a CTA night shift, Joshua met George Johnson. Johnson was just beginning his business with Ultrasheen, which today is the number-one seller on the minority hair-care market. "We just got to talking. We had things in common. You know, chemistry is chemistry." The conversations stirred his curiosity. Shortly, from his basement came a hair-care product, instead of insect poisons. A jar of his experiments' results—Raval—sits in his office today.

By 1967 Joshua could afford to drop his bus job. Still making Raval, he went to work as plant manager for another hair-care manufacturer. "That's where I learned more about the business side," he recalls. In 1973 he left that job, sold Raval, and moved to California, working for another company until it was sold in 1976.

That is when he started J.M. Products, manufacturing Style-crest—and when his cancer was diagnosed. Feeling "too far away," in September 1977 he moved his family and business to Arkansas, where he was born and reared until he was six.

The enterprise was in a storefront on East 14th Street in Little Rock, and he and those who were with him then still talk about the open stove burners and converted coffee makers they used to boil up the chemicals and fill the jars by hand. Now more than 20 full- and part-time employees work in a 25,000-square-foot production facility. The equally low-budget marketing—the same folks filling jars loaded them in trailers and "took off in different directions"—soon paid off. Beauty supply houses began to call and ask to stock the product. Now there is a sophisti-

J.M. Products markets Isoplus, a line of 56 cosmetic hair-care items, which are constantly being tested and improved upon.

cated network of sales people, brokers, and technicians across the country, directed by Anthony Riney.

Joshua was not always on the site as the company grew. He was often directing operations, or suggesting formulas from his hospital bed when his cancer recurred. He talks most—in telling the firm's story—about his gratitude to his wife and children, both for help in the illness he has now "arrested" and in their assistance with the operation. "It's a family business. I retired in 1984 and now I let the youngsters run it," he says, speaking of Riney plus sons Ernie Jr., plant manager, and Michael, vice-president. But his dreams still direct the organization. His idol is George Johnson, his old coffee-drinking buddy, and he wants an equal corporation. About his projected $20-million year in 1986 he states, "Our growing is just beginning."

From headquarters in Little Rock, Isoplus is shipped nationwide and to Canada, England, France, Africa, and the Caribbean.

MONARCH MILL AND LUMBER COMPANY

It was a sawmill and a manufacturer of finished lumber. It was deep in the woods, and went no farther than its own backyard for the trees that it cut, dried, planed, and sold. It was Pritchard Lumber Company, which—when it was hit by financial difficulties after 16 years—was acquired by two men who worked there, who incorporated it as Monarch Mill and Lumber Company, in 1919.

Monarch never moved from that site—but it is no longer deep in the woods. Today the five-acre lumberyard and mill is a stone's throw from downtown Little Rock, just west and down the hill from the Arkansas State Capitol, and near a crosstown freeway.

The enterprise has grown through the days of handsaws, mule wagons, and green lumber stacked to air-dry to powered equipment, forklifts, and kilns. For the ancient art of milling wood, it recently purchased a milling machine that represents a $50,000 investment. Most sawmills that once dotted the forests west of Little Rock did not have the chance to mature to such sophistication.

Mack Price, who retired as president of Monarch in 1981, has a memory of the company from 1946. That was the year he went to work there, a young veteran of World War II, learning the trade of draftsman for a $25-per-week salary. Price's recollections are of both the life of the old lumberyard and the business' genealogy.

According to Price the two men who created Monarch Mill and Lumber Company in 1919 were R.H. Sutton, president until 1954, and A.C. Davidson, who served in that position for the following 10 years. The firm's subsequent presidents were E.C. Rorex, 1964-1978; Price, 1978-1981; and James F. Hall, who came in 1981 from a Fort Smith lumber company. Some of the original stockholders were men whose names are familiar in local history: George Worthen,

DeMatt Henderson, Dr. O.K. Judd, and Frank Niemeyer.

When Price arrived in 1946 the mill was cutting its timber in the forests of what is now the Kingwood neighborhood in Little Rock. The company also purchased timber tracts in the Ouachita National Forest. After 1963 Monarch bought its lumber finished, from the large timber operations in Arkansas' forests.

In contrast to the one man who now works in the yard, in the mid-1940s Monarch hired up to 40 people, says Price. He remembers their stamina, pivoting lumber off rail cars and onto stacks that they built 10 feet high. In particular, he recalls the man called Shorty who drove the mule wagon. When the wagon was full and Shorty was riding atop the load, he looked for all the world like a Roman charioteer, Price recalls. They were a fixture at the mill until 1954, the year that both of them—the mule and Shorty—died.

Price laughs about the steam boiler, fired with wood shavings, that powered all the tools in the yard when he first arrived. "OSHA would drop out in horror," he declares. The steam engine had a flywheel, seven feet in diameter, with an 18-inch belt, running the length of the whole mill. A system of pulleys and belts connected all the facility's machinery to the flywheel's belt. A diesel engine replaced the steam engine in the early 1950s, and later in the decade each piece of equipment was fitted with its own electric motor. New equipment began to replace the old in the 1960s.

Two events beyond its control have changed the physical nature of Monarch. One was the digging of the underpass on West Seventh Street in 1936, so local traffic would go under the railroad tracks. The company lost half of a building and some of its property in that dig, but with the money it was reimbursed the firm constructed its current office and salesroom. Another loss of buildings was not as carefully planned—when a tornado touched down nearby in the 1960s.

Today Monarch employs 50 people—in sales, administration, clerical, and delivery, as well as in the mill shop and door manufacturing. The mill custom-manufactures items such as teller counters, checkstands, stairways, mantles, and cabinets. In 1963 Monarch began making prehung doors—the door is built within its frame, leaving a carpenter with little to do but set it in its opening and nail trim around it.

The company's revenue source, Price estimates, is split evenly between the millwork and retail lumber business, with residential construction taking up most of the lumber items. It is an organization in touch with the building needs of today, benefiting from the memory of one who can tell the story of its evolution.

This is Seventh Street with a railroad crossing and Monarch Mill and Lumber Company in the background, in the early 1930s. In 1936 the street was excavated to pass under the railroad tracks. Monarch lost some of its property in the excavation but was compensated by the city.

KARK-TV

To children of the 1950s the memory is indelible. If there was no television at their own home, they found a friend who had one. They had to have their afternoon dose of KARK-TV, Channel 4, the National Broadcasting Corporation's local affiliate. They may not have explained it quite that way, however. More likely they were shouting, with the show's host, "It's Howdy Doody time!"

It was 6 p.m., April 15, 1954, when KARK came on the air. Besides "Howdy Doody," the programming, all in black and white, included "Mr. Peepers" with Wally Cox, "This Is Your Life" with Ralph Edwards, "The Life of Riley" with William Bendix, and "The Paul Winchell Show" with Winchell and Jerry Mahoney.

Within 18 months color telecasting came to Arkansas. The phenomenon might have gone unheralded by the general public, except for the World Series. It was September 28, 1955, and KARK-TV was broadcasting the opening game of the series. It was in color. At the time, TV distributors estimated that only 15 color television sets were owned in the entire central Arkansas area, although they had more orders than they could fill. Consequently, viewers were given an invitation to see the World Series games—for free—at

A KARK-TV camera at a live remote during the 1950s.

the Robinson Auditorium, where RCA had installed color sets.

The man who made that possible, the founder of KARK-TV, was Colonel T.H. Barton, a wealthy El Dorado oilman. The first office for the station was at 10th and Spring streets, where 52 people worked for the firm in its first year. While viewers may not have been aware of other transactions since Barton's founding of the company, in 1966 KARK-TV became part of Mullins Broadcasting, a firm owned by Denver entrepreneur John C. Mullins. At his death the Mullins family sold the station to Karl Eller, of Phoenix, Arizona, and it became a part of Combined Communications Corporation in 1972.

A merger of Combined Communications with the Gannett Corporation in 1979 made KARK-TV a subsidiary of the largest communications company in the United States.

Four years later, on April 13, 1983, SouthwestMedia, Inc., a group of central Arkansas businessmen, purchased the station. KARK-TV was again a locally owned corporation, for the first time since its original ownership. In 1985 the principals of SouthwestMedia, Inc., formed the hold-

ing company, United Broadcasting Corporation, of which KARK-TV became a subsidiary.

Since 1977 KARK-TV, Channel 4, or, as it is also called, NEWS-CENTER 4, has been one of the top five NBC stations in the top 100 markets in America. Its locally produced "Eyewitness News" has consistently been Arkansas' most-watched television newscast. In addition to providing its entertainment and news programming, the company has been deeply involved in other commitments to the community. Examples of its service include the Community Service Awards that recognizes citizens for their volunteer work; the "Letters to Santa" project that provides toys, food, and clothing to families in need during the Christmas season; and the Easter Seal Telethon.

The organization, now operating with 120 employees, continues with technological innovations. From the first station to bring the state color broadcasting of the World Series, in 1955, came stereo broadcasting in 1985. The installation of a new circular polarized antenna and transmitter in November of that year allowed NBC programs that were broadcast in stereo to be similarly transmitted to viewers.

"Dialing for Dollars" at noon during the late 1960s on Channel 4.

STEBBINS & ROBERTS, INC.
MANUFACTURERS OF STERLING 12 STAR PAINT

It only seems fitting that paints coating the first Arkansas State Capitol as well as the state's newest and tallest office building—the 40-story Capitol Tower—were manufactured nearby in the capital city of Little Rock. The subtle hues gracing the Old State House and Capitol Tower are products of Stebbins & Roberts, Inc., which produces its Sterling 12 Star Paint line for distribution to more than 600 retail outlets spread across a nine-state area that encompasses southern and southwestern regions of the United States.

In recent years the firm—which traces its founding back to 1914—has emerged as the largest paint manufacturer in Arkansas and one of the top regional coatings producers in the country. All products are produced at Stebbins & Roberts' modern manufacturing plant on East Sixth Street in Little Rock, a facility spread over three city blocks that includes a sophisticated research laboratory, manufacturing plant, and warehouse facility. In addition, the company operates distribution centers in Fort Worth, Texas, and Oklahoma City, Oklahoma.

Recently, the graphic appeal of Sterling 12 Star Paint products was enhanced with a new signature and colorful labels for paint cans and packaging materials. Yet these new Sterling graphics represent only the tip of improvements, since formulas for virtually all of the firm's products have been enhanced in recent years to provide Sterling Paints with state-of-the-industry qualities for durability and protective coverability.

That's quite a record for a company that traces its origins to a sideline business initiated by A. Howard Stebbins, Sr., in a basement at the old Arcade Building on Louisiana Street in Little Rock. Actually, making paint was a spin-off from a sign business Stebbins began in 1911. Paint production began in 1914, and by 1921 the

business (known then as Stebbins & Goldsmith) had grown to the point that Benjamin Moore & Company, an international paint manufacturer, selected it to become Arkansas distributor for Benjamin Moore paints.

When Gardner Goldsmith retired later in the 1920s, Lindsey Roberts, a brother-in-law to Stebbins, took Goldsmith's place and the corporate name was changed to Stebbins & Roberts, the name that continues to this day, although Roberts sold Stebbins his interest in the enterprise in the 1930s.

During the Depression Stebbins & Roberts expanded its paint manufacture in order to supply the WPA and other projects of the federal government. The increasing demand for paints manufactured by Stebbins & Roberts eventually prompted officials at Benjamin Moore to ask its Arkansas distributor to cease production of these competitive paints. Instead, Stebbins & Roberts accelerated production, introducing a full line of products and marketing them exclusively. In 1946 the company built its Little Rock production facility on East Sixth Street, which later was expanded several times to become Stebbins & Roberts' present home office and manufacturing and distributing center.

The most repeated explanation

for selecting "Sterling 12 Star" as the company's product banner is that Howard Stebbins wanted to honor Sterling Adamson, the company's enterising young sales manager during the Depression era, by naming the paint line after him. Stebbins added the "12 Star" designation to denote one star for each of the products then produced under the Sterling label.

Sterling Adamson eventually became the firm's president, expanding the company to its nine-state distribution area. Upon the death of Adamson in 1973, his son-in-law, attorney Thomas J. Bonner, continued the Adamson family leadership as president until his death in 1982. At that time Bruce Lively, who had joined Stebbins & Roberts in 1975 as sales manager, assumed presidency of the organization and—together with James S. Adamson, M.D., Sterling Adamson's son, who became chairman of the board of the company in 1983—formed an advisory leadership council and guided Stebbins & Roberts to its current position as one of the country's leading regional paint manufacturers.

Sterling 12 Star products, such as the ones featured below, are marketed in a nine-state area. Over 500 independent paint dealers are serviced from distribution centers in Little Rock, Fort Worth, and Oklahoma City.

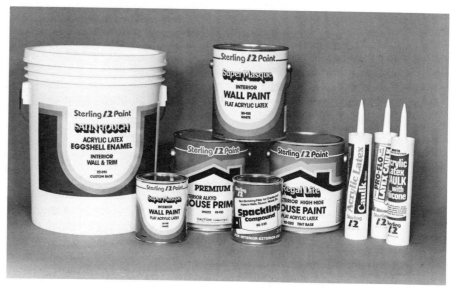

NATIONAL OLD LINE

Bill Darby had vacation time coming in 1929, after five years of working in the press room of *Detroit Free Press.* He used it to drive, in his new Model-T Ford, back home to Arkansas: He wanted his new wife, Maurine, to see his home state. Detroit was soon part of his past, and he was traveling Mississippi County—representing a new, Arkansas-owned insurance company, National Old Line. Darby was to help mold it into one of the nation's top insurance firms.

National Old Line had started three years earlier, in 1926, founded by a group of visionary businessmen who prided themselves on their "conservative outlook." W.F. Ault, the first president, characterized himself as "a capitalist who is conservative enough to be safe, yet progressive enough to be successful." Admonishing early customers to "keep their reserve capital at home," the enterprise saw great growth potential in the South and its upcoming generations.

The optimism of the early days was challenged, however, when the Great Depression struck. Nonetheless, the company managed to survive, even in its infancy, while much larger firms were forced into bankruptcy. The Depression, before the era of the New Deal, brought home to many families the dire straits they could face if the only breadwinner was lost or injured.

It was about that time, armed with a National Old Line rate book and his own belief that insurance was good for others, that Darby set out in drought-stricken Mississippi County. He was not to be daunted. When given the challenge of selling one million dollars of insurance in a year, he met the goal in 128 days.

Darby met and exceeded all the goals that were set for him over the next several years. In 1945 his determination, knowledge of the business, and energy were rewarded. He was pulled out of the

field and made president of National Old Line. His first proclaimed goal in that position was to advance the total insurance in force from $11 million to $100 million by 1954. The goal was met a year early.

The company's growth necessitated new headquarters, built in 1955 facing the Arkansas State Capitol. It was designed with expansion in mind; and 10 years later, when the main office work force had grown to 200, an additional wing and stories were added. That spurt of growth was accounted for, in part, by a merger in 1960 with National Equity Life Insurance Company, which extended operations into a total of 30 states.

By the time of Darby's 1966 retirement as president, National Old Line was among the top 7 percent of insurance companies nationally. Three years later another milestone was passed—having one billion dollars of insurance in force. The second billion was achieved in 1971; the third in 1975.

Throughout its 60-year history National Old Line has maintained its headquarters in Little Rock, moving to this building across from the Arkansas State Capitol in 1955.

Throughout its 60 years the firm has maintained its headquarters in Little Rock. With five billion dollars in assets, National Old Line was purchased in January 1982 by the ENNIA group, a Dutch holding company comprised of organizations engaged in life insurance, general insurance, and noninsurance operations. In 1983 the group became known as Aegon, with headquarters at The Hague, in the Netherlands. Today Arkansas' homegrown insurance agency is part of the second-largest insurance organization in the Netherlands, and one of the largest in the European economic community.

With the vision of its early founders and Bill Darby's energetic expertise, National Old Line Insurance Company has made its impact on the insurance industry felt well beyond Arkansas' borders.

JONES TRUCK LINES, INC.

When the Missouri-Arkansas Railroad went on strike in 1918, Harvey Jones went to work. What the railways didn't haul, he would. He hitched up one red mule and one black mule to a Springfield wagon, loaded it with groceries and hardware from wholesale houses in Rogers, Arkansas, and hauled the loads to Springdale, Arkansas, 10 miles away. The round-trip ride took him from 10 to 14 hours.

Adding Fayetteville-Springdale to his rounds later in the year, the 18-year-old Arkansas farm boy doubled the distance and time he was traveling.

Jones' commitment to hauling was sealed the next year when he sold his wagon and both mules, and bought a truck—a used, hard-tired Federal—to haul lumber and lime. Calling himself the Jones Transportation Company, the young man expanded his route and began to serve the towns of Fort Smith, Arkansas, and Joplin and Springfield, Missouri.

The enterprise kept growing. In 1933 it became Jones Truck Lines, with terminals at Fort Smith and Little Rock, Arkansas; Joplin, Springfield, and Kansas City, Missouri; and Tulsa, Oklahoma. The old Federal truck had had numerous successors by then. In 1936, the same year a new masonry office was built in Springdale, Jones Truck Lines had an inventory of 33 International trucks.

Some of those vehicles were cool enough for hauling meat long distances, because Jones Truck Lines was a pioneer in refrigerated transportation. In 1935—with 55-gallon drums loaded with ice and sawdust in the corners of 22-foot trailers—the company started hauling meat from Swifts in Kansas City to Fort Smith, Little Rock, and northwest Arkansas, where it picked up chickens in Springdale and hauled them back to Swifts. Ice remained the coolant until 1943, when the first mechanical refrigeration units were put into use.

Above
Jones Truck Lines' present-day equipment. This 1985 photo shows a set of over-the-road units called doubles.

Right
Harvey Jones is shown in his first truck in 1919. He is honorary chairman of the board today.

In the early part of World War II, Jones purchased routes to St. Louis and Memphis; then expansion halted until three years after the war, at which time the firm acquired a route between Fort Smith and Oklahoma City, with a stop in Muskogee. By the time it was incorporated in 1949, Jones was the largest individually owned and operated truck line in the country—a long way from its first mule-drawn wagon days, but not as large as it was to become.

Jones Truck Lines is now a computerized, 2,600-vehicle trucking company that specializes in transporting what is called general commodity, less-than-truckload (LTL) freight. It operates in 21 states of the South, with blanket service to Arkansas, Tennessee, Mississippi, Illinois, Alabama, and Louisiana. With 115 terminals and 2,500 employees, the corporation in 1984 grossed more than $153 million.

A Memphis employee collected the 1984 company statistics, and made a graphic metaphor of the work done by Jones: The 2,183,394,000 pounds of freight that the firm hauled over 38 million miles that year was, said the employee, equal to six trips around the world at the equator, every day.

Jones not only carries many pounds over many miles but does it well, according to *Distribution* magazine's Carrier Marketing Awards. It gave the company top-10 billing in best in service, best in pricing, best in promotion/communication, and best in convenience categories among regional carriers. Jones was called, in 1984, 1985, and 1986 the leading regional carrier in the country.

Sun Carriers, Inc., a part of Sun Oil Company, bought Jones Truck Lines in 1980. With four other regional trucking firms as subsidiaries, Sun Carriers allows Jones to be linked with all parts of the nation. However, growth and computerization does not mean that the Springfield wagon days have been forgotten. The wagon is on display near Grove, Oklahoma, at Har-Ber Village—the pioneer village that Harvey and Bernice Jones began in the late 1960s, open to visitors for free. And Springdale, Arkansas, where it all began, is still the Jones Truck Lines headquarters.

COLEMAN DAIRY, INC.

Eleithet B. Coleman, founder, making deliveries from his horse-drawn wagon through the streets of downtown Little Rock.

The intersection of University and Asher in Little Rock, with a shopping center on each corner, has little hint of the pastoral calm of a dairy farm. However, W.C. "Buddy" Coleman, Jr., chairman of Coleman Dairy, remembers one nearby. He remembers a herd of cattle grazing there, and his parents rising at three o'clock each morning to milk the cows. His recollections also include horse-drawn delivery wagons and, later, one of the three pickup trucks he drove as a teenager, stopping at an ice house to pack down the milk before heading into town.

Buddy Coleman does not remember his grandfather or great-grandfather, just stories about them. The latter, Eleithet B. Coleman, established the family dairy in the 1860s. Like other farmers with dairy cows near Little Rock, Eleithet drove to town in his wagon—stopping at houses and pouring his raw milk into containers that customers brought out from their homes. An accident at Seventh and Scott streets, when his own horse kicked him in the head, ended Eleithet's life, but not the dairy operation. His son, Fred, continued; then W.C. Coleman, Sr., in the next generation, took over.

Recalling five other family dairies that were within 10 miles of his family's farm when he was growing up, Buddy Coleman is not sure why, today, his forefathers' enterprise is the last of such dairies its size in the state—but he attributes it to his father's and brother's foresight.

In the late 1930s his brother, Boots, agreed to join the operation on the condition that the dairy pasteurize its milk. Despite a fear that the new process could ruin the milk's taste, the dairy made the change—and with the change, began to mature as a business. The father and son erected a new plant on the farm in 1946 and, when sales increased, decided to sell their own herd and buy milk from local producers. They made their first merger in 1948 with the neighboring C.S. Douglass Dairy.

The 1950s brought a giant spurt of growth to the firm, partly attributable to sponsorship of the Annie Oakley television show. Owned by Gene Autry, the show starred a Little Rock native and friend of the Coleman family. At commercial breaks the young actress told viewers, "When I'm back home in Arkansas, I drink Coleman milk." The dairy's name recognition boomed. Locally, a company employee visited the city's newcomers, giving them sample products and encouraging their use of Coleman's delivery service.

The Quality Chekd Dairy Products Association selected Coleman as the Quality Chekd Dairy for Arkansas in 1960, giving it a common trademark used by other independent dairies in the United States and Canada. In the late 1960s and 1970s growth continued through consolidations with OK Dairy and Ice Cream Company in Pine Bluff, Dixon and Midwest Dairies in Little Rock, and Ouachita Valley Dairy in Camden.

Boots Coleman was president and chairman of the organization when he died in 1971. Buddy, who joined the company in 1953, is the current chairman; his son Walt succeeded him as president in 1985. Two other sons, Cherb and Bob, are transportation manager and ice cream sales manager, respectively. They are the fifth generation of the family to run the operation, and they—as the Colemans before them—grew up within 20 yards of the dairy facilities.

It is a different dairy from the one of milk pails and crocks, though it stands on the same site 12 decades later. Now there is a fleet of 107 trucks, a roll of 300 employees, and daily processing of 50,000 gallons of milk. Branch facilities are in Batesville, Camden, Forrest City, Hot Springs, Jonesboro, Morrilton, and Pine Bluff. Coleman emerged from a family farm to become a leader among dairies in the Southwest, and a sixth generation is in grooming to maintain the family tradition.

The 200-acre Coleman Dairy Farm, located on what is now Asher Avenue and just east of University Avenue, as it looked during the 1930s. Today Coleman Dairy operates one of the most modern dairy and ice cream processing and distributing plants in the United States on this same site.

BEACH ABSTRACT COMPANY

The mystery of old Spanish land grants and Indian burial grounds is part of a Beach abstracter's work everyday. So is the drama of contested wills and neighbor suing neighbor. E.A. Bowen, president of Beach Abstract Company, contends there is even humor in the mass of material that an abstracter pulls together. That mystery, drama, and humor—plus the Little Rock history that comes to life in a title search—are part of what has kept Bowen fascinated with his job since 1947.

The purpose of abstracts may, admittedly, sound dry: to assure owners of land that they have a clear and unencumbered title to their property. That is determined by checking every legal transaction for a piece of property, including ownership changes (by grants, purchase, inheritance, or forfeit), mortgages, lawsuits, and taxes—paid or unpaid. All of this information is recorded and filed at the courthouse. The abstracter then copies the information into his own books, which are organized by the legal description of a piece of property.

Beach Abstract Company has been doing this kind of work longer than any other abstract firm in Little Rock. The business got its start in 1877 when Beach, a civil engineer and native of New York, came to Little Rock. He was 28 years old and had just returned from a government surveying job in Panama—where a canal would eventually be dug. Beach incorporated his company in 1882.

Twelve years later he was one of the original directors and organizers, and second vice-president, of Peoples Building and Loan Association (later Peoples Savings and Loan, which merged with First Federal). Beach died in 1909, and that year his firm was merged with the Arkansas Abstract Company. It retained the Beach name, and W.E. Lenon was elected its president. Lenon also was president of Peoples Savings Bank (later First National Bank, now First Commercial). Chancellor Frank Dodge and John E. Martineau, governor of the state and later a federal district judge, were directors on the Beach Abstract Company board in the early 1900s. Today the board chairman and chief executive officer is George Pitts.

Since 1877 the firm has had four addresses, always within the same two-block area of downtown, bounded by Markham, Louisiana, Second, and Center streets. In the late 1970s Beach Abstract Company opened its first branch office, in North Little Rock. Later offices were opened on West Markham and in Benton in 1981, and in Hot Springs in 1985.

Bowen says that today only 10 percent of the firm's work involved literally making abstracts. The balance is title insurance and escrow. Title insurance involves the same examination of records, but the abstracter only describes on a search sheet what was found and does not type up the voluminous book that an abstract often becomes. Lending institutions, especially out-of-state organizations, require the title insurance rather than an abstract because they consider it safer. Beach Abstract represents agents for several of the largest title insurance companies in the nation. However, the predominance of title insurance in the firm's history is relatively new. Even in 1977, Beach Abstract Company's 100th year, the call for abstracts made up 50 percent of its work.

A model of the future home of Beach Abstract Company, to be completed in December 1986.

JACUZZI INC.

Jacuzzi is an international corporation, headquartered in Little Rock, taking pride in its decision to become part of the strength of Arkansas. The company began its fruitful association with the state in 1963, bringing its own illustrious history from California, together with an honored reputation for quality and value, ingenuity and invention. In fact, in the pumps and water systems industry and other water-related fields, Jacuzzi had become known as "The Innovator."

The company's roots were planted around the turn of the century when seven immigrant brothers from Casarsa, Italy, a small town near Milan, started to look for a place to use their extraordinary talents and abilities to full advantage. First two of them and then singly, they came to the United States, and finally the entire Jacuzzi family, brothers, sisters, and parents, settled around the San Francisco Bay area.

The brothers immediately had set out to find work—on farms, in machine shops, anywhere they could. Rachel was the oldest, and only one word can describe him—genius! He determined that the new aviation industry was where he could best use his scientific expertise and inventiveness, and he perfected a way of manufacturing wooden airplane propellers by laminating them of layers of wood.

This proved the starting point for Jacuzzi Bros. Inc. In 1915 Rachel was awarded a contract by the infant Army Air Corps, and his brothers quickly joined him in the new business venture. With the U.S. declaration of war in 1917, thousands of the new propellers came pouring out of the hastily provided Jacuzzi facilities. But when World War I ended, propeller orders quickly faded.

Manufacturing propellers for warplanes, however, had whetted the brothers' interest in aviation. Soon their energy and ingenuity

The Jacuzzi brothers founded Jacuzzi Bros. Inc. in 1915 to manufacture airplane propellers for the newly formed Army Air Corps.

were busily engaged in the private sector of the new industry. With Rachel as the guiding genius, the brothers designed and built a tiny, single-seat monoplane that was quickly followed by a second plane, recorded in aviation history as the first successful, fully enclosed high-wing monoplane to be built and flown in the United States. After several flights, the plane proved to be of sound design and the Jacuzzi brothers made plans to manufacture it, but when 26-year-old Giocondo Jacuzzi was killed while a passenger on the final test flight, the surviving brothers, upon the urging of their parents, abandoned aviation plans and turned to other things.

The following period was a difficult one for the young firm, even threatening its existence. However, the inventiveness and perseverance of Rachel and his brothers began to pay off in the development of other products. One of the many experiments concerned the application of the tip-jet principle of powering propeller-driven aircraft and an early version of the helicopter. A tiny steam injector used in this research produced the germ of an idea that proved the turning point for Jacuzzi Bros. Inc. The idea eventually resulted in the jet or injector pump which revolutionized the pumps and water systems industry!

In 1926 the company built its first jet pump, and Jacuzzi had begun its long relationship with the pumps and water systems industry. Buyers quickly recognized that these new pumps were more durable and efficient than the pumps offered by competitors. In recognition of this entirely new product, Jacuzzi in 1930 was awarded a gold medal for "Meritorious Invention" by the State of California. Soon a variety of Jacuzzi pumps—turbines, centrifugals, submersibles—began to appear in the marketplace as innovation followed innovation. Then in 1937 Rachel Jacuzzi died at the early age of 51. But even the loss of this key figure in the company's early life didn't slow its progress.

As more was learned through experience and experimentation, new developments and inventions crowded one upon the other. Increasingly, Jacuzzi was looked upon as "The Innovator," and new and improved products became expected from the firm. California wine makers, for example, liked Jacuzzi pumps, but they wanted filters to go with them. So, Jacuzzi entered the filter business, presaging their eventual advance into the swimming pool equipment market.

With buyers demanding more and more Jacuzzi products, the company outgrew its early facilities, which consisted of a 10-room house and rented stores in Berkeley, California. New headquarters were located in a brick factory on Berkeley's San Pablo Avenue.

World War II necessitated a temporary halt to pump production, and Jacuzzi aided the war effort by supplying submarine valves to the U.S. Navy. But war's end saw a pentup demand for pumps, and production soared. By 1947 the company expanded to a $2-million factory on 10 acres in Richmond, California; and by this time eastern states vied with the West in demanding Jacuzzi pumps. To serve them Jacuzzi opened a factory in St. Louis.

The old plant in Berkeley, however was still retained. It was needed to manufacture the product that was to make Jacuzzi a household word—the famous Jacuzzi Whirlpool Bath. The product was developed by Candido Jacuzzi to provide hydrotherapy for his youngest son, Kenny, who had been stricken by arthritis at two years of age. From this beginning, which grew out of a small boy's need, a new industry has been created, adding an entirely new dimension to leisure living.

In 1955 Jacuzzi, already providing pumps and filters to the swimming pool industry, entered fully into that market, offering distributors and dealers a complete line of swimming pool equipment. At the same time the firm was producing new improvements and patents on Jacuzzi pumps—ideas that incidentally were quickly adapted by the rest of the pump industry. Today approximately two-thirds of all domestic pumps sold in the world are jet pumps, all lineal descendants of that first Jacuzzi Jet Pump invented by Rachel Jacuzzi.

In 1962 Jacuzzi developed a marine jet drive unit for the boating industry in a range of sizes to power anything from a small pleasure boat to the largest work boat.

Some of the 410 people employed at the Jacuzzi Inc. plant at Little Rock.

A modification of the mixed flow turbine pump, this unit was selected by the U.S. Navy during the Vietnam War to equip a fleet of newly developed light patrol boats, the first time in naval history that jet propulsion was used.

The constant growth soon convinced Jacuzzi executives that a new location was needed for the international headquarters. In 1963 Little Rock was chosen. The California site, it was felt, had been giving the company a West Coast image rather than a national one. Additionally, Jacuzzi decided it could service its eastern distribution outlets better from this new central location.

Ray Horan, who in 1968 had become the first Jacuzzi president outside of the family and who only recently retired from the presidency of Jacuzzi Inc., recalls that when he and other company members were scouting for a new location they had had a pleasant surprise in the attitude of the Little Rock community and in the cooperation of the Chamber of Commerce and city and state officials. He says, "The then-new Arkansas Industrial Development Commission under Winthrop Rockefeller's leadership was well structured and quite effective. The incentives were appealing to a new industry." He speculates, "Without such a plan as that in effect, we would not have ended up locating here."

In 1979 the Jacuzzi family decided to sell their entire organization to a group of companies with the corporate name of Kidde, Inc. The companies share Kidde's financial strength, but remain highly auton-

omous. They make the day-to-day decisions on what products to make and what markets to serve.

As a result of the Kidde acquisition, Jacuzzi Bros. Inc. was reorganized to become Jacuzzi Inc., a wholly owned subsidiary of Kidde, Inc. As the corporate policymaker, Jacuzzi Inc. coordinates the operations of the Jacuzzi Bros. Division in Little Rock; Jacuzzi Whirlpool Bath, Inc., in California; Jacuzzi plants in Brazil, Chile, Canada, Italy; and the Jacuzzi Export Division, headquartered in Little Rock. The corporation also owns an interest in Jacuzzi Universal, S.A., in Monterrey, Mexico.

Jacuzzi Bros. Division, employing 410 people, is headed by Harold Phillips, who joined Jacuzzi in 1983 as executive vice-president and general manager and was named president in 1986. Phillips states categorically that Jacuzzi is still dedicated to the innovative policies of its founders. As a graphic illustration, he presents Jacuzzi's latest innovation—solar-powered pumps. These are of special interest to Third World countries lacking electrical power. Mainland China, for example, was so interested that it sent a special delegation to Little Rock to contract with Jacuzzi for its new solar pumps.

From today's solar pumps to yesterday's famous Jacuzzi "toothpick" airplane propellers—Jacuzzi has always meant innovation; and if anyone would like further proof of the company's ingenuity and invention, he or she need only visit the U.S. Patent Office, which can document approximately 300 patents in the company's name.

BEST FOODS
A DIVISION OF CPC INTERNATIONAL INC.

In 1977 Little Rock welcomed to Arkansas one of the best-known food brands in America—Skippy peanut butter. Best Foods, a division of CPC International Inc., had chosen the state and a site in Little Rock's Port Authority Industrial Park for its newest peanut butter-producing facility.

Local and even national interest in the new Skippy plant was keen from the beginning. Not only did the plant boast a highly sophisticated technical system for peanut butter production, it was also the proving ground for a new system of plant organization—one in which production and office employees assume broad responsibilities traditionally allocated to supervisors.

A philosophy statement, issued while the plant was under construction, said this: "The goal is to develop a plant society that encourages each individual to maximize his or her contribution to the objectives of the organization while, at the same time, satisfying his or her needs as an individual." In practice, this means that employees at Best Foods' Little Rock plant are encouraged to develop skills and experience that earn them increasingly important roles in work-place problem solving and decision making.

The facility's approximately 110 employees work in teams, within which individual employees take on various assignments, depending upon the group's objectives. In addition to the necessary operational tasks, these might include making work assignments, handling people-related problems, scheduling work to meet production needs, or training other employees in new skills.

This system of "participative management" has attracted the interest of various publications and many professionals in organizational planning. One publication described the plant as "an example of the new, sociotechnical systems that will transform both the U.S. work place and the American work force—if the idea catches fire."

Skippy peanut butter was first commercially produced in 1933 in Alameda, California, under the banner of the Rosefield Packing Company. J.L. Rosefield, the

The Best Foods plant in Little Rock, Arkansas.

firm's president, had earlier perfected a process to prevent oil separation in peanut butter by using hydrogenated peanut oil as a replacement for a portion of the natural peanut oil. Skippy quickly took a leading position among the several dozen peanut butter brands then on the market.

Over the following 20 years additional innovations and patents in peanut butter processing provided Skippy with advantages in shelf life, flavor, and spreadability. In 1955 Best Foods—today's producer of such well-known products as Hellmann's and Best Foods mayonnaise, Mazola corn oil, Mazola margarine, and Karo syrups—acquired Rosefield Packing and the Skippy brand. Under Best Foods, Skippy expanded its markets while maintaining its insistence on the highest-quality ingredients and manufacturing practices.

The production of Skippy today begins with the purchase of U.S. Grade Number One peanuts, primarily of the "Runner" variety. Their quality is rigorously controlled—along the chain of testing that carries them from the farmer's field through the USDA con-

An employee examines peanuts before they are processed into Skippy peanut butter. Every peanut must be of the highest quality.

trol laboratories and then through Best Foods' own inspection system.

The actual manufacturing process involves, first, roasting the raw shelled peanuts. The peanuts are cooled; then their outer skins are removed and they are split. Again, they are inspected, both visually and electronically.

Next, the peanuts are ground (twice, in fact, to ensure smooth texture), and small, carefully controlled amounts of salt, dextrose, and sugar are added for the distinctive Skippy flavor. Chunk-style peanut butter is made by adding bits of chopped peanuts to the finished creamy-style mixture. Finally, Skippy is packed and shipped.

The Little Rock Best Foods plant supplies nearly 100 million pounds of Skippy annually to outlets primarily in the central part of the United States. Some Little Rock-produced Skippy travels, however, as far as the East and West coasts. Sister plants in Portsmouth, Virginia, and Santa Fe Springs, California, supply the northeastern United States and the West Coast, respectively.

Best Foods' roots in the Little Rock area continue to grow. A landscape award, presented by the City Beautiful Commission of Little Rock in 1984, recognizes the visual and environmental contribution the handsome one-story plant and its 25-acre site have made to the community. As employer and as neighbor, Best Foods and Skippy peanut butter are at home in Arkansas.

A Best Foods employee checks to be sure that each jar of Skippy peanut butter contains the correct amount of the product.

ARKANSAS BLUE CROSS AND BLUE SHIELD, INC.

In Dallas, Texas, in 1929, a group of teachers developed an agreement with Baylor University Hospital. They each paid the hospital 50 cents per month, and in turn were guaranteed three weeks of hospital care annually.

The teachers were voluntarily prepaying medical and hospital expenses, to offset unexpected bills, and their idea quickly gained attention in the nation. By the mid-1930s the first Blue Cross Plans had been established in New York and Minnesota.

It was in the late 1940s in Arkansas that the need for voluntary prepayment of health care expenses attracted the notice of a group of farm and business leaders, physicians, and hospital administrators. They selected the Blue Cross and Blue Shield concept, and, in December 1948 Arkansas Medical and Hospital Service, Inc.—later changed to Arkansas Blue Cross and Blue Shield, Inc.—was formed. Its initial financing was from a $14,425 loan from the Arkansas Hospital Association, a $5,000 loan from the Arkansas Medical Society, and a $5,000 loan from the Arkansas Farm Bureau Federation.

Under the leadership of Jack L. Redheffer, the first full-time director; Ellery C. Gay, M.D., the first president; and a founding board of 18 trustees, the company began offering memberships. For a family premium of $4.35 per month, the first group contracts offered hospital benefits of $5 per day, for up to 30 days, and medical benefits of up to $175 for surgery. The firm operated from a one-room office on the eighth floor of the Rector Building, in downtown Little Rock; however, by the end of its first year of operation, with a membership of 32,000, the staff had increased to 15 people and the one-room office was outgrown.

In 1955—when John Rowland was executive director, and Arkansas membership had risen to 200,000—Arkansas Blue Cross and Blue Shield constructed its own two-story home office building at Sixth and Gaines streets. By this time enrollment nationally was 50 million. Voluntary prepayment had taken hold as a concept, and Blue Cross Blue Shield was the recognized leader.

In 1966 the Medicare program was instituted, and Arkansas Blue Cross and Blue Shield was selected to administer the state's operation. By the end of the 1960s, under the leadership of Sam Butler, president, and Waldo Frasier, chairman of the board of trustees, membership had doubled to 400,000.

The 1970s presented the organization with volatile changes in health care delivery and financing. With advances in medical science and technology, additional—better—care was available. However, inflationary spirals hit the economy at the same time, and health insurance became an essential—but a very expensive—commodity.

Leading Arkansas Blue Cross and Blue Shield at this time were Robert P. Taylor, president from 1971 to 1975, and John P. Price, M.D., chairman of the board of trustees during most of the decade.

By the company's 25th anniversary in 1974, membership exceeded 500,000. Private claim payments were more than $50 million, and Medicare claim payments were about $100 million. A staff of 600 had processed one million claims.

A landmark event came with the dedication of the new 11-story structure alongside the headquarters building.

When Dr. George K. Mitchell-current president of Arkansas Blue Cross and Blue Shield—took office in 1975, he was confronted with a 20-percent increase in the cost of medical care services. For the company and its customers, such costs had reached crisis proportions.

In his first annual report Dr. Mitchell addressed cost containment as the number-one corporate priority. At the same time he pointed out that rational and effective cost containment would require a proactive coalition among those who receive care, those who provide it, and those who pay for it. He wrote, "For medical care is but one ingredient in the broader issue of health care and the cost of good health care for our state and nation is a product not only of medical care cost but the interwoven consequences of our total economy, medical technology, health care planning, public education, housing, politics—even our

When Arkansas Blue Cross and Blue Shield first flew this banner over the Main and Markham streets intersection in downtown Little Rock, it was just beginning to be known in Arkansas. Today Blue Cross and Blue Shield serves nearly half of the people who call Arkansas home.

Three men who have given Arkansas Blue Cross and Blue Shield its direction are Sam Butler (left), who served as executive director from 1958 to 1972; H.T. Gardner (center), executive vice-president and chief operating officer, who joined the plan in 1950; and Dr. George K. Mitchell (right), president and chief executive officer since 1975.

habits and life-styles."

The search in the latter half of the 1970s for more effective cost-containment measures resulted in a variety of initiatives designed to strengthen corporate influence, public accountability, and utilization controls. At the policy level, public representation on the board of trustees was increased from six to 13 members. A network of eight Subscriber Advisory Councils around the state was created to gain broader customer input into the planning and operations of the organization. A "Feeling Good" campaign was launched for the purpose of encouraging more wholesome life-styles. Company spokesmen were speaking out more clearly about the costly consequences of the growing excess in hospital bed supply in the state.

Then, in 1979 and 1980, these and other cost-containment efforts were overshadowed by the devastating effects of the general economy. Double-digit inflation was the major cause of dramatic increases in health care costs. During these two years alone, benefit payments exceeded income by more than nine million dollars.

Despite the eventual economic recovery, concerns over continued high costs for the future prompted the formation of the Arkansas Commission on Health Care Cost Effectiveness in 1981.

Through the company's leadership, including that of the new board chairman, Louis L. Ramsay, Jr., Arkansas Blue Cross and Blue Shield extended a $100,000 grant for the establishment of this independent study commission. Its report in 1983 comprised a variety of recommendations to improve access and control costs. Many of those recommendations were subsequently implemented by the corporation.

During the first half of the 1980s, the firm devoted most of its efforts toward positively influencing the structure and behavior of the health care delivery and financing system. Innovation and adaptation through sound planning were the key ingredients. In addition, the competitive climate, plus the interest and cooperation of increasing numbers of physicians and hospitals in developing alternate delivery and financing systems, paved the way for a broader portfolio of health care and fringe benefit products.

Diversification and broadening the product portfolio included the formation of a life insurance subsidiary, Life of Arkansas; the introduction of the Preferred Payment Plan, in which more than 85 percent of the state's physicians participate; and establishing alternate delivery systems such as the Pri-

mary Care Network and HMO Arkansas. For customers who were self-funded, the company established a subsidiary third-party administrator operation that would offer administration of both traditional and alternate delivery products. During the 1980s the organization also became one of the country's most efficient and low-cost contractors in the Medicare program.

By its 35th anniversary the company had positioned itself as the leading health and fringe benefit provider in the state. From its infancy it has grown to the point of employing more than 1,000 Arkansans, with an annual payroll of nearly $22 million in 1986. In addition to 650,000 private customers served in the state's sesquicentennial year, there are 360,000 Medicare beneficiaries. More than six million claims are processed, with private and government program benefits exceeding one billion dollars.

The Arkansas sesquicentennial is a proud period for the state and its people. Arkansas Blue Cross and Blue Shield shares in this pride and is pleased to have been one of many Arkansas enterprises that have contributed to and benefited from our Land of Opportunity. In the memory of the organization's determined founders, and on behalf of its leaders, customers, and employees over the years, Arkansas Blue Cross and Blue Shield, Inc., joins in celebrating the past and in shaping a bright future for Arkansas and its people.

ARKANSAS MODIFICATION CENTER

About twice a month two pilots fly out of England in an unpainted, uninsulated, 10-passenger plane— bare of seats, walls, floors—and head for Little Rock, Arkansas. The plane has no radar or automatic pilot. Its instrument panel is even borrowed for the flight. The cockpit, defined by a lead curtain that hangs behind the pilots, is heated by a hand-rigged hose bringing air from the engine to the cockpit. By the time the pilots land in Little Rock, the interior on the other side of the lead curtain is often glazed in ice.

Fifteen weeks later that same airplane is one of the most stylish corporate offices in the world, and beneath its carpeted floor is wiring for the most sophisticated aviation technology available. The plane can guide itself from one airport to another, and make adjustments along its route if turbulence ensues. It has an instrument panel custom designed for the pilot of the plane. The cabin—now completely insulated for sound and temperature—is color coordinated from its ultra-suede cornices to its sometimes handwoven carpets, with custom-designed wood cabinetry and touches of leather and gold. One of its seats is likely contoured to the body of a frequent passenger— usually the chief executive officer of one of America's largest corporations.

Like the British ferry pilots, the

The empty, unpainted planes flown to Ark Mod from England or Canada are called "green airplanes." Fifteen weeks later they have been painted with the company's corporate identity and wired with the latest aviation technology.

chief executive officer will have flown into Little Rock, too—to be fitted for the seat and, while there, to discuss the design of the cabin as it is being conceived and executed.

The tranformation from an empty ice-coated plane to an office-in-the-sky for one of America's corporate leaders is called airplane modification. The industry concensus is that the best airplane modification available in the country is at Arkansas Modification Center— or Ark Mod, as it is called. It is one of only two independent modification centers in the country, and small, by industry standards. It does its work on two planes—the

Hawker, made by British Aerospace, and the Canadair Challenger from Canada. It also refurbishes planes completed earlier.

In a world where streamlining and mass production is the by-word, this company breaks the rules—and, because it does, wins contracts with the country's industrial giants. They appreciate the personal service and the consideration given their tastes. Sometimes they send their own interior designer to work with Ark Mod's designers because they want the plane's interior coordinated with the design of the corporate headquarters. This is possible at Ark Mod, where every part of a plane's interior—seen and unseen—is custom designed.

"We use as few outside vendors as possible," says Dennis Davis, president of Ark Mod since 1983. "We like being self sufficient. I guess we're sort of old-countryish." It's an ironic label to give a company that won distinction in 1984 for assembling the first all-digital business jet in the world. But there is truth in the label. After buying metal frames for the planes' seats, for instance, Ark Mod upholsterers, working with six different densities of foam, contour it onto the frames, then cover it with the customers' choice of fabric or

Most Arkansas Modification Center employees, who complete business jets for America's corporate giants, come from central Arkansas.

Almost everything done to complete business jets at Ark Mod is done on the premises; little is subcontracted. They are handcrafted planes in a high-tech industry.

leather. They usually build in the integral headrest that they invented for seats—meeting an FAA regulation with creativity. Meanwhile, other employees are at Ark Mod's own vacuum press, molding frames for the airplanes' windows, and others are painting—applying a corporate identity to the planes' exteriors with specially designed colors and stripes. The cabinetmakers are building storage compartments, walls, the galley, applying wood veneer to composites or basswood—mindful of weight limitations. The engineers are making four copies of the schematic drawings of all the electrical systems with the aircraft, while other engineers are actually wiring the planes. In two hangars and three buildings at Little Rock's Adams Field, Ark Mod has creative people at work in many fields of the arts and sciences, all in an effort to bring high technology and luxury to busy corporate leaders.

Business aviation is an industry that dates to the mid-1940s, just after the war. Industries with satellite companies in remote parts of the country—as the South was then—needed private planes for access to their factories. In recent years airline deregulation again makes small communities harder to reach by commercial travel. The need for corporate jets continues, saving executives hours, even days, of time.

The investment in their time-saving vehicle is high. Customers have already paid from $7 to $12 million for a plane before delivering it to Ark Mod, where the engineering and interior completion costs anywhere from $1.5 to $2 million.

With aerospace centered on the West Coast and the bulk of corporate America in the North and Northeast, how is it that British and Canadian corporate jets, chief executive officers of *Fortune* 100 and 200 companies, even Saudi Arabian millionaires are flying into

Little Rock for this service?

It's "all coincidence," Davis says, but he sees advantages to Ark Mod's being in Arkansas, now that it has grown up here. In a building at Adams Field now occupied by Falcon Jet of France, a company called Little Rock Airmotive started a fixed-base operation in 1960, also selling aircraft. They added the modification service later. When Fred Smith, a relative unknown at the time, began operating Federal Express in Little Rock, he contracted with Little Rock Airmotive for modification of the jets he was using—he needed cargo doors where the passenger doors were. Smith eventually bought the company.

Four men who were working with Little Rock Airmotive wanted to stay in the industry, but also wanted to stay in Little Rock, and Smith was moving to Memphis. In 1974 the four—Lucien Taillac, Roland Corriveau, Dick Copeland, and Ed Hendon—began Arkansas Modification Center. They had one customer with one plane, but built the company to modifying 20 to 24 planes a year.

It is those four who set the standards that made Ark Mod unique in the industry (there were about nine other independent centers at the time) and, in the early 1980s, when they were considering selling the business, they wanted buyers who would maintain the smallness and personal touch that allows Ark Mod its quality work. Dennis Davis and Warren Stephenson, Davis' partner until recently, shared the belief in that value. The firm still modifies fewer than 30 planes per year. "We could have grown larger, and doubtless will, but very, very gradually," Davis says, contrasting the care that his employees give their work with that of someone in a larger, more impersonal factory.

That is when he mentions the value of the Arkansas location for the company. "People here in the South, in Arkansas, have a work

ethic that you don't find on the coasts," Davis observes, adding that outsiders also have an image of quality craftsmanship coming out of Arkansas. He calls it "down home care. It has a tremendous amount of appeal."

Not only does it have appeal, but the customers appreciate it. Davis quotes a corporate president, after visiting with the man making his plane's card table, "Hey, you people really take personal pride in what you're doing." The value of that contact goes both ways. The chief executive officer is impressed, and the woodworker gets to know the person who will use the table—and inevitably puts more into the piece. If the firm grew too large, that special communication would be lost, and it's the personal trust that Ark Mod develops with its clients that makes the company, Davis says.

Asked to comment on Ark Mod's role in the state's economy, Davis replies, "I always say we're an importer of money. These people bring us something they bought, we load it up, and then they leave—never even using our highway system—and they leave money. It provides a good living for 250 people." The Ark Mod employees are mostly from central Arkansas, a point Davis likes to stress. "We could bring them in from the West Coast, but they'd be gone in a year or two," he says. So it remains to Arkansans to keep giving "down home care" to the nation's top business leaders. Judging by the repeat business, it is care they appreciate.

BEMBERG IRON WORKS, INC.

One of the present leaders of Bemberg Iron Works says he didn't know his grandfather, the firm's founder. "But, oh, I wish so many times that I had known him. They say he was such a gentle man—quite a businessman along with that—but such a gentle man."

Then a memory comes back of a "great big man," with "a great big mustache," always wearing "a great big black hat." It is his young-boy impression of the grandfather who died when he was six, who sometimes took him to the First Lutheran Church at Eighth and Rock, to the eight o'clock German service.

However, he didn't know "gran'pa," Julius Bemberg, in his prime, as the head of Bemberg Ironworks—the position he, Herman Bemberg, Jr., holds today. Stories have survived, though. Herman Jr. cautions that it is "word-of-mouth" history, but he thinks that it is accurate.

Julius Bemberg was working for Krupp Ironworks in Essen, Germany—"the armorers of the world at that time"—when Otto Von Bismark's interest in conscripting young Germans into his Prussian Army convinced the young man that it was time to move on. Like many Germans in the 1870s and 1880s, he found his way to Arkansas, settling in Little Rock and working for the Iron Mountain Railroad.

In 1885 Bemberg established a blacksmith shop at Second and Rock streets. The work ranged from horseshoeing, wagon repair, and building iron fences to projects for heavy industry, the major part of the business. There was much demand at the time for boiler repair, for instance, for steamboats and sawmills as well as other industries that used steam for power.

Outgrowing the shop, in 1912 the entrepreneur purchased 10 acres of a cotton field and constructed a new facility. It was near Thibault Milling Company—one of the few structures there at the time, and still there now—just southwest of the Ninth and Bond streets intersection in Little Rock.

Julius Bemberg died in 1929. His four sons inherited the operation, but two of them left during the Depression. Herman Sr. became president. His son remembers him as "a very quiet man, a workaholic, no-nonsense person," who went to night school after the eighth grade to complete his education, and learned engineering from his own library. "He was a brilliant man," Bemberg relates, and recalls another young-boy impression: that his father wore a tie everyday, "whether it was 20 or 120 degrees, inside boilers or wherever he was working."

On a tour through the plant, Bemberg points to a piece of equipment his grandfather used ("We say it came from the Ark") and an old anvil ("Nobody uses it, except to sit on"). He then notes seams in the concrete floor that mark the original exterior walls of the first "old wooden shop from gran'pa's time," before his father had it enlarged in the 1950s.

The facility continues to grow, day by day, and in it 35 workers are cutting, bending, and welding steel, aluminum, and other metals to create what industry and agriculture need from ironworkers, boilermakers, and welders today. Fifty percent is bid work, the remainder is negotiated, Bemberg explains, and adds that the firm also does maintenance and repair for contractors who simply drop in.

The business is a family corporation owned and operated by brothers Herman Jr. and Gordon, along with wives Lois and Mary. The fourth generation is also at work there—two of Herman's sons assist in purchasing and traffic control, and Gordon's two sons aid their father as shop superintendent and design engineer.

The original blacksmith shop. The tall man with the mustache is founder Julius Bemberg and the man at right (with hands on hips) is Julius Bemberg, Jr. (1892-1963). The boy at left (with his hand on the big steam-driven forging hammer) is Herman Bemberg, Sr. (1898-1963). Photo circa 1910

This stainless steel separator shell is part of a wet scrubber system for collecting air pollutants at a local bauxitic clay-processing plant. The vessel is in the process of being shop fitted, after which all joints will be welded.

GENERAL TELEPHONE COMPANY OF THE SOUTHWEST

In June 1918 John F. O'Connell, Sigurd L. Odegard, and J.A. Pratt pooled their savings and purchased Richland Center (Wisconsin) Telephone Company, which eventually became GTE Corporation—a worldwide leader in developing, manufacturing, and marketing telecommunications, electrical and electronic products, as well as network services and systems.

The 18 GTE telephone operating companies provide many types of communications services, ranging from telephone service for the home or office to highly complex voice and data services for industry and national defense.

What is now General Telephone Company of the Southwest (GTSW), which serves the four-state area of Arkansas, Texas, Oklahoma, and New Mexico, was incorporated with headquarters in Lubbock, Texas, in June 1926.

GTSW has 48 exchanges in its Arkansas division, which serve more than 60,000 customers. By the end of 1986 approximately 25 percent of those customers will be served by digital switching equipment—offering the most advanced telecommunications service possible.

Headquartered in Jacksonville, the firm has 15 service locations throughout the state. Operations centers are in Pocahontas, Stutt-

E.L. "Buddy" Langley, president of General Telephone of the Southwest, which acquired most of its Arkansas exchanges in a 1968 merger.

gart, and Texarkana.

The original enterprise was known as the State Telephone Company of Texas. It served approximately 7,000 telephones in some 40 towns near Lubbock and a portion of southeastern New Mexico.

The firm expanded into Oklahoma in 1930; the following year it was merged with three other independents to form the Southwestern Associated Telephone Company.

The corporate headquarters was moved to Dallas in 1949 to be nearer the geographic center of the company's operations, which were soon to include operations in Arkansas. At the end of 1950 it served 100,000 customers and had approximately 1,900 employees.

In 1952 the name of the organization was changed to General Telephone Company of the Southwest to achieve closer identification with the General Telephone System—with which it had been affiliated since 1935. GTSW returned its headquarters to West Texas in 1953 with the acquisition of the San Angelo Telephone Company.

Growth continued, including mergers with Texas Telephone Company and Oklahoma Telephone Company, both subsidiaries

of Theodore Gary Company and Southwestern States Telephone Company of the Western Utilities Corporation—gaining GTE most of its Arkansas exchanges in 1968. In May 1973 the firm installed its one-millionth telephone. In the mid-1980s its 10,700 employees serve almost 1.2 million customers.

Recognizing its continued growth in the Dallas metropolitan area, the corporation again has a headquarters presence there. While maintaining its general office in San Angelo, GTSW also established offices at Las Colinas in Irving, Texas, in 1985. According to president E.L. "Buddy" Langley, the office was necessary in the new deregulated environment so GTE can be near its fastest-growing market. Some 25 percent of the company's customers are already in the Dallas area, and that figure is expected to grow to almost a half-million customers by 1990.

Growing with Arkansas and the Southwest, GTE looks forward to continuing its tradition of being a full-service provider of quality service at competitive prices, progressive management, and community involvement.

General Telephone Company of the Southwest (GTSW) serves 60,000 Arkansas customers. The headquarters building (shown here) is in San Angelo, Texas. The Arkansas headquarters is in Jacksonville, with operation centers in Pocahontas, Stuttgart, and Texarkana.

ARKANSAS' ELECTRIC COOPERATIVES

The success of rural electrification is due as much to determined people as it is to the program that made it possible.

Power lines now reach to even the most remote areas of Arkansas. Most were built by electric cooperatives. The 18 electric cooperatives that serve in Arkansas have combined service areas encompassing more than 62 percent of the state's land area, primarily the more thinly settled rural sections.

Getting electric service for rural residents was no easy task. But there were few complaints from the men and women who walked backcountry roads in the 1930s, visiting isolated farms and homes to explain how rural families could "get the lights" by organizing electric cooperatives.

"No more pumping water and having to carry it from the well," the visitor might remark, looking at the pump beside the house. Then, nodding toward the ever-present privy at the back of the lot, "You can even have an inside bathroom." And, pointing at the washtubs on the back porch, "You can have a washing machine, too."

Everybody agreed that electricity

ARCHITECTS OF THE REA PROGRAM. President Franklin D. Roosevelt is flanked by (left) Representative Sam Rayburn, D-Tex., and Senator George Norris, R-Neb., the chief proponents of the Rural Electrification Act passed by Congress in 1936. It was Roosevelt's May 11, 1935, executive order creating a national Rural Electrification Administration that made electric service possible in the nation's thinly settled sections.

would be beneficial.

"An electric refrigerator will service in the 1930s. There were precious few power lines in rural sections, however. Power companies, for the most part, saw no profit potential there. The cost was too great to serve in rural areas, they said, and it took too long to recover the expense involved.

Indeed, there was little to attract investment in rural areas in the 1930s. Flood, drought, and the Depression had reduced many farming operations to the poverty level. Southern states were particularly hard hit. Electricity, for most farmers, was just a dream. In Arkansas, only 5,121 of the state's 242,334 farms had central station electric service in 1930, less than 2 percent of the total.

Recognizing the need for improved living standards in the nation's farming areas, President Franklin D. Roosevelt on May 11, 1935, signed an executive order creating a national Rural Electrification Administration.

REA, as most people called it, was to be an agency that would lend money to rural folks so they could organize nonprofit associations and build their own electric systems. The rates charged for energy could be just enough to repay the loans, pay the interest, and keep the lines in operation. Service would be the motivation, not profit.

Congress passed a comprehensive rural electrification act in 1936, clearing up some of the earlier questions about just how the program was to be carried out. A year later the Arkansas General Assembly provided legislation needed to permit the organization of electric cooperatives that could participate in the REA program.

The state's major agricultural groups—Farm Bureau, Extension Service, and others—had been promoting the rural electrification idea for a long time. They had held numerous meetings all across

"Here's where your farm is, and here's where the high line will likely go," they would explain, using a rough map to show the locations. Then, pointing to another spot on the map, "This is where Sam (or whomever it might have been) lives. He's already signed up." Sam could have lived half a mile or so on down the road, or on the far side of a hill. No matter. He was the nearest neighbor.

keep the milk, butter, and eggs from going bad so quickly in the summer. Meat, too. Can't sell sour milk or spoiled meat." There was no arguing with that fact.

Most of all, though, rural families wanted electric lights. Those who have tried to read, mend clothes, or do anything else by the dim, flickering glow from a kerosene lamp know why that was so.

Cities and towns had electric

POLE-SETTING CEREMONY. The first pole set by an electric cooperative in Arkansas was raised by First Electric Cooperative during ceremonies held October 20, 1937. The pole was located in a field near Jacksonville, directly across Highway 161 from the present-day general office facilities of First Electric Cooperative.

the state. Maps had been prepared to show farm and home locations. The leadership cadre was ready to go into action when the last "i" was dotted and last "t" crossed.

Power line right-of-way had to be acquired. Arrangements had to be made to buy energy at wholesale from a power company or municipal electric system. Poles had to be set, and lines strung.

The first pole set by an Arkansas electric cooperative was raised into place near Jacksonville on October 20, 1937. It went up in a field directly across Highway 161 from the cooperative's present-day general office building.

First Electric Cooperative was quickly joined by six similar systems. They, too, were sponsored by the Farm Bureau and Extension Service. There was Arkansas Valley Electric at Ozark; Carroll Electric, Berryville; Craighead Electric, Jonesboro; Farmers Electric, Newport; Southwest Arkansas Electric, Texarkana; and Woodruff Electric,

Forrest City.

Four more were initiated in 1938: C & L Electric, Star City; Clay County Electric, Corning; Mississippi County Electric, Blytheville; and Ozarks Electric, Fayetteville. North Arkansas Electric at Salem and Ouachita Electric, Camden, were organized in 1939.

Another three were incorporated in 1940: Petit Jean Electric, Clinton; South Central Arkansas Electric, Arkadelphia; and Riceland Electric, Stuttgart. Ashley-Chicot Electric, Hamburg, was established in 1941.

World War II brought a halt to most electric cooperative activity. While there was relatively little

line construction in Arkansas during the war years because of material shortages, one new system— Rich Mountain Electric at Mena— was set up in 1945, as the war began coming to a close.

Once the war was over, extensive expansion programs were begun as rapidly as the necessary materials became available. Central station electric service in rural Arkansas— only a few years earlier available to a relative handful of families— had become the rule rather than the exception.

Electric cooperatives continue to serve the state's farming areas. Much of Arkansas' industrial growth will take place in those same non-urban sections. The need for an adequate and dependable source of electric energy will be even more important in the future than in the past. Electric cooperatives will meet that need.

Rural electrification in Arkansas is far from completed. It's really just beginning!

3M COMPANY

Late in the 1930s, sensing that the South was the country's next growth area, 3M sent a team of geologists to the southern states. They were searching for a mineral suitable to be ground into bits of granule for asphalt roofing tiles. It needed to be tough and durable, plus accessible, near railroad lines, and plentiful. Plans were to build a plant nearby to serve southern roofing manufacturers.

What the geologists found was the only deposit of a hard granite—called syenite—between Canada and Mexico. It was just south of Fourche Creek in Little Rock and was owned by the Big Rock Stone Company, which quarried the syenite for riprap. The quarry was available and for sale, and it also met the essential requirements of being accessible, close to rail lines and predicted to last for more than a century.

The company was ready to locate in Little Rock when World War II began. The war interrupted, but did not change, 3M's plans to build. By December 1945 plant construction at the eight-acre site was under way. It was the first major commercial construction in Little Rock after the war.

Operation began April 24, 1947, and the first carload of granules was shipped that same day. That first year 150 employees produced enough granules to weatherproof the roofs of 600,000 homes.

Today one of the most diverse companies in the world, 3M en-

The Little Rock quarry, where mineral is blasted and loaded into 35-ton trucks.

tered the roofing granule business with its 1929 purchase of a small sandpaper firm in Wausau, Wisconsin. The purchase included a hill containing quartzite, used for making sandpaper and other abrasive materials.

With more mineral in the hill than 3M could use for abrasives, laboratory teams began researching uses for this and other mineral. They developed a process of encasing stone granules in a colorful ceramic coating. The process filled a need in the roofing industry which, until then, did not have granules with the durability nor the choice of colors that the ceramic coating provided. The company now has five roofing granule plants—four in the United States and one in Canada.

3M believes that no matter where it operates, it should endeavor to be a good neighbor. It believes in employing local people, actively participating in community activities, and financially supporting qualifying worthy community-wide projects. Over the years 3M has invested many thousands of dollars in support of various agencies and projects to help develop the Little Rock area.

Scores of 3M employees have served as presidents or on boards of directors of various clubs, associations, and councils throughout the greater Little Rock area. W.H. Walters, plant manager from 1951 to 1977, was city mayor from 1973 to 1975.

The 240 employees who are now at the Little Rock 3M operation are working in one of the largest hard-mineral quarries in the world— a little-known fact among local citizens. By the end of 1985 the plant had, according to its present manager Dean Skaer, quarried and crushed enough syenite since 1947 to roof more than 40 million homes.

The facility has gone through several expansions over the years, and continues to be a major reliable supplier to the roofing industry throughout the South.

The Little Rock granule plant, where mineral receives its final crushing and is colored for shipment.

ETHYL CORPORATION

The Ethyl Corporation Bromine Chemicals Division is located in Magnolia on U.S. Highway 79. Its people are an integral part of the social and economic sectors of their community and the state of Arkansas.

Beneath the rolling pines and holly grove lowlands of southern Arkansas, far beneath the land surface of Columbia and Union counties, a discovery was made in 1945 that would change the face and economy of that part of the state. It was just after the end of World War II that the subterranean brines of the southwest corner of Arkansas, in what is known geologically as the Smackover Formation, were found to contain some of the richest known bromine reserves in the world.

It would have surprised the citizens of the area at that time to hear that, four decades later, their corner of the state would lead the nation in the production of bromine—as well as related products—and would even provide about one-half of the world's such needs.

On the pine-tree-bordered and winding U.S. Highway 79, just a few miles north of the Louisiana border, is the world's largest bromine plant, Ethyl Corporation's Bromine Chemicals Division.

The facility was built seven miles south of Magnolia in 1969 as a one-product venture devoted entirely to supporting the company's tetraethyl lead business. Growth since that time has been consistent, diversifying nearly every year into new product lines. To-day Ethyl's Magnolia plant is a multiproduct specialty chemicals operation, specializing in flame retardants, oil field completion fluids, and a number of intermediate products for industrial and agricultural businesses.

A versatile element, bromine is the basic raw material of this industry, found throughout the world in oceans, in briny lakes and inland seas, in salt beds and subsurface brines, as well as in fruits, vegetables, and animals, including man. It is produced worldwide, but the foremost production today

Ethyl's Magnolia plant is a multiproduct specialty chemicals operation, specializing in flame retardants, oil field completion fluids, and a number of intermediate products for industrial and agricultural businesses.

comes from the brine wells of Columbia and Union counties in southern Arkansas.

The area is unique because the geological structure permits the economic extraction of large quantities of brine through systems of deep wells. These wells are a wonder in themselves—they are 1.5 miles deep and require motors and pumps of extraordinary capacity to pump the thousands of barrels of brine per day from this great depth.

Ethyl's people at Magnolia are proud of their plant and their jobs, proud of their accomplishment of continuing growth, and especially proud of their corporate and individual roles in the social and economic sectors of their community and their great state.

The operation is a part of Ethyl Corporation, a Virginia-based organization listed in the top half of the *Fortune* 500 that is a worldwide producer of performance chemicals for the petroleum industry, high-technology chemicals, plastics, and aluminum products with interests in oil, gas, and coal. Ethyl, which also owns First Colony Life Insurance Company, had sales in 1985 of $1.55 billion and net income of $117 million.

ALUMAX/MAGNOLIA DIVISION

Many adults today can recall eating meals from a dinette set popular after World War II, in which the kitchen table featured sleek aluminum trim. Such trim had not existed until the late 1940s, after a new process called aluminum extruding had been developed.

The state of Arkansas has a historical link with that process: A plant in Magnolia, known then as Southern Extrusions, and operated now by Alumax, Inc., was the first aluminum extrusion plant in the region, the 19th built in the United States.

Although known for centuries, aluminum became commercially available only in the 1890s. The extrusion process, similar to pushing toothpaste out of a tube, expanded the many known uses of the metal. In the extrusion process aluminum, which has been formed into billets or logs using a "direct-chill" process to assure uniform strength throughout, is heated and then pushed in its plastic state through a die. The process requires a large amount of concentrated pressure and results in a continuous, uniform product that is seamless and can be almost any shape.

Founded by three young men from Michigan, Southern Extrusions in Magnolia began operation on July 12, 1949. Its first payroll had nine hourly employees and three management personnel, with starting wages of 65 cents per hour. The founding partners were Joe Ida, Ralph Sullivan, and H.N. Sebring.

Sebring designed and built the first extrusion press, which by today's standards was a miniature press. With only 350 tons of pressure, it extruded an aluminum billet three inches in diameter and 13 inches long that included shapes for dinette trim as well as counter moldings, stair nosings, thresholds, carpet edging, and weather-stripping.

With an auspicious beginning, the firm three years later added a

second, much larger press and began a branch operation at Louisville, Kentucky. Also in 1952 Ida and Sebring purchased Sullivan's interest. In 1956 Ida left the concern, and Sebring then acquired two new partners who brought important skills and experience to the operations.

One of the new partners was a Russian-born metallurgist named Victor Sheshunoff, who had a small aluminum casting business in Magnolia called Arkansas Alloys and Castings. His venture was merged with Southern Extrusions when he came on as a partner; and that branch of the operation continues today, producing with modern machinery over 50 million pounds of billets each year.

The other new partner, K.E. Gordon, had been in Texarkana, Texas, operating a small business, Texas Metal Processing, Inc., that polished and anodized aluminum. He relocated the business in Magnolia and put Southern Extrusions into the polishing and anodizing business.

The operation grew, and in the early 1960s a new office building and extrusion press plant were completed. A new press was added in 1961, the year the company acquired a related business, the Smithcary Corporation. Smithcary

The new officers for Southern Extrusions in 1966 were (left to right) Joe Dees, vice-president/finance; Charles Taylor, vice-president/sales and marketing; H.N. Sebring, chairman of the board; John Smith, president; Lloyd Cary, vice-president/engineering; and Jack Rogers, vice-president/manufacturing.

was a local fabricator of bath enclosures and sliding glass doors, and it brought a new and important product line to Southern Extrusions.

During 1962 a major rebuild of the cast house was completed, and Southern Extrusions began casting the world's longest horizontal direct chill extrusion logs, with lengths up to 150 feet. Within two years the firm constructed a second plant nearby, housing a much larger extrusion press that was a 3,000-ton model capable of handling billets 11 inches in diameter and up to 32 inches long. This capacity put the company into competition with large presses elsewhere, and a year later it purchased a brand-new plant with an automated paint line at Hutchinson, Kansas.

By the mid-1960s Southern Extrusions' growth demanded a new management approach. In a reorganization in 1966, Sebring, who had been president since 1949, be-

The newest Alumax extrusion plant, built in 1985.

came chairman of the board; John Smith, of the Smithcary group, was named president; and Charles Taylor, a Reynolds Metals sales executive, joined as vice-president of sales and marketing.

Taylor is credited with moving the organization in a new direction—toward custom fabrication and finished products, instead of just lineal extrusions. He also developed new products—including stadium seating, scaffold boards, picnic tables, and aluminum transmission towers.

In 1968 the custom fabrication work burgeoned: The plant manufactured and installed 72,000 all-aluminum stadium chairs at the Cotton Bowl in Dallas, and outfitted Denver's Mile High Stadium with aluminum seat boards with backrests. That same year Arkansas Power and Light Company used Southern Extrusion aluminum transmission towers for power lines across southern Arkansas.

The firm was sold in 1971 to the Howmet Corporation, a wholly owned subsidiary of Pechiney Corporation of Paris, France, and a major supplier of raw aluminum for Southern Extrusions. Smith remained as president until 1973. Taylor became division manager in 1973, followed by Jack Rogers in 1979 and Henri Fine in 1982. In 1983—the year that Alumax Aluminum Corporation acquired

Howmet's aluminum operations, including the Magnolia plant—Jimmie G. Davis became the division manager, and he continues in that position.

Under Alumax Corporation, the fourth-largest primary aluminum producer in the United States, the Magnolia operation has continued to expand, always maintaining an emphasis on quality, controlling every aspect of production from raw material to finished product. The Alumax Magnolia Division can extrude and fabricate virtually any shape up to 12 inches wide. The company offers complete machining capabilities, and its engineers and craftsmen work with clients in designing and making prototypes of their new products.

The finishing capabilities at the plant are extensive. Alumax can supply whatever color, finish, or texture is needed or desired for the product. The plant can etch, Brite-dip, anodize, or paint to

specifications; and silkscreen a logo, instructions, or other information on the product. Final fabrication is also performed at the facility by assembling component parts.

While the products are always expanding, the primary products of the Magnolia operation are stadium seating, bath and shower enclosures, scaffolding, interior door frames, and ceiling grid systems. Custom finish and fabrication also makes up a large portion of the business. With these and other lines the 1985 sales from the plant were over $50 million. The Magnolia plant is part of a vast enterprise.

Alumax is headquartered in San Mateo, California, and operates 111 facilities throughout the United States, Canada, and Europe with over 13,500 employees.

The Magnolia plant has come a long way from the early days of Southern Extrusions. The payroll has increased from 12 employees to being the largest employer in Columbia County, with more than 600 people. And from modest beginnings that helped to seat families around a dinette table, aluminum extrusions from the plant now seat tens of thousands of people and provide important products to a wide range of industries.

This 3,000-ton extrusion press is the latest state-of-the-art equipment installed in the new extrusion plant.

DOW CHEMICAL COMPANY

The Dow Chemical Company was founded by Herbert Henry Dow in 1897 in Midland, Michigan. Dow had developed an electrolytic process for the extraction of bromine from brine and, after several years of experimentation, became the first man in the world to produce bromine in commercial quantities using this process. Bromine is a liquid element akin to chlorine

R.S. Chamberlin, plant manager at the Dow Magnolia plant, stands with 10 Cotton Belt Railroad officials at the first EDB shipment from the plant on June 5, 1967.

Dow Fee #1—The first brine well is being drilled at the Dow Chemical USA Magnolia plant in 1966.

that has a variety of uses and applications.

The rich bromine-laden brine reserves deep beneath southwest Arkansas were discovered in 1945. Making use of one of the world's most abundant subterranean sources of brine was the sure attraction for Dow Chemical as it looked in the 1960s for the right place to expand its operations.

By 1966, when Dow came to Magnolia, its experience in Arkansas and in the brine and chemical industries was extensive. Attracted by the rich brine reserves in Columbia and neighboring Union counties, the company made a substantial investment in southwest Arkansas.

The Magnolia Brine Chemicals plant has been in operation since 1967, but Dow's investment in Arkansas and in the growth and evolution of the chemical industry go back well beyond that, utilizing a waste product to make sodium hydrosulfide, a material used in manufacturing paper.

Dow's use of waste material emphasizes the firm's commitment to responsible stewardship of the land. The two large tanks that hold the brine after it has been ex-

tracted from 1.5-mile-deep wells are the largest free-standing plastic tanks in the world, built at a cost of one million dollars each. Although there were less costly ways to build the tanks that would have met all regulations, Dow went to the expense of building the most durable and the safest containers for the brine.

Not surprisingly, they were built from a Dow product, a vinyl ester resin with the trademark Derakane®. Dow also built a water-collection system around the tanks to ensure that nothing harmful would ever enter the surrounding soil.

The same attitude is shown in Dow's handling of nonusable hazardous wastes. These are incinerated, not put into landfills. This is another expensive but responsible choice. It costs an average of $300 to incinerate every ton of waste, compared to just $24 for landfilling. However, Dow is committed to protecting the Magnolia environment.

The second plant at the Magnolia site was a Styrofoam® brand plastics foam plant in 1968. Few Arkansans, or for that matter people from elsewhere, realize that the Styrofoam® is used to insulate their homes. This plant produces 100 million board feet of Styrofoam® annually. More than 100 different types, sizes, and colors of this plastic foam, which has

become a household word, are shipped out of the Magnolia plant.

The work force at the Dow plant in Magnolia is now 125 full-time and 50 contract workers, contributing five million dollars annually in salary to the community and another $14 million in materials and supplies. Those employees work in a safe environment. According to the National Safety Council, the chemical industry is 2.3 times safer than industry in general and Dow has a record 10 times better than the rest of the industry. By mid-1986 the Magnolia plant had not lost any time due to accidents in over three years, and the commitment to maintaining that record is reinforced with monthly safety training sessions and continuous safety monitoring.

Dow's plant in Magnolia in 1966, and an aerial view of the expanded plant today (inset) where the company drills brine to make bromine and where Styrofoam is made and shipped—100 million board feet per year.

Reaching to the community with its safety programs, Dow employees work with the fire and sheriff's departments, the local police, and the local hospital to ensure that an effective plan is in place to respond to any emergency the community might face. The company and its people are also active in other community concerns. They sponsor school programs about science and safety, participate in groups such as the United Way and Educators-in-Industry, and contribute to science education in local schools and colleges.

Dow's first venture in Arkansas, however, was not in Magnolia. Dow was a partner in a joint venture known as DowSmith that opened a plant in Little Rock in 1963. The plant, one of the first in the new industrial park at 65th Street, was making a revolutionary new product called Red Thread pipe. The pipe is made of a material that has continuously wound glass filaments embedded in a thermoset epoxy resin. This blend of materials makes it strong, light, and resistant to corrosion. It has proved ideal for use in petroleum-handling operations, gas distribution, and chemical and electrical applications. Dow has developed the special epoxy resins while its partner, the A.O. Smith Company, had developed the winding process to make the material. The plant still operates in Little Rock although Dow is no longer associated with it.

That same year, 1963, Dow had made another commitment to Arkansas, contributing to a poultry research farm that had just been established at the University of Arkansas. The farm carried out research on the prevention of coccidiosis and in determining the feed affects of amino acids. The farm consisted of a feed mill and broiler

Dow's plant in Russellville, built in 1970, where chlorine cells are made.

houses that produced about 28,000 birds a year. This work, so crucial to the large broiler business in the state, continued for 10 years.

In 1970 Dow again chose an Arkansas site for production of another Dow product, and began construction of a new plant, this time in Russellville. Here Dow makes chlorine cell components used in the manufacture of chlorine. The location was centrally situated and close to the Arkansas River and the interstate highway network, for shipping products throughout the United States and Canada. When the plant achieved full operation in 1973, it began employing 185 people in the Russellville area. At Russellville Dow shows the same concern for its people and its community, and has provided a park and pavilion for local use and a soccer field. Safety is a high priority in the Russellville plant, where employees participate in quality circles to put the personal touch on plant problems and productivity.

Dow's investment in Arkansas is continuing today. Another plant is beginning operation in Magnolia in 1986 and the existing plant is being modernized, at a cost of $30 million. The new plant will produce 120 million pounds of calcium bromide annually and employ another 17 people. Calcium bromide is a clear brine fluid used in the oil drilling industry.

Dow's almost 25 years of investment in Arkansas and its people has paid off—in jobs, community service, and in valuable products that are manufactured in Arkansas for applications around the world.

® Trademark of the Dow Chemical Company

UNION MEDICAL CENTER

People who are living alone—perhaps elderly, perhaps convalescing—call there in the morning, to tell someone how they are feeling. Diabetics find other diabetics there, and they talk in a support group. Smokers go for help in stopping their habit. Parents-to-be go to prepare for childbirth, and can return later for tips on child care.

Union Medical Center in El Dorado takes an extra step to act on its founding principle, that the mission of a hospital is service. For some of the services described above, it has earned national recognition. The American Hospital Association named it one of 45 hospitals in the nation "outstanding" in "contribution to furthering the leadership role of hospitals in developing community health promotion programming." The volunteers who operate the morning phone-in project, called TEL-CARE, won the Arkansas Hospital Association's award for "Most Outstanding Auxiliary Inservice Project."

These programs help to explain a hospital director's comment, "The story about Union Medical Center is not in the number of beds, it's about our growth in services," which she followed with details of outpatient services that go even beyond the hospital facilities. The hospital's home health care, allowing patients to convalesce at home, helps them spend less time in the hospital, yet stay under the direction of their physician. This and other outpatient services— one-day surgery, a pulmonary rehabilitation program, diagnostic testing, physical therapy—go far in reducing a patient's medical care costs.

It is hard to avoid mentioning beds in a Union Medical Center story since, in its first year, it had enough demand to open its fourth floor and grow from 66 to 96 general care beds. That was in 1964. In 1967 a 10-bed intensive care unit was added, the first in El Do-

rado. The year 1973 brought a south wing, and in 1983 a north wing provided space for a new intensive care/coronary unit, updated nuclear medicine and radiology departments, and the one-day surgery area.

The facility, first called Union Memorial Hospital, was built with funds from a county bond issue plus a 2.5 percent millage tax. But in 1975 all tax support ended, as the founders had envisioned. While still owned by Union County and governed by a seven-member board of governors appointed by the county judge, the hospital is totally self-supporting. In 1978 the board of governors changed the name to Union Medical Center. They felt the name change better reflected the hospital's expanded role in Union County, south Arkansas, and north Louisiana. With 79 physicians and 17 dentists on its staff, it is accredited by the Joint Commission on Accreditation of Hospitals and is designated, for purposes of the Medicare system, as a Regional Referral Center.

Affiliations that Union Medical Center has within the state have helped to expand the treatment it provides. As the regional hospital networking with Arkansas Children's Hospital, it operates a Level II neonatal intensive care nursery, with treatment once available only in Little Rock. This statewide networking effort has reduced by two-thirds the number of newborn deaths in the state. It provides clinical facilities for the University of Arkansas for Medical Sciences through the Area Health

The American Hospital Association named Union Medical Center one of 45 hospitals in the nation "outstanding" in "contribution to furthering the leadership role of hospitals in developing community health promotion programming." Located in El Dorado, the center serves Union County, Arkansas, and north Louisiana.

Education Center-South Arkansas (AHEC), and its family practice residency program. Other students also train there, including Southern Arkansas University students enrolled in the radiologic technologist and the Associate Degree Registered Nursing programs and Oil Belt Vocational Technical School students in the LPN program.

Union Medical Center has consistently kept up with the best of technology. It was the first hospital in the state to have a linear accelerator for radiation treatment of cancer patients, a machine donated to the South Arkansas Radiation Therapy Institute (SARTI) when it opened in 1983. The hospital's Cerebral/Carotid Doppler Scanner identifies potential stroke victims without the use of invasive techniques.

To continue to provide the best in care, the hospital has set up an independent foundation for contributions. The gifts are used exactly as the donor designates. The hospital's auxiliary, which by 1985 had donated an astounding 335,120 hours of volunteer service, is a significant contributor to Union Medical Foundation, raising funds through rummage sales, Christmas bazaars, and the hospital gift shop.

UNIVERSITY OF ARKANSAS AT LITTLE ROCK

"Why don't you ask me to give it to you?"

"All right, how about giving it to us?"

"All right. I'll give it to you."

That conversation between Raymond Rebsamen, who owned the land where the main campus of the University of Arkansas at Little Rock now stands, and John A. Larson, dean of Little Rock Junior College, was the solution to a problem in 1947: LRJC did not have $30,000 to buy Rebsamen's land.

Larson, head of a school that had existed for 20 years without owning a building or an acre of land, saw the acquisition as the first step in forming "the great university that is to come."

More than 10,000 students enroll at University of Arkansas at Little Rock each fall.

The school had been founded in 1927 by the Little Rock Board of Education using vacant classrooms in Little Rock High School (now Central High School) to accommodate about 100 students taught by eight instructors. In 1931 LRJC moved into the old U.M. Rose School structure, renting it for 50 dollars a month.

The same year Rebsamen and Larson struck their deal, LRJC began a $650,000 fund drive to pay for construction of three buildings. The Little Rock business community responded, and Larson closely supervised construction. He demanded that trees be cut only when absolutely necessary, and even then was known to trade the timber on the spot for building materials.

By 1949 LRJC was on the new campus, finally occupying its own facilities.

The school in 1957 became a four-year, private, liberal arts college named Little Rock University. LRU grew slowly but steadily, and by 1969 there were 3,500 students taught by 75 full-time faculty members in 11 buildings—with others under construction.

After years of negotiations between the two boards of trustees, LRU—at the University of Arkan-

sas' request—agreed to a merger that was approved by the legislature in 1969. The University of Arkansas at Little Rock came into being with the legislative action.

Today UALR enrolls more than 10,000 students, has 450 full-time faculty members, and there are 25 buildings on the main campus, plus a downtown School of Law. The main campus houses nine colleges and schools—Liberal Arts, Sciences, Communication, Education, Business Administration, Fine Arts, Engineering Technology, Graduate School, and Graduate School of Social Work.

The institution's growth has come under eight chief executives: R.C. Hall (1927-1930); John A. Larson (1930-1950); Granville Davis (1950-1954); E.Q. Brothers (acting president 1954-1956); Carey V. Stabler (LRU president 1956-1969, and UALR chancellor 1969-1972); James H. Fribourgh (interim chancellor 1972-1973, 1982); G. Robert Ross (1973-1982); and James H. Young (1982-present).

Larson undoubtedly would agree that his "great university that is to come" is coming along very well.

Ottenheimer Library is at the geographical and intellectual center of the university.

WESTARK COMMUNITY COLLEGE

The largest of the 12 two-year institutions of higher education in Arkansas is located in Fort Smith and has been a part of Arkansas history since 1928.

Today Westark is a truly comprehensive community college with approximately 3,500 students enrolled in university-parallel (college transfer) and vocational-technical programs. In addition, the college annually enrolls over 15,000 persons in noncredit courses, and another 20,000 area residents come to the campus each year to attend plays, concerts, sporting events, meetings, seminars, workshops, and extension classes. Westark is, indeed, the educational and social hub of Sebastian and surrounding counties.

When Grover C. Hardin—a Fort Smith attorney and school board member—proposed the creation of a two-year college in 1923, his plan was simply to provide two additional years of education on the high school campus for graduates of Fort Smith High School. When the controversial concept was eventually adopted and Fort Smith Junior College opened in the fall of 1928, it was housed briefly in what is now Darby Junior High School. There were 34 students enrolled in that first class. When the new Fort Smith High School (now Northside High School) opened in the spring of 1929, the college moved there and remained for 24 years.

During that era the superintendent of Fort Smith schools served as president of the college, and the principal of the high school doubled as the college dean.

J.W. Ramsey was the founding president and served until 1952 when the founding dean, Elmer Cook, assumed the presidency.

While the college operated as an extension of the public school system, enrollment peaked at 211 in 1946 and had declined to 123 in 1950 when the courts ruled that public school funds could not be used for higher education. Defying an attempt in the early 1950s to close the institution, Elmer Cook left the public school system and moved his struggling private college to the location of its current campus, a former "county poor farm," at Grand Avenue and Waldron Roads in the Fort Smith suburbs.

J.W. Ramsey, the college's first president.

Joel R. Stubblefield, the current Westark president.

Despite a serious and continuing problem with finances, the college grew steadily during its private era, from 1952 until 1965, and relied on tuition, fees, and philanthropy for its operating budget. Meetings of the college board of trustees often concluded with members contributing hundreds of dollars each to meet payrolls or to make insurance payments. Area leaders such as T.L. Hunt, Ed Louise Ballman, and Melanie Speer were among those who helped sus-

Eighteen modern buildings now comprise the Westark campus.

Old Main, a former Sebastian County "poor farm" building, became a college classroom facility in 1952. It was demolished in 1966.

tain the struggling institution.

In 1958 Dr. E.T. Vines assumed the presidency of the college. Probably his most notable achievement was the initiation of technical training in 1961. Early programs were machine shop, electronics, auto mechanics, welding, and drafting. Today Westark is the state's largest technical training institution with seventeen such programs—including data processing, computer repair technology, word processing, and nursing.

President Vines led a community drive in 1965 that resulted in the creation of a special community college district (with boundaries concurrent with those of Sebastian County) and the passage of a local tax levy to provide capital facilities at the college. This action altered the status of the institution from private to public. Shortly thereafter, the name was changed from Fort Smith Junior College to Westark Junior College.

The initial nine-member board of trustees of the public college was appointed by the governor, with subsequent members being popularly elected to six-year terms. One of the primary strengths of the institution has been the outstanding quality of its trustees, comprised of leading businessmen and women with a community-wide outlook. Board members serving in 1986 were Conaly Bedell, Shanon Bridges, James Burgess, Larry Clark, Nancy Llewellyn, Edward Sanders, Mike Shaw, Sam Sicard, and Lucille Speakman.

Following Dr. Vines' death in 1968, Shelby Breedlove was appointed president and led the development of Westark into a truly comprehensive community college. To reflect the increasingly comprehensive nature of the institution, the name was changed again in 1973 from Westark Junior College to Westark Community College. The following year the institution reached another milestone when it received initial accreditation from the North Central Association's Commission on Institutions of Higher Education.

In 1973 Governor Dale Bumpers promoted, and the General Assembly adopted, legislation implementing a plan drafted by president Breedlove to establish community colleges around the state.

Upon Dr. Breedlove's death, leadership of the college passed to its fifth president, Dr. James M. Kraby. During his tenure several building projects were completed, and Westark's reputation as a leading community college in the state and nation was strengthened.

In 1983 the board named to the presidency Joel Richard Stubblefield, a Fort Smith native who had returned to the area three years earlier as Westark's vice-president for finance and administration. Stubblefield's leadership has focused on enhancing and strengthening the college's reputation for top-quality instruction and student counseling, the launching of two major building projects, and acquiring adjacent property for long-range expansion.

Among all the colleges and universities in Arkansas, two- and four-year, public and private, only four have larger enrollments than Westark. Gone are the three original buildings on the "poor farm" in which the college first operated on its present campus. In their place are 18 modern structures.

Positioned in the fastest-growing area of the state, Westark is prepared to continue providing a variety of top-grade educational and training opportunities to the people of western Arkansas and serving as a catalyst for the economic and cultural development of the area.

An aerial view of Westark Community College.

MAYBELLINE COMPANY

As a young man, T.L. Williams moved to Chicago from his native Kentucky, looking for work and business opportunity. By 1915 he had begun to parlay a mail-order novelty business into some profits, and his sister, Mabel, traveled to Chicago to work with him. Her mind wasn't all business, though, and one night she was primping in front of the mirror when her brother stopped by to chat. "What are you doing?" he asked. "I am applying Vaseline on my eyelashes and eyebrows to keep them healthy and make them show up more," she answered.

Subsequently, the enterprising young businessman and a chemist friend took Mabel's makeshift cosmetic idea and, with it, prepared to enter the newly developing cosmetic industry. They wasted no time marketing their new product, developing an ad with an eye illustration that read: "Beautify your lashes with Lash-Brow-Ine; send 25 cents." The little company began to grow, and before long Williams decided to add color to the cosmetic to darken eyebrows and lashes. This he named in honor of his sister, and the firm has carried the name of Maybelline since.

Maybelline's 70 years of success have been built on its founder's basic concept. He said his products must be easy to use; create an instant, observable beauty change; be of high quality but reasonably priced; and be nationally advertised.

It all worked well. Maybelline's product line and sales expanded at amazing rates. By 1967, when the company was sold, it was the undisputed leader in eye-makeup sales—with stock valued at $102 million.

The corporation that purchased Maybelline had a similar beginning. Plough, Inc., was founded by Abe Plough in Memphis with $125 he borrowed. The entrepreneur sold his own concoction, Plough's

In 1967 Maybelline Company chose this 106-acre site in North Little Rock's Galloway Industrial Park for its new plant. Today virtually all of Maybelline's more than 500 products are made in and shipped from this facility.

Antiseptic Healing Oil, door to door. In 1915 he started selling malaria tonics, and soon after added a little-known pain reliever, aspirin, to his wares. When his customers were not interested in the aspirin, Plough offered it as a bonus with a "liver regulator" known as St. Joseph's. Soon St. Joseph's Aspirin became Plough's bread and butter. By 1929 he was known as "the multimillionaire drugstore clerk" because he was still working behind the counters in his very successful business.

When Plough acquired Maybelline in 1967, he maintained the plant and offices in Chicago. By the mid 1970s it was apparent the sales growth, multiplicity, and sophistication of the products demanded a new facility. Schering-Plough (Plough had merged with the Schering Corporation of New Jersey) chose a 106-acre site in North Little Rock's Galloway industrial park for its new plant. Today virtually all of Maybelline's more than 500 products are made in and shipped from that facility.

The Maybelline operation is a wonderland of cosmetic production. Mascara formula cooks in 500-gallon stainless steel tanks; waxy, shiny lipstick formulas are mixed in the large tanks as well; powdered colors run in pipelines through the plant; robotic forklifts, guided by computers and wires buried beneath the floor, carry materials and products from place to place; and white-coated technicians assist and test every stage of every product.

The plant, which opened in 1975 with 300,000 square feet of space and 596 employees, has expanded to more than 775,000 square feet with more than 1,200 employees; its annual payroll is over $20 million. Filling about 1,000 orders a day for shipment, Maybelline—true to its primary consumers—has a work force that is over 80 percent female.

DOCTORS HOSPITAL

When a group of Little Rock physicians built Doctors Hospital for their place of practice in 1975, they had something that doctors in earlier decades did not have when they teamed up for such a facility. The Little Rock physicians had the choice of selling the management of the hospital to an organization specializing in that field. When that original company was purchased in 1981, Doctors Hospital became an owned affiliate of Hospital Corporation of America (HCA), the largest publicly owned health-care company in the world.

The benefits of Doctors Hospital's affiliation with HCA go to its patients, employees, and physicians alike. Efficiencies result due to the purchasing power of a large corporation; the staff has access to special education and training; and the most advanced technology is more easily accessible to the physicians.

At the same time, HCA has a "decentralized" philosophy, so Doctors Hospital is still a local hospital, managed by a local administrative team and a board of trustees comprised of area physicians and community leaders.

During its 10th year in 1985, Doctors Hospital celebrated its anniversary in both large and small

ways. On the large scale, it had an open house to dedicate its newly renovated and expanded facilities, which had added another 24,000 square feet of space to the 341-bed acute care facility. The improvements included a new parking deck, ophthalmology center, coronary care and intensive care units, outpatient surgery unit, emergency department, endoscopy lab, clinical laboratory, radiology and special procedures department, nuclear medicine department, and oncology center. This was the second major construction at the facility since it was first erected.

On the smaller scale, the institution initiated a Care Card Preregistration Program. Under this plan necessary information is preregistered with the hospital, and the Care Card is presented upon admission. The patient simply verifies that the information on file is correct. Tangible benefits, besides saved time, come to Care Card holders: discounts at the hospital's cafeteria and gift shop.

Outpatient Surgery is another Doctors Hospital feature that can spare patients some anxiety—as well as time and costs. Recently added, the Outpatient Surgery "Plus" Program offers the extra cost savings of flat-rate pricing plus a choice of spending the night in the hospital after the surgery with a 50-percent discount on the charge for the room, meals, and nursing care.

Doctors Hospital reaches out to

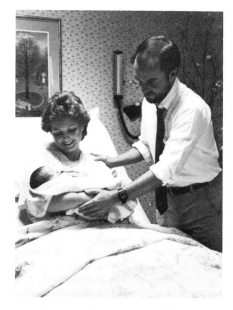

Photographed in the birthing suite, a home-like room for labor, delivery, and recovery. Doctors Hospital prides itself in being an innovator and being responsive to the needs of the patients and their families. The hospital has been the first in the central Arkansas area to provide such obstetric services as the birthing suite, sibling-attended birth, big brother/big sister classes, infant CPR, and the mother-to-mother program.

the community, and Safety Town—the auxiliary's safety awareness program for pre-kindergarten children—is an example of its community care. With the help of the Junior League of Little Rock, the hospital contributes to a child's understanding about transportation on city streets, streetlights, school buses, fire safety, and stranger awareness.

The institution is confident about its service, so much so that it has initiated a Guaranteed Patient Services Program. If a patient reports within 24 hours a dissatisfaction with food, cleanliness, nursing care, or ancillary or emergency departments, and is paid in full on past accounts, he or she may notify the hospital and the charges for such services will not be billed. Such a guarantee could only come from an institution that has total trust and confidence in its employees and services, as Doctors Hospital does.

Doctors Hospital following the expansion and renovation project completed at the end of 1984. In the foreground is the easily accessible 24-hour emergency department.

CITY OF HOT SPRINGS

For over five centuries people have been traveling to the "Valley of the Vapors" to soothe away aches, pains, and tension, or simply to relax. The famous thermal water flows from the ground at an average temperature of 143 degrees Fahrenheit.

After President Thomas Jefferson made that smart buy from Napoleon Bonaparte—the 1803 Louisiana Purchase—Lewis and Clark were not the only adventurers he sent forth to explore it. There was an expedition sent straight into the Ouachita Mountains which, as part of its charge, was to find and report on the hot springs of which Jefferson had heard. Word came back from the trip that the water, in some places too hot to touch, "tasted like spice-wood tea."

While new to European-background Americans, in 1803 those hot springs were ancient knowledge to the native Americans who, as legend has it, had long made it neutral ground for their tribes to gather, for rest and healing. The hot springs gave Spaniard Hernando DeSoto and his band of weary men a month of healing rest, in 1541, before they pushed on in their feverish search for gold in the New World. After DeSoto, the only nonnative visitors to the springs for many years were French trappers.

In 1832 Congress approved a bill by Arkansas' territorial delegate, Ambrose Sevier, for the United States to buy four sections of land, with the hot springs at the center, as a national land preserve for recreational purposes. It makes Hot Springs National Park the oldest federally held and protected recreation area in the country.

The waters drew settlers and visitors alike, and a bathing industry developed in the young town. Rights to access and use of the springs were not reserved to the National Park until 1876, and earlier development was somewhat haphazard. For a time it even threatened to pollute the springs themselves.

By the 1880s, with direct rail service, the spa was flourishing as the meeting spot for the "upper crust" from around the country, and Bathhouse Row began to develop along Central Avenue. The wooden structures were gradually replaced, beginning at the turn of the century and through the 1920s, by the elegant facilities that make up Bathhouse Row today.

Hot Springs was not only a city for bathing. In the early part of the century, the precursor to Oaklawn Park began offering a season of thoroughbred racing each year. Lakes Ouachita, Hamilton, Catherine, Greeson, and DeGray were gradually built around the city and, cumulatively, offer over 70,000 watery acres for fishing, camping, resorts, and water sports. The Park Service erected a tower 216 feet above Hot Springs Mountain that visitors can climb—for a panorama of the Ouachita Mountains, the five lakes, and the city itself.

The racing, the lakes, the elegant hotels, plus other side attractions began to attract more of the tourists' attention when the bathing industry faced hard times in the late 1950s. Modern medicine had usurped reliance on the healing power of the waters, and modern life was accelerating to a pace that no longer accommodated taking the baths.

Determined to keep life both on Bathhouse Row and in the distinctive commercial buildings that face it, the mid-1980s have brought preservation forces together. The National Park Service is working to find new uses that will preserve the grandeur of the bathhouses. Local businessmen, city officials, and state and federal agencies are joining to revitalize Central Avenue.

Nationally known Arkansas author Dee Brown wrote an anecdotal history, *The American Spa,* for the Hot Springs Reservation's 150th birthday in 1982, sponsored by the Arkansas Bank and Trust. Its last chapter is "Sojourners," in which Brown concludes that "apparently everybody who is or was anybody visited Hot Springs at least once."

Magnolia- and holly-bordered Bathhouse Row is the showplace of Hot Springs National Park, Arkansas. Declared a national reservation in 1832, the 47 hot springs have since been protected by the federal government and are still flowing at a rate of nearly a million gallons per day.

CROW-BURLINGAME COMPANY

W. Robert Crow was a salesman for the Karcher Candy Company; J.G. Burlingame was a grocer. It was 1918, in Little Rock, and—by the account of Fletcher Lord, Jr., Crow's grandson—the two men got to figuring how to make some money. Crow went to St. Louis to purchase a car and came back—without a car. He told Burlingame that the real opportunity was not in buying cars, but in buying the accessories.

Back then, when cars came from the manufacturer, they were not exactly ready for the road. Shipped by rail, they were minus steering wheels, lights, tops—even tires. "You had to have the accessories," Lord says. "It was like building a kit. The manufacturer just shipped the basics—a body, a transmission, axles. And that's the way they started the business. They bought the accessories and sold to dealers."

Crow-Burlingame, as the men named their company, was organized in 1919 and was one of the first automobile accessory dealerships not only in the state but in the nation. Within a few years, however, car manufacturers began to "add" the "accessories" before the cars left the factory. While this eliminated the necessity for accessory distributors, there was a growing market for automobile parts; consequently Crow-Burlingame continued operation to meet that demand. As major markets developed in the state, the firm established branches: El Dorado, Pine Bluff, Hot Springs, Stuttgart, and Texarkana were the first. The enterprise expanded steadily into the Depression, and, ironic as it may sound, the economic crisis made the business grow significantly.

By the 1930s the automobile had become popular enough that American life-styles were dependent on it. Even in their poverty, people needed to keep their cars running. It was a stimulus to the parts industry that lasted until World War II, which boosted sales

W. Robert Crow was the first president and co-founder of Crow-Burlingame. His grandsons are now active in the firm.

J.G. Burlingame, the original vice-president and treasurer of Crow-Burlingame, was in the grocery business before beginning his automobile accessories and parts business.

even more.

The government had everything on allocation, everything going to the war effort, so people had to patch up what they had and keep going. All that is the seedbed of the parts industry of today. It was still very small. The business really took off when the economy rebounded after the GIs came home from the war.

Since the 1973 oil embargo the story has been less about growth and more about change in how and where parts are distributed. Service stations, once the primary customer of the parts industry, suffered in the 1970s. Forty percent went out of business, and many of the remainder, Lord points out, "sell milk and bread and are self-service." General-service garages are growing in

number but are having to compete with shops that specialize in a single service, such as tune-ups, and the do-it-yourself trend has opened up more retail stores.

Lord, current president of the company, sees a consolidation mode now. "The number of players in the industry is shrinking. We sense it's a positive thing for us." With 61 outlets—40 in Arkansas and the rest in East Texas, Louisiana, and Missouri—Crow-Burlingame expects to keep growing, primarily by buying competitors who are the best in their marketplace and teaming up with them. The industry is headed to high volume, high efficiency. So without computerization or sophisticated inventory-control systems, it'll be hard to survive.

GARVER AND GARVER, P.A.

In the spring of 1918 Neal Garver, a professor of civil engineering at the University of Illinois, made it known he would be available for "war work" in the summer—to "help defeat the Huns." A Chicago engineering firm responded with a job in Little Rock, Arkansas, assisting the supervising engineer on construction of an explosives plant producing picric acid.

The professor went to Little Rock for the summer; and when the job lasted beyond three months, he requested a leave of absence from his teaching post. Asked to write the final report on the $7-million project and present it to the Navy, he accepted the assignment—and resigned from the university.

After the report was completed, Garver decided to remain in Arkansas. There were "architects . . . here in sufficient number to design buildings," he wrote in an autobiography, "but few could design complicated structural features." He opened an office in the Gazette Building, but later moved to the Donaghey Building when ex-Governor Donaghey

This 1920s photo shows the construction of a fixed span bridge crossing the Arkansas River. The location is a historic site, Dardanelle Rock having been noted and named by de LaHarpe, the French explorer. The man in the photo is not identified, but Neal Garver was the engineer of record on the project.

An aerial view of a 27-million-gallon-per-day wastewater-treatment plant for the City of Little Rock, Arkansas. The plant utilizes the activated sludge process and its effluent flows to the Arkansas River. Photo circa 1979

offered free rent in exchange for engineering advice. It was his ability in bridge design, however, that shaped his new career: The State Highway Department named him bridge engineer in 1921. He worked half-time, but by 1926 he was asked for three-quarters of his time.

This increased work load for the highway department affected Garver's private practice. In 1922 he had asked W.T. Morrow, a colleague from Illinois, to join him as a partner. Morrow willingly took on more of the firm's projects after 1926, and the two remained partners until the Depression. Garver then took full-time employment with the highway department, and Morrow joined the Tennessee Valley Authority staff. Buildings standing today that the two men engineered include Little Rock Central High School, North Little Rock High School, Immanuel Baptist Church, the Wallace Building, and, at the University of Arkansas, Fayetteville, the science, agriculture, and library buildings.

In 1948, after several thousand Arkansas highway bridges had been designed and constructed under his supervision, Garver returned to consultant status with the highway department. He created a new firm in 1954 with his son, Mark, a journalist as well as an engineer. Mark had edited the England, Arkansas, newspaper early in the Depression, then held three professional engineering posts before serving in World War

II. He worked in Texas after the war, returning to Little Rock in 1950 when he became the city's first traffic engineer.

Garver and Garver incorporated in 1959 with Sanford Wilbourn and Tandy V. Allen, joined later by Gordon Grayson and William J. Driggers. The organization continued work for the State Highway Department, and Wilbourn—the company's president since 1970—recalls one of the his first assignments in the 1950s being the Eighth Street Expressway, which evolved into Little Rock's I-630, completed in 1985.

Neal Garver—who in his career was president of the Mid-South Section of the American Society of Civil Engineers, the Little Rock Engineers Club, and the Arkansas State Board of Registration for Professional Engineers—retired in 1966 and died, at age 92, in 1969. Mark Garver retired in 1970; he died in 1982.

Garver and Garver has grown from a father-son partnership to a large and diversified engineering concern with more than 100 employees. It offers engineering and planning services for industrial facilities; environmental studies and facilities; highways, bridges, railroads, airports, and river ports; and land development.

ARKLA, INC.

Although Arkansas is almost 100 years older than Arkla, their names are almost synonymous and their growth is almost parallel. In 1934, when Arkla was founded, Arkansan Dick Powell lighted American movie screens in *Flirtation Walk.* That same year radio performers Lum and Abner brought Ozark life to the nation and Arkla brought gas services to over 70,000 customers.

By early 1984, when the National Basketball Association named Arkansan and Arkla board member Sidney Moncrief the Defensive Player of the Year, *Investment Decisions* named Arkla the "best-managed utility in the United States." Now in Arkansas' sesquicentennial year, Arkla serves almost 730,000 customers in a five-state area. Arkansas and Arkla have come a long way together.

In the nineteenth century American cities used expensive manufactured gas to illuminate streetlights. Various chemical processes, including burning coal or pine knots, produced the manufactured gas. By the 1860s Little Rock had manufactured-gas streetlights. And, by 1882, Little Rock paid dearly for manufactured gas—four dollars per month for each streetlight.

After Shreveport, Louisiana, converted its streetlights to natural gas, two oil wildcatters formed the Arkansas Natural Gas Company and, in 1911, completed a 160-mile gas line connecting the gas sources in northern Louisiana and Little Rock.

This pipeline supplied 5,000 customers in Little Rock and serviced many towns along its route. Although some of the early gas lines were made of wood and hollow logs, this pipeline was made of 16- and 18-inch metal pipes.

As exploration and drilling escalated between 1906 and 1934, the industry developed the technology to produce the pipes, fittings, meters, and compressors, and the ability to transport and deliver natural gas over a wide area.

Arkansas Louisiana Gas Company, now Arkla, Inc., evolved from a merger of three companies, all subsidiaries of ANG, on November 30, 1934. J.C. Hamilton, president until his death in 1957, led the organization from 71,437 customers in 1936 to 177,003 in 1949.

W.R. "Witt" Stephens became director and chairman of the board in 1957. Stephens led the company in three mergers in the 1960s, adding 178,000 customers in Arkansas, Louisiana, Texas, Oklahoma, and Kansas. In the same decade Arkla acquired huge natural gas reserves in the Arkoma basin of eastern Oklahoma and western Arkansas. By 1963 Arkla had more than 500,000 customers, and in 1966 the firm completed its corporate headquarters, Arkla Plaza, in Little Rock.

D.W. Weir, who started with the company in 1935, became chairman of the board in 1973. Weir served as co-chief executive with Sheffield Nelson, an attorney who began in Arkla's management-trainee program during his college years. Weir retired in 1979, Nelson in 1984. They began in the early 1970s to divest Arkla of some of its nonproductive and nongas-related properties, and continued the process through 1984, when the firm's focus again became acquiring, transmitting, and distributing natural gas.

When the national gas industry faced shortages during the 1970s, Arkla began development in the Anadarko Basin, in western Oklahoma, and the Texas Panhandle. A large Oklahoma discovery in 1979 further improved gas reserves. On the stock market, in 1981, Arkla had its fourth two-for-one split since 1957 when its stock first sold in the public marketplace. As a result, 100 shares purchased in 1957 had grown to 1,000 shares.

Thomas F. "Mack" McLarty

Thomas F. "Mack" McLarty leads Arkla through a reorganization program aimed at solid growth in the natural gas industry.

succeeded Nelson at Arkla, Inc., in 1985. In his first year, McLarty received the *Wall Street Transcript's* 1985 Bronze Award in competition for the top chief executive officer in the gas producer, pipeline, and distribution industry.

In 1986 McLarty led Arkla in aggressively pursuing the acquisition of Mississippi River Transmission Company of St. Louis to strengthen the company's position in the industry.

In Arkansas' sesquicentennial year, Arkla operates in five states with 80 percent of the gas reserves in the lower 48 states. Arkla has a 9,700-mile pipeline system and a 16,000-mile distribution system. In 1984 the organization delivered 117.4 billion cubic feet of gas to its customers, who have among the lowest rates in the nation.

As Arkansans use natural gas for heating homes, preparing meals, or for any of the more than 25,000 uses of natural gas, they know Arkla will continue to make discoveries, developments, and distributions to improve the quality of life for all its customers. Arkla's 50-plus years complement Arkansas' 150 years. The names belong together—Arkla and Arkansas.

POLYVEND

It was just a screw, or an auger, more accurately. Nothing unique or special about that, unless it was used in a revolutionary way. The concept was to motorize this long screw-type mechanism and, each time it made a full turn, have something drop off its end. What products might be suitable?

Pat Stoltz took the bare-bones idea and soon matched it with a use: dispensing snack items from vending machines. With the concept of attractively presenting the snacks behind glass, Stoltz made a proposal to Tom's Peanuts in Columbus, Georgia.

Tom's listened. Others called it folly. Vandalism was inevitable, they said, with food in full view and accessible with just a blow to the glass. Tom's wasn't ready to commit, but, with Stoltz's enthusiasm, it was willing to experiment. Stoltz made some machines, and the firm put the first-ever glass-front vending machines on the grounds at the 1964 New York World's Fair.

It seemed they had something. A man had to be put to work full-time just to keep the machines filled, and that was with five-cent snacks being sold for a quarter.

An aerial view of Polyvend's 250,000-square-foot production facility.

J.P. Stoltz, founder.

After a few more test models, Tom's was ready to place a production order. Pat Stoltz was about to revolutionize the vending machine industry, and it was all happening from Conway, Arkansas.

Stoltz had been recruited to Arkansas when an industrial search committee sought a firm to manufacture the state's car license plates. His experience in metal fabricating and novelty license plates in Pennsylvania qualified him for the venture. He moved from Pennsylvania to Arkansas, and began Custommade Products in Lonoke in 1955.

Three years later the entrepreneur sold the company to the S.G. Adams Company of St. Louis, which was then acquired by Universal Match Corporation. Interested in opening another plant in Arkansas to expand its product line, Universal asked Stoltz to stay on as a vice-president and general manager for the proposed facility. He was told it could be in the town of his choice.

Stoltz accepted the offer and chose Conway. His son, Steve, says he once asked why he decided on that community. His father mentioned its proximity to Little Rock and its accessibility to good transportation. The Arkansas River was opening to navigation, and rail lines were close by—and he had his family in mind. Conway had good schools, two colleges, and a strong Catholic community.

After two years of heading Universal, Stoltz was ready to be on his own again. He reverted to what he knew best, and in February 1962 opened up a 20,000-square-foot facility called Metal Stamping Corporation—and again began making Arkansas license plates. The firm then bid and was awarded similar contracts in other states, and by the late 1960s it was the largest commercial manufacturer of license plates in the world. Two shifts were producing more than 100,000 plates per day. The company made other products, too, such as electrical control boxes, truck bodies, gas lamp posts, and deep-fat fish fryers.

Vending machines, after 1964, gave Metal Stamping a new direction. The heyday of license plate manufacturing was eventually to wane: States began issuing small reflectorized stickers with the year's date on them, and only they needed annual replacement.

Stoltz's interest and growing understanding of the vending indus-

try soon took him more deeply into it. In 1976 he launched a program that again led vending in a new direction. He started thinking small—designing machines that dispensed coffee and cold drinks for small locations, such as offices.

During this period Steve Stoltz, the eldest boy of the nine Stoltz children, joined the operation. This fulfilled his father's desire to maintain a family operation by involving the second generation. Steve had begun to learn the business at 14, starting with the proverbial broom, and had worked in each department by the time he entered Notre Dame—where he graduated in 1974 with a degree in business administration.

He was in sales with a Memphis company in 1975 when his father suggested that, if he was considering returning to the family company soon, now was a good time. He would be there from the start of this new vending venture, which they were calling Cooperative Service Vending (CSV).

Steve returned in 1975 as national sales manager, then vice-president of sales and a member of the board of directors. One of the decisions that he and his father made was to change the corporate name. As the growth of the organization was in vending, they chose the name Polyvend ("poly" being the Latin derivative of the word for "many").

In the late 1970s the corporation opened itself to the international market, creating two subsidiaries. Polyvend International is the marketing arm that sells vending equipment worldwide; Polyvend Ltd. is a base operation in England from which the vending equipment, manufactured in Arkansas, is sold and serviced in the United Kingdom.

In the midst of putting CSV on

Polyvend currently manufactures a vast array of products.

the market, founder Pat Stoltz died, in 1977. Steve assumed the presidency. Within a few years the national economy caused him to reshape some long-range planning of the company. Interest rates were 22 percent, and many vending customers were merging, or going under, and therefore not buying new vending machines. He decided Polyvend was too vulnerable as a one-industry operation.

Knowing its strength in manufacturing, he began to solicit fabrication and assembly contracts from national firms. One of the first it was awarded was a Black and Decker Corporation order for 500,000 belt sanders that was needed for the Christmas season—an order its own factories could not produce. Polyvend did it.

"That proved to us that we could produce for even consumer products companies with their rigid specifications, quality standards, and high volume," Stoltz says. "That convinced us. We got very aggressive in contract manufacturing and discovered that we were well equipped to produce a variety of products under contract. Our skills in sheet metal, fabrication, and painting, and our internal engineering support lent themselves very well to other types of manufacturing. Now it is a fundamental premise within our long-range plans that we do both: grow our proprietary products in vending while continuing to pursue certain types of contract work."

So, in addition to its oldest customer, the State of Arkansas, for

A prototype of the first glass-front vending machine produced by the firm.

whom Polyvend continues to make license plates; and its next oldest, and largest, customer, Tom's Foods, which has bought more than 150,000 glass-front merchandisers, Polyvend is adding many more names to its client list.

Steve Stoltz praises the crew of 400 people who work for Polyvend in Conway (the original 20,000-square-foot facility is now 250,000 square feet), who have the flexibility to adapt well to both types of production. There are another 50 employees at the Polyvend headquarters in England. All of them are contributing to a company that has more than once put Arkansas on the map for manufacturing distinction—in capacity and creativity.

CMW, INC.

When John Cline was 13 years old, his father traded the family's property in Illinois to a stranger in town for 120 acres that he had never seen in Fallsville, Arkansas. An unheralded event at the time, about 1908, the move is valued now by Clarksville residents who can recall John's part in their community. He was a character, a well-loved leader, a man who could fix things. And through his little machine and welding shop, opened in 1929, he left them an unusual legacy—the seedbed for Arkansas' most "high-tech" industry of the 1980s.

As far as education, John Cline finished seventh grade, read constantly, and tinkered. His father noticed his mechanical bent early; and when the boy was ten he gave him his own shop, instructing him in metals, tools, and forging. Tinkering later became Cline's livelihood. Once married and settled in Alix, a coal-mining town near Altus, he worked on coal-cutting machinery, converting plane bearings to ball bearings. Then he expanded his garage and repaired America's newest gadgets—automobiles and airplanes. He rebuilt an entire plane once, taught pilots, and only stopped his own flying when he tired of airsickness.

Cline moved his business to Clarksville in 1929. Four years later the local paper featured him as

John Cline, founder of Clarksville Machine Works, today's CMW, is the third adult from the left in the back row of this Depression-era photograph. His son Jack, who later took over leadership of the company, is the boy wearing a cap at left. Mrs. Cline and the Cline daughters are also in the photograph. Courtesy, Jack Cline

"one of the nation's most interesting men," writing about his patented inventions that had drawn people to his Clarksville Machine Works from all over the United States.

Although it was the height of the Depression, 1933 was a year of expansion for Cline, who enlarged his building and was keeping 39 employees busy. Prohibition had just ended, and suddenly the machine he had invented to make barrel staves for beer and bourbon kegs was in high demand. Earl Bean, who came to work for Cline in 1943, recalls that the shop was still making staving machines and

converting the mining machinery during World War II. It also had some contracted "defense work," which, by law, had first priority. It was enough work for 15 employees; but after the war and without defense contracts, times were slow until the new Small Business Administration offered more government contracts.

"He was a very energetic person—had to be," Bean says of Cline, and recalls, "I've worked with him until two in the morning, trying to get something ready for people to work on at seven in the morning. He was that kind of a person; he'd stick with you."

Jack Cline's recollection of his father is similar—that four hours of sleep was a long night, and that he was busy the other 20 hours of the day, and not just with mechanical matters. According to his son, John Cline had stayed an avid reader, was a marksman of note, a self-taught musician with a third-place prize in a national fiddling contest and a seat in the violin section of Clarksville's Little Symphony, a pilot (he took up flying again at 55), Clarksville's first airport commissioner, "the best softball pitcher in town," and a man who could spell anything.

Jack Cline invented the Hydro-Cooler in 1949 for a Clarksville peach grower. Today he sells them internationally since CMW, the family company he sold in 1978, sold production rights back to him. He makes them in the original 1929 shop, also pictured. Courtesy, Jack Cline

"I've never in my life seen someone as well loved as that man, by everyone he ever touched," Jack says of his father. "He was a man a long time ahead of his time . . . and more of a genius than he was a businessman," he adds, noting that his machines made millionaires of more than one customer.

After serving in World War II, son Jack returned to Clarksville, and to his father's business, in 1945. Soon he followed in John's inventive footsteps, and produced the world's first Hydro-Cooler.

As his father had with his inventions, Jack was responding to the need of a customer. A local peach grower asked Jack to fly to the University of Michigan to check out its research on using ice water to preserve peaches. The research showed that the fruit lasted longer, and thus could be shipped farther, if cooled by 33-degree water for 15 minutes. The cooling permanently stopped the natural respirative process that produces ethylene gas and raises a fruit's temperature. Cline became a believer and came home to design, build, and deliver the grower a Hydro-Cooler.

"That thing started something," Cline says. "In this day you can't sell a fruit or vegetable that has not been hydro-cooled." In 1949 it was a brand-new concept, and Cline's machines caught nationwide attention. Orders came unsolicited. In 1959 he had to build a larger building across town to make the Hydro-Coolers. "There's nothing patentable about them," he says, "but this is the Cadillac." The Canadian government toured the United States in the 1970s and settled on Cline's Hydro-Coolers as the ones they would order in mass, then sell to Canadian farmers, subsidized according to the farmers' needs.

When Jack erected the new building, his father sold his half of the machine works business, choosing to concentrate on his hardwood flooring company. Four years later,

in 1963, the elder inventor died.

Hydro-Cooler production continued, but Clarksville Machine Works was headed for a new era—the result of still another customer request. A local brick manufacturer wanted a machine to strap his bricks up for shipment. Cline and his crew designed and built the machine. Soon the firm supplying the brick company with its steel strapping bands was asking questions. Why the enormous orders for strap from Clarksville, Arkansas? When he saw the new machine, the regional salesman saw opportunity for his Chicago company, Signode Steel Strapping. Signode would market the machines if Clarksville Machine Works would make and service them. Cline agreed. "That's what made this company," Cline says now. With over 100 employees aboard, he began to fill orders both nationally and internationally, and Signode sold strap to every customer.

Signode was the company's major account when Jerry Stokes came to apprentice under Cline, a year before the latter's retirement. Cline had sold his operation in 1978 to Robert L. Kietzman and Don E. Dixon, who later made it part of Advanced Manufacturing Systems, Inc., which became a public company in 1985. After the sale they shortened the corporate name to CMW, and in 1981 sold Hydro-Cooler production back to Cline.

CMW has positioned itself in the high-technology market. "But we relate to John Cline," Stokes—president since 1980—says, "because he helped customers solve problems. He did it mechanically. We do it with many different tech-

nologies." The corporation's customers include some major names in the U.S. manufacturing industry: General Electric, Whirlpool, LTV Aerospace and Defense, Acme Brick, Brown and Root, and Signode. They have come to CMW to automate their operations and make use of the latest manufacturing technology. CMW engineers visit their plants, then custom design systems for them, systems that are a combination of many machines, with robots, lasers, computers—systems that can even diagnose themselves if something goes wrong.

In all, CMW does about six million dollars of business in a year. Stokes is proud that this sophisticated work is designed and produced by local people. "If a kid in high school shows interest in engineering, electronics, or computers, we have him here in the summers and after school. Our people are as capable as anyone in the country." Eighty employees are on CMW's rolls.

When Stokes talks about the company's future, the adventuresome and inventive Cline spirit is still apparent. "We're still moving," Stokes says. "A year from now we'll be doing things we haven't even thought of."

AFFILIATED FOOD STORES, INC.

In the mid-1940s ten independent Little Rock retail grocers, who invested $1,000 each, formed the nucleus of what was later to become Model Markets, Inc. Through that firm they were able to work cooperatively in purchasing food products at wholesale prices, as well as instituting a group advertising program.

The foresight of the individuals who directed Model Markets and the subsequent leadership over the past 40 years has contributed to Affiliated Food Stores emerging as one of the largest, most modern and efficient wholesale food cooperatives in the southwest United States. With distribution centers in Little Rock and Van Buren, Affiliated currently services 250 member supermarkets located in Arkansas, Louisiana, Mississippi, Tennessee, and Oklahoma. The initial $10,000 investment of those 10 retailers created more than $317 million in sales in 1985, and the four people employed in 1948 were supplemented with another 708 employees in 1986.

The growth of Model Markets, Inc.—which became Associated Wholesale Grocers Warehouse in 1957 and Affiliated Food Stores, Inc., in 1972—has been phenomenal. In 1957 independent retail grocers in Little Rock had less than 5 percent of the market share; today Affiliated Food Stores claims about 30 percent of the market.

Foresight and good management have obviously been at play in the development of this nonprofit cooperative. Four of the original Little Rock grocers who formed Model Markets, Inc., were C.H. McCrory, A.B. Corder, Eldron Taylor, and O.E. Fiser. Each of them, at one time, served as chairman of the board. Currently the chairman of the board and chief executive officer is C.E. "Doc" Toland, who came to work for Model Markets in 1948. He had worked for two years with a Little Rock food broker, and before being drafted for service in World War II had owned his own grocery store for two years with his brother-in-law.

Toland tells the history of Affiliated Food Stores with clarity, never taking credit for shaping its history; but many who have worked with him suggest that it is so. He does chuckle at his longevity with the company, noting that when he became general manager in 1957, he was the youngest in that position among the national associated grocers. In 1986, his retirement year, he holds the distinction of being the oldest of his contemporaries.

In explaining Affiliated Food Stores, Toland begins by placing it in the context of food distribution in general. There are national chains—a classification given to a company that owns 11 or more grocery stores—which operate their own warehouses. There are voluntary wholesalers, who sell to everyone; and there are retailer-owned cooperatives, which sprang from the same idea in the 1940s that prompted the organization of Model Markets, Inc. The national owners have 50 percent of the trade, and the voluntaries and retailer cooperatives split the other half evenly. In the whole of the United States, there are "90 warehouses like ours," says Toland. "We're classified as a medium/large food distribution center."

Available to any Affiliated member retailer are over 16,000 items located within the distribution

Current chairman of the board of directors, C.E. "Doc" Toland (center), with Bain Corder of Little Rock (left) and O.E. Fiser of Sheridan, Arkansas (right).

centers. Virtually state-of-the-art computer purchasing systems are employed to ensure a continuous supply of product for the 250 stores serviced through the facilities. The organization maintains an impeccable record of high service.

Attending the 1965 ground-breaking ceremony for the current Affiliated Food Stores Warehouse at 12103 Interstate 30 in Little Rock were (left to right) Bain Corder, Harry Booe, Paul Bone, J.T. McKinnon, C.E. "Doc" Toland, O.E. Fiser, Everett Ward, Allen Bellamy, and George Bruno.

A tour of the Little Rock warehouse defies old perceptions of warehousing. Affiliated's Little Rock Warehouse—now in its fifth location—is a whole world under one roof. A variety of climates provides for different storage needs: the cool, dry room with the crisp apples; the cool, damp room that houses green, leafy vegetables such as cabbage and lettuce; the antarctic room with acres of frozen foods; the jungle section with still-green bananas fresh from South America; and the child's fantasy room, with every confection sold on the market, stacked four stories high.

As Affiliated is located near railroad tracks, it was once serviced by rail; however, all its items now come in and go out by truck. The firm's own 44-foot trailer trucks do triple duty—delivering orders as well as mail to the 250 stores it serves, and hauling inbound merchandise on the return trip.

While food and dry goods are the largest space users at the company's headquarters, there is more to the story of what Affiliated does for its member stores. It can begin assisting the member even before a store is built. If an independent grocer wants to build a new unit, Affiliated has a department that can survey a location, draw plans, then lay out the merchandise when the store is constructed. It boasts an investment corporation, which can provide adequate financial assistance, and an advertising and print shop, which can—among other services—develop a six- to eight-week promotion for a new outlet.

For its established stores Affiliated has a supermarket equipment company that purchases equipment and sells, at a substantial savings, to its members. It also gives host support to front-end scanners in supermarkets—or, in layman's terms, the computers talk to each other in the night and can, in turn, enable Affiliated to change prices on items in different stores—

eliminating the time-consuming and costly can-by-can hand pricing.

Affiliated Food Stores provides an insurance agency, Arkansas Retail Grocers Insurance Services (ARGIS), and the Grocers Financial Services Credit Union.

The firm is not always just the middle man, but a producer as well. Toland speculates that the company's Gold Star Dairy, located in Little Rock, is the most modern in the world. Begun in 1979, Gold Star is the largest user of raw milk in Arkansas. It was also the first dairy worldwide to deliver milk in disposable cardboard crates, a practice that other dairies in the nation are beginning to adopt. Winnsboro Beverage Packers in Winnsboro, Louisiana, an additional Affiliated subsidiary, provides private-label soft drinks for the corporation as well as for other distribution centers located throughout the country.

Affiliated Food Stores, Inc., currently services Thriftway, Food 4 Less, Skaggs Alpha Beta, Piggly Wiggly, Jitney Jungle, Smitty's

Affiliated Food Stores' trucks become rolling billboards for its Shurfine and Shurfresh Private Label Brand Program. The Affiliated fleet travels over five million miles annually.

Food King, Williams, and Independent Affiliated Food Stores.

Toland summarizes the Affiliated story with the cooperative's role in Arkansas' history and economy. The largest population it directly affects is the consumer in Arkansas who can "buy food at a lower cost, including a better variety, at improved supermarkets." The organization has enabled the independent retail grocer not only to survive but to progress; it has created a number of successful satellite companies and subsidiaries; and with 712 people on its rolls, it is a substantial employer.

Automation within Affiliated Food Stores' distribution center enables supermarket products to move efficiently from warehouse to retail supermarket shelves. Automation results in keeping food costs down.

CAMELOT HOTEL

The business and professional community realized its dream of making Little Rock a convention center when ground was broken for the Camelot Hotel in March 1971.

Anyone who was there for the groundbreaking of the Camelot Hotel remembers it well: It was a Monday in March 1971, and with the crowd of well-wishers were armored knights on white horses carrying swords to break the earth, with trumpeters to blow the fanfare. They embodied the theme of the hotel about to be built.

Everyone remembers the rain too. The heavens opened up and poured on the well-wishers, the knights, the horses, the spot of earth to be dug, the trumpeters, and buildings in the block on Markham Street, just west of the Old State House, that soon would be demolished to make way for a spectacular change in the streetscape and in Little Rock's ability to be hospitable.

Many years and tenacious dreaming preceded this groundbreaking. The fact that Kinark Corporation had come to Little Rock with an interest in developing the Camelot Hotel made possible the rest of the construction happening on the block, in addition to the hotel. It involved remodeling the Robinson Memorial Auditorium, as it was then called, plus building a long-needed parking lot that would be underground, with a brick plaza covering it. The auditorium was funded by an Eco-

nomic Development Act grant, the parking lot by the City of Little Rock, and the plaza by the Little Rock Housing Authority. Another part of the construction, just east of the hotel, was the Arkansas Bar Center, headquarters for the Arkansas Bar Association.

It was the idea for the latter facility, suggested eight years earlier, that had the groundbreaking happening in this particular site. However, the dream for a hotel and convention center area—which the Robinson Auditorium was being remodeled for—had been alive even longer.

In the 1950s and 1960s Little Rock's grand hotels were old—not a bad quality in itself, except there was no promise of their being refurbished. No facility in the city could satisfy the needs for a large convention, and Little Rock was missing its chances for what some cities were finding a profitable enterprise—hosting not only state but regional and national meetings.

At one point the Little Rock Housing Authority, operating with federal urban renewal funds, tore down the Victorian buildings between the Marion and Manning hotels (in the block the Excelsior Hotel and Statehouse Convention Center now occupy), hoping that the management of the hotels

would develop and manage a convention space there. It never happened.

Then, in 1963, William S. Mitchell, president of the Arkansas Bar Association, called his friend Edwin Cromwell, an architect, asking advice. He wondered about the feasibility of restoring the old Rose law firm building, just west of the Old State House, for the bar association's state headquarters. Cromwell went to look it over.

Conscious of the city's search for a way to host conventions, Cromwell saw the site in that context and began to dream of a combination of the bar center and other facilities on the block that then had old houses and industrial facilities on it. He suggested that the attorneys delay plans for their headquarters and to consider the broader scope of possibilities. Cromwell involved others in this vision, such as the City of Little Rock and the Chamber of Commerce. When the city was approached for permission to close Spring Street, north from Mark-

ham Street, to build a 550-car parking lot for the auditorium Mayor Martin Borchert listened to the plans and suggested a hotel should be a part of it all. The plans also spurred the development of the Little Rock Parking Authority.

With everyone's contribution in, Cromwell's architectural firm and the Chamber of Commerce funded a model of the complex and began to circulate it around the city, in bank lobbies and the like, where citizens could see the possibilities for the convention area—if only there were a developer for the hotel shown on the model.

Eventually the model, well circulated about town, was retired to the back workroom of the Chamber of Commerce. And, as had been happening all along, Hot Springs continued entertaining about 90 percent of the convention trade in the state.

One day a man came to town representing a company called Kinark Corporation, a Tulsa-based oil and gas firm that was branching into the hotel industry. With a successful venture in Tulsa, it was looking at Little Rock for its next such development. The Chamber of Commerce had escorted the man, Abe Hessler, all over Little Rock, but he was not encouraged with anything he saw and went back to their offices to wait until his plane left. When offered a cup of coffee, he went to the workroom to help make it—and there was the hotel site he was looking for in the retired two-year-old model with the auditorium, bar center, parking deck, and plaza.

The Cromwell Firm was nearby, Hessler was told, and within minutes he had cancelled his plane trip and arranged to talk with representatives of the firm and, in March 1971, there was a groundbreaking. It took having this developer to make the rest of the package work—a complicated package, according to the memories of those involved, with grants,

bond issues, and multiple leases having to mesh, which George Millar, then the administrative head of the Chamber of Commerce, orchestrated with skill. What is built on the two-block stretch of Markham, between Broadway and the Old State House, is much as the model showed it.

The Camelot Hotel not only gave Little Rock 303 new hotel rooms, it provided the Great Hall where 800 people could sit for a banquet and 1000 for a meeting. The largest space until then had been the Marion's ballroom which could crowd in 300 people for a meal; however, the Marion had closed in 1969. The Great Hall's 8,720 square feet divide into four small rooms, and another four rooms are available for meetings as well. In combination with the exhibit and meeting space at the adjacent Robinson Center there is a total of 40,000 square feet. The music hall at the Robinson Center seats 2,655 and the 21,237-square-foot exhibit area is also used for large meetings and banquets. The Camelot is the official caterer for functions at the Robinson Center.

The Civitan International Ozarks District made a place in the history of the Camelot Hotel when it hosted its first meeting there, just after the hotel opened on June 1, 1973. By September 1973, when the Robinson Center was finished, the convention of the Central State Shrine Association brought 16,000 people to the facility. It was a function so large that Little Rock and Hot Springs split the hosting duties. Conventions continued to come to the Camelot, the earliest ones planned some years before the hotel was actually completed.

In February 1971—a month before the groundbreaking—Barry

The Camelot Hotel is at the center of activity in Little Rock. Besides offering convenient accommodations and entertainment facilities, it also has restaurants and a coffee shop that overlook the Arkansas River.

Travis, now head of the Little Rock Convention Center, became the third person on its staff. To illustrate what the combination of the new convention center and Camelot Hotel started, in combination with other factors (a mixed drink law in 1969, the establishment of the Advertising and Promotion Commission in 1970, and the opening of other inns and hotels in the early 1970s), he compares the three-person staff he joined to the 84-person staff he now manages. In 1970 there were 84 meetings or conventions in central Arkansas compared to 531 in 1985. Most telling of the effects of the Camelot and other factors is that in 1971 the people who came to meetings spent $2,635,390 in central Arkansas and in 1985 they spent $42,503,891.

The Camelot is in the center of activity of the Little Rock convention and meeting trade, feeding people in its Country Squire coffee shop that overlooks the Arkansas River, and in the King's Court, known for its prime rib. Jester's Lounge features live entertainment nightly and there is no estimation of how many well-known people these facilities have fed, the Camelot having been host to most of the entertainers who come to Little Rock and use the Robinson Center's stage. They find it convenient, as all Camelot guests do, to the airport, the major interstates, the Riverfront Park, and the center of downtown Little Rock, with its restored neighborhoods and historic museums.

ARTHUR YOUNG & COMPANY

A sophisticated display of the works of Arkansas artists hangs on the walls of the Arthur Young offices in Little Rock. Each month, in boardrooms of the statewide museums and performing arts organizations, members of the Arthur Young firm give attention and advice as directors of the boards. Arthur Young & Company contributes leadership in the Downtown Partnership and the Arkansas Repertory Theatre; has volunteers at Riverfest, the symphony, and Arts Center events; and gives support to its employees competing in sports teams—even chili cookoffs.

This support, leadership, and volunteerism is all a part of the good corporate citizenship that Arthur Young fosters as an organization and encourages in its employees. A close relationship with the community is as important to the company as the close relationship it nurtures with its clients.

Arthur Young has a long record of helping Arkansas—it is the largest and oldest accounting operation in the state, founded in December 1923 by the late Russell G. Brown. Brown, who died in 1981, was one of the state's first licensed CPAs and served as president of the Arkansas Society of CPAs and the State Board of Accountancy. Known since 1982 as Arthur Young & Company, today the firm has 130 people working in offices in Little Rock and, to serve the northwest part of the state, Fayetteville. It works with a diversity of clients, and offers them a diversity of services—services far beyond the scope of an accountant's work in the late nineteenth century when, in Chicago, founder Arthur Young established his accounting enterprise in 1894.

In those days accounting was hardly more than bookkeeping, a condensed balance sheet and summary income statement sufficing for most companies. A burgeoning economy in the early 1900s brought changes—not only examination of the accounts but closer attention to the firm's accounting techniques. By the late 1920s accounting had established a professional identity, and in 1933 the federal Security Act required that the annual statement of all listed corporations be accompanied by certificates of opinion from independent accountants.

Other federal regulations from the 1930s increased corporate needs for accountants; however, the Depression economy, followed by World War II, delayed recognition of the accountant's vital role until the 1950s. Since that time, especially with the new computer technology, accounting has forever buried its old bowler hat and wire-rimmed glasses image.

At Arthur Young a person deft only in numbers is obsolete. Its professionals see themselves as more than an accountant, auditor, tax professional, or consultant. They see themselves as trusted business advisors.

Edwin Hanlon, managing partner for Arkansas' Arthur Young, explains the importance of this concept. "An audit should be a confirmation of what we already know," he says. "Evidence of a deficient relationship is when an audit generates a surprise." The basic responsibility of financial and management consultants is to advise their clients about the risks involved in their business activities, he continues. "In a fully developed client situation, we become their sounding board, whether they are seeking a recommendation on which accounting principles to follow or something as major as acquiring another company."

Hanlon, describing the company as "a conservative organization that has devoted itself to highly personal, extremely high-quality products, particularly in the areas of audit and tax advice," adds, "At the same time, we have always been one of the firms closest to the cutting edge in the development of

Spectacular fireworks have become a hallmark of huge outdoor events in Arkansas, many of which are sponsored by Arthur Young & Company.

new technologies."

Arthur Young believes that specialization in certain specific areas is beneficial to its practice as well as to its clients. In Arkansas it has identified areas where it has unique, marketable proficiencies, and is concentrating on building upon the broad base it has already established. The practice has become so proficient in the areas of agribusiness that it is now the national resource on the topic of agricultural cooperatives for all Arthur Young offices in the United States.

The firm has a large base of banks and saving and loan associations as clients in Arkansas, and

Arthur Young & Company is a leader in support of the arts in the state, including performances by the Arkansas Repertory Theatre.

its financial services group is continuing to better serve not only financial institutions but all its clients. In addition, Arthur Young maintains a highly specialized tax department that in itself is a large operation.

Technology magazine named the organization to its "Technology 100" list of the top innovators in America for one of its achievements in adapting microcomputer technology to its audit practice. Its "audit computer" was the first in use within the profession.

The computer technology means that time once spent "crunching numbers" now goes into planning, identifying problems quickly, and analyzing alternative tax-saving strategies. In the analysis, performed during the regular audit work, a company can find out whether there is a cause and a remedy for unfavorable trends—or can confirm that everything is fine.

In consulting, use of the new technology means that the firm can help a company develop, for example, systems that will not only give its executives more up-to-date information for better planning

power but will enable them to do analyses and projections. The management consulting services from Arthur Young range from systems development, industrial engineering, and compensation/benefit planning to financial planning and control, cash management, and productivity studies.

Arthur Young also has an entrepreneurial services group to serve owner/operated businesses—who in many cases do not have the luxury of in-house expertise in such areas as computer technology, taxes, or financial management. "We've taken some clients from their early days, all the way to going public," said a local employee. "It's exciting for our people—we go to New York with them when they're admitted to the big board."

One of the "Big Eight" international CPA firms, Arthur Young—whose growth has primarily taken place within the last 20 years—is headquartered in New York City. It has 83 offices in the United States and more than 200 offices abroad. In the past 10 years it has had the best record of all of the Big Eight firms in attracting *For-*

tune 500 industrial companies as clients; has had four of its partners elected chairman of the American Institute of CPAs in the last two decades—more than in any other organization; and has been selected to perform more peer reviews of large acounting firms than any other.

Arthur Young's offices are organized into five geographic areas, each of which is under the direction of a regional managing partner. The Arkansas practice is part of the Southwest region. The company views the state as having the potential for major economic growth in the next decade. "Arkansas' motto as 'The Land of Opportunity' is certainly a correct statement," Hanlon says. "Arkansas has nothing but opportunities. And we are prepared to do all we can to assist and share in the economic developments that lie ahead."

Hundreds of thousands of people each year visit the Riverfest celebration along the Arkansas River in Little Rock over Memorial Day weekend.

MOUNTAIRE FEEDS, INC.

When Hayes Grain and Commission Company began doing business in 1914, feed mills were a familiar part of daily life. Feeding the family horse then was as routine as filling up the family car today. Many families kept a small flock of chickens, perhaps a dairy cow, in their backyard, for their own supply of milk and eggs. Whether they drove their wagon right up to the mill's loading dock for sacks of grain and garden seeds, or bought from a general feed store, people were aware of the mill's importance to their daily lives. The flour for their bread even came from there.

The importance of a feed mill has never changed—only its visibility is different, says Ronnie Cameron, president of Mountaire Feeds, Inc., the successor of Hayes Grain and Commission Company. With just two percent of the population directly involved in food production, he notes, few people are considering what horses, chickens, and cows are eating. Mountaire Feeds has stayed aware of their nutritional needs, and continues to provide high-quality feed for livestock, shipping within Arkansas and out to surrounding states—as it has for more than seven decades.

Cameron's grandfather, Guy Cameron, was a minority partner, with the Reverend James Thomas, in C.E. Hayes' Grain and Commission Company. A native of Gallatin, Missouri, Cameron had moved to Little Rock in 1905, nine years before the grain business started. In 1931 he purchased his partner's interest in the business and changed its name to Cameron Feed Mill. The partners had relocated the mill in the early 1920s from Little Rock to its current North Little Rock location. In 1923 a fire destroyed the original mill, and they built a concrete and steel structure to replace it.

Guy Cameron's son, Ted, born in 1917, began an early apprentice-

Ronnie Cameron is the third generation to head the family's feed business, now known as Mountaire Feeds.

ship as a general helper at his father's feed mill. Officially Ted joined the company after he had earned a degree in business administration at Washington University in St. Louis in 1937. He eventually worked in all of the major departments, learning the business from the ground up—production, sales, finance, nutrition, and merchandising.

As an illustration of the role feed mills play in the nation's economy, Ronnie recalls that his father tried to enlist in World War II but was told by the government that his work at the mill was essential to the war effort, so he stayed home with the family business. In 1948, a few years after the war's close, founder Guy Cameron passed away. In the following three decades his son, Ted, greatly expanded the scope of the business.

Today Mountaire Feeds, Inc., as Cameron Feed Mills was renamed in 1971, is one of four related industries within the Mountaire Corporation, headed by Ted's son, Ronnie, who assumed the presidency in 1973. Ted, then chairman of the corporation, died in 1978.

The mill produces bulk and bagged "Prime Quality Brand" feeds for all animals, including horse, fish, and poultry, manufactured from raw ingredients that come to the mill. The feed is marketed primarily in Arkansas, Oklahoma, Texas, Louisiana, and Mississippi.

Also part of Mountaire Corporation is a vitamin premix operation, started in 1964 at the North Little Rock mill. Called Mountaire Vitamins, Inc., it sells microingredients, to mix with animal feed, to mills throughout the southern states, with some exports to Central and South America.

The two other industries in the firm are Mountaire Foods, a food distributorship in San Antonio acquired in 1973—which markets poultry and meat products, eggs, cheese, and other food items in San Antonio and the surrounding area—and Mountaire of Delmarva, Inc., an integrated poultry operation in Delaware and Maryland, acquired in 1977.

The sophisticated nutritional research behind today's feed products was not known in the mill's early days, but the company showed

This concrete and steel structure was built in 1923, replacing one that had burned. In 1984 Mountaire added a 28,000-square-foot warehouse, which can store up to 2,500 tons of feed.

an awareness of the health benefits of mixing grains in certain proportions. The company also showed an early savvy for the advertising benefits of correctly mixed feeds. In 1922 Hayes Grain and Commission published *Horse Sense,* a pamphlet for the merchants who sold their product. The booklet reveals the company's sense of the political times, boasting on the front cover to sell "Arkansas Feeds for Arkansas Needs." It told merchants: "Boost your home state that you and yours may prosper! Sell the Hayes line of feeds that your customers may be tied to you with the iron bonds of quality!"

Advertising copy is not the only thing that has changed in 60 years. Some of Mountaire's longtime, present employees recall the old 100-pound cotton and burlap bags of grain that came in and were shipped from Cameron Feed Mill. They also remember the unloading that was done by hand, with workers "all over the place" pushing five bags at a time on two-wheelers. That is a contrast to the ton of grain that a man can now move at one time with a fork lift, the grains bagged in paper sacks of 25 and 50 pounds. Paper replaced the cloth bags in the 1950s.

In those sacks today may be as many as 200 different formulas that the mill manufactures in a given month, according to Bob DeClerk, a vice-president and Mountaire Feeds' general manager. Grains come into the mill daily, and with formulas researched for more than two decades, the mill mixes the ingredients and, when called for, uses the appropriate milling machines to make the mixture into pellets, or to roll or grind it. As far back as 1919 the mill was manufacturing molasses feeds, and today the sugar by-product is still brought in and used in many of the feed mixtures.

In time the company began the manufacture of dairy feeds and, in October 1924, went into the pro-

For twenty-one years there have been no better feeds made for Livestock and Poultry than—

HAYES QUALITY FEEDS

Manufactured by

HAYES GRAIN & COMMISSION CO.,
Little Rock, Arkansas

In order that the style of this firm may reveal the true ownership and character of the business, THE NAME IS BEING CHANGED TO—

CAMERON FEED MILLS

If you are a buyer of feed, you are already familiar with the high quality of our products. This quality will absolutely be maintained, and you cannot afford to overlook figuring with us when buying feed.

CAMERON FEED MILLS

LITTLE ROCK, ARKANSAS

Guy Cameron, President   W. W. Knight, Vice Pres.

Joe E. Scott, Treasurer

(Mill located Fifth and Poplar, North Little Rock)

A 1932 newspaper advertisement announces Mountaire's first name change from Hayes Grain & Commission Co. to Cameron Feed Mills, reflecting a change of ownership.

duction of poultry feeds. After a period of concentrating on the poultry industry, Mountaire Feeds has found a special niche in the feed market, manufacturing an especially high-quality feed line for all animals. About three-quarters of its feed is sold in bags, to about 250 dealers, and the rest is sold in bulk to large fish farmers and cattle and dairy farmers. "The warehouse turns over about once a week," says DeClerk.

For the volume of feed it handles, Mountaire erected a new 28,000-square-foot warehouse in late 1984. It allows the mill to store up to 2,500 tons of animal and poultry feed and vitamin premixes for immediate shipment to customers. The last warehouse had been built in 1957.

The firm represents a long legacy of feed manufacturing—with a history actually bigger than itself. As it has adapted to the changing marketplace, added trucking to the traditional rail transportation for receiving and delivering, and distinguished itself in the vitamin premix industry, it tells a partial story of the whole feed industry. One all-too-common chapter it has not entered: absorption into a larger, nationally familiar feed company. It remains today with the third generation of a local family, adding jobs with its expansions and delivering quality Arkansas products to the state and throughout the South.

In North Little Rock since the early 1920s, Mountaire is strategically placed next to rail lines, once the only way grains were transported. Today trucks have become essential, and some grains even arrive by way of barges on the Arkansas River.

BALDWIN & SHELL CONSTRUCTION CO.
LITTLE ROCK, ARKANSAS

Bob Shell was a mail boy at Fones Brothers in 1950 when he heard that the Baldwin Company needed a timekeeper. It was a 10-month job, at Ninth and Picron in Little Rock. The company was constructing a housing project for the Little Rock Housing Authority. Shell left Fones Brothers—the first employment he had found after returning home from the Navy—for the new job.

According to schedule, at the end of 10 months Shell was no longer employed. However, he took notice that the payroll clerk had left her job at the office. "It dawned on me, I could do that job," he recalls, noting that, if they hired him, he would be the company's first male payroll clerk.

Shell was given the job. From that position he "got into accounting, into estimating," and, in 1962, he became a board member and officer for the company. Now he is president of Baldwin & Shell, general contractors.

The men who trusted Bob Shell and guided him in the ways of the construction business were the Baldwin Company's three founders, Werner C. Knoop, P.W. Baldwin, and Olen A. Cates. "They were very good to me. They took me in and were willing to spend time to teach me," Shell says appreciatively as he recalls their stories.

They were three of the most experienced men in the construction field. The late Werner C. Knoop, whose name is familiar from the 1950s and 1960s as a mayor of Little Rock and as president of both the school board and the Chamber of Commerce, was a civil engineer who came to Little Rock from Iowa in the 1920s. An original founder of the Capital Steel Company, Knoop had a widespread practice as a consulting engineer. He was structural engineer for the Veteran's Hospital on Roosevelt Road, which, just after World War II, was one of the biggest projects ever built in the city. It was

The management team of Baldwin & Shell Construction Co. (left to right): James B. Hardin, vice-president/secretary; John S. Copas, vice-president; Robert J. Shell, president; and Henry L. John III, vice-president.

one of a number of multimillion-dollar projects that he contracted with the Corps of Engineers to plan and supervise, in combination with several architects and engineering firms.

Shell remembers Knoop saying that he began to like the idea of having a construction business and thought P.W. Baldwin, whom he had come to know through working together on several projects, would be a good team member. Baldwin was then with the George H. Burden Company. "Mr. Baldwin was a construction person—recognized in Arkansas and the South as the best. He was the job superintendent for the Arlington Hotel [in Hot Springs]; he built the Robinson Auditorium. He knew construction," says Shell. Cates, a man with extensive financial expertise, became the accountant. The firm still operates on the cost accounting system that he set up. Clearly, even before their 1946 incorporation as the Baldwin Com-

pany, the team represented considerable experience and a strong reputation. Four decades later the company has maintained the reputation. "We have been, and still are, selective in the work we do," says Shell. "We really do the prestigious jobs in Arkansas, the landmarks." The organization has completed more than 800 projects.

Clients have included financial institutions, educational facilities, every arena where the Arkasas Razorbacks play basketball, churches, hospitals and other medical facilities, commercial and industrial construction projects, plus shopping centers, motels, office buildings, and residential centers.

During 1986 Baldwin & Shell

Baldwin & Shell Construction Co. is known throughout Arkansas for such projects as the Barnhill Field House in Fayetteville (above), the Murphy Oil Corporation headquarters in El Dorado (above, right), and the Lafayette Office Building in Little Rock, whose elegant lobby is shown here (right).

cranes were prominent in one of Arkansas' oldest business districts, Little Rock's Main Street. Some of the work was new—two parking decks—and some was renovation on older buildings, between Fifth and Sixth, for the $9-million Main Street Market project. Shell enjoys the restoration work. "I've always been interested in old things. The real challenge is to try to get a duplication of quality, to be able to say, 'We did it just as good as they did.' If you take care, you still can do as good as the original," he adds. The company's first restoration job was before Shell's time, in the 1940s, on the Old State House. In the 1970s and 1980s Baldwin & Shell restored Central High School ("Every room and closet, 12 classrooms at a time."), the Legacy Hotel (formerly the Sam Peck), the Lafayette Office Building and the Rose Law Firm (the old YWCA).

Bob Shell's care for quality has been recognized by the Arkansas Associated General Contractors, who awarded him its Distinguished Service Award. Only 10 Arkansans have received the award, one of whom was Werner Knoop.

Since 1969 three more men have been learning the construction

trade at Baldwin & Shell. James Hardin, who had been an engineer at the Little Rock Air Force Base, joined in 1969 and is vice-president and secretary of the company now. Henry Johns joined the firm in 1975 and is vice-president in charge of the estimating department; John Copas began his association two years later as an estimator, became a project manager, and is now a vice-president.

In the 1970s Baldwin & Shell was one of the forerunners among Arkansas contractors to follow a national trend of doing negotiated, instead of bid work. Bid work puts the owner and contractor in an adversary position, Shell explains, and in negotiated work the owner and contractor are a team. "The main thrust is to save money, to get through quickly and still do quality work. The owner gets a better product at less cost," he says, estimating that 70 percent of their work is now on a negotiated basis.

"But we always want to do bid work, to stay abreast of market conditions and instill in our own people a competitive drive."

Baldwin & Shell is not only competitive in the marketplace, it has a reputation for bringing its projects in on time, almost always ahead of schedule. Client satisfaction is clear from the volume of repeat business. Part of the Baldwin & Shell client satisfaction may come from its interest in its workers' satisfaction. "We try to maintain dedicated, quality-minded people," says Shell, referring to a core of 60 or 70 people. The payroll ranges from 100 to 250 people, depending on the jobs. He can even name a few people who have been on the construction side of the company for decades. That is unusual for the construction trade, where workers usually do a project and move on. "We try to instill in our people a sense of pride, a sense of accomplishment in what they do. We want them to do a job that, years later, they can drive past with their kids and say 'I had a part in this.'"

In the mid-1970s Baldwin & Shell decided it could best maintain its high-quality work by sticking with projects within the state. So, while licensed in six states, it has worked in none but Arkansas. Was it the right decision? "The jobs we've had speak for themselves," says Shell, naming the company's prestige and quality projects. "It's become an important part of our business philosophy, and we know it's sound."

ST. VINCENT INFIRMARY

Little Rock was spared the yellow fever epidemic that ravaged Memphis and other parts of the South in 1878. The protection was an answer to the prayers of Mr. and Mrs. Alexander Hager, who h?d vowed that if the town escaped the fever they would leave their estate to establish a hospital.

Ten years later five Sisters of Charity of Nazareth traveled from Kentucky to Little Rock to carry out the Hagers' will. Bishop Edward Fitzgerald of the Arkansas diocese had set their journey in motion, inviting the Sisters to come, and purchasing the George House on East Second Street (still standing today), for their home and hospital. The $21,000 purchase price was provided from the estate.

The Mississippi River ferry delayed the last leg of the Sisters' travels—the train trip from Memphis lasted 13 hours—but the Bishop met them at the station and then drove them by open carriage to their new home. There they found groceries on the table, women at work sewing sheets and pillowcases for their beds—even a washtub and irons "that we might wash our clothes and caps."

They came to know more of the community as they set about making the house a hospital, finding carpenters to remodel it, and arranging for wooden beds to supplement the 10 iron beds donated by one of the local bankers. They found some particularly hospitable businessmen in town who had received kindnesses from the Sisters while in Kentucky during the Civil War.

The Sisters chose a name for the hospital by drawing lots. By coincidence the name drawn was St. Vincent, their patron saint. However, the Bishop warned of possible anti-Catholic prejudice and suggested calling it Charity Hospital for awhile.

As it happened, the Sisters' first patient came to them on St. Vincent's Day, in the third month

The original St. Vincent Infirmary, established in 1888, was in the former George residence, which still stands on Second Street.

after their arrival. Referred by Dr. James A. Dibrell, she was a "charity patient from the country." One of the Sisters later wrote, "After our first charity case, the patients began to pour in, all charity. An epidemic of dysentery was all through the country, and we had patients and deaths every day .... St. Vincent gave us plenty to do."

The Bishop's concern about their acceptance was relieved, perhaps when in less than a year the *Arkansas Gazette* noted: "Probably no other institution ever established in Little Rock in the same length of time has become so well known throughout the state and the entire south west as the Charity Hospital of this city." It reported its new name—the Little Rock Infirmary.

Some of the early Sisters who served at St. Vincent Infirmary (from left): Sisters Bernard, Mary Patrick, Rose Genevieve, Virgilea, Hortense (Superior), Mary Damian, Mary James, and Mary Philip. Two, Sister Hortense and Sister Mary James, were of the original five.

Conditions were never ideal at the converted house, and it was a disguised blessing that the Rock Island Railroad decided to buy the structure for its offices. The Sisters had six months to move, and for two years squeezed into two houses on Center Street while work was underway for a new 50-bed infirmary at 10th and High streets.

They moved into their new facility—with furniture and 36 railroad

St. Vincent Infirmary, in Little Rock, has grown to a full-service, state-of-the-art regional medical center.

patients—in September 1900. Six years later the Sisters opened the first training school for nurses in the state of Arkansas, graduating seven in 1909.

The hospital kept growing—an annex in 1910 that increased its bed capacity to 150; a nurses' home in 1923; a chapel and Sisters' home in 1925. Its equipment was also improving—including a clinical X-ray laboratory in 1919. In 1921 the American College of Surgeons ranked the hospital as "Class A," the first in the state to have that distinction.

The Depression days were trying times at the hospital, but there was a new children's department in 1936, the Golden Jubilee in 1938 (celebrating 50 years of history), and, in 1939, dedication of a 50-bed maternity annex. When the goverment asked for more nurses with the outbreak of World War II, St. Vincent's enlarged its school of nursing. In 1946 the hospital began negotiating for a 40-acre tract of land along two dirt roads in western Little Rock—Markham and Hayes (now University Avenue). Before moving to the new site in 1954, St. Vincent's had to quickly rearrange its quarters to respond to the 1949 polio epidemic in Arkansas. With the assistance of the Red Cross nurses, as many as 48 polio patients were cared for at one time.

Planning and construction at the new site were made possible by the combination of a public campaign for a half-million dollars and an application for federal funds. During December 2-5, 1954, more than 10,000 people toured the new 325-bed hospital—the newest medical facility in the state, and by far the tallest structure in the west Little Rock woods. A laundry, nurses'

residence, Sisters' quarters, and chapel were missing from the completed complex. The Korean War had made material costs escalate. However, they did have the quarters and laundry by 1961, and a chapel in 1969.

Expansion has been the rule since: an intensive coronary care area in 1964 (greatly expanded later), a northwest wing, bringing capacity to 500 beds in 1969, and new laboratories and special care units. Patient bed capacity was increased to 691 beds in the early 1980s, and two professional buildings for physicians, a parking deck, and a guesthouse were added. St. Vincent Infirmary has grown to a full-service, state-of-the-art regional medical center. Its services extend to patients throughout Arkansas and surrounding states. Licensed for 691 beds and 26 intensive care nursery beds, the hospital provides virtually all medical and surgical specialties except obstetrics. As evidence of its cutting edge technology, St. Vincent recently became the 14th hospital in the United States to offer extracorporeal shock wave lithotripsy—a near-miraculous new method of eliminating kidney stones without surgical intervention.

In a physicians and services directory, the hospital's services fill 50 pages of explanation, all important contributions to patients' care and, in some cases, special services to the community. One is the St. Vincent Health Clinic East, opened in 1971. Operated by St. Vincent—under contract with the City of

Little Rock—the clinic furnishes general medical services, dental services, and a special child health program in the low-income eastern neighborhoods of the city.

Attendant to professional training since 1906, the hospital operates three schools—medical technology, nuclear medicine technology, and radiologic technology—and numerous other education programs, some in cooperation with other Arkansas colleges and universities.

Compared to the 1,800 patients the Sisters treated in their first 12 years in Little Rock, some 23,000 inpatients and 58,000 emergency and outpatients are now seen in a single year. The changes in medicine through the century are staggering. Even the present hospital site, built in the woods, is a haven of green amidst commercial development—and no more than 20 minutes from anywhere in Little Rock. The constant in this change is the spirit of caring that the Sisters of Charity spread throughout the Infirmary, the caring that brought them to Little Rock so long ago and guided them in the development of this well-recognized medical center.

The Sisters of Charity's spirit of caring has been a constant in St. Vincent's almost 100-year history.

341

BALE CHEVROLET COMPANY

The year 1929 was a tenuous time to start a business, but months before the stock market crash Hardin Bale left 17 years as a partner in a Ford dealership and purchased Little Rock's Chevrolet dealership. The next year he had a $200,000 construction project under way at Second and Broadway, to house the growing business.

Community spirit ran deep in Hardin Bale. Little Rock even has an elementary school named for him. His community spirit was at work when Bale made plans for his new building in 1930. He insisted on using Arkansas materials in its construction, and he noted in the *Arkansas Gazette* that the construction was a step toward solving Little Rock's unemployment problems. The showroom opened in time to display Chevrolet's new 1930 models. Bale's brochure for the grand opening pointed out that "the new institution is purely a home concern—home owned, home operated," built with "native materials and home labor."

The Depression did, of course, profoundly affect Bale Chevrolet. Hardin Bale "mortgaged his life insurance and borrowed anything he could to build the new building," his son, John Bale, Sr., recalls. He also had strong support from his family; but, mostly, "my father made it through the Great Depression because of hard work. He closed up the place at night and would open it up the next day."

Before anyone had realized the severity and longevity of the Depression, the company anticipated an annual payroll of $75,000 for its 75 employees. An employee recollected the day the senior Bale called his workers together and explained his plan for getting through the Depression, with everyone on board. "Mr. Bale came to us and said, 'I'm in trouble and can't pay you full wages. But I am going to pay you enough to get along.' And he said he was going to make all

parts and service deals only for cash, and divide the money among his employees."

In 1881, when he was eight years old, Hardin Bale and his family left Kentucky for Texas. Along the way they stopped to visit friends in Washington, Arkansas—and stayed for 10 years. When Hardin was 18 he went to Searcy Business College, dropped out to marry, moved to Winthrop, Arkansas, and began work in the lumber industry, associating with Long-Bell Lumber Company at the turn of the century. His first son, William Eugene, was born in Winthrop.

In 1911 Bale brought his family to Little Rock, working for Niemeyer Lumber Company. The following year, as John Bale puts it, his father "saw opportunity to become part of something that would be important to our economy." He left the lumber company and, on June 10, 1912, in association with two others, opened the state's first Ford automobile dealership, one of the first in the South. Six months later the associates were gone,

leaving Bale with dim prospects in his new venture. Then along came a financier, C.E. Shoemaker, who had the backing to secure the business. He also owned a building that suited the needs of the dealership, at the corner of Markham and Arch streets. He and Bale joined forces, forming Shoemaker-Bale Company.

It was in the days that tops and windshields were extra equipment, carbide lamps lit the night roads, and Hardin Bale even had to teach some of the new car owners how to drive. Good business, according to national standards for the day, was a dealer selling 50 cars per year. In its first year Shoemaker-Bale, in a territory of Saline, Faulkner, Lonoke, and Pulaski counties, averaged more than 10 car sales per month.

In 1928 Ford Motor Company had no production, hence sent no cars to Little Rock. With the other family factors already in force, this was a push to send Bale in pursuit of his new car dealership with Chevrolet. He bought the dealer-

Bale Chevrolet still services cars in the same area it used in 1931—but the models and methods have changed considerably.

ship from Jim Green, and changed the name to Capitol Chevrolet, at 411-413 West Capitol (where the First Federal Savings building is now). For a few months the business was operated by his son-in-law, Joe D. Byars, who later served as sales manager for Bale Chevrolet. He acquired the Second and Broadway property in 1929, asking Wittenberg & Delony, architects, to draw plans for his new facility.

While the Depression colored his first 10 years in business, Bale headed next into the unusual economy of World War II. The U.S. goverment had restrictions on rubber, gasoline, and other items necessary to the automotive business. It even restricted the number of cars that could be sold. Perhaps that restriction did not mean so much, in light of the reality of the market. When John Bale, Sr., joined the Navy in 1940, Bale Chevrolet had a total of four new cars for sale. He came back in 1945, and three of those cars were still in the showroom. The war had caused such government restrictions that

only one car had sold.

Car owners did have to keep the cars they had in working order. "We were able to stay in business through our service and parts departments," John recalls, adding that sales boomed—for the first time for this dealership—after the war.

In 1948 the founder of Bale Chevrolet died. He was 75, and had been active as president up until his death. Working with his father since the early 1920s, William Eugene (Gene) Bale succeeded him as president of the company. John became vice president. Each of the brothers had attended Georgia Tech, and each was active in the community, as their father had been. Even the firm reflected the Bale family spirit of community service. Between 1953 and 1961 its employees contributed more than $10,000 to various organizations through a voluntary employees'

charity fund.

There were 109 employees at Bale in 1962, and the organization's annual payroll was $600,000. Its sales the year before had run $5.5 million. The company estimated that in its history it had serviced over one million cars and trucks.

Hardin Bale's oldest son, Gene, died in 1975, and his brother John assumed the role of president of the firm. In 1981 he chose retirement, passing leadership on to his sons. Those two grandsons of Hardin Bale decided on some restoration work in 1983, and all of Little Rock smiled when the neon began glowing and the canvas awnings went back up on the art deco Bale Chevrolet Building at Second and Broadway. Wittenberg, Delony and Davidson, Architects, directed the restoration—on the building it had designed originally. The work brought official recognition from the Quapaw Quarter Association, the local preservation association, and nomination to the National Register of Historic Places.

Car sales and car maintenance continue as the third generation works in "this luxurious terminal, conveniently located on the city's busiest boulevard," as it was described in 1930. Broadway is not the city's busiest boulevard anymore, but Bale is convenient to the almost 50,000 people coming downtown to work each day. When they drive into Bale's service area, they find a vaulted steel and glass structure that is the same their grandparents knew. The waiting room displays photographs from the old days, indicating a decided difference in the times, but the words of the 1930 brochure convey the same message today: "The Bale Company is a modern-day motor center—a place where every type of repair and replacement may be secured—a friendly institution where interested executives and sales people will discuss your motoring problems with you."

ARKANSAS GAZETTE

In America's pioneer days young William Woodruff and other printers headed for the western frontier with hand presses, ink, and cases of type. However, none other has Woodruff's place in journalism history: founder of the oldest newspaper west of the Mississippi and the oldest business in Arkansas, which, in its second century, would win two Pulitzer prizes.

William E. Woodruff

The young man's arrival at the Arkansas Post on October 31, 1819, hardly foretold his later acclaim as "the father of Arkansas journalism." Ending a six-week river trip from Tennessee, he disembarked from a hollowed out pirogue, unloaded his secondhand press, and set up shop in a rented log cabin, one of the 30 or so houses in the village.

Within three weeks he had printed the first *Arkansas Gazette,* four pages long, pronouncing its alignment with the Republican (now Democratic) party, but prudently choosing neutrality in local politics.

While only 24 years old at the time, Woodruff had started in printing nine years earlier—serving an apprenticeship in his native New York, then venturing west as far as Nashville. After a year at that city's local paper, he set forth for the new Arkansas territory.

The first printer to arrive, he knew, was guaranteed appointment as the public printer for the territory—a way to support himself while beginning his own newspaper.

In 1821 Woodruff and his *Arkansas Gazette* followed the territorial government in its move upriver to Little Rock. When that government's office holders and aspiring office holders evolved into seriously opposing factions in 1827, Woodruff found himself breaking the *Gazette*'s neutrality. He had to arm himself that year, as a result. His opposition to Secretary of State Robert Crittenden brought a threat to cut his throat and prompted the *Gazette*'s first opposition newspaper, the *Advocate,* begun in 1830.

Other papers followed. In 1838, wanting to retire from political combat, Woodruff sold the *Gazette.* In 1846 he was creating a new paper, dismayed at the new *Gazette*'s political policies. In four years he was able to buy back his original paper and restore it to its former editorial outlook.

Woodruff sold the *Gazette* again in 1853, this time to Captain C.C. Danley. Ten years later Little Rock was occupied by Union forces in the War Between the States, and the Yankee commander pro-

The first office of the Arkansas Gazette.

posed to Danley that the *Gazette* continue—but in support of the military occupation. Danley refused. For two years the Union army used the newspaper's plant to put out the *Unconditional Union.*

Danley resumed publishing the *Gazette* in 1865, but within a year both he and his partner had died and the paper was back in the Woodruff family, this time pur-

George Washington hand press.

chased by William Woodruff, Jr. He kept the paper for 10 years, editorializing strongly against the Reconstruction regime. At the end of that era, he sold the *Gazette,* finally ending the Woodruff family connection.

In the decade that followed came a succession of owners and editors. In 1888 leading Democrats formed a stock company to buy the paper, wanting to ensure an effective political voice for their party. The paper managed to hold to its editoral stance, but the absence of an owner with a personal interest in its financial well-being weakened the business side of the operation.

In June 1902 the *Gazette* returned to family ownership; today it remains wholly owned by the descendants of that family. A prominent Tennessee judge put up most of the purchase price for the paper, and his two sons came to lead it. John Netherland "J.N." Heiskell became president and editor of the *Gazette*, titles he still had at 98 years of age. He arrived in Little Rock at age 30, already an experienced journalist. His brother Fred was managing editor; Fred W. Allsopp, with a minority interest in the paper, became the business manager. The Heiskells bought his interest after his death in 1946.

J.N. Heiskell brought the *Gazette* into the twentieth century. He moved advertising from its front page, added sports and society sections, color comics, and a Monday edition, giving the paper a

Article announcing statehood.

365-day publishing schedule. He also imbued the paper with his own humane, progressive, and gentlemanly quality, a quality that a reporter in the 1920s sensed when later he wrote of the *Gazette*: "... She ... is one of the nation's most literate voices speaking for

one of our most illiterate states. Never does she write down to the people, but only up to them."

Heiskell loved Arkansas. He believed the *Gazette*'s role as the original, and often the only surviving, source of the state's historical record imposed an institutional obligation, and he assembled a collection of "Arkansiana" that grew to the point of needing a curator. In the early 1980s the collection was donated to the University of Arkansas at Little Rock.

World War II was taxing on the paper's staff and facilities—as it was on all newspapers—and also brought the death of Heiskell's son, Carrick, who had been in grooming for leadership at the *Gazette*. Heiskell had a son-in-law, Hugh B. Patterson, who had worked in commercial printing before the war. Patterson accepted his father-in-law's invitation to join the paper and to fill a new post, the office of publisher. Now 75, Heiskell was also looking for a "deputy" editor, and from the *Charlotte News* hired Harry S. Ashmore, called by *Time* magazine "one of the South's most realisitic and readable editorial writers." *Time* had quoted him as saying of the South "... it is high time we joined the Union." Ashmore, with Heiskell and Patterson, soon had a highly visible part in guiding the South toward a new history.

The *Brown* vs. *Board of Education* case, decided by the U.S. Supreme Court in 1953, declared public school segregation unlawful. When Governor Orval Faubus threw Little Rock into international headlines by defying court-ordered desegregation at Central High School, then closing the city's high schools one year later, the *Gazette* boldly opposed him. Its condemnation of Faubus cost subscribers and advertisers. It also brought the paper an unprecedented double Pulitzer Prize and numerous recognitions for its service to the community. Faubus' 12-year reign

The first Arkansas Gazette.

ended in 1966, with the reformist administration of Winthrop Rockefeller, a Republican, receiving the *Gazette*'s editorial support.

Another era ended in 1972 when J.N. Heiskell died—at 100 years of age. Today his grandson, Carrick Patterson, who joined the *Gazette* as a reporter in 1968, is editor. Under his guidance the *Gazette* was one of the first papers in the nation to switch to computers. This move into a new technology happened in the 1970s within the Beaux Arts walls of the office building Heiskell had commissioned in 1908, where the editorial and administrative offices remain.

It is a growing understanding of the newspaper as a service that has prompted not only broader reporting and new sections but the *Gazette*'s involvement with education in the schools, research and marketing for its advertisers, and improved billing to its subscribers. This is nothing more, however, than extension of the service the vigorous and outspoken *Gazette* has always given Arkansas—enlightening its citizens and bringing national honor to the state by insistence on journalistic excellence.

345

UNION NATIONAL BANK

This photograph was taken at the grand opening of the Union Trust Company Building, which later housed the bank until 1969.

Electronic banking and credit cards are concepts that would have baffled William J. Turner in his day. He was a Little Rock businessman in the 1880s, the man who started the two financial institutions to which Union Bank of Little Rock traces its beginnings. A former deputy in the state treasurer's office, Turner opened a private banking, brokerage, and real estate loan business in 1885. It was the town's fifth—and smallest—bank, with a capital of $7,500.

From Markham Street, Turner moved in 1887 to a new office he had built at Second and Louisiana. The next year he was one of four incorporators of Guaranty Trust Company, the other institution that launched Union's history. The company loaned money from eastern investors for Little Rock real estate, with interest rates that were very low for the times.

William Turner died in 1893. His executors sold the good will of his private banking business to Sydney Johnson, a confidential clerk for Turner and the secretary/treasurer of Guaranty Trust. Changing the name of the business to S.J. Johnson and Company, Bankers and Brokers, Johnson brought in his brother Allen as a partner. Six years

later Sydney Johnson died; Allen became president, and soon purchased and absorbed Guaranty Trust.

Working for the Johnson brothers since 1894 was Samuel W. Reyburn, the most influential man in the Johnson Company's 1902 incorporation as Union Trust Company. Just out of law school when the Johnsons offered him a position as rent collector, Reyburn had already unknowingly distinguished himself in Little Rock as the young man who—even though a poor student—insisted on making good his father's debt with a local merchant. Distinction continued to follow him. Upon Allen Johnson's death in 1905, Reyburn became president of Union Trust Company. In 1914 J.P. Morgan asked him to come to New York to help the financially troubled Lord and Taylor department stores. Reyburn went, taking a year's leave from Union.

The bank's growth under Reyburn was rapid. At its 1902 incorporation Union Trust had capital of $50,000 and deposits of $120,000. By 1910 the capital stock was $250,000, the surplus and undivided profits were $124,376, and deposits were $1,108,394. At the end of his year

in New York, Reyburn decided to remain there, becoming president of the Associated Dry Goods Corporation. Several years later, in 1923, when a third Union employee followed Reyburn's path and left for a New York banking career, the *Arkansas Gazette* made note of the departure: "It is a testimonial to the character of the Union Trust Company's organization that this institution has given strong men to the metropolis and has never ceased to grow stronger itself."

Reyburn's successor at Union in 1915 was Moorhead Wright, who also had begun with the Johnson brothers as a rent collector in 1894. In 1919 he led the bank in purchasing the Mercantile Trust Company, making it Union and Mercantile Trust Company, and increasing its capital to $400,000. The name changed back to Union Trust in 1923.

When Alfred Kahn was named president in 1928, changes were imminent. Union purchased prop-

The bank's present lobby features art and sculptures by prominent Arkansas artists.

erty that year at Fourth and Louisiana (just north of its current site) and began construction of a new bank. Only months before the move the stock market crashed.

Union National Bank, which the Trust Company became in 1933, distinguished itself in its service to its Depression era depositors. By 1943 it had repaid every depositor in full, with an additional 9 percent interest. Kahn was still president of the bank, serving until January 1950—when he became chairman of the board, and H.C. Couch, Jr., became president.

Hints of modern banking customs began in Couch's time. Union built the state's first drive-in bank facility just behind its headquarters in 1951. In the late 1950s it had its first branch bank—at Markham and Hayes (now University).

Upon Couch's death in 1963, Zack Wood was appointed the chairman of the board and Earl McCarroll assumed the presidency. Their tenures saw the purchase of Union's current site and a 1967 ground breaking ceremony. The actual ribbon cutting for the new building came in a tumultuous time in Union's history, while Harlan Lane was chairman of the board and Don Couch was president for two years.

Union National Bank presently occupies a modern 21-story building located in the downtown financial section of Little Rock.

Confidence and depositors lost in that time returned when Herbert McAdams became chairman of the board in October 1970. An attorney and banker, McAdams was heading Citizens Bank of Jonesboro—the largest bank in eastern Arkansas—when some of Union's board members urged him to consider taking leadership at the troubled bank. He came to Union, with Cliff Wood serving as president.

Within two years of the new management, Union National Bank had grown faster than any other financial institution in Arkansas, more than doubling its resources—to $200 million. New departments were added, one that linked Union to the world—the international division—providing customers the only place for full-service international banking in that state. Another state first was its automated bookkeeping in the Trust Department.

Electronics and deregulation were revolutionizing the banking industry in the early 1970s, and Union's management was ready to work with the changes. Making full use of the capabilities of electronic banking, Union began to establish itself as a leader in consumer banking. Many of its services were unique to Union and drew thousands of new accounts to the bank.

Ranked as Arkansas' second-largest consumer bank by 1981, Union expanded its marketing territory to a regional scope and led the nation in the creation of major new banking services. Union and Dillard's Department Stores pioneered the use of a bank credit card authorization and charge system that was all electronic, completely paperless. The bank's promotion for two of its services—the investor account and Union express cash—were so successful that the data-processing packages for both,

developed by the operations division, were used and marketed nationwide. It also marketed the personnel department's own successful personnel programs, developed to enhance employee performance. That department had another major first in American banking—establishing a personnel consulting agency for people in the financial field.

By 1984 Union was second among all commercial banks in the United States in servicing mortgage loans. It had become a national center for credit card service. Its express banking network had grown to a statewide system with more than 100 locations and then beyond the state, in an agreement with two national automated teller machine networks. It gave Union customers access to their accounts at hundreds of locations outside Arkansas. In 1985 banks and savings and loans in Little Rock began to enter into arrangements for their customers to use the express machines.

Union's management team, led by McAdams, president Robert Connor, and executive vice-president Hall McAdams, has used banking computer technology with vision. It merits the bank's national recognition. It also ensures that continued growth, with the best in personal customer service, will continue to be the Union story.

ARKANSAS CHILDREN'S HOSPITAL

"All children benefit from the existence of Arkansas Children's Hospital, whether they are ever admitted as patients or not. We provide an important element of security and comfort for parents throughout the state. After all, we're only a telephone call, a helicopter flight or a car ride away from every child in Arkansas."

This assessment by Dr. Randall O'Donnell, Chief Executive Officer of Arkansas Children's Hospital, echoes a 76-year tradition of service to all the children of Arkansas. The tradition began when the Arkansas Home Finding Society was established in Morrilton in 1910, and continues today and into the future.

During the years since the society was founded, many people have worked to mold it into today's Arkansas Children's Hospital. Through a century of revolutionary change in medicine, Children's Hospital has combined medical expertise and loving care to evolve into one of the 20 largest pediatric hospitals in the country. It is a regional medical center for infants and children from every county in Arkansas and from many surrounding states.

The Arkansas Home Finding Society was established by a Morrilton real estate dealer, Horace Pugh, to provide a home for orphaned and neglected children throughout the state. When Dr. O.P. Christian became superintendent of the Society in 1916, he moved the facility to Little Rock because of its central location.

Christian also was the first to note the need for a health care facility to care for the youngsters at the Home, many of whom suffered the effects of malnutrition, physical and mental handicaps and abuse. "We feel that it is a shame and a crime to allow children to go through life maimed when they might be fully restored; to remain a sufferer, when pain can be removed," Christian said in addressing the need for a hospital.

The first hospital building for the Arkansas Children's Home and Hospital. The home was established in 1910, with this hospital facility added in 1926.

The Board of Trustees of the Home Finding Society voted in 1920 to build a hospital, with funding coming from private donations, bequests, the sale of real estate and a $50,000 loan. The hospital opened in 1926, and the Pulaski County Medical Society provided the staff physicians, all of whom retained their private practices and received no pay for their work at the hospital.

The following years were ones of financial struggle for the new Arkansas Children's Home and Hospital, although the hospital never closed its doors. Dr. Christian retired in 1934 with the hospital facing foreclosure proceedings.

Ruth Beall of Rogers succeeded Christian and served as superintendent for the next 27 years. Tenacious in seeking support, she asked physicians to donate their services, community leaders to raise funds, other counties to appropriate funds, and revived the Ladies Auxiliary. By 1938, the hospital's income exceeded expenses by more than $2,000.

By that time, the hospital had

Patients in the "Girls' Ward" at Arkansas Children's Home and Hospital enjoy a Christmas party in the 1940s.

The main lobby of today's Arkansas Children's Hospital is a three-story atrium, which includes a unique electronic mobile to delight children of all ages.

been fully accredited by the American College of Surgeons, and the mortgage was finally paid off in 1944. The 1940s brought new challenges—much of the medical staff left for wartime service, and polio became widespread—but there also were promising developments. A pediatric burn center, the only one of its kind in the nation, was established in 1948.

The 1950s, a decade of prosperity for the nation, also were good years for Arkansas Children's Home and Hospital, with major donations coming from private sources and the state legislature. The decision to phase out the home placement function and become solely a hospital was made, and the name officially was changed in 1955 to Arkansas Children's Hospital. In order to meet the institution's growing needs, the hospital then was completely rebuilt and remodeled, with the new facility including a dental clinic and a speech and hearing clinic in addition to all previous services.

Ruth Beall retired in 1961, having pushed and pulled the hospital into solvency and extended its range of services. Also during the 1960s, the Salk vaccine had greatly reduced the incidence of polio, and the hospital again was at a point of setting new directions to meet the changing needs of Arkansas children.

Those changes occurred in the late 1960s and early 1970s, when three important developments fell into place at the same time, ac-

cording to Dr. Betty Lowe, who has been the hospital's medical director since 1975. First, Leland McGinness, who served as hospital administrator and then chief executive officer from 1972 to 1983, and the Board of Trustees recognized the need to develop a children's medical center that could provide the most technologically sophisticated care for Arkansas children. McGinness and Dr. Robert Fiser, chairman of the Department of Pediatrics at the University of Arkansas for Medical Sciences, began developing new medical services and recruiting top pediatric specialists from throughout the nation to head those programs.

Secondly, pediatricians throughout the state became convinced that their patients' needs could be met in Arkansas and, thirdly, the University took a leadership role in developing pediatric health care as part of its educational mission.

A milestone was reached in October, 1969, when Arkansas Children's Hospital entered an educational affiliation with UAMS to serve as the primary pediatric teaching facility in the state for medical students, post-doctoral residents, nursing students and paramedical professionals.

McGinness pursued this new era with vigor. "The idea, the concept was so good that no one could be against it," he said. "We felt that there were no problems too great for us to overcome; that was inherent in our quest for excellence."

The commitment to quality care and education has paid off. For example, over the past seven years, Arkansas' newborn mortality rate decreased from 39th in the nation to 15th, the best ranking of all Southern states.

In its current role as a regional medical center, Arkansas Children's Hospital last year admitted nearly 7,000 infants and children, and the hospital's 46 specialty clinics had more than 90,000 outpatient visits.

Another major step forward was the establishment of the hospital's emergency transport system, which in September, 1986, passed the half-million-mile mark in distances traveled to bring critically ill and injured children to Children's Hospital. *Angel One,* the emergency transport helicopter, as well as a specially equipped twin-engine airplane and transport van, make more than 70 trips each month to all corners of the state.

The hospital's continuing expansion of services and sophistication of technology are creating new opportunities and challenges for the future. The hospital will remain at the cutting edge of medical technology, and will complete construction of a new Education and Research Building in 1987.

Dr. O'Donnell, who has served as chief executive officer since 1983, emphasizes that the Arkansas Children's Hospital of today and tomorrow "is an all-encompassing, regional medical center that is truly for *all* the children of Arkansas. Parents gain an important feeling of security from our existence because they know that we'll be here whenever they need us, whether their child's problem is critical or less serious."

Today's Arkansas Children's Hospital is one of the 20 largest pediatric hospitals in the country. The hospital's emergency transport helicopter, Angel One, is in the foreground, and construction for the Education/Research/Laboratory Building to be completed in 1987 can be seen in the background.

METROPOLITAN NATIONAL BANK

Metropolitan National Bank has been the nearby and neighborly bank in southwest Little Rock since October 19, 1970. Today president Lunsford Bridges adds, "We're still nearby and neighborly—we're just nearby and neighborly to more people."

Metropolitan, with corporate headquarters for 15 years in southwest Little Rock, moved into downtown Little Rock in 1983 with a branch bank. In 1985 it consolidated the branch into its new headquarters, also in downtown Little Rock, on the first and second floors of the Rogers Building. The summer of 1986 brought more expansion. Metropolitan opened a branch in the Pulaski Heights neighborhood of Little Rock and a motor bank at the corner of Broadway and I-630.

Despite its growth, Metropolitan's identity with southwest Little Rock remains strong. Its biggest customer base is still in the University Avenue branch, Bridges says. "We're not forgetting our roots. We're just putting out more roots, establishing branches where it looks like it will be profitable."

Full-service branch banking was not allowed in Arkansas in 1968, when attorney William J. Smith hit upon the idea of creating a new bank in Little Rock. He decided it was a good idea because southwest Little Rock was virtually neglected in banking services. Smith helped to assemble a board of directors. The Comptroller of the Currency gave preliminary approval for the bank on April 1, 1970. Seven months later Metropolitan Bank opened its doors to customers. Its capital, at the beginning of its first day, was $1,213,104.89. At the close of the day its total assets were $2,720,046.72.

The bank opened in a portable building and operated there for 18 months, when the permanent headquarters, just behind the first building, were ready for occupancy. "That accounts for our profitability," says Mack Taylor, the vice-president and cashier when it opened. "There's always a strain on a new bank if it has the added expenses of a new building when it first opens."

As it was, Metropolitan paid its start-up expenses in three months, which was the last quarter of 1970, and in 1971 was showing a profit. Most new banks, according to industry statistics, take three years to operate in the black.

Another new-bank statistic in the industry is the common "life expectancy of new management," as Taylor puts it. The average is nine months. "We beat the odds," says Taylor, who, with president Weldon McWirter, stayed for 15 years.

The day the bank opened McWirter, Taylor, six other staff members and one guard were on duty—"not enough for a group insurance plan," recalls Taylor. By the time the permanent building on South University was ready, the staff had grown to 15 and the bank's assets were $20 million. By 1975 Metropolitan had a branch bank on Baseline Road.

Members of the bank's original board of directors were chairman Ben Allen, president Weldon McWirter, Stanley Bauman, W.G. Clark, Jr., Herschel Friday, Boyd Montgomery, Harry Oswald, Dave Parr, Carl S. Petty, Jay Smith, William J. Smith, E.C. "Doc" Toland, and Frederick D. Walker.

Today two original members continue to serve the board—Toland and Montgomery. The chairman is real estate developer Doyle Rogers, of Batesville, who bought controlling interest in the bank in 1983. Other directors are president Lunsford Bridges, Paul Hoover, Jr., Tommy Lasiter, Dwight Linkous, Leger Parker, and Doyle Rogers, Jr.

Metropolitan National Bank is Little Rock's youngest bank. In 16 years it has grown from a staff of nine to a staff of 85; from assets of $1,213,000 to assets of $98,522,441, as of June 30, 1986; and from headquarters of 1,200 square feet to headquarters of 30,000 square feet. The new downtown headquarters was designed specifically to strike a balance between the bank's suburban clientele and its growing stature in the banking community. Wanting to blend with the Rogers Building's polished mahogany and black Andes granite, the bank has created a space in its new headquarters that facilitates efficient banking operations and conveys calm sophistication with personalized attention—the attention that has built the bank and won it great client loyalty.

EXCELSIOR HOTEL

When Doyle Rogers talks about the Excelsior Hotel, he spends no time on its room count, nor does he dwell long on President Ronald Reagan's overnight stay there. Instead, Rogers reflects on the consequences of the multi-million investment he and the city of Little Rock made—$54 million counting the city's bond issue for a convention and conference center. He suggests it has spurred other investments in downtown Little Rock that are at least that much—and more.

He is right. As noted in another story among these pages, the restoration of the historic Capital Hotel was officially feasible, and other renovations along Markham Street were made realistic, only when the Excelsior Hotel established its impressive new presence.

It does not stop at restorations. The hotel and convention center have attracted people, and their buying power, to the streets of downtown Little Rock. That has spurred new construction directly attributable to the hotel and convention center's influence—parking decks. The squeeze that came from so many people coming to so many events downtown made the parking decks a must.

In the late 1970s two old-beyond-their-use hotels stood on the block where the Excelsior Hotel is now. Studies had suggested their restoration was out of the question. They had once been monuments: the oldest, the Marion Hotel, the grandest gathering spot in the state. When Doyle Rogers made a package deal with the City of Little Rock—with Finley Vinson working in the city's behalf, as chairman of the Advertising and Promotion Commission—those hotels were in the way. The arrangement with the city was that Little Rock would build a convention center, funded through a $28-million bond issue, and Rogers would lease the airspace above the center and build a 19-story hotel with his own financing.

The first step in the construction was the well-attended Sunday-morning demolition of the old hotels, on February 17, 1980. Then the 19-story, 462-room Excelsior Hotel could be built, atop the 63,000-square-foot exhibition hall of the convention center.

Throughout its two-year construction, up to its grand Arkan-Celebration opening November 18-21, 1982, the media followed the construction of the convention center and Excelsior Hotel, reporting on all the fine details of the structures as they were released. The complex, designed and engineered by a team of four architectural firms from Little Rock (Blass, Chilocte, Carter & Wilcox; Cromwell, Truemper, Levy, Parker & Woodsmall; Robinson, Wassell & Savage; and Wittenberg, Delony & Davidson), was erected by the Pickens-Bond Construction Company. It rises 225 feet above its La Harpe Boulevard level, with a 17-story atrium above its lobby—a lobby with a floor of imported Mexican marble. Depending on which bronze and glass elevators guests choose, their view during the ride is either the entire height of the atrium or an exterior view of western Little Rock along the Arkansas River. Those choosing the atrium side are presented with a close-up look at the 40-foot-long spiral crystal chandelier that hangs at the top of the atrium. It was designed by Louis Baldinger and Sons of Brooklyn, who disassembled and shipped it to Little Rock in no less than 150 boxes.

The carpet contractors were counting, too. The ones who laid the carpeting in the public areas of the hotel and convention center added up 25,000 yards of carpet. The man in charge of the "plant-scape," not only the forest of trees in the lobby but the boxes lining the balconies of the atrium, provided 2,000 plants. When seen all at once some of those details may be missed, such as the 1,600 prisms in each of the chandeliers of the ballroom.

The 11,000-square-foot ballroom divides into three sections, but undivided seats up to 1,100 for banquets. In total the Excelsior has six bar lounges and dining rooms. Its lobby spills into an avenue of retail shops, beyond which is a well-equipped continuing education center, with three main lecture auditoriums and other rooms.

The combination of these facilities makes convention-going convenient and elegant in Little Rock. Hotel guests have a world under one roof and skylight, with access to the city's newest park at the hotel's backdoor, along the riverfront.

The city's focus literally picked up and moved when the Excelsior Hotel was opened, with an impact larger by far than the usual combination of 462 rooms.

DOYLE ROGERS COMPANY

It is a circuitous route that brought Doyle Rogers to being the developer who rents more space to retail stores than any other developer in Arkansas. He did not start in real estate. He had thought—after childhood jobs running paper routes, selling movie tickets, and delivering groceries—that he was moving on to be a physical education coach.

But life intervened.

First it was World War II. Before the United States officially entered the war, Rogers took off with some buddies to join the Royal Canadian Air Force. When the United States did become involved in combat, Rogers returned to enlist in the U.S. Army Air Corps. He spent most of his time in the United States, but he had one special assignment in Burma, where he established a money order unit for troops who were having a difficult time getting their military pay home.

Next it was the Railway Express Company. He began learning the ropes in the Newport office, found himself fascinated by it, kept asking for more responsibility, and soon was sent to relieve agents on leave all through northeastern Arkansas. When he was acting agent at the office in Jonesboro, a major station, he thought for sure he would be made agent. Men in Little Rock were recommending him for the job. But he was in his twenties and, despite his record, company management passed him by—too young, they said.

Ironically, when it looked at its new competition and assessed its position in the marketplace, the firm decided a few years later that its management needed to be younger. It was agent Doyle Rogers, now in the Batesville office, that the business tapped. Railway Express made him the youngest division supervisor they'd ever hired—the first one under 45 years of age.

For two years he regularly traveled 3,000 miles of rail line, supervising 129 Railway Express offices—always riding into Newport on Saturdays, then out again on Sundays, to have weekends with his wife and family.

In a different town every night and with no family on weekdays, Rogers made productive use of his circumstances. His rail route became a sales route for the Masonic Bible. He established a large network of Bible salesmen and checked in with them at every evening's stop, after he had finished the day's business with Railway Express.

With a promising career at the firm, Rogers looked at the travel, the time away from home, the logical next step—relocating in St. Louis—and announced his resignation. When his boss wondered aloud about his ambition, Rogers replied that there was more than one way to measure ambition. He went back to Arkansas to settle in Batesville.

Rogers kept his Bible business, became partners in a Batesville restaurant, started mining manganese that the government was stockpiling, and began working in real estate, earning his license in 1953 and opening an office in 1954. It was far from coaching, but it was close to Newport, where he and his wife grew up, and it was where he wanted to be.

The choice of real estate was, in a way, a sign of respect for his father-in-law. Jackson County's tax collector, a former schoolteacher and a self-taught lawyer, Rogers' father-in-law frequently recalled that the only people making money in the Depression were the ones with something to sell—real estate, usually. Rogers took that observation to heart as he shaped his new career.

He also put into action a maxim his mother was fond of quoting: "If you're going to do it, do it right, and to the best of your ability—or don't get involved." Rogers did it right in real estate. For one thing, he advertised. The other two agents in town did not. His first residential development was the 200-acre College Heights subdivision, near Arkansas College in Batesville, where he and his wife still live. He looked for the best advice available before he began the project, going to Little Rock to the Federal Housing Administration office to ask about Arkansas' best example of a successful subdivision. The FHA steered him to Elbert Fausett, who was developing Broadmoor, Little Rock's first big subdivision.

Fausett did more than talk to Rogers; he took most of the day to drive him out there, show him the plats, explain what was working and what to avoid. It was the beginning of a valuable friendship for Rogers. He recalls Fausett saying at the end of the day, "There's one more thing you need to do now.

Go to Batesville and dig a tunnel to a bank." Because private financing was scarce in the 1950s, Rogers developed the streets and utilities in the subdivision and then sold the lots, built the houses, and handled the loans.

Rogers' first commercial development was a service station for Lion Oil Company in Batesville. He created a pattern with that first project that he continues. He built the station not for the local distributor, but for the oil company itself. He always builds for a large national tenant. A Kroger in Batesville was his next project. He rarely sells his commercial property, either. Rogers owns the building he built for Lion, for that first Kroger, and every other development project he created.

"All the properties we've developed in 30 years, we've built because of pride in what we do," he says. "I've always felt like I wanted to see the property paid off. There's greater potential in owning than in selling. Generally, developers build and sell for tax advantages. We've overcome taxes by continuously building new properties."

Rogers' name became known in central Arkansas when he built the Excelsior Hotel, and the City of Little Rock built the Statehouse Convention Center in a joint project in the early 1980s. His company's first work in Little Rock, in the early 1970s, was hardly so heralded. It was his development of Colony West shopping center, on Rodney Parham, which most people predicted was too far west of town. No one in Little Rock would risk making a loan on the project. He's been proved the visionary on that project.

In Batesville, Little Rock, and throughout Arkansas and the South, Rogers' firm has developed large single-tenant stores, malls, shopping centers, and other commercial and residential developments. "We don't pick our locations;

we have tenants who are telling us where they need to build," he says, explaining his long term relationships with national tenants such as Kroger, Safeway, Wal-Mart, JCPenney, and Magic Mart. He has worked with each of those businesses through the years, and won their confidence.

The Doyle Rogers Company has 15 people on its staff, with Rogers' son-in-law advising him on legal matters and his son a partner. Not on the staff, but someone he mentions throughout the story of his life and business, is his wife, Josephine "Raye" Jackson Rogers. She was still in high school when they met. They courted two and a half years, then married.

Raye was the first recipient of a mail order from Burma, and they still have it, helping remind them where they started—it was worth five cents. Rogers has another story from those days. Raye worked at the telephone company while he was in the service and she was saving enough money, from her salary and what he sent home, that they had enough to pay for a new car, in full, when he came home. It was her surprise for him, and he's as proud of it today as he was then.

"She wanted, also, to do the best, to be a success," Rogers says of his wife. "And she's helped me be successful. Everything I've done, she's done with me. You make the right decision when you pick someone who helps you make the right decision," he says, imply-

ing his good fortune in picking her.

"The best time we have," he adds, "is the hour and 45 minutes it takes to drive between Batesville and Little Rock. We talk and visit. When we fly, that's just 25 minutes, and it's not enough time."

That drive, or flight, is necessary many times a week, because Rogers keeps offices in Little Rock—at the FirstSouth Building that he constructed—and in Batesville. The couple has a suite in the Excelsior for their stays in Little Rock. Raye's sophisticated decorating talent is evident in both the office and suite.

Rogers takes credit for his smart choice of a spouse. Many other events in his life he attributes more to happenstance. "You have to pick something that has a future in it. It's not so much how capable you are, or even how hard you work. I'm sure there are those who work at it a lot harder than I do. It's how everything meshes together, how the times are . . . . I've been fortunate that the things I've been involved in have potential." Then he gives one other of his personal traits some credit. "Lots of people are smarter than I am—I've got enthusiasm."

CROMWELL TRUEMPER LEVY PARKER & WOODSMALL INC.

Some call Charles L. Thompson a pioneer. In 1886 he preferred a job offer in Little Rock to others in New York—Little Rock, he said, was "farthest in the wilderness." He came as a draftsman for architect Benjamin J. Bartlett, who had been in the community for a year, designing projects such as the School for the Blind at 18th and Center, and needed help with his work load.

Once in Little Rock, Thompson pioneered simply by staying. Architects in those days were more often itinerant, following work to their next project. That is, in fact, what Bartlett did. He was in three cities before he moved to Little Rock, and was on the road again, to Mississippi, within five years.

Bartlett, 55, turned over the practice to his 21-year-old partner, Charles L. Thompson, never knowing what he had started. Thompson turned out to be a prolific designer, a disciplined businessman, and a good citizen. The business Bartlett left behind has become Arkansas' oldest and largest architectural firm—one of the 17 oldest in the country. Rightfully, Thompson gets most of the credit as the founding father, and is considered by many to be the father of the architectural profession in Arkansas.

With Bartlett's departure Thompson created a partnership with Fred Rickon, an engineer. It was one of the earliest professional associations of an architect and engineer. Rickon changed careers in 1897, and Thompson practiced for the next 19 years with numerous

employees—but no partners. One of his projects was an assignment from Governor Donaghey to oversee the completion of the Arkansas State Capitol. Thompson also became known for his courthouse designs, including the Washington County Courthouse, and designed 15 in all.

Of Thompson's 2,000 projects, however, it is the residences that stand out. He and his associates skillfully executed the popular styles of the day in houses that are landmarks, still, in Arkansas' towns and countryside. In 1982, 131 of his structures were placed on the National Register of Historic Places in the United States, and a book by F. Hampton Roy was published, *Charles L. Thompson and Associates: Arkansas Architects 1885-1938.*

Thompson's professional business practices were out of the ordinary for architects of his time. He ran a well-managed office, which Thomas Harding guided when he joined as a partner in 1916. When Harding left in 1925 Thompson found two former draftsmen interested in merging firms—Theo Sanders and Frank Ginocchio. It is from the Thompson, Sanders & Ginocchio operation that the elder

architect retired in 1938, almost 70 years old.

Three years later, when Theo Sanders retired, Ginocchio looked to the younger generation for a new partner. He found Ed Cromwell, coincidentally a son-in-law of Thompson. Practicing in Little Rock since 1935, Cromwell had high sights for the state, as well as his new firm—but immediately in the future was the completion of many military projects for World War II.

With the end of the war came a healthy economic climate—and new commissions, including the first master plan and buildings at the new location of Little Rock Junior College (now the University of Arkansas at Little Rock). The firm also designed the Governor's Mansion—on the site of Benjamin Bartlett's School for the Blind.

John Truemper, Jr., the current chairman, who came to work full time in 1950 after an apprenticeship there that began in 1942, describes the firm's designs in the late 1940s as safe, conservative, and popular, but not a match for "the ambition of Ed Cromwell . . . who set out to find a first-rate designer to thrust the firm—and Arkansas architecture—into a new era of design excellence." In 1950 he found the designer: Dietrich Neyland, trained in the international style of architecture.

The Engineering Technology Building at the University of Arkansas at Little Rock.

School for the Blind, Little Rock, Arkansas.

Projects that Ginocchio, Cromwell and Associates worked on in the 1950s set the venture in directions it continues to follow. Its design for the Arkansas Children's Colony, in 1955, was cited as the finest facility of its type in North America, and has led to the company's continued work with health care facilities nationwide. These include projects in Mountain Home, Searcy, Mena, Blytheville, Osceola, Hot Springs, and Jacksonville, Arkansas; Jasper, Alabama; Memphis, Tennessee; West Point, Mississippi; Hammond and Kenner, Louisiana; and as a joint venture member for the John L. McClellan Memorial Veterans Hospital in Little Rock.

Aware of the state's new aggressiveness with industrial recruiting, the firm became equally aggressive in seeking projects from the new industries, a field that had been shunned by other architectural enterprises. Industrial facility design remains a specialty of the firm, whose clients include Maybelline, USS Chemicals, Orbit Valve, Rockwell, General Electric, AT&T, Southwestern Bell Telephone, Jacuzzi, Vought, Whirlpool, Sanyo, and Johnson & Johnson.

Winthrop Rockefeller's new home and ranch on Petit Jean Mountain was another 1950s project, and it led to the consulting engineer, Ben Dees, joining the firm in 1954, the first modern-day association in Arkansas of architects and engineers—a parallel to Thompson and Rickon's association. In the early 1970s the organization incorporated interior design into its services.

Ed Cromwell's personal interest in historic preservation guided the firm toward numerous projects, some of them helping to revive Little Rock's old Markham Street. The grandest restoration was the Capital Hotel.

In 1973 the Arkansas Public Building Authority asked the firm to create a master plan to provide more space for state agencies. The first phase of the 25-year plan, known as One Capitol Mall, was finished in 1976 on the state capitol grounds. Some other recent examples of the firm's work in Little Rock are the Airport Terminal, Engineering Technology Building at UALR, One Spring Street Building, Beach Abstract, Camelot Hotel, Superior Federal Bank, and as part of a joint venture for the Excelsior Hotel and the FirstSouth Building.

During the 1970s and 1980s the company began expanding its marketplace, seeking more federal and out-of-state private work, and today has a national and international clientele, particularly among the military. Commissary facilities have been designed for a number of locations in the United States and three foreign countries. A current major research facility is being designed for Fort Leavenworth, Kansas. In 1980 it grew to the point of consolidating its eastern Arkansas branches into The Cromwell Firm, Inc., in Memphis, a sister firm that is now one of the largest architectural and engineering firms in that city. Altogether, 110 people work for the Cromwell firms.

For the firm's 100th anniversary, John Truemper wrote *A Century of Service, 1885-1985.* In its epilogue Gene Levy, president of the organization and Ed Cromwell's son-in-law, wrote that he saw no recognizable company style. "There is, probably, a design 'spirit'," he noted, "which might be characterized as an ongoing search for excellence." It is a spirit that came naturally to Charles L. Thompson, Ed Cromwell, their partners and successors, and is manifest in their work. It is a spirit that permeates Arkansas, through the buildings designed and built, and ideas given birth, during Cromwell Truemper Levy Parker & Woodsmall Inc.'s century of service.

FIRM GENEALOGY

1885
Benjamin J. Bartlett
1888
Bartlett & Thompson
1890
Charles L. Thompson
1891
Rickon And Thompson
1897
Charles L. Thompson
1916
Thompson and Harding
1925
Charles L. Thompson
1927
Thompson, Sanders and Ginocchio
1938
Sanders and Ginocchio
1941
Ginocchio and Cromwell
1947
Ginocchio, Cromwell and Associates
1961
Ginocchio, Cromwell, Carter, Dees & Neyland
1962
Ginocchio, Cromwell, Carter & Neyland, Inc.
1969
Cromwell, Neyland, Truemper, Millett & Gatchell, Inc.
1974
Cromwell, Neyland, Truemper, Levy & Gatchell, Inc.
1981
Cromwell Truemper Levy Parker & Woodsmall Inc.

Belvedere, a project by the City of Little Rock commemorating the Arkansas Sesquicentennial in 1986.

AMFUEL®
AMERICAN FUEL CELL AND COATED FABRICS COMPANY

Amfuel® acquired the business in 1983; all former personnel remained with Amfuel and today design and produce fuel bladders and fuel and water containers for use around the world at its 71-acre complex in Magnolia, Arkansas, opened in 1965.

It all started when the U.S. Army Signal Corps began developing aircraft for military use in 1917-1918. One of the most dangerous things an airplane could carry was its own fuel tank. The potential offensive and defensive uses of aircraft were almost unlimited, but losses kept mounting as planes burned and exploded when the gas tanks were hit.

The Army turned to Firestone Tire and Rubber Company for a solution. The firm developed a rubber compound that, when applied to the metal fuel tanks, would seal off bullet wounds. The product worked; however, with World War I winding down, there was little use or development until World War II made it a necessity. From that day to this the refinement and applications of the first product have led to a major industry supplying military and industrial users with containers that can receive, store, dispense, and transport fuel and water under almost any conditions.

The evolution of Amfuel and its personnel, experience, and resources with its products parallels the history of modern aviation. Before World War II the firm's personnel developed the first fuel cells for the P-47 Thunderbolt and for the P-51 Mustang being built for Great Britain. The 85-gallon cells developed for use in the Mustang's wings helped make it the fastest plane of its day.

The first self-sealing cells were aboard the B-17 Bomber, and the first lightweight fuel cells of synthetic rubber-coated nylon fabric helped give the B-36 Bomber the world's longest range.

Following World War II Amfuel

Amfuel employs over 400 people in the Magnolia area for the manufacture of containers for military and industrial use that can receive, store, dispense, and transport fuel and water under almost any conditions.

helped pioneer fuel containment systems for America's first military jets. The P-80 and B-47, America's first jets, carried Amfuel cells, as did the F-104, the first production plane to sustain supersonic speeds in level flight in 1956. In the mid-1960s fuel cells were developed for the Hughes OH-6 helicopter and the first crash-resistant cells for the Bell OH-58 helicopter.

Amfuel continues today as a leading supplier of fuel cells for military and commercial aircraft and land vehicles, completely designs, manufactures, tests, and delivers its products. Starting at the beginning, Amfuel maintains total control and accountability in each process, from raw materials to the finished product.

In addition to its fuel cells, which are used in tracked vehicles, as well as airplanes, Amfuel makes a wide range of Fabritank® containers for fuel and water. Flexible, highly portable, easy to install, and durable, these units have gained worldwide acceptance. Self-supporting tanks range in size up to 50,000 gallons, while tanks that

employ earthen embankment support are available in capacities of up to two million gallons. The latter are used primarily for the storage of waste, potable, process, and fire protection water. Hundreds of installations have included plant facilities, housing developments and municipalities, city-run utilities, and sewer plants.

Locally, the firm employs over 400 people with an annual payroll of over five million dollars. The process and product that grew out of a need to keep early military aircraft flying have grown with the century. Now Amfuel, using the best in personnel and technology at its Magnolia plant, makes products that enable jets to fly while using the same know-how to develop land-based tanks of enormous proportions that are used around the world.

THE McMATH LAW FIRM, P.A.

Sidney S. McMath, governor of Arkansas from 1948 to 1953.

Sidney McMath grew up in Hot Springs, a town controlled politically by Mayor Leo P. McLaughlin. He set up law practice there in 1937, after graduating from law school at the University of Arkansas at Fayetteville. However, his first venture ended after three years. War clouds were gathering in Europe and in 1940 McMath volunteered to return to the U.S. Marine Corps and was commissioned a second lieutenant.

After World War II, in which McMath earned hero status, the young attorney went back to Hot Springs, determined to have a fair professional chance in the city. So too were other of his old classmates home from the war, and their pooled frustration and efforts to clean up the town magnified into "The GI Revolt." The young men each declared their candidacy for a local office, controlled still by the McLaughlin machine. McMath was the only one of nine candidates to win the primary; but when the others ran as independents in the general election, many of them won office. Their successful campaign, headed by McMath,

led to similar electioneering in Arkansas.

While most of his colleagues had run simply to oust the incumbents, McMath used the local race for prosecuting attorney as a launch into state politics. In 1948 he ran successfully for governor, and served through 1952 in an administration of progressive leadership.

McMath's second venture into law practice was in 1953, following defeat in his race for a third term. This time he had a partner, Henry Woods, his former executive secretary. They were soon joined by Leland Leatherman, who had begun his chairmanship of the Public Service Commission in McMath's second term. All three were Hot Springs natives, but opened the McMath, Leatherman and Woods firm in Little Rock.

McMath's politics as governor stressed the common man and liberal issues, and the firm's clients initially reflected his administration's policies.

The Honorable Henry Woods was appointed to a federal judgeship in 1973.

Leland F. Leatherman, one of the original partners in the McMath, Leatherman and Woods law firm.

McMath stayed active in politics. In 1954 he had run second in a close race against incumbent Senator John McClellan. Eight years later he ran against Orval Faubus, who, in earlier days, had been a young, liberal Democrat on McMath's staff. They parted ways when Faubus fomented the race issue for his political gain in Little Rock's Central High crisis. Faubus won, and that was McMath's last race.

McMath's successful law firm has come to be known as The McMath Firm, P.A. Henry Woods accepted an appointment to a federal judgeship in 1973. Partners in the firm today are Sidney McMath and three sons—Sandy, Phillip, and Bruce—and Leland Leatherman and Mart Vehik. Their practice covers generally trial practice: negligence, toxic torts, trials, public utility law, workmen's compensation, admiralty law, and environmental litigation.

McMath's political career is carefully documented in a biography by Jim Lester, entitled *Sid McMath - A Man For Arkansas.*

FRIDAY, ELDREDGE & CLARK

By tracing the legal representation of the Missouri Pacific Railroad in Arkansas, the Friday, Eldredge & Clark law firm traces its own history to December 1, 1871, when attorneys George E. Dodge and Benjamin S. Johnson formed a partnership for the practice of law, representing what was then known as the St. Louis, Iron Mountain and Southern Railroad, one of Arkansas' first major legal clients. Since that time the firm has maintained an unbroken record of representing Arkansas' dominant railroad, the Missouri Pacific Railroad, acquired a few years ago by the Union Pacific Railroad.

Like the railroad, the law firm has changed names through the years, due to deaths, resignations, and reorganizations, but the changes have not adversely affected the firm's practice. Its clients— the railroad, truck lines, utilities, banks, contractors, manufacturers, investment houses, insurance companies, professional organizations, governmental agencies, school districts, improvement districts, estates, and individuals—have continued to seek the firm's services, and today it is the state's largest law firm.

In the 1870s Dodge and Johnson took on a new partner and changed the name to Winfield, Dodge and Johnson. The firm first appeared as counsel for the railroad before the Arkansas Supreme Court in 1880, in the case of *St. Louis, Iron Mountain and Southern Railroad* v. *Morris,* 35 Ark. 622. The case had originated in the Jackson County Circuit Court in July 1876.

A second name change came when Winfield died and the firm was again Dodge and Johnson. After the 1904 death of George Dodge, Benjamin Johnson worked with a number of partners and associates. One of them was Judge Thomas M. Mehaffy, who joined Johnson in 1907 and later served as a justice on the Arkansas Supreme Court.

Pat Mehaffy, who joined the firm in 1941, accepted an appointment by President John F. Kennedy to the United States Court of Appeals of the Eighth Circuit in 1963.

Others in the early part of the century included J.E. Williams, a candidate for governor in 1904 on the Prohibitionist ticket; E.B. Kinsworthy, once Arkansas' attorney general (his Little Rock home, known as the Villa Marre, is restored and open for touring); Lee Miles, later the solicitor general for the United States Postal Department; R.E. Wiley; and W.R. Donham.

Pat Mehaffy, son of Judge Tom Mehaffy, joined Henry Donham and Martin Fulk as a law partner at the beginning of 1941, when Donham needed help with his work on the Missouri Pacific account, as well as People's Bank (later First National Bank), a thriving insurance company practice, and some general law practice. From 1942 through 1952 other lawyers joined the Donham, Fulk and Mehaffy firm in their quarters in the Boyle Building, either as associates or sharing facilities, practicing independently.

Donham died in 1951 and Mehaffy organized the Mehaffy, Smith &

Williams firm on June 1, 1952. William J. Smith, a native of Texarkana, had been an associate with Donham, Fulk and Mehaffy since 1946. An active Democrat, Smith served Governors Homer Adkins, Ben Laney, Francis Cherry and Orval Faubus as legislative advisor. John T. Williams had worked in the prosecuting attorney's office under Mehaffy and was in private practice in Marianna.

Associates in the Mehaffy, Smith & Williams firm were Ben Allen and Herschel Friday, at the time a clerk for a federal district judge in Fort Smith, who immediately began working on bond issues.

After their military service, William A. Eldredge, Jr., and Bill S. Clark joined the firm in 1953. Eldredge developed a specialty in trial work and railroad representation, and Clark eventually devoted most of his practice to labor relations. In 1954 William H. Bowen, an Altheimer native, was hired from the tax division of the Justice Department and became the first lawyer in Arkansas to devote his practice solely to taxes. William L. Terry, son of former Congressman David D. Terry, with whom Mehaffy had shared an office in 1927, joined in 1954, developing a specialty in real estate. When Robert V. Light was hired in 1955 the firm was double its size of three years earlier.

Mehaffy, Smith & Williams was the first law firm in the state to develop several departments of two or more attorneys devoting most of their time to a specialty. Over a period of time the firm established departments in the fields of taxation, bonds, securities, trial work, commercial law, and labor law.

At its Boyle Building office, and now at its First Commercial office, the firm's red carpeting has become a trademark. The carpet was recommended to Mehaffy by actor Dick Powell, his friend and a Lit-

William J. Smith served on the Arkansas Supreme Court in 1959.

tle Rock native, as a mark of distinction.

The firm became Mehaffy, Smith, Williams, Friday & Bowen, then the Smith, Williams, Friday & Bowen firm after Mehaffy accepted an appointment by President John F. Kennedy to the United States Court of Appeals of the Eighth Circuit in 1963. William Bowen left in 1971 to become president of Commercial Bank, now merged with First National and known as First Commercial Bank, N.A., where he serves as chairman of the board and chief executive officer. With his leaving, the firm became Smith, Williams, Friday, Eldredge & Clark. After 1974, when both Smith and Williams retired to be of counsel to the firm, it took the name it uses today, Friday, Eldredge & Clark.

Besides Mehaffy and Bowen, other partners and associates have left to pursue further public service. In 1953 Harvey Combs left the firm to become insurance commissioner for the state of Arkansas; in 1958 William J. Smith left to serve the unexpired term of Justice Minor Milwee on the Arkansas Supreme Court, returning in January 1959; State Senator R. Ben Allen, who started his public career in the House of Representatives, left in 1969 to devote full time to personal business and to governmental affairs, which has included service as president pro tem of the Senate and acting governor.

The firm's most extensive period of growth, to 60 attorneys, has come while Herschel Friday has been the senior partner. In 1954 Friday was the youngest lawyer elected to the House of Delegates of the American Bar Association, which he still serves. He has had many other leadership roles in the American Bar, including four years on its board of governors. President of the Arkansas Bar Association in 1976-1977, he was named

Man of the Year in Arkansas by the *Arkansas Democrat* and Outstanding Lawyer by the Arkansas Bar in 1971.

Contributions of other members of the firm to their profession and community are extensive. John Williams, now of counsel to the firm, has been the chancellor for the Episcopal Diocese of Arkansas since 1972. Bill Eldredge, outstanding in medical malpractice law, was named an Outstanding Alumnus of the University of Arkansas School of Law in 1983. Meredith Catlett, the first woman in the firm, was a delegate to the 1986 USA-USSR Emerging Leaders Conference. Bill Clark is a member of the Section of Labor and Employment Law of the American Bar Association and the Committees on the Developing Labor Law and on Collective Bargaining and Arbitration for the American Bar. Laura Ann Hensley is president of the Board of Our Way Inc. Bill Terry is a past president of the Pulaski County Bar Association. "Buddy" Sutton is a Fellow of the American College of Trial Lawyers and is on the board of Directors of the Arkansas Baptist Medical System, which he served as president in 1982. Elizabeth J. Robben is co-chairman of the Arkansas Bar Association's Practice Skills Seminar. Since 1963 George E. Pike, Jr., has been secretary/treasurer of the Harvard Law School Association. James W. Moore, head of the

firm's Labor Law Department, is on the board of directors of the Arkansas State Chamber of Commerce. Bill Patton, Jr., is a past president and past chairman of the board of the Arkansas Arts Center. Byron Eiseman is a trustee for the Pulaski Heights Baptist Church and for the Baptist Medical System Foundation. Mike Thompson is a member of the American Board of Trial Advocates and served on the steering committee for the March of Dimes Walk America Campaign in 1986. Paul Benham III serves the Little Rock Chamber of Commerce on various committees. This is just a representative list—the firm's members and associates have always recognized their civic, church, and governmental activities above and beyond their practice of law.

In 1983 two 1977 Harvard Law graduates issued *The Best Lawyers in America.* From the Friday firm Herschel Friday, Bill Clark, Bill Terry, Buddy Sutton, Jim Moore, and Byron Eiseman, Jr., are listed under their areas of expertise. It is further assurance to the firm's hundreds of business clients, who represent almost every field of activity, and the hundreds of individuals who come for matters such as estate planning, business affairs, and family matters, that they are represented by a firm of outstanding legal experience.

Herschel H. Friday, senior partner, has undertaken many leadership roles in the American Bar Association and was president of the Arkansas Bar Association in 1976-1977.

RICELAND FOODS, INC.

Riceland Foods' first rice mill, located at Stuttgart.

Riceland Foods, Inc., headquartered in Stuttgart, Arkansas, is the world's largest processor of rice and the nation's fifth-largest grain company. Each year it stores, transports, processes, and markets approximately 100 million bushels of grain as raw grains and products.

The firm provides the total crop marketing service for rice, soybeans, wheat, milo, corn, and oats grown by more than 10,000 farmers in Arkansas and nearby states. A network of 36 grain elevators receives farmers' crops, which may be processed at plants in Stuttgart or Jonesboro or merchandised as whole grains.

With the turn of the twentieth century, a wave of rice cultivation began to sweep over eastern Arkansas' Grand Prairie. The silt-loam soil has an impervious clay layer four to six inches under the surface, making it ideal for rice cultivation.

In the spring of 1904 a 70-acre field of rice was planted in Lonoke County. By 1920 Arkansas harvested a crop of 8.6 million bushels of rice from 175,000 acres.

World War I disrupted traditional supply lines and caused increased demand for U.S. rice. Prices rose and attracted more and more Arkansas farmers to rice growing.

Prices dropped just as quickly after the war. In 1920 rice sold at three dollars per bushel during the growing season, then plummeted to 30 cents a bushel after harvest. The world agricultural Depression

of the 1920s came suddenly to Arkansas.

Farmers began looking for a solution to market instability, and concluded that they could competitively market their grain only through cooperative action. On September 23, 1921, they formed The Arkansas Rice Growers Cooperative Association, the forerunner of Riceland Foods, to cooperatively market their rice.

Benefits to growers were evident. First, by pooling members' rice by varieties and grades until prices improved, growers found ready markets for their crops. Through pooling, they received cash advances on delivery at harvest time, instead of settling for the low prices that generally prevailed. Members also benefited in that they were able to gain greater dominance in the market as a cooperative than as individual growers.

The young cooperative, realizing it must take a larger role in rice processing, acquired its first rice mill in 1928, in Stuttgart. A second mill was purchased in Jonesboro in 1939.

After two decades of gradual formation and stabilization, Riceland entered a second phase—one in which technology spurred rapid organizational change.

Initially, farmers cut the stalks and left the green shocks of rice in the field to dry, risking damage from wind and rain. The development of the mechanical combine to harvest the grain reduced field losses.

With mechanical technology Riceland set up the first commercial rice-drying plant in 1944. That same year the company began assisting in the development of local grain-drying cooperatives that were affiliated closely with the marketing organization. In just five years eight such ventures were established to serve as the basis of Riceland's grain-drying division.

The firm's technological advancements also resulted in being among the first mills that switched from steam-powered equipment to electrically driven machines. It became a leader in the application of Japanese rice-milling technology in the U.S. rice industry.

Following World War II rice was still in such short supply that it was rationed. U.S. millers enjoyed

The Jonesboro, Arkansas, Riceland facility is the world's largest rice mill.

Sling loading of rice into barges was introduced by Riceland in an effort to become more competitive in the export market.

a seller's market; but technological advances on the farms, as well as at the rice mills, provided a larger volume of rice to market. To move this volume the cooperative began packaging under the Riceland Rice label in 1946 and began advertising its products.

As soybeans became an important crop to Arkansas farmers, Riceland members wanted the cooperative to market it for them. On August 29, 1958, the Arkansas Grain Corporation was incorporated as a sister cooperative. It was structured to share common receiving, drying, storing, and administrative facilities.

Riceland's introduction to soybean marketing prompted interest in soybean processing. The cooperative built a soybean processing plant in Stuttgart and began producing soybean meal and vegetable oil in 1961.

As progress was made in that field, Riceland again saw the value of developing a branded line of consumer products. Chef-way was chosen as the name of the new vegetable oil and shortening products.

Lecithin, a by-product of soybean processing, grew in importance

to the processed food industry. Riceland built the second granular lecithin plant in the United States in 1978 to serve this growing demand.

The cooperative saw grain marketing as an opportunity to take advantage of the state's position relative to export markets. To maximize that position, Riceland constructed its Pendleton Terminal on the Arkansas River near Dumas in 1980.

A second export terminal—this one on the Mississippi River at West Memphis—was added in 1985 to help move soybeans, wheat, and milo, as well as milled rice, to foreign customers. Riceland's position as a grain processor and merchandiser provides the flexibility needed for it to serve its farmer/members to best advantage.

Two thousand Riceland employees work together to market daily more than two million dollars in food products and grain across the United States and in more than 100 foreign countries. The organization's growth and development have distinguished it among Arkansas companies. An aggressive marketing effort earned it the Presidential Export Star award, the first presented to an Arkansas firm. Riceland Foods, Inc., also ranks in the *Fortune* 500 listing of leading corporations.

Riceland and Chef-way products have been successfully marketed in retail and food-service markets for many years.

CAMPBELL SOUP COMPANY

The Campbell Soup Plant in Fayetteville, Arkansas, makes fried chicken dinners, freezes and packages them, and ships them out under the Swanson label. It has done so since 1955, the year that Campbell Soup Company and C.A. Swanson Company merged. The merger brought the famous soup maker into the growing market of the frozen industry—an industry that Swanson had helped to pioneer.

The firms were no strangers. They shared both a 30-year business association and a common lineage, each with Swedish founding fathers. The Swanson side of the union goes back to the 1899 partnership of John Hjerpe and Carl Swanson. Swanson—20 years old at the time—borrowed $125 to invest in Hjerpe's Commission Company. A former grocer, Hjerpe operated a one-wagon commission business handling eggs, milk, and poultry. He drove out to the farms for the supplies and sold them to hotels and grocery stores.

The enterprise expanded its territory and soon went from dealing in wagon loads to trainloads. It grew so much that at different times in his career Carl Swanson was labeled both the butter king and the turkey king of America. In the 1920s it began processing food on a large scale and bought poultry processing plants, including, in 1929, a plant on Spring Street in Fayetteville. It was still the Jerpe Commission Company ("Jerpe" because of a sign painter's mistake that was too expensive to correct in 1900), although Hjerpe had sold most of his stock to Swanson in 1928.

One of Swanson's two sons, Gilbert, 23, was sent to head the Fayetteville creamery and poultry plant, which had been losing money. Gilbert added a feed mill, a hatchery, and began working with the University of Arkansas College of Agriculture and Home Economics, urging poultry breeders

This 1950 photograph shows a feed station for the C.A. Swanson Company, where farmers brought their chickens before processing. Today, managed by Herider Farms, growers on contract with Campbell Soup produce 600,000 broilers per week in climates that are much more sophisticated than this feed station.

to adopt hybrid genetics to improve feed use and attain desirable growing characteristics. The work began to pay off by 1934, and by 1944 the Arkansas plant, with a payroll of 500, was the largest, most profitable branch in the company chain. Northwest Arkansas became for a time the country's No. 1 supplier of broilers, and Swanson methods helped upgrade the local dairy products. Although Gilbert was called back to Omaha in 1939, he kept a strong Arkansas connection forever—marrying Roberta Fulbright, sister of U.S. Senator Bill Fulbright.

World War II changed Swanson's direction, while it chiefly produced food for the armed forces. It emerged from the war needing—and seeing—a brand-new market: families looking for convenience in the kitchen, who were buying refrigerators with the newly available freezer. Already packaging frozen foods under the Birds Eye label, using the quick-freeze machines

invented by Clarence Birdseye, it asked permission to lease and use his machines for its own label (changed to "Swanson" in 1944). Birdseye felt the more frozen food on the market, the better. So, in 1951, Swanson produced its first frozen chicken pot pies. It soon patented the label "TV Dinner," beginning a new age in American eating. In the year of the Swanson-Campbell merger it produced 25 million frozen packages per year, well over a third of the market.

Campbell Soup was 86 years old when it added the frozen food

A 1952 scene in parts packing for C.A. Swanson, on Spring Street in Fayetteville. Today, at a new plant, Campbell's employees on four assembly lines can create 1,000 dinners per minute.

Campbell Soup Company is the industry leader in poultry research centered in Fayetteville in this 40-person staff poultry research facility. Emphasis is on feed quality, health of the birds, and genetics. Food technologists also conduct research there.

business to its product line. It had begun as a canning and preserving business in 1869, founded in Camden, New Jersey, by Joseph Campbell, a fruit merchant, and Abram Anderson, an ice box manufacturer. Its canned condensed soups were originated in 1897 by Dr. John T. Dorrance, later a company president, and in 1900 the soup won a gold medallion in the Paris International Exposition— the medallion that is still on the familiar red and white label. The Campbell Kids were created in 1904. Officially named Campbell Soup Company in 1922, the organization is highly diversified. Its merger with Swanson is just one of many it has made over the years. The firm that the world knows for its soup sells more than 1,000 items in the United States and 120 foreign markets.

Between the 1955 purchase from Swanson and 1963, Campbell's production in Fayetteville tripled. By 1965 it had outgrown its Spring Street plant and constructed a new one; by 1986 that facility had been expanded five times. The plant does, indeed, have a large order to fill, supplying all of the Swanson-

label fried-chicken products west of the Mississippi, all the boneless-chicken products in the country, and supplying all plants west of the Mississippi with the turkey meat they use for turkey dinners.

The Fayetteville facility is one of seven plants nationwide producing Swanson products, but it is more than the processing plant. The company supplies all its own poultry. Herider Farms, one of three Campbell Soup farms, has 200 farmers on contract, all within 35 miles of Fayetteville, from whom it buys eggs—hatched in the farm's hatchery—and with whom it places day-old chicks to be raised. The farm buys Arkansas crops to make its own feed—sorghum, corn, soybeans, rice—which runs as much as 3,000 tons a week, and helps farmers with supplies and supervision. Ninety people work with Herider Farms, headed by Chuck Reis.

Dr. R.H. Forsythe, head of Campbell Soup's poultry research facility in Fayetteville, says the firm has always been technically oriented, believing if it can grow a better product than it can buy, it should grow it. "Nobody else comes close to us, commercially," Forsythe concludes. "Our research information goes to Canada and three other domestic locations." He acknowledges benefits in Campbell's proximity to the University, which he calls the leading poultry academic institution. Most of the field representatives in Herider farms are U of A graduates, as are most of the professional staff on the research team.

The research involves improving the feed quality, the health of the birds, "finding the best genetics available and developing innovative poultry processing."

There are also food technologists on the 40-person staff who research the processing and products development phase. Their efforts have enabled workers on four assembly lines to produce 1,000 dinners per minute. Weekly, 100,000 to 125,000 cases are shipped out in 65 trucks. The plant makes 16 different dinners (no longer in aluminum, but in microwave-safe trays).

There are 1,200 people employed at the facility. L.M. Brown, manager, stresses that 31 percent of its salaried staff are quality-control personnel. Line inspectors inspect every unit before it is packaged, and a bacteriological laboratory must approve all ingredients before they are used.

Wages and benefits that Campbell's paid in 1985 were $25 million, local expenditures another $20 million—a significant part of the Fayetteville economy. It also contributed generously to four major campaigns in 1985: $43,400 to the Fayetteville United Fund; $30,000 to the Fayetteville Development Foundation; $15,000 to the University of Arkansas "Campaign for Books"; and $30,000 to the Northwest Arkansas Radiation Therapy Institute.

Campbell Soup Company's plant in Fayetteville has undergone expansions since it was built in the mid-1960s.

MARTINOUS ORIENTAL RUG COMPANY

Carl and Dorothy Martinous never had to coerce their son, David, to help at the store. He was captivated by the Oriental rugs his parents sold. His fascination eventually became his profession. Today David Martinous owns and operates the Little Rock store that is a successor to the stores his parents opened, the first in 1939 in Fort Smith.

The Martinous family tradition of marketing Oriental rugs is a long one. David's grandparents emigrated from Lebanon at the turn of the century and settled in West Mineral, Kansas. Grandfather Thomas Martinous opened a general dry-goods store there. A sudden fire destroyed the building and wiped out the family business—in those days there was no insurance for small businesses—and then the family itself was broken with Thomas' death. His widow, with their four sons, left Kansas for Springfield, Missouri, where there were relatives.

Carl was 10 at the time of the move. In 1923, at age 18, he began working for a cousin, Mr. Malick, an Oriental rug merchant. In that era the business required frequent travel. A favorite city was Fayetteville, Arkansas, where Carl and Mr. Malick used to call on the Fulbright family; at that time Bill Fulbright was president of the University of Arkansas. After Mr. Malick and Carl would sell some of their rugs to the Fulbrights, the Fulbrights would invite them to stay for dinner and Carl would tell stories about the old country. These stories always fascinated Bill. Another family, the McElroys, also purchased rugs from Carl and Mr. Malick.

All of the Martinous brothers eventually opened Oriental rug businesses. Carl's, in Fort Smith, was in the city's first shopping center on Rogers Avenue. His wife, Dorothy, managed the office and helped repair rugs. She remembers that the salary for their one employee was $25 per month, rent on

Carl J. Martinous (above) and wife Dorothy J. (right) established a reputation for providing fine imported Oriental rugs through 60 years of service.

the building was $35, and utility deposits were $10.

In the early 1940s Carl opened a store in Little Rock at 23rd and Arch streets. He later erected his own building on East 21st Street and operated it and the Fort Smith store until his death in 1958. Dorothy continued to run the businesses, and David, now 12, helped. When he finished his third year at the University of Arkansas in Fayetteville, David moved to Little Rock to take over operation of that store and finish his degree at UALR. Dorothy then sold the Fort Smith Building, but continues to appraise Orientals. In 1976 David moved the store to a new shopping center on Cantrell Road. He remained there until the spring of 1985, when he opened a new 5,000-square-foot building in western Little Rock.

Martinous Oriental rugs come from Iran, India, Rumania, Pakistan, China, and Turkey. All of those countries now weave the old traditional Persian patterns as well as patterns native to their own region. David explains that he carries rugs in the traditional colors—reds, dark blues, wines—plus colors that have come into fashion through the contemporary tastes of American buyers. Importers even work with American fabric companies today, he explains, to coordinate the colors that they ask their

weavers to use. While the store handles mostly new rugs, it does have antique rugs for sale. New or old, David says that the rugs he sells—if well maintained—only appreciate in value.

Rug maintenance, not coincidentally, is and has been part of the Martinous business. When wall-to-wall carpeting came into vogue in the 1940s, Carl introduced professional carpet cleaning to the state of Arkansas. Likewise, David has a large section of his building devoted to rug cleaning. The rugs are washed, rinsed, combed, and hung to dry in a room especially equipped with a timed heater and special fans. They are dry within 24 hours.

David Martinous stresses the family tradition of his business. His father left a heritage of honor and ethics in fulfilling commitments.

Inspired at a very early age, David K. Martinous carries on the family tradition as president of Martinous Oriental Rug Company in Little Rock.

Patrons

The following individuals, companies, and organizations have made a valuable commitment to the quality of this publication. Windsor Publications and the Arkansas State Capitol Association gratefully acknowledge their participation in *Arkansas: An Illustrated History of the Land of Opportunity.*

Affiliated Food Stores, Inc.*
Air Distribution Products, Inc.
Alumax/Magnolia Division*
Amfuel®*
Arkansas Blue Cross and Blue Shield, Inc.*
Arkansas Children's Hospital*
Arkansas Eastman Company
Arkansas' Electric Cooperatives*
Arkansas Gazette*
Arkansas Modification Center*
Arkansas State Capitol Association*
Arkla, Inc.*
Charles Rodney Baker
Baldwin and Shell Construction Co.*
Bale Chevrolet Company*
Beach Abstract Company*
Bemberg Iron Works, Inc.*
Best Foods
    A Division of CPC International Inc.*
Mr. and Mrs. Hugh H. Brewer
George W. Browning, Jr.
Bryan, Worley & Co., Inc.
Camelot Hotel*
Campbell Soup Company*
Capital Hotel*
Central Flying Service*
City of Hot Springs*
CMW, Inc.*
Coleman Dairy, Inc.*
Columbia-Lafayette-Ouachita-Calhoun Regional Library
Crittenden County Historical Society
Cromwell Truemper Levy Parker & Woodsmall Inc.*

Crow-Burlingame Company*
Doctors Hospital*
Dow Chemical Company*
Dr. and Mrs. Ben M. Elrod
Ethyl Corporation*
Excelsior Hotel*
Fairfield Communities, Inc.*
The FASWEET Company
Orval E. Faubus
Friday, Eldredge & Clark*
Garver and Garver, P.A.*
General Telephone Company of the Southwest*
Gordos Arkansas, Inc.
Hope Brick Works
Q. Byrum Hurst, Jr.
Harold Ives Trucking Company
Jackson Cookie Company*
Jacuzzi Inc.*
J.M. Products, Inc.*
Johnson County Republican Women
Jones Productions, Inc.
Jones Truck Lines, Inc.*
KARK-TV*
Koppers Co. Inc.
W.A. Krueger Company
Lennox Industries
Life Insurance Company of Arkansas
Dwight and Lynda Linkous
Glen McLaughlin
The McMath Law Firm, P.A.*
Martinous Oriental Rug Company*
Maybelline Company*
Mechanics Lumber Company
Metropolitan National Bank*
Mitchell, Williams, Selig, Jackson & Tucker
Monarch Mill and Lumber Company*
Mountaire Feeds, Inc.*
National Old Line*
New Subiaco Abbey
Ozark Folk Center State Park
The Paisley, Blackwell, McKinney Family Group
Pine Bluff Warehouse Company
John B. Plegge

Polyvend*
Porbeck Printing Co., Inc.
William Loyd Price
Mr. and Mrs. John G. Ragsdale
Miriam Day Raney
Riceland Foods, Inc.*
Pat M. Riley
Doyle Rogers Company*
Hampton Roy M.D.
St. Vincent Infirmary*
Simmons First Bank of Jonesboro
Snell Prosthetic & Orthotic Laboratory*
Southwestern Bell Telephone Company
Southwestern Energy Co.
Stebbins & Roberts, Inc.
    Manufacturers of Sterling 12 Star Paint*
Stenograph Institute of Arkansas
SunBay Resort, An Affiliate of Independence Federal Bank
300 Spring Building
3M Company*
Twin City Bank*
Union Medical Center*
Union National Bank*
University of Arkansas at Little Rock*
Opal F. Wallace
Mr. & Mrs. Bill Weidman
Westark Community College*
Arthur Young & Company*

*Partners in Progress of *Arkansas: An Illustrated History of the Land of Opportunity.* The histories of these companies and organizations appear in Chapter 9, beginning on page 277.

Arkansas Post County Museum offers visitors a glimpse into Arkansas' past utilizing a nineteenth-century farmstead and a display of agricultural equipment. Photo by Robyn Horn, courtesy, Arkansas Department of Parks and Tourism

Bibliography

Alexander, Charles C., Jr. *Invisible Empire in the Southwest: The Ku Klux Klan in Texas, Louisiana, Oklahoma, and Arkansas, 1920-1930.* 1962.

Allard, Chester. *Who's Who in Arkansas.* 1959.

Angelou, Maya. *I Know Why the Caged Bird Sings.* 1969.

Arnold, Morris. *Unequal Laws Unto a Savage Race: European Legal Traditions in Arkansas 1686-1836.* 1985.

Baird, David. *The Quapaws: A History of the Downstream People.* 1980.

Bartley, Newman. *The Rise of Mass Resistance.*

Bates, Daisy. *The Long Shadow of Little Rock: A Memoir.* 1962.

Baxter, William. *Pea Ridge and Prairie Grove.* 1864.

Bearss, Edwin. *Steel's Retreat from Camden and the Battle of Jenkins Ferry.* 1967

Bearss, Edwin and A.M. Gibson. *Fort Smith: Little Gibraltar on the Arkansas.* 1969.

Biographical and Historical Memoirs of Arkansas. 7 vols. Chicago: Goodspead Publishing Co., 1890.

Bishop, A.W. *Loyalty on the Frontier.* 1863.

Boyette, Gene W. *The Whigs of Arkansas, 1836-1856.* 1972.

Clayton, Powell. *The Aftermath of the Civil War in Arkansas.* 1915.

Daniel, Pete. *Deep as they Come: The 1927 Mississippi River Flood.* 1977.

Davis, Hester and Charles Robert McGimsey. *Indians of Arkansas.* 1969.

Dimitry, John and John Harrell. *Confederate Military History.* Vol. 10. 1899.

Donaghey, George. *Building a State Capitol.* 1937.

Dougan, Michael. *Confederate Arkansas.* 1976.

DuVall, Leland. *Arkansas: Colony and State.* 1973.

Ellenburg, Martha Ann. *Reconstruction in Arkansas.* 1967.

Ferguson, John. *Arkansas and the Civil War.* 1957.

Ferguson, John L. and James H. Atkinson. *Historical Arkansas.* 1966.

Fletcher, John Gould. *Arkansas.* 1947.

Gerstacker, Frederick. *Wild Sports in the Far West.* 1854.

_____. *Western Lands and Western Waters.* 1864.

Grubbs, Donald. *The Cry From Cotton.* 1971.

Hallum, John. *Biographical and Pictorial History of Arkansas.* 1887.

Harington, Fred H. *The Hanging Judge.* 1951.

Harrell, John M. *The Brooks-Baxter War.* 1893.

Harrington, Mark R. *Certain Caddo Sites in Arkansas.* 1920.

_____. *The Ozarks Bluffs' Dwellers.* 1960.

Hempstead, Fay. *A Historical Review of Arkansas.* 3 vols. 1911.

_____. *A Pictorial History of Arkansas from the Earliest Times to the Year 1890.* 1890.

Herndon, Dallas T. *Annals of Arkansas.*

_____. *Centennial History of Arkansas.* 3 vols. 1922.

Holley, Donald. *Uncle Sam's Farmers: New Deal Farmers in the Lower Mississippi Valley.* 1975.

Hull, Clifton. *Shortline Railroads of Arkansas.* 1969.

Johnson, Boyd. *The Arkansas Frontier.* 1957.

Lapin, Deirdre. *Hogs in the Bottom: Family Folklore in Arkansas.* 1982.

League of Women Voters. *Government of Arkansas.* 1976.

Leeper, Wesley Thurman. *Rebels Valiant.* 1964.

Lester, James. *A Man for Arkansas: Sid McMath and the Southern Reform Tradition.* 1976.

McKnight, O.E. and Boyd Johnson. *The Arkansas Story.* 1955.

_____. *Living in Arkansas.* 1951.

McNutt, Walter S. *A History of Arkansas.* 1933.

Masterson, James R. *Tall Tales of Arkansas.* 1943.

Mitchell, H.L. *Mean Things Happening in this Land.* 1979.

Moore, Waddie W. *Arkansas in the Gilded Age, 1874-1900.* 1976.

Niswonger, Richard L. *Arkansas Democratic Politics, 1896-1920.* 1973.

Nutall, Thomas. *A Journal of Travels into Arkansas Territory.* 1966.

Paine, Alfred B. *The Arkansas Bear.* 1925.

Penick, James. *The New Madrid Earthquake of 1811-1812.*

Pope, William E. *Early Days in Arkansas.* 1845.

Quapaw Quarter Association. *The Quapaw Quarter: A Guide to Little Rock's 19th Century Neighborhoods.* 1976.

Randolph, Vance. *Ozark Folklore.* 1972.

_____. *Ozark Magic and Folklore.* 1964.

_____. *Ozark Mountain Folks.* 1932.

_____. *The Ozarks.* 1931.

Reynolds. *Makers of Arkansas History.* 1918.

Richards, Ira and Don Richards. *Story of a Rivertown: Little Rock, in the Nineteenth Century.* 1969.

Ross, Margaret S. *Arkansas Gazette.* 1969.

Russell, Jerry and Bessie Newton Allard. *Who's Who in Arkansas.* Vol. II. 1968.

Secretary of State. *Historical Report of the Secretary of State.* 3 vols. 1978.

Segraves, Joe. *Arkansas Politics, 1874-1918.* 1974.

Shinn, Josiah. *Pioneers and Makers of Arkansas History.* 1908.

Shirley, Glenn. *Law West of Fort Smith.* 1957.

Staples, Thomas S. *Reconstruction in Arkansas, 1862-1874.* 1927.

Stokes, D.A. *Public Affairs in Arkansas, 1836-1850.* 1966

Taylor, Orville W. *Negro Slavery in Arkansas.* 1958.

Thomas, David Yancy. *Arkansas and Its People: A History, 1541-1930.* 4 vols. 1930.

_____. *Arkansas in War and Reconstruction, 1861-1874.* 1926.

Thompson, George. *Arkansas and Reconstruction: The Influence of Geography, Economic and Personality.* 1976.

Waltz, Robert. *Migration into Arkansas, 1834-1880.* 1858.

Ward, John. *The Arkansas Rockefeller.* 1978.

White, Lonnie J. *Politics on the Southwestern Frontier: Arkansas Territory, 1819-1836.* 1964.

Williams, Leonard. *Cavorting on the Devil's Fork: The Pete Whetstone Letters of C.F.M. Noland.* 1979.

Woodruff, William. *With the Light Guns in '61-65.* 1903.

Worley, Ted R. and Eugene Nolte. *Pete Whetstone of Devil's Fork.* 1957.

Worthen, William B. *Early Banking in Arkansas.* 1906.

367

Pea Ridge National Military Park is one of Arkansas' many historic monuments that help Arkansans today understand the events of the past that forged the future. Courtesy, Arkansas Department of Parks and Tourism.

Index

White, Mary, *163*
White River, 12, 28, 34, 35
White River District, *57*
White's Citizens Council, 258
Widney, G.C., 10
Williams, Aubrey, 198
Williams, Claude, 205
Willys-Knight Overland, *8*
Wilson Farm, *191*
Wilson's Creek, 70, *103*
Wingo, Effigene Locke, *209*, 213
Wingo, Otis Theodore, 209
Winrock Farms, 264

Woman's Chronicle (newspaper,) 141
Women; in government, 268, 269-270; rights, 141; suffrage, *142*, 164, 167, 171; in the workforce, 215, 322
Women Democrats for Rockefeller, 262
Women's Christian Temperance Union, *163*
"The Wonder State," 213
Woodruff, William E., *55*, 56, 277
Woods, Henry, 229

Woodsmall Brothers, 195
Working Men's Union of the World, 204
Works Progress Administration (WPA,) 201, 205, 207, 208, 211
World War I, *166*, *180*, *188*
World War II, *200*, 215-218, 278

Y
Yell, Archibald, 50-51, *51*, 52-54, 56, 58-59
Yellville, *237*

Books in the Windsor Series

ALABAMA

The Valley and the Hills: An Illustrated History of Birmingham and Jefferson County
by Leah Rawls Atkins
1981, 248 pp., $21.95
ISBN 0-89781-031-7

Historic Huntsville: A City of New Beginnings
by Elise Hopkins Stephens
1984, 216 pp., $22.95
ISBN 0-89781-096-1

Mobile: Sunbelt Center of Opportunity
by Cathalynn Donelson
1986, 224 pp., $22.95
ISBN 0-89781-200-X

Mobile: The Life and Times of a Great Southern City
by Melton McLaurin and Michael Thomason
1981, 200 pp., $22.95
ISBN 0-89781-020-1

Montgomery: An Illustrated History
by Wayne Flynt
1980, 196 pp., $24.95
ISBN 0-89781-10-4

Tuscaloosa: An Illustrated History
by G. Ward Hubbs
1987
ISBN 0-89781

ARIZONA

Scottsdale: Jewel in the Desert
by Patricia Myers McElfresh
1984, 136 pp., $22.95
ISBN 0-89781-105-4

Tucson: Portrait of a Desert Pueblo
by John Bret Harte
1980, 186 pp., $19.95
ISBN 0-89781-012-0

ARKANSAS

Arkansas: An Illustrated History of the Land of Opportunity
by C. Fred Williams
1986, 384 pp., $29.95
ISBN 0-89781-182-8

CALIFORNIA

Heart of the Golden Empire: An Illustrated History of Bakersfield
by Richard C. Bailey
1984, 160 pp., $22.95
ISBN 0-89781-065-1

Burbank: An Illustrated History
by E. Caswell Perry
1987
ISBN 0-89781-204-2

Butte County [Chico]: An Illustrated History
by Bill Talbitzer
1987
ISBN 8-89781-208-5

California Wings: A History of Aviation in the Golden State
by William A. Schoneberger with Paul Sonnenburg
1984, 192 pp., $24.95
ISBN 0-89781-078-3

Los Angeles: A City Apart
by David L. Clark
1981, 254 pp., $19.95
ISBN 0-89781-017-1

Long Beach and Los Angeles: A Tale of Two Ports
by Charles F. Queenan
1986, 208 pp., $24.95
ISBN 0-89781-178-X

Merced County: An Illustrated History
by Delores J. Cabezut-Ortiz
1987
ISBN 0-89781-209-3

The Monterey Peninsula: An Enchanted Land
By Randall A. Reinstedt
1987
ISBN 0-89781-199-2

Napa Valley: From Golden Fields to Purple Harvest
by Denzil & Jennie Verardo
1986, 160 pp., $22.95
ISBN 0-89781-164-X

The Golden Promise: An Illustrated History of Orange County
by Pamela Hallan-Gibson
1986, 432 pp., $27.95
ISBN 0-89781-160-7

Pasadena: Crown of the Valley
by Ann Scheid
1986, 288 pp., $24.95
ISBN 0-89781-163-1

Redding & Shasta County: Gateway to the Cascades
by John D. Lawson
1986, 184 pp., $24.95
ISBN 0-89781-187-9

Harvest of the Sun: An Illustrated History of Riverside County
by James T. Brown
1985, 256 pp., $24.95
ISBN 0-89781-145-3

Sacramento: Heart of the Golden State
by Joseph A. McGowan and Terry R. Willis
1983, 160 pp., $24.95
ISBN 0-89781-066-X

San Bernardino County: Land of Contrasts
by Walter C. Schuiling
1984, 207 pp., $22.95
ISBN 0-89781-116-X

San Diego: City with a Mission
by Dan Berger
1987
ISBN 0-89781-212-3

[San Francisco] International Port of Call: An Illustrated Maritime History of the Golden Gate
by Robert J. Schwendinger
1984, 160 pp., $22.95
ISBN 0-89781-122-4

Santa Clara County: Harvest of Change
by Stephen W. Payne
1987
ISBN 0-89781-185-2

Stockton: Sunrise Port on the San Joaquin
by Olive Davis
1984, 160 pp., $22.95
ISBN 0-89781-093-7

Ventura County: Land of Good Fortune
by Judy Triem
1985, 232 pp., $22.95
ISBN 0-89781-156-9

COLORADO

Life In The Altitudes: An Illustrated History of Colorado Springs
by Nancy E. Loe
1983, 128 pp., $22.95
ISBN 0-89781-051-1

Denver: America's Mile High Center of Enterprise
by Jerry Richmond
1983, 256 pp., $29.95
ISBN 0-89781-082-1 AE

CONNECTICUT

Only in Bridgeport: An Illustrated History of the Park City

by Lennie Grimaldi
1986, 304 pp., $24.95
ISBN 0-89781-169-0
We Crown Them All: An Illustrated History of Danbury
by William E. Devlin
1984, 144 pp., $22.95
ISBN 0-89781-092-9
Hartford: An Illustrated History of Connecticut's Capital
by Glenn Weaver
1982, 192 pp., $24.95
ISBN 0-89781-052-X
New Haven: An Illustrated History
edited by Floyd Shumway and Richard Hegel
1981, 224 pp., $19.95
ISBN 0-89781-033-3
Stamford: An Illustrated History
by Estelle F. Feinstein and Joyce S. Pendery
1984, 192 pp., $22.95
ISBN 0-89781-114-3

DELAWARE
The First State: An Illustrated History of Delaware
by William Henry Williams
1985, 216 pp., $24.95
ISBN 0-89781-158-5

DISTRICT OF COLUMBIA
Washington, D.C.: The Making of a Capital
by Charles Paul Freund
1987
ISBN 0-89781-205-0

FLORIDA
Fort Lauderdale and Broward County: An Illustrated History
by Stuart McIver
1983, 236 pp., $24.95
ISBN 0-89781-081-3
Palm Beach County: An Illustrated History
by Donald W. Curl
1986, 224 pp., $24.95
ISBN 0-89781-167-4

GEORGIA
Columbus: Georgia's Fall Line "Trading Town"
by Dr. Joseph Mahan
1986, 256 pp. $24.95
ISBN 0-89781-166-6

Eden on the Marsh: An Illustrated History of Savannah
by Edward Chan Sieg
1985, 224 pp., $24.95
ISBN 0-89781-115-1

IDAHO
Boise: An Illustrated History
by Merle Wells
1982, 208 pp., $22.95
ISBN 0-89781-042-2
Idaho: Gem of the Mountains
by Merle Wells and Arthur A. Hart
1985, 256 pp., $24.95
ISBN 0-89781-141-0

ILLINOIS
Chicago: Center for Enterpise
by Kenan Heise and Michael Edgerton
1982, 600 pp. (2 Vols), $39.95
ISBN 0-89781-041-4
Des Plaines: Born of the Tallgrass Prairie
by Donald S. Johnson
1984, 136 pp., $19.95
ISBN 0-89781-095-3
Prairies, Prayers, and Promises: An Illustrated History of Galesburg
by Jean C. Lee
1987
ISBN 0-89781-194-1
Prairie of Promise: Springfield and Sangamon County
by Edward J. Russo
1983, 112 pp., $19.95
ISBN 0-89781-084-8

INDIANA
At the Bend in the River: The Story of Evansville
by Kenneth P. McCutchan
1982, 144 pp., $22.95
ISBN 0-89781-060-0
The Fort Wayne Story: A Pictorial History
by John Ankenbruck
1980, 232 pp., $22.95
ISBN 0-89781-015-5
Indiana: An Illustrated History
by Patrick J. Furlong
1985, 232 pp., $24.95
ISBN 0-89781-152-6
Muncie and Delaware County: An

Illustrated Retrospective
by Wiley W. Spurgeon, Jr.
1984, 144 pp., $22.95
ISBN 0-89781-104-6
Terre Haute: Wabash River City
by Dorothy J. Clark
1983, 112 pp., $19.95
ISBN 0-89781-089-9

IOWA
Cedar Rapids: Tall Corn and High Technology
by Ernie Danek
1980, 232 pp., $19.95
ISBN 0-89781-021-X

LOUISIANA
River Capital: An Illustrated History of Baton Rouge
by Mark T. Carleton
1981, 304 pp., $21.95
ISBN 0-89781-032-5
So Mote It Be: A History of Louisiana Freemasonry
by Glenn Jordan
1987
ISBN 0-89781-197-6
New Orleans: An Illustrated History
by John R. Kemp
1981, 320 pp., $24.95
ISBN 0-89781-035-X
The History of Rapides Parish
by Sue Eakin
1987
ISBN 0-89781-201-8

MARYLAND
Baltimore: An Illustrated History
by Suzanne Ellery Greene
1980, 325 pp., $19.95
ISBN 0-89781-009-0
Maryland: Old Line to New Prosperity
by Joseph L. Arnold
1985, 256 pp., $24.95
ISBN 0-89781-147-X
Montgomery County: Two Centuries of Change
by Jane C. Sween
1984, 232 pp., $24.95
ISBN 0-89781-120-8

MASSACHUSETTS
Boston: City on a Hill
by Andrew Buni and Alan Rogers

1984, 240 pp., $24.95
ISBN 0-89781-090-2
The Valley and Its Peoples: An Illustrated History of the Lower Merrimack River
by Paul Hudon
1982, 192 pp., $22.95
ISBN 0-89781-047-3
South Middlesex: A New England Heritage
by Stephen Herring
1986, 248 pp., $24.95
ISBN 0-89781-179-8
Heart of the Commonwealth: Worcester
by Margaret A. Erskine
1981, 208 pp., $19.95
ISBN 0-89781-030-9

MICHIGAN
Battle Creek: The Place Behind the Products
by Larry B. Massie and Peter J. Schmitt
1984, 136 pp., $19.95
ISBN 0-89781-117-8
Through the Years in Genesee: An Illustrated History [Flint]
by Alice Lethbridge
1985, 144 pp., $22.95
ISBN 0-89781-161-5
In Celebration of Grand Rapids
by Ellen Arlinsky and Marg Ed Conn Kwapil
1987
ISBN 0-89781-210-7
Jackson: An Illustrated History
by Brian Deming
1984, 148 pp., $19.95
ISBN 0-89781-113-5
Kalamazoo: The Place Behind the Products
by Peter J. Schmitt and Larry B. Massie
1981, 304 pp., $19.95
ISBN 0-89781-037-6
Out of a Wilderness: An Illustrated History of Greater Lansing
by Justin L. Kestenbaum
1981, 192 pp., $19.95
ISBN 0-89781-024-4
Michigan: An Illustrated History of the Great Lakes State
by George S. May
1987
ISBN 0-89781-181-X

Muskegon County: Harbor of Promise: An Illustrated History
by Jonathan Eyler
1986, 200 pp., $22.95
ISBN 0-89781-174-7
Saginaw: A History of the Land and the City
by Stuart D. Gross
1980, 200 pp., $19.95
ISBN 0-89781-016-3

MINNESOTA
Duluth: An Illustrated History of the Zenith City
by Glenn N. Sandvik
1983, 128 pp., $19.95
ISBN 0-89781-059-7
City of Lakes: An Illustrated History of Minneapolis
by Joseph Stipanovich
1982, 400 pp., $27.95
ISBN 0-89781-048-1
Saint Cloud: The Triplet City
by John J. Dominick
1983, 168 pp., $22.95
ISBN 0-89781-091-0
St. Paul: A Modern Renaissance
by Virginia Kunz
1986, 200 pps., $29.95
ISBN 0-89781-186-0
St. Paul: Saga of an American City
by Virginia Brainard Kunz
1977, 258 pp., $19.95
ISBN 0-89781-000-7

MISSISSIPPI
The Mississippi Gulf Coast: Portrait of a People: An Illustrated History
by Charles L. Sullivan
1985, 200 pp., $22.95
ISBN 0-89781-097-X

MISSOURI
From Southern Village to Midwestern City: Columbia, An Illustrated History
by Alan R. Havig
1984, 136 pp., $19.95
ISBN 0-89781-138-0
Joplin: From Mining Town to Urban Center, An Illustrated History
by G.K. Renner
1985, 128 pp., $19.95
ISBN 0-89781-153-4

At the River's Bend: An Illustrated History of Kansas City, Independence and Jackson County
by Sherry Lamb Schirmer and Richard D. McKinzie
1982, 352 pp., $24.95
ISBN 0-89781-058-9
Kansas City: The Spirit, The People, The Promise
by Patricia Pace
1987
ISBN 0-89781-211-5
Springfield of the Ozarks
by Harris and Phyllis Dark
1981, 240 pp., $19.95
ISBN 0-89781-028-7

MONTANA
Montana: Land of Contrast
by Harry W. Fritz
1984, 200 pp., $24.95
ISBN 0-89781-106-2

NEBRASKA
Lincoln: The Prairie Capital
by James L. McKee
1984, 192 pp., $24.95
ISBN 0-89781-109-7
Omaha and Douglas County: A Panoramic History
by Dorothy Devereux Dustin
1980, 200 pp., $19.95
ISBN 0-89781-011-2

NEVADA
Reno: Hub of the Washoe Country
by William D. Rowley
1984, 128 pp., $22.95
ISBN 0-89781-080-5

NEW HAMPSHIRE
New Hampshire: An Illustrated History of the Granite State
by Ronald Jager and Grace Jager
1983, 248 pp., $27.95
ISBN 0-89781-069-4

NEW JERSEY
Hudson County: The Left Bank
by Joan F. Doherty
1986, 168 pp., $22.95
ISBN 0-89781-172-0
Morris County: The Progress of Its Legend
by Dorianne R. Perrucci
1983, 216 pp., $24.95

ISBN 0-89781-075-9
The Hub & the Wheel: New Brunswick & Middlesex County
by Gary Karasik
1986, 136 pp., $22.95
ISBN 0-89781-188-7
New Jersey: A History of Ingenuity and Industry
by James P. Johnson
1987
ISBN 0-89781-206-9
A Capital Place: The Story of Trenton
by Mary Alice Quigley and David E. Collier
1984, 160 pp., $22.95
ISBN 0-89781-079-1

NEW MEXICO
New Mexico: The Distant Land
by Dan Murphy
1985, 184 pp., $24.95
ISBN 0-89781-119-4

NEW YORK
Albany: Capital City on the Hudson
by John J. McEneny
1981, 248 pp., $24.95
ISBN 0-89781-025-2
Broome County Heritage
by Lawrence Bothwell
1983, 176 pp., $24.95
ISBN 0-89781-061-9
A Greater Look at Greater Buffalo
by Jim Bisco
1986, 480 pp., $35.00
ISBN 0-89781-198-4
Buffalo: Lake City in Niagara Land
by Richard C. Brown and Bob Watson
1981, 336 pp., $27.95
ISBN 0-89781-036-8 [Hard Cover]
　　　　$12.95
ISBN 0-89781-062-7 [Soft Cover]
The Hudson-Mohawk Gateway: An Illustrated History
by Thomas Phelan
1985, 184 pp., $22.95
ISBN 0-89781-118-6
A Pictorial History of Jamestown and Chautauqua County
by B. Dolores Thompson
1984, 128 pp., $19.95
ISBN 0-89781-103-8

Between Ocean and Empire: An Illustrated History of Long Island
by Dr. Robert McKay and Carol Traynor
1985, 320 pp., $24.95
ISBN 0-89781-143-7
Harbor and Haven: An Illustrated History of the Port of New York
by John G. Bunker
1979, 302 pp., $25.00
ISBN 0-89781-002-3
A Panoramic History of Rochester and Monroe County, New York
by Blake McKelvey
1979, 264 pp., $24.95
ISBN 0-89781-003-1
Syracuse: From Salt to Satellite
by Henry W. Schramm and William F. Roseboom
1979, 244 pp., $19.95
ISBN 0-89781-005-8
The Upper Mohawk Country: An Illustrated History of Greater Utica
by David M. Ellis
1982, 224 pp., $22.95
ISBN 0-89781-054-6

NORTH CAROLINA
Asheville: Land of the Sky
by Milton Ready
1986, 136 pp., $22.95
ISBN 0-89781-168-2
Greensboro: A Chosen Center
by Gayle Hicks Fripp
1982, 216 pp., $24.95
ISBN 0-89781-056-2
Made in North Carolina: An Illustrated History of Tar Heel Business and Industry
by David E. Brown
1985, 248 pp., $24.95
ISBN 0-89781-157-7
Raleigh: City of Oaks
by James E. Vickers
1982, 128 pp., $22.95
ISBN 0-89781-050-3
Cape Fear Adventure: An Illustrated History of Wilmington
by Diane Cobb Cashman
1982, 128 pp., $22.95
ISBN 0-89781-057-0

OHIO
Butler County: An Illustrated History

by George C. Crout
1984, 128 pp., $19.95
ISBN 0-89781-123-2
Springfield and Clark County: An Illustrated History
by William A. Kinnison
1985, 152 pp., $22.95
ISBN 0-89781-146-1

OKLAHOMA
Oklahoma: Land of the Fair God
by Odie B. Faulk
1986, 344 pp., $29.95
ISBN 0-8978-173-9
Heart of the Promised Land: An Illustrated History of Oklahoma County
by Bob L. Blackburn
1982, 264 pp., $24.95
ISBN 0-89681-019-8

OREGON
Lane County: An Illustrated History of the Emerald Empire
by Dorothy Velasco
1985, 168 pp., $22.95
ISBN 0-89781-140-2
Portland: Gateway to the Northwest
by Carl Abbott
1985, 264 pp., $24.95
ISBN 0-89781-155-0

PENNSYLVANIA
Allegheny Passage: An Illustrated History of Blair County
by Robert L. Emerson
1984, 136 pp., $22.95
0-89781-137-2
Erie: Chronicle of a Great Lakes City
by Edward Wellejus
1980, 144 pp., $17.95
ISBN 0-89781-007-4
Life by the Moving Road: An Illustrated History of Greater Harrisburg
by Michael Barton
1983, 224 pp., $24.95
ISBN 0-89781-064-3
The Heritage of Lancaster
by John Ward Willson Loose
1978, 226 pp., $14.95
ISBN 0-89781-001-5 [Hard Cover]
　　　　$9.95

ISBN 0-89781-022-8 [Soft Cover]
The Lehigh Valley: An Illustrated History
by Karyl Lee Kibler Hall and Peter Dobkin Hall
1982, 224 pp., $24.95
ISBN 0-89781-044-9
Pennsylvania: Keystone to Progress
by E. Willard Miller
1986, 640 pp., $35.00
ISBN 0-89781-171-2
Pittsburgh: Fullfilling Its Destiny
by Vince Gagetta
1986, 624 pp., $35.00
ISBN 0-89781-189-5
Never Before in History: The Story of Scranton
by John Beck
1986, 144 pp., $22.95
0-89781-190-9
Williamsport: Frontier Village to Regional Center
by Robert H. Larson, Richard J. Morris, and John F. Piper, Jr.
1984, 208 pp., $22.95
ISBN 0-89781-110-0
The Wyoming Valley: An American Portrait
by Edward F. Hanlon
1983, 280 pp., $24.95
ISBN 0-89781-073-2
To the Setting of the Sun: The Story of York
by Georg R. Sheets
1981, 240 pp., $22.95
ISBN 0-89781-023-6

RHODE ISLAND
Rhode Island: The Independent State
by George H. Kellner and J. Stanley Lemons
1982, 208 pp., $24.95
ISBN 0-89781-040-6

SOUTH CAROLINA
Charleston: Crossroads of History
by Isabella G. Leland
1980, 136 pp., $17.95
ISBN 0-89781-008-2
Columbia, South Carolina: History of a City
by John A. Montgomery
1979, 200 pp. $17.95
ISBN 0-89781-006-6

Greenville: Woven from the Past
by Nancy Vance Ashmore
1986, 280 pp., $24.95
ISBN 0-89781-193-3

SOUTH DAKOTA
Gateway to the Hills: An Illustrated History of Rapid City
by David B. Miller
1985, 136 pp., $19.95
ISBN 0-89781-107-0

TENNESSEE
Chattanooga: An Illustrated History
by James Livingood
1981, 206 pp., $19.95
ISBN 0-89781-027-9
Metropolis of the American Nile: Memphis and Shelby County
by John E. Harkins
1982, 224 pp., $24.95
ISBN 0-89781-026-0

TEXAS
Abilene: The Key City
by Juanita Daniel Zachry
1986, 128 pp., $22.95
ISBN 0-89781-150-X
The Golden Spread: An Illustrated History of Amarillo & the Panhandle Plains
by B. Byron Price & Frederick Rathjen
1986, 168 pp., $22.95
ISBN 0-89781-183-61986
Austin: An Illustrated History
by David Humphrey
1985, 376 pp., $27.95
ISBN 0-89781-144-5
Beaumont: A Chronicle of Promise
by Judith W. Linsley and Ellen W. Rienstra
1982, 192 pp., $22.95
ISBN 0-89781-053-8
Corpus Christi: The History of a Texas Seaport
by Bill Walraven
1982, 136 pp., $22.95
ISBN 0-89781-043-0
Dallas: An Illustrated History
by Darwin Payne
1982, 400 pp., $29.95
ISBN 0-89781-034-1
City at the Pass: An Illustrated History of El Paso
by Leon Metz

1980, 126 pp., $19.95
ISBN 0-89781-013-9
Where the West Begins: Fort Worth and Tarrant County
by Janet L. Schmelzer
1985, 152 pp., $22.95
ISBN 0-89781-151-8
Houston: Chronicle of the Supercity on Buffalo Bayou
by Stanley E. Siegel
1983, 296 pp., $29.95
ISBN 0-89781-072-4
In Celebration of Texas
by Archie P. McDonald
1986, 488 pp., $29.95
ISBN 0-89781-165-8
Waco: Texas Crossroads
by Patricia Ward Wallace
1983, 136 pp., $22.95
ISBN 0-89781-068-6

UTAH
Ogden: Junction City
by Richard C. Roberts and Richard W. Sadler
1985, 288 pp., $24.95
ISBN 0-89781-154-2
Salt Lake City: The Gathering Place
by John S. McCormick
1980, 130 pp., $19.95
ISBN 0-89781-018-X

VERMONT
Vermont: An Illustrated History
by John Duffy
1985, 264 pp., $24.95
ISBN 0-89781-159-3

VIRGINIA
Norfolk's Waters: An Illustrated Maritime History of Hampton Roads
by William Tazewell
1982, 224 pp., $22.95
ISBN 0-89781-045-7
RICHMOND: An Illustrated History
by Harry M. Ward
1985, 544 pp., $29.95
ISBN 0-89681-148-8
Virginia Business and Industry
1987

WASHINGTON
King County And Its Queen City:

Seattle
by James R. Warren
1981, 314 pp., $24.95
ISBN 0-89781-038-4
Where Mountains Meet the Sea:
An Illustrated History of Puget
Sound
by James R. Warren
1986, 288 pp., $24.95
ISBN 0-89781-175-5
A View of the Falls: An Illustrated
History of Spokane
by William Stimson
1985, 160 pp., $22.95
ISBN 0-89781-121-6
South On The Sound: An Illustrated
History of Tacoma and Pierce
County
by Murray and Rosa Morgan

1984, 199 pp., $22.95
ISBN 0-89781-0474-0
Vancouver on the Columbia: An Illustrated History
by Ted Van Arsdol
1986, 200 pp., $22.95
ISBN 0-89781-194-1

WEST VIRGINIA
Charleston and the Kanawha Valley: An Illustrated History
by Otis K. Rice
1981, 136 pp., $19.95
ISBN 0-89781-046-5
Huntington: An Illustrated History
by James E. Casto
1985, 160 pp., $22.95
ISBN 0-89781-101-1
Wheeling: An Illustrated History

by Doug Fethering
1983, 120 pp., $19.95
ISBN 0-89781-071-6

WISCONSIN
The Fox Heritage: A History of
Wisconsin's Fox Cities
by Ellen Kort
1984, 256 pp., $22.95
ISBN 0-89781-083-X
Green Bay: Gateway to the Great
Waterway
by Betsy Foley
1983, 168 pp., $22.95
ISBN 0-89781-076-7

WYOMING
Cheyenne 1987

Canada

Brampton: An Illustrated History
by Helga Loverseed
1987
ISBN 0-89781-207-7
Brantford: Grand River Crossing
by Janet Kempster and Gary
Muir
1986, 200 pp., $29.95
ISBN 0-89781-184-4
Calgary: Canada's Frontier Me-
tropolis
by Max Foran and Heather
MacEwan Foran
1982, 400 pp., $29.95
ISBN 0-89781-055-4
Edmonton: Gateway to the North
by John F. Gilpin
1984, 320 pp., $29.95
ISBN 0-89781-094-5
Halifax: Cornerstone of Canada
by Joan Payzant
1985, 224 pp., $27.95
ISBN 0-89781-149-6
Hamilton: A City in Symphony
by Sherry Sleightholm
1986, 168 pp., $29.95
ISBN 0-89781-195-X
Hamilton: Chronicle of a City
by T. Melville Bailey
1983, 184 pp., $24.95
ISBN 0-89781-067-8
Kitchener: Yesterday Revisited

by Bill Moyer
1979, 150 pp., $19.95
ISBN 0-89781-004-X
The Forest City: An Illustrated
History of London, Canada
by Frederick H. Armstrong
1986, 336 pp., $29.95
ISBN 0-89781-180-1
Mississauga: An Illustrated History
by Roger E. Riendeau
1985, 184 pp., $24.95
ISBN 0-89781-162-3
Oakville, A Place of Some Impor-
tance
by Clare & Joseph McKeon
1986, 136 pp., $24.95
ISBN 0-89781-170-4
Where Rivers Meet: An Illustrated
History of Ottawa
by Courtney C. J. Bond
1984, 176 pp., $24.95
ISBN 0-89781-111-9
Regina: From Pile O'Bones to
Queen City of the Plains
by William A. Riddell
1981, 232 pp., $24.95
ISBN 0-89781-029-5
Saint John: Two Hundred Years
Proud
by George W. Schuyler
1984, 200 pp., $27.95
ISBN 0-89781-108-9

Saskatoon: Hub City of the West
by Gail A. McConnell
1983, 128 pp., $27.95
ISBN 0-89781-070-8
The Sudbury Region: An Illustrated
History
by Graeme S. Mount
1986, 144 pp., $24.95
ISBN 0-89781-177-1
Toronto: The Place of Meeting
by Frederick H. Armstrong
1983, 304 pp., $29.95
ISBN 0-89781-077-5
Vancouver: An Illustrated Chro-
nology
by Chuck Davis & Shirley
Mooney
1986, 288 pp.,
$29.95, (USD)$24.95
ISBN 0-89781-176-3
Beyond the Island: An Illustrated
History of Victoria
by Peter Barkerville
1986, 144 pp.,
$27.95, (USD)$22.95
ISBN 0-89781-192-5
Winnipeg: Where the New West
Begins
by Eric Wells
1982, 288 pp., $29.95
ISBN 0-8971-039-2

In 1881 photographer T.W. Bankes produced "Bankes' Gallery of Noted Arkansans," which included the greats of early Arkansas. Courtesy, Arkansas History Commission

This book was set in Helvetica and Century types. It was printed on 70-lb. Mead Enamel Offset and bound by Walsworth Publishing Company